MOLOTOV REMEMBERS

MOLOTOV REMEMBERS

Inside Kremlin Politics

CONVERSATIONS WITH
Felix Chuev

EDITED WITH AN INTRODUCTION
AND NOTES BY
Albert Resis

Ivan R. Dee
CHICAGO 1993

Library of Congress Cataloging-in-Publication Data:
Chuev, Feliks Ivanovich, 1941–
[Sto sorok besed s Molotovym.   English]
Molotov remembers : inside Kremlin politics : conversations with
Felix Chuev / edited with an introduction and notes by Albert Resis.
p.   cm.
Includes index.
ISBN 1-56663-027-4 (cloth : alk. paper)
1. Soviet Union—Politics and government.   2. Soviet Union—
Foreign relations.   3. Molotov, Vyacheslav Mikhaylovich,
1890–1986—Interviews.
I. Molotov, Vyacheslav Mikhaylovich, 1890–1986.
II. Resis, Albert.   III. Title.
DK266.C47513   1993

320.947—dc20

93-11253

CONTENTS

PREFACE

Viacheslav Mikhailovich Molotov has a special place in my memory. I met with him regularly during the last seventeen years of his life, from 1969 until 1986. We had 140 in-depth talks, each on the average four to five hours. No matter how Molotov may be judged, his opinions are important, his life is inseparable from the history of his country. He worked with Lenin, was a member of a Military Revolutionary Committee that prepared the October armed uprising in Petrograd (Saint Petersburg) and deputy chairman of the State Committee of Defense during the Great Patriotic War (World War II). He filled high posts in the party and the government, headed the foreign ministry, and met almost all the major figures of the twentieth century.

His judgments are subjective and often conflict with what is today published and asserted as "truth." The subjects of my talks with Molotov were quite various, but they involved the most tense moments in the post-Revolutionary history of our country. All these years I kept a special diary, recording in detail every talk, every statement, and questioning and clarifying them in later meetings. From 1970 to 1977 the historian Shota Kvantaliani took part in half our meetings.

Molotov's view of events was unchanging. He was a censor to himself. The angle of a question might change, but the extent of his answer remained the same. This is why one piece of information may be followed by several dates. Molotov was exact in his choice of words and sometimes picked at unimportant details. He liked to dig down to the roots of matters and was stubborn and consistent in conversation. He talked little about himself.

He understood that I would write a book about him. Molotov did not leave memoirs. "I'm not interested in who said what and where, who spat on what. . . . Lenin didn't write memoirs, nor did Stalin. . . . There are people who say they have seen my book. I don't write memoirs, I write about socialism—what it is and, as peasants say, 'what we need it for.'"

Even in 1969, when I first visited him at home, he was already approaching eighty. A man of a medium height, sturdily built, with a big, stubborn forehead, sharp, bright hazel eyes, not faded from aging. A wiry grey mustache—everyone in the Politburo had mustaches in his time.

What you noticed at once was his modesty, meticulousness, and thrift. He saw that nothing would be wasted—for instance, the light would never be on for no reason in other rooms. He wore clothes for years—in the same hat and coat he appears in official government pictures over years' time. At home, a thick brown shirt; on a holiday, a grey suit, a dark tie. He had an excellent memory until the end of his life.

"Not everything has happened as we thought it would," Molotov told me. "Much has turned out the other way. Many things have been done wonderfully, but that's not enough."

I am looking at a picture of Lenin's funeral while he says this: Stalin is bent under the weight of the coffin, Molotov is supporting it with his young shoulder. The leaders were as young as the country itself.

Molotov spent his last twenty years on a state-owned dacha in Zhu-kovka. Two cheerful women took care of him after the death of his wife in 1970—his wife's niece Sarra Golovanevskaya, and Tatiana Tarasova.

We talked usually from noon till 4 p.m. He would say, "Eat shchi (soup) with slices! It's an old Russian meal. I remember it since childhood. You cut slices of brown bread into the soup and eat. . . . Have these pears—they sent them to us from Georgia. Pour yourself brandy, as Stalin used to say—for the groundwork! But I could have a drop."

"I am a man of the nineteenth century," Molotov said. "What superstitions people carried with them into the new century: they were afraid of everything!"

"There certainly will be failures and frustration along the way," he said. "But imperialism is falling to pieces!"

He died at age ninety-six on November 8, 1986, on the day when exactly sixty-nine years earlier he had stood beside Lenin as he was proclaiming Soviet power. Molotov's will was opened. There was a savings book in an envelope: 500 rubles for the funeral—that was all of his savings.

FELIX CHUEV

INTRODUCTION

Russia never ceases to amaze, astound, and confound. On November 7, 1917, at 10 a.m., a seeming gang of jailbirds led by an obscure revolutionary, alias Lenin, proclaimed the overthrow of the Russian Provisional Government headed by Alexander Kerensky and the transfer of all power to the Soviets of Workers' and Soldiers' Deputies. The Soviet government headed by Lenin managed to survive against all odds: counterrevolution, armed intervention, blockade, famine, epidemic, and total breakdown of the economy. Under Stalinist despotism, the Russians and the "fraternal peoples" of the Union of Soviet Socialist Republics transformed the most economically undeveloped major country of Europe into the world's second greatest industrial power and declared it "the first socialist society." They defeated Hitler in World War II. Now a superpower, they pioneered the development of nuclear-tipped intercontinental ballistic missiles, making it clear by 1957 that if war broke out between the two superpowers, the United States would not emerge unscathed. Incredibly, the party-state juggernaut that crushed the slightest manifestation of political nonconformity, much less dissidence, produced two great, de-Stalinizing reformers, Nikita Khrushchev and Mikhail Gorbachev. Suddenly in 1991 the USSR collapsed. All of this happened often contrary to the expectations of outsiders, indeed, often to the astonishment of Soviet leaders themselves. Russia, most certainly, is not a country easy to comprehend.

The greatest barrier to understanding Russia has been the obsessive secrecy imposed by the Soviet regime. Closed societies make it virtually impossible to ascertain the real state of affairs. And the Soviet Union was the ultimate in closed societies. Unlike a normal state, the USSR regarded virtually all public business as a state secret. Because secrecy enabled officials at all levels to camouflage malfeasance or falsify affairs, even Soviet leaders could not know with any degree of certainty the true state of the union. Reality was further obscured by the regime's dictating a highly idealized view of the Soviet Union as the best of all possible worlds. Further compounding this false vision, the regime also arranged a grossly falsified version of the past designed to buttress the roseate official view of the present. This secrecy went so far that the Soviet government did not even permit the publication of uncensored, candid political memoirs. In the USSR the citizen could find no political memoirs, diaries, or autobiographies, written by past and present Soviet leaders or their aides, which might inform and deepen understanding of the country's polity. Public discourse, such as it was, suffered from the absence of political memoirs, civil society's vital link connecting the recent past and present politics.

Obsessive secrecy was not the only reason for the dearth of political memoirs. Early death in battle or in purges or in overwork prevented many revolutionaries from committing their thoughts to paper. Or memoirs, if actually written, found publication barred by the Soviet security mania and may still be gathering dust in KGB archives. Or key memoirs had to be smuggled out of the country for publication abroad, as was true with Khrushchev's recollections. But there was another formidable barrier to the writing and publication of candid memoirs: self-censorship. The ideological mind-set of Soviet leaders militated against such individualistic literary activity. For their doctrine taught that they were mere instruments of the inexorable, inevitable forces of history in which the individual (except for a Lenin or a Stalin) counted for little and the masses for everything. The most notable exception was Trotsky, who in exile abroad wrote and published *My Life*. That book used to be cited in Moscow as further proof of Trotsky's egoism, bourgeois individualism, and "anti-Leninist" line.

The urge to set the record straight or, more precisely, to leave one's version of events for posterity, cannot always be resisted. Once censorship ended and the ideological blinders fell away with the crumbling of Soviet power, political memoirs began to appear. In the past five years we have seen publication of memoirs by two former ministers of foreign affairs, Andrei Gromyko and Edvard Shevardnadze, and a rising tide of autobiographical works or political memoirs, including those by Boris Yeltsin, Mikhail Gorbachev, Alexander Yakovlev, Gorbachev's principal adviser, and Yegor Ligachev, Gorbachev's chief critic within the former party.

Valuable as these works are, they fill none of the blank pages in the history of the era of Lenin and Stalin. For that we now have this testimony from V. M. Molotov who served Lenin as secretary of his chancery and served Stalin as his second in command. Expelled from the Communist party and in forced retirement since 1962, the aging pensioner had become a familiar figure at Reading Room Number One of the Lenin Library, where for a time he busied himself at writing his memoirs. But no journal would publish portions he submitted. The party leadership had banned Molotov's writings because he persisted in assailing the foreign and domestic policies pursued by Khrushchev (1953–1964) and Brezhnev (1964–1982). The ban on publishing anything short of total repudiation of his most deeply felt views impelled him to give up writing his memoirs.

Moreover, the regime had a heavy club over his head. In the twenty-two years following his expulsion from the party, Molotov frequently petitioned for readmission, which he insisted must be backdated to 1962, expunging the record of his ever having been cast into outer darkness. Molotov refused to publish an anodyne, sanitized version of his memoirs tailored to fit the current line, of the sort Andrei Gromyko and Anastas Mikoyan had published. And an attempt to publish the views expressed in this book would have nullified his chances of reinstatement in the party, which he believed inevitable once the party returned to the "correct" path. He was finally informed that his petitions for reinstatement had been rejected on two counts: he was still held culpable for the murderous part he played in the terror of the 1930s and for his participation in the "antiparty group" which nearly unseated Khrushchev in 1957. He not only rejected a *mea culpa*, he continued privately his stout defense of the most horrible crimes of the Stalin regime—forced collectivization, the Great Terror, and pervasive repression—as necessary and positive, though he conceded that the terror was marked by "errors" and a bit of overdoing.

As the years passed Molotov claimed that the "antiparty" charge against him had become moot. He and his "antiparty" confreres, Malenkov, Kaganovich, Bulganin, and Shepilov, could claim foresight in their failed effort to remove Khrushchev from office in 1957. After all, the party itself removed Khrushchev seven years later. Ironically, Molotov was reinstated in the party in 1984 by General Secretary Konstantin Chernenko, whom Molotov had privately ridiculed as a nonentity, a wholehearted participant in the Brezhnev leadership's binges of mutual medal-bestowing.

But why, then, the conversations sedulously recorded from 1969 to 1986 by Felix Chuev with Molotov's knowledge and permission? Molotov and his principal interlocutor, Chuev, too had an eye to posterity. In the last thirty years of his life Molotov believed that Stalin's successors were betraying the Revolution—and his own life's work. He wanted to set the record straight and help return the party to the true Leninist-Stalinist faith. Thus he agreed to meet frequently over a seventeen-year period with Chuev who faithfully recorded Molotov's remarks and thoughts, his resounding affirmations of the virtual infallibility of Lenin and Stalin and of the "scientific" correctness of the system they created in contrast to their successors' alleged concessions to Western "imperialism" and perversion of "socialism."

And why the publication of this book in Moscow in 1991? And why the claimed press run of 300,000 copies on smooth paper and in sturdy binding—most unusual for publications in the last days of the USSR? Although Terra, the book's publisher, is one of the few high-quality publishing firms in Moscow today, it is quite possible that this book was intended to rally neo-Stalinists and other hard-liners in a movement to oust Gorbachev and establish a quasi-Stalinist regime. Indeed, if the conspirators who engineered the failed coup of August 1991 ever read anything, this might have been their favorite book.

But the significance of this book goes beyond contemporary politics. It is first of all a significant historical source, for it offers invaluable firsthand information on Lenin and Stalin and their times.

Molotov had worked closely with Lenin in Lenin's last two years. He had worked so closely with Stalin that he was long regarded by many as Stalin's most likely and logical successor. As Soviet foreign minister from 1939 to 1949, and again from 1953 to 1956, he had negotiated with Hitler and Ribbentrop, Churchill and Eden, Roosevelt and Hopkins, and their postwar successors to boot. As an unrepentant Stalinist he had broken with Khrushchev and was expelled from the party in 1962, yet had survived into the Gorbachev era. Thus Molotov offers us an unparalleled insider's view of Kremlin political history over most of its life. Indeed, this is the first, and undoubtedly the last, inside account of top-level Soviet politics to cover the entire Lenin-Stalin-Khrushchev era. And as Molotov relates his recollections in response to the occasionally probing questions posed by Chuev and his friends, we gain an insight into a singular mentality and morality, that of an unregenerate Stalinist.

Molotov, né Viacheslav Mikhailovich Scriabin, was born February 24 / March 9, 1890 (old and modern calendars), in the village of Kukarka, Viatsk Province (now Sovetsk, Kirov oblast [region]). His mother came from a fairly well-off family, the Nebogatikovs; her three brothers owned a prosperous general store, in which Molotov's father worked as a clerk, in the neighboring town of Nolinsk. The Scriabin family moved there in 1897. Molotov was the ninth of ten children, three of whom died in infancy. One brother became an army surgeon. Another brother, Nikolai, attended a gymnasium and university and became a composer. To avoid confusion with a distant relative, the famous composer Alexander Scriabin, Nikolai changed his surname to Nolinsk.

Molotov failed in his gymnasium studies (he did not explain why), then enrolled in a Realschule, a modern secondary school, in Kazan. There a leading Bolshevik married to a cousin of Molotov's apparently completed Molotov's political conversion. In 1906 he joined the Bolshevik wing of the Russian Social-Democratic Workers party, despite the stronger Menshevist influence prevailing among exiles sent to Nolinsk. In 1909, on the eve of Molotov's graduation, he and three comrades were arrested for revolutionary activity. He was expelled from the Realschule and exiled for two years to Vologda. There Molotov supplemented his income in exile (eleven rubles subsistence per month paid by the government) by playing the mandolin in a quartet that performed in restaurants for a ruble per night and in movie theatres.

Molotov was permitted to take his Realschule graduation examinations as an extramural student. He passed them in 1910 and the next year enrolled in the Saint Petersburg Polytechnic Institute to study economics. Formal enrollment until 1916 enabled him to avoid the draft and provided cover for clandestine revolutionary work. A former exile residing illegally in the capital, in 1912 he assisted in the founding of Lenin's newspaper *Pravda*. In 1915 he moved to Moscow to work as an organizer of the underground party organization there. He then adopted the alias "Molotov," derived from the Russian word for hammer. Arrested that year and sentenced to three years of exile in Manzurka, Irkutsk Province, he managed to escape in 1916 and made his way back to Saint Petersburg (renamed Petrograd in 1914).

In the decade following the Revolution of 1905, the tsarist government had managed to shatter all revolutionary organizations. The regime drove senior revolutionary leaders to seek asylum abroad or exiled them to the remotest margins of the empire. In 1914 repression was redoubled when the Bolshevik party adopted Lenin's antiwar position, "Transform the imperialist war into civil war." Lenin and Zinoviev had fled to Switzerland. Trotsky and Bukharin found haven in New York. Stalin and Kamenev were exiles in Siberia. On the eve of 1917 not a single member of the Bolshevik party's Central Committee was in the capital. The party had some 24,000 members with 3,000 in Petrograd. In 1916 the "Russian Bureau of the Central Committee" was set up in Petrograd to exercise on-the-spot leadership and to maintain liaison with Central Committee members abroad. The bureau consisted of three very junior party leaders: Molotov and two former workmen, Alexander Shliapnikov and Peter Zalutsky.

The bureau members played no direct part in the overthrow of the tsarist government. But Molotov and his two comrades, faithful Leninists, immediately condemned the newly created Provisional Government as a counterrevolutionary combination of capitalists and landlords. Molotov opposed the support, however conditional, given this government by the Petrograd Soviet of Workers' and Soldiers' Deputies, then headed by moderate socialists, the Mensheviks and the Social Revolutionaries (SRs). Notwithstanding, Molotov was brought into the executive committee of the Petrograd Soviet by none other than Alexander Kerensky, who would enter the new government as its minister of justice and future head from July to November 1917.

Upon their return to the capital from Siberian exile at the end of March, Central Committee members Stalin and Kamenev reversed Bolshevik opposition to the Provisional Government. Contending that the party should endorse the Petrograd Soviet's support of the Provisional Government as long as it sought peace, they overruled Molotov and removed him from the editorial board of *Pravda*. Flouting Lenin's desperate letters from Switzerland demanding that the party refuse to support the Provisional Government, Stalin pursued a policy of conditional support. In fact Stalin and Kamenev abandoned Lenin's position which held that only worldwide proletarian revolution could achieve a lasting peace. They took up instead the moderate socialist antiwar position which assumed that popular pressure could compel existing governments, including the newly formed Provisional Government of Russia, to negotiate an immediate, just, democratic peace. On Lenin's return to Russia in April he succeeded in persuading the party to reverse itself and adopt his line: no support whatever to the Provisional Government—"All power to the Soviets!" Molotov's position was vindicated, though he had not yet gone as far as Lenin in demanding a Soviet government. Stalin was never able to live down this lapse into Menshevism, except by exterminating most of the old Bolsheviks who remembered it, Molotov being the major exception.

Lenin's demand that the party move Russia directly from the bourgeois democratic revolution to socialist revolution temporarily stunned Molotov as well as most of the other Bolsheviks. For several weeks they opposed Lenin's new course. In November Lenin led the party into power. Thereafter Molotov, unlike most of the old Bolsheviks who were an independent, contentious lot, never opposed or deviated a hair's breadth from any major policy shift Lenin proposed, even when he, Molotov, did not immediately understand the reasons for it. Only once in the Politburo did Molotov later vote against Lenin—when Lenin proposed closing down the Bolshoi Theatre as an economy measure.

For his dogged devotion and services Molotov received a series of rapid promotions to ever more responsible work. By 1930 he had risen to the pinnacle of power in the Soviet state, chairman of the Council of People's Commissars (Sovnarkom), by assisting Lenin then Stalin in removing Bolsheviks who had fallen into disfavor. In the 1920s Molotov stepped into the boots of men he had helped turn into political corpses. In the 1930s he zealously helped Stalin turn them into corpses, period.

Although Molotov was a member of the Military Revolutionary Committee, chaired by Trotsky, that planned and executed the insurrection, he played a relatively small part in that event. No fiery revolutionary tribune or theoretician, his talents lay rather in the humdrum work of administration, and he came into his own in the 1920s. For he was the ideal *apparatchik* and *chinovnik*, party and state bureaucrat. Not for nothing would he be dubbed, supposedly by Lenin, "stone-bottom" or "iron-ass."

In the civil war, 1918–1921, Molotov held a number of posts in Petrograd and in the provinces where in 1919 he came to the favorable attention of Krupskaya, Lenin's wife.

1921 proved an important year for Molotov. He was elected a full member of the party's Central Committee, was named secretary of the CC, and was elected a candidate member of the Politburo (composed of full members Lenin, Trotsky, Stalin, Kamenev, and Zinoviev, and candidate members Kalinin, Bukharin, and Molotov). As secretary he served as Lenin's chief of staff until 1922, when the newly created office of general secretary went to Stalin. Molotov then acquired the title of second secretary of the Central Committee, deputizing for Stalin. In 1921, no longer living out of a suitcase, Molotov settled down to marry Polina Semenovna Zhemchuzhina, a Bolshevik who had worked in the Ukrainian underground during the Revolution and civil war.

The death of Lenin in January 1924 sharpened the struggle for power within the Communist party. Despite earlier differences with Stalin and the fact that Stalin had superseded Molotov as chief administrator of the party in 1922, Molotov became Stalin's most loyal servitor. Indeed, he figured as one of Stalin's point men, so to speak, in the struggle against the three major opposition groups within the party in the 1920s: Trotskyist, Zinoviev-Kamenev, and Bukharinist. In 1926 Molotov was elected a full member of the Politburo, a position he retained until 1952 when he figured among the next round of Stalin's purge victims. In 1930, at the age of forty, Molotov became chairman of Sovnarkom, succeeding the defeated rightist Alexander Rykov. In Soviet political power Molotov was now second only to Stalin and acted as his chief spokesman.

Molotov accordingly played a crucial and bloody role in the main domestic events of the 1930s which accompanied the crash program of industrialization under the Five-Year Plans launched in 1929: total collectivization of agriculture with its attendant horrors of famine and mass "de-kulakization" (the kulaks were better-off peasants) and the Great Terror.

In 1928–1930 Molotov helped Stalin defeat the Bukharin-Rykov-led opposition to the Stalin-Molotov resumption of compulsory grain requisitioning and the drive for total collectivization. Stalin had launched the effort at the end of 1929 with the pronouncement that the time had come for "liquidating the kulaks as a class." This was a logical consequence of Molotov's charge in September that emboldened kulaks had moved from obstructionism to mounting an offensive against collectivization of the peasantry. Since "kulak" was a social category never clearly defined, any peasant, however poor, who showed insufficient enthusiasm for the collective farm could be accused of having kulak "proclivities."

In January 1930 Molotov was appointed head of the Politburo commission on collectivization which mapped out the chief antikulak measures. Molotov boasted that he personally designated the areas from which tens of thousands of so-called kulak families were selected for expropriation and deportation. Precise figures are still lacking, but the victims may have numbered an estimated ten million people sent into internal exile in Siberia, the far north, and other inhospitable locales. Perhaps one-third of them perished under the harsh conditions of transportation and exile. Molotov also shares with Stalin direct responsibility for the man-made famine of 1932–1933 caused by total collectivization and forced grain procurement. Molotov told Chuev that on his inspection tours he saw no evidence of famine in the Ukraine, conceding that there might have been "hunger" in certain other areas. The famine of 1932–1933 took an estimated five million lives in the Ukraine, one million in the North Caucasus, and one million in Kazakhstan and elsewhere.

By 1934 Stalin had routed all oppositionists; his power was almost absolute. But in February at the XVIIth Party Congress, as Molotov recounted it, a small group of delegates asked the extremely popular Sergei Kirov, faithful Stalinist and party boss in Leningrad, whether they could run him as a candidate for general secretary against Stalin. Horrified, Kirov declined and reported the incident to Stalin. Molotov recalled that Kirov, mindful that he was not up to the responsibility of general secretary, had no such aspirations. Thus Molotov denies that the congress came close to voting in Kirov instead of Stalin, which would have given Stalin a reason to do away with Kirov.

Even if Molotov's version is correct, would Stalin have let the matter of Kirov's popularity rest there? Whatever the case, Kirov was assassinated in December 1934. *Cui bono?* The assassination of Kirov eliminated Stalin's likeliest replacement and provided a pretext for the ensuing Great Terror, 1936–1938. Many esoteric and sophisticated theories have been propounded to explain the terror. Molotov offers the crudest: it eliminated a potential "fifth column." But his argument implicitly lends credence to the theory which holds that Stalin engineered the terror to eliminate all individuals who in the coming crisis of war might form or support an alternative to the Stalin government.

Although Molotov was party to the slaughter and exile of millions of peasants, he may initially have opposed applying the death sentence to the first batch of Old Bolshevik purge victims, including Zinoviev and Kamenev. Moreover, Molotov disagreed with Stalin over some questions of theory posed in drafting the new constitution then under discussion. When *Pravda* published a list of Soviet leaders whom the "terrorists" had "confessed" they were conspiring to assassinate, Molotov's name was not on the list—a sure sign of disfavor with Stalin. Unless the omission was inadvertent, which is most unlikely, Molotov apparently faced elimination in the summer of 1936. But the next year his name was included in the list of targets of the accused conspirators brought to trial. What proof of an attempt on Molotov's life did the prosecutors adduce? In 1934 an automobile carrying Molotov had skidded into a ditch. Three years later this ordinary accident was transformed by the prosecutors into an "attempt" on Molotov's life.

The prisons and the *Gulag*, the forced labor camps, swollen by hapless peasants, were now further swollen by "enemies of the people," victims of the terror that reached its peak in 1937. Again precise numbers of victims are lacking. Estimates of the number of those "repressed" (arrested, shot, imprisoned, exiled) in the 1930s range from five to twenty million.

Despite the horrors of collectivization, famine, and terror, the USSR won unprecedented sympathy abroad, thanks largely to Soviet foreign policy. Commissar for Foreign Affairs Maxim Litvinov's campaign for "collective security" in the League of Nations and for a grand alliance with the democracies against the aggressor states of Nazi Germany, Fascist Italy, and militarist Japan seemed to show a democratic, progressive, humane side of the USSR. This impression was reinforced by the drive of the Comintern (the Communist International, the central organization of the world communist movement, headquartered in Moscow) to mobilize in every country a "Popular Front" of parties and organizations against fascist aggression and tyranny. The Soviet Union, in contrast to the appeasers, seemed to be the only country willing to stand up to Hitler and his allies.

In the spring of 1939, however, Litvinov's negotiations with Britain and France for a mutual defense alliance against aggression stalled. On May 3, at a crucial juncture in these talks and when behind the scenes the possibility of a German-Soviet rapprochement had sprouted, Stalin replaced Litvinov with Molotov as commissar for foreign affairs.

Although Molotov had no experience whatever in diplomacy, he represented Stalin's ideal candidate for the post of commissar for foreign affairs. In every way Molotov was the opposite of Litvinov. Molotov was Russian. He was provincial. He had never been outside the USSR except for a brief sojourn in Czechoslovakia and Italy in 1922. He had only a smattering of foreign languages and was fluent in none. He had never had much contact with foreigners with the possible exception of some foreign communists. He was decidedly anti-Western. Initially he knew virtually nothing about foreign countries and was almost totally ignorant of political geography. And his wife was not a foreigner (though her Jewish origin almost doomed both of them in Stalin's last years). Molotov, the most intransigent Stalinist type, was in a sense the punishment Stalin inflicted on the West for spurning Soviet conditions for a grand alliance.

Although Molotov lacked the conventional education for the post of foreign minister, he had moved to the top through the cruelest, most grueling and perilous political survival course: Stalinism. That experience seems to have served Molotov well. From 1939 to 1949 and again between 1953 and 1956 he did more than hold his own in negotiations with major world leaders and highly trained, widely experienced foreign ministers. He began his career as foreign minister with a diplomatic revolution: the 1939 German-Soviet Nonaggression Treaty and Supplementary Secret Protocol that divided Eastern Europe into German and Soviet spheres of interest. His career ended in 1956 when Khrushchev dismissed him for his efforts to block or reverse the new policy of "peaceful coexistence" with the West.

In foreign affairs, how effective was Molotov? He saw his main task as foreign minister "to extend the frontier of the Fatherland to the maximum." Moreover, he was a powerful proponent of "Red Army Socialism," the establishment and consolidation of communist regimes largely by Soviet military power in countries around the Soviet perimeter. He boasted that Stalin and he had coped well with this task.

Outside appraisals of Molotov's record as foreign minister vary. D.C. Watt, a leading British diplomatic historian, has called Molotov "one of the most inexorably stupid men to hold the foreign ministership of any major power in this century. Beside him, Ciano, Beck, even Ribbentrop, seem masters of intelligence, quick-witted, well informed, and of impeccable judgment." But two statesmen who dealt directly with Molotov would not agree. According to Winston Churchill, Molotov "was a man of outstanding ability and cold-blooded ruthlessness," robotlike, yet "an apparently reasonable and keenly polished diplomatist." In the conduct of foreign affairs, "Mazarin, Talleyrand, Metternich would welcome him to their company." And John Foster Dulles, who squared off with Molotov from 1953 to 1956, wrote, "I have seen in action all the great international statesmen of this century. I have never seen such personal diplomatic skill at so high a degree of perfection as Molotov's."

But a full evaluation of Molotov the statesman, domestic as well as international, must also take into account his perverted ethos. He asserted the outrageous proposition that Stalinist morality was more humane than bourgeois morality. The regime had destroyed millions of lives for what Molotov saw as the noblest purpose, the building of full "socialism." On close inspection, Molotov's vision reveals the social equality of the anthill and little else. Stalinist morality was also superior, he claimed, because the repression of actual and potential "enemies of the people" ultimately saved lives in the coming war. But he also favored the resumption and continuation of repression. A "permanent purge" was needed to prevent the final triumph of rightists, like Khrushchev, who, inspired by kulak ideology, pandered to the "philistine" desire of the majority of the people to live a peaceful, comfortable life in freedom and justice as well as in social equality.

In Molotov's ethos the means—unlimited violence—had swallowed up the ends—socialism and communism, that is, a world without violence. Nevertheless, Molotov in his last days proved to be a prophet. He predicted the triumph of the Bukharinist "right" in the USSR, which turned out to be an apt description of Gorbachev.

In Molotov, never has a prime minister or foreign minister of a great country more zealously, proudly, and effectively served a more monstrous master and his legacy.

A word about the text and translation of the Russian-language *One Hundred Forty Conversations with Molotov, From the Diary of F. Chuev.* Between 1969 and 1986 Chuev, who since childhood had idolized Molotov, met with him at Molotov's flat in Moscow or dacha at Zhukovka 139 times; the 140th "conversation" was Molotov's funeral. Between 1970 and 1977 Chuev and Molotov were joined by the Georgian historian Shota Kvantaliani. The questions posed by the interlocutors covered every aspect of Molotov's life and career, each conversation lasting on the average four to five hours, after which Chuev recorded them in his "Molotov Diary." Only seven hundred of the more than five thousand typewritten pages of this diary went into his book.

Occasionally Molotov was asked a very pointed question, but his interlocutors did not press hard for a candid response, nor did they often dispute him. Perhaps that is why the publisher took the unusual step of asking the well-known Soviet historian Sergei Kuleshov to write a fifty-page afterword commenting on the book. The publisher noted that Chuev did not share Kuleshov's position—that the horrors Molotov and Stalin inflicted on the people of the USSR originated with Lenin. This judgment is still novel in the USSR but is quite familiar in the West, consequently the Kuleshov afterword is not included in this translation. Generally, material not originating with Molotov or having little or no bearing on him has been omitted. This entailed excising banal details, lengthy statements by third persons, and extended quotations from books having little relevance to Molotov. Nothing significant from Molotov himself has been omitted. Occasionally I have added explanatory information in brackets in the text.

Chuev on the whole arranged this material topically. The dates appended to the various conversations indicate the dates the conversations took place. I have moved some of the material so as to order the whole into chronological historical periods. I have, however, let the section on "International Affairs" open the book as it does in the original.

The reader should bear in mind that these are conversations; they are at times discursive, repetitive, even self-contradictory, and often range over entire historical periods.

A very rough draft translation was done in Moscow by Jane Ormrod, Lisa Patrick Wilson, and Toby Perlmutter. I have, however, entirely reworked this draft and retranslated large sections of the Russian original. The degree to which the translation accurately conveys the letter and spirit of the original is my responsibility.

The reader unfamiliar with Soviet politics and government may appreciate some guidance through the maze of titles and agencies and institutions referred to throughout the book.

The USSR was governed by two vast hierarchical, parallel political structures: the Communist party and the Soviet governmental structure. The real governing body of the country was the party, which exercised its authority through the state mechanism. Submission to party discipline was the overriding obligation of party members wherever they worked and lived.

Molotov's rise and fall in this system can be briefly traced. After the Revolution he rose quickly up the ladder of Bolshevik politics. In 1920 he was elected as a candidate (nonvoting) member of the party Central Committee (CC), the executive committee that ran the party in the period between party congresses. The congresses, held annually at first, then irregularly, passed on matters of policy, strategy, and tactics, and elected the members of the Central Committee. In 1921 Molotov was elevated to full membership in the CC and elected a candidate member of the Politburo, the steering committee of the party and the real locus of power. The next year Politburo member Stalin was elected to the newly created post of general secretary of the CC, a position he held until his death in 1953. Molotov now hitched his career to Stalin's.

That Stalin became the absolute ruler of the USSR without holding any executive office in the government is a measure of the power he amassed as general secretary. In 1926 Molotov reached the highest echelon of power: he was elected a full member of the Politburo, a position he held until he lost favor with Stalin in 1952. He recovered this position in 1953, the day after Stalin's death, but lost it again in 1957 by opposing Khrushchev's de-Stalinization drive and conception of peaceful coexistence. Molotov's opposition to Khrushchev's party program, which pledged the achievement of communism by 1980, precipitated Molotov's expulsion from the party and his removal from all offices in 1962. Ironically, the Khrushchev system that Molotov reviled pensioned off Molotov, the oppositionist. Under the Stalinist system that Molotov revered, he would have been "repressed." He finally won reinstatement as an ordinary party member in 1984. Thus he held membership in the party for eighty of its ninety-three years of history (1898–1991).

On the formal governmental side, the cabinet that Lenin formed on the heels of the insurrection was called the Council of People's Commissars (Sovnarkom) with Lenin as chairman. When Lenin died in 1924, Alexander Rykov succeeded him as chairman of Sovnarkom. Rykov, a defeated "right-winger," was removed from office in 1930. Molotov said he had urged Stalin to assume the post, but Stalin declined saying it ought to go to a Russian. Although Molotov had no ministerial experience, he came to the post of chairman of Sovnarkom, which he held until May 1941. In May 1939 Molotov added the position of commissar for foreign affairs to his chairman's portfolio.

Signaling the approaching crisis, in 1941 Stalin himself replaced Molotov as chairman of Sovnarkom. From 1941 until his death in 1953 Stalin held the two most powerful positions in the country. Titular chief of state was the chairman of the presidium of the Supreme Soviet, a purely ceremonial position occupied by Mikhail Kalinin until his death in 1946. During the war Molotov was deputy chairman of Stalin's inner war cabinet, the State Council of Defense. After the war Sovnarkom was renamed the Council of Ministers, changing Molotov's official title to minister for foreign affairs.

No doubt for most of the period from 1930 to 1952 Molotov was second only to Stalin in the USSR.

After Khrushchev removed Molotov from top positions in the party and state, Molotov was appointed ambassador to the Mongolian People's Republic, 1957–1960. There he was too close to Mao Tse-tung for Khrushchev's comfort, so Khrushchev transferred him to Vienna where he acted as Soviet representative to the International Atomic Energy Commission. That posting was not as outlandish as it seems, inasmuch as Molotov played a prime part in the initial development of the Soviet atomic bomb program.

One key agency, the secret police, is ubiquitous in these conversations. This agency passed through a series of name changes and reorganizations. In December 1918 Lenin established the Cheka, the Russian acronym for the full name of the secret police, the Extraordinary Commission to Combat Counterrevolution, Sabotage, and Espionage. Through the years it was renamed several times and known by the following initials: GPU, OGPU, NKVD (1934–1946), MVD, and MGB. Downgraded after Stalin's death, it was named the Committee of State Security (KGB). Molotov often referred to it nostalgically as the Cheka.

Finally we come to Molotov and the basic institutions of Soviet agriculture. One must bear in mind that the Revolution, by abolishing private property in land and turning over former privately owned estates to the peasants, extended and consolidated the traditional system of peasant agriculture in Russia. This was based on communal land tenure with periodic repartition of land allotments. In other words, the villages owned the land and the peasants had use rights to equal shares of it. Every so often the assignment of plots was adjusted to reflect changes in the size of families. After fifteen years of trial and error, two forms of socialist agriculture won Stalin's favor: the kolkhoz and the sovkhoz. Kolkhoz is the Russian acronym for collective farm. It was nominally a self-governing producers' cooperative, resembling the prerevolutionary artel. The members' land allotments, implements, farm buildings, and livestock were pooled with ownership vested collectively in the kolkhoz. Members were permitted to own some poultry and a few animals for meat and milk (but no draft animals), and each household was allowed a small plot for a kitchen garden. The sovkhoz was the acronym for state farm. All land and productive property were owned by the state which appointed the farm director. Sovkhoz members were simply agricultural wage workers, though they too were permitted small garden plots and some farm animals for family use. The sovkhoz might be viewed as a kind of socialist "factory-farm."

Two other types of collective farming, the TOZ and the commune, fell by the wayside. The TOZ was an elementary agricultural producers' cooperative in which only heavy implements were owned in common. In the commune all property was held in common. Work and daily life were conducted communally. Work was not compensated by wages or other forms of distributed income, since theoretically the commune was supposed to provide for all the needs of its members.

The authorities favored the sovkhoz over the kolkhoz because the sovkhoz, as state property, was theoretically owned by all the people of the USSR, the broadest form of social ownership. That is why Molotov blindly thought that the solution to the problems of Soviet agriculture lay in turning the kolkhozes into sovkhozes.

Now to Molotov himself.

ALBERT RESIS

MOLOTOV REMEMBERS

One

INTERNATIONAL AFFAIRS

M OLOTOV, who had no previous experience in diplomacy, was appointed commissar for foreign affairs by Stalin in May 1939, just when the Soviet Union entered the most critical period in its diplomatic history since Brest-Litovsk. In this section Molotov and Chuev focus on three key problems: (1) Stalin's German policy, 1939–1941, including a defense of the German-Soviet Nonaggression Pact and an explanation of why the German invasion of June 1941 took the Stalin leadership by surprise; (2) alliance with the West, 1941–1945, and the onset of the cold war; and (3) Molotov's opposition to Khrushchev's version of peaceful coexistence.

Molotov insists that Stalin and he had no illusions about Hitler. Molotov defends the Nonaggression Pact because it gave the USSR another twenty-two months to prepare for a German invasion that Stalin and he knew was sooner or later inevitable. In November 1940 Molotov went to Berlin where he sharply complained to Hitler and Ribbentrop that the Germans, by stationing troops in Finland and Rumania, were violating the German-Soviet secret spheres-of-interest agreements (the existence of which Molotov continued to deny in these conversations). Moscow, fully aware of the weakness of the Red Army compared with the Wehrmacht, desperately played for more time to continue its military buildup. When May 15, 1941, passed without the German invasion predicted by Soviet intelligence, Soviet leaders thought the country was more or less safe until the summer of 1942. For surely Hitler would not launch an invasion toward the end of June, which would entail a winter campaign and a war on two fronts to boot. Thus the USSR, it seemed, had gained another year in which it could reach peak military strength. But the Kremlin erred badly, Molotov admits. They should have recalled that Napoleon had launched his invasion of Russia as late as June 24, 1812.

Molotov regards the Grand Alliance of 1941–1945 as another fruit of the German-Soviet Nonaggression Pact. The pact, he contends, divided the imperialists against themselves and precluded the formation of an imperialist anti-Soviet, united front. Consequently, when the German

5

invasion came, the USSR had Great Britain and the United States on its side as allies and friends. But Molotov also believed that the Western democracies intended to allow their Soviet ally to be bled white by the Germans. Moscow desperately needed an Allied second front in Western Europe. Molotov reveals here that Stalin and he were perfectly aware that the United States and Britain could not successfully launch a second front in Western Europe in 1942 or in 1943 for that matter. Nevertheless, Molotov in May–June 1942 extracted from Washington and London pledges to launch a second front in 1942. The pledge helped lift the morale of the Soviet people. Equally important, according to Molotov, Western failure to deliver a second front in 1942 or 1943 put Roosevelt and Churchill in bad light with their own electorates. Subsequent public pressure forced a step-up of Lend-Lease assistance to the USSR and fulfillment of the second-front pledge in 1944.

Most revealing are the very first pages of this section on Soviet concerns in the first postwar year. Stalin in a *tour d'horizon* concluded that the USSR in victory had achieved international security around its entire perimeter—except in the direction of Turkey and Iran, which were neither Soviet satellites nor allies. Molotov concedes here that Stalin went too far by calling for Soviet military bases at the Dardanelles, delaying evacuation of Soviet troops from northern Iran, and laying territorial claims to parts of eastern Turkey. The West consequently hardened its policy toward the USSR, and the Grand Alliance, which Molotov never had much faith in, was sundered.

Yet Molotov bitterly charges his predecessor and rival, Maxim Litvinov, with treason for opposing this policy then. On June 18, 1946, Litvinov in his deputy foreign minister's office confided his oppositionist views to the American correspondent Richard Hottelet. Litvinov said that worsening relations with the United States was caused by the Kremlin's false conception of security based on territorial expansion, prompted by the belief that war with the West was inevitable. (Three weeks after Litvinov died, Hottelet published the contents of his Litvinov interview in the *Washington Post*, January 21–25, 1952.) The conversation was secretly recorded by Soviet security services, and on August 23, 1946, Litvinov was dismissed from his post as deputy minister for foreign affairs.

Litvinov's opposition raises a significant question about the origins of the cold war. Litvinov stated that Soviet leaders in 1946 believed that war with the West was inevitable. But at the very same time Stalin was publicly declaring that such a war was not inevitable and that peaceful coexistence between East and West was quite possible.

Throughout these conversations Molotov evinces little faith in peaceful coexistence and the possibility of preventing a new war. Indeed, other Soviet sources show that Molotov believed the U.S. military buildup in 1946 was intended for an attack on the USSR, notwithstanding Stalin's protestations that war was not inevitable.

Where did Litvinov get the idea that Soviet leaders believed an East-West war was inevitable—from Stalin, from his immediate boss Molotov, or from both? Was Stalin dissembling when he publicly professed faith in peaceful coexistence? Or did he really believe in it? If he so believed, did Molotov disagree with him on this vital question? It would seem so, judging by Molotov's 1946 views revealed recently in other Soviet sources and by his vehement opposition to Khrushchev's version of peaceful coexistence.

In sum, Molotov dared argue with Hitler, and despite Molotov's notoriety as a servile, Stalinist yes-man, he even dared disagree with Stalin.

■ A New Map ■

It's good that the Russian tsars took so much land for us in war. This makes our struggle with capitalism easier.

[1-14-75]

My task as minister of foreign affairs was to expand the borders of our Fatherland. And it seems that Stalin and I coped with this task quite well.

. . . I recall a story told by A. Mgeladze (first secretary of the Central Committee of the Communist party of Georgia during the last years of Stalin's life), supplemented by Molotov.

It's about a map with new borders of the USSR that was brought after the war to Stalin's dacha. The map was very small—like those for school textbooks. Stalin pinned it to the wall: "Let's see what we have here. . . . Everything is all right to the north. Finland has offended us, so we moved the border from Leningrad. Baltic states—that's age-old Russian land! —and they're ours again. All Belorussians live together now, Ukrainians together, Moldavians together. It's okay to the west." And he turned suddenly to the eastern borders. "What do we have there? . . . The Kuril Islands belong to us now, Sakhalin is completely ours—you see, good! And Port Arthur's ours, and Dairen is ours"—Stalin moved his pipe across China—"and the Chinese Eastern railway is ours. China, Mongolia—everything is in order. But I don't like our border right here!" Stalin said and pointed south of the Caucasus.

[11-29-74]

In this matter we admittedly went a bit too far, but something has been brewing in the south. You have to understand that there are limits to everything, otherwise you can choke.

The problem of the Baltic states, western Ukraine, western Belorussia, and Bessarabia we solved with Ribbentrop in 1939. The Germans reluctantly agreed to our annexation of Latvia, Estonia, and Bessarabia. A year later when I was in Berlin, in November 1940, Hitler asked me,

8

"Well, good, you are uniting the Ukrainians, uniting the Belorussians, all right, and the Moldavians, that's reasonable—but how are you going to explain the Baltic states to the whole world?"

I said to him, "We'll explain."

Communists and the people of the Baltic states favored joining the Soviet Union. Their bourgeois leaders came to Moscow for negotiations but refused to sign such an agreement with the USSR. What were we to do? I must tell you confidentially that I pursued a very hard line. I told the Latvian minister of foreign affairs when he came to visit us, "You won't go home until you sign the agreement to join us."

A popular minister of war from Estonia came to see us—I've forgotten his name. We told him the same thing. We had to go to such extremes. And to my mind, we achieved our aims quite satisfactorily.

This sounds crude in the telling, but in fact everything was done more delicately.

But the first one could have warned the others.

There was no escape for them. A country somehow has to see to its security. When we laid down our demands—you have to act before it's too late—they vacillated. Of course bourgeois governments could not join a socialist state with alacrity. But the international situation was forcing their decision. They found themselves between two great powers—fascist Germany and Soviet Russia. The situation was complicated. That's why they wavered, but finally they made up their minds. And we needed the Baltic states. . . .

We couldn't do the same with Poland. The Poles were irreconcilable. We negotiated with the British and French before talking to the Germans. If the West had permitted our troops in Czechoslovakia and Poland, then of course we would have fared better. They refused, thus we had to take at least partial measures; we had to keep German troops at a distance.

If we hadn't moved toward the Germans in 1939, they would have invaded all of Poland right up to our old border. That's why we came to an arrangement with them. They had to agree. They took the initiative on the nonaggression pact. We couldn't defend Poland because it didn't want to deal with us. Inasmuch as Poland would not deal, and war was close at hand, give us just that part of Poland that we believe indisputably belongs to the Soviet Union.

And we had to protect Leningrad. We didn't make the same demands on Finland as on the Baltics. We talked to them only about their ceding to us a piece of the territory near Leningrad. From Viborg. They were very stubborn.

I had to talk at length with Ambassador Paasikivi—he later became president. He spoke a bit of Russian but was understandable. He had a good library at home, he read Lenin. He realized that without an agreement with Russia, Finland would be in trouble. I sensed that he wanted to meet us halfway, but he had many opponents.

[7-24-78]

How merciful we were toward Finland! We were smart not to annex it. It would have been a festering wound. Not because of Finland itself, but because that wound would have afforded a pretext for anti-Soviet action.

People are very stubborn there, very stubborn. Even the minority could have been dangerous there.

But little by little we are now consolidating our relations. Just as with Austria, we were unsuccessful in making Finland democratic.

Khrushchev handed over Porkkala-Udd to the Finns. I doubt we would have done this.

Port Arthur wasn't worth spoiling relations with the Chinese. And the Chinese kept within limits, didn't bring up their territorial problems. But Khrushchev pushed. . . .

[11-28-74]

We never recognized Bessarabia as Rumanian. Remember how it was shaded on our maps? So when we needed it I summoned the Rumanian minister to the USSR. I gave him a deadline for withdrawal of their troops, after which we would move ours in.

You summoned the Rumanian ambassador?

Yes, yes.

"Let's come to an agreement. We never recognized Bessarabia as yours, and it would be better to resolve these problems now." He replied immediately, "I have to consult my government." He went limp, of course. "Consult and come back with an answer," I said. He came back later.

Did you discuss with the Germans whether they would stand in your way in Bessarabia?

We came to an agreement when Ribbentrop visited us. At the same time we were talking directly with Rumania; we had contacts there.

Hitler told them: "Give it to them, I'll return it to you soon!"

They took their cues from him all the time. . . . I didn't know geography well at the time of Ribbentrop's visit. I didn't know the geography of the borders between Russia, Germany, and Austria-Hungary. I demanded we draw the borders so that Chernovitsy would go to us. The Germans said to me, "But you've never had Chernovitsy, it's always belonged to Austria. How can you demand it?"

"The Ukrainians demand it! Ukrainians live there, they ordered us to do this!"

"But it has never been Russian, it's always been part of Austria and then of Rumania!" Friedrich von der Schulenburg, German ambassador in Moscow, said this.

"Yes, but the Ukrainians must come together!"

"There aren't many Ukrainians. . . . Let's not discuss this question!"

"We have to make a decision. And the Ukrainians are now both in Trans-Carpathian Ukraine and in an area to the east—all of this belongs to the Ukraine, and you want to leave out a chunk? Impossible. How can this be?"

"What is it called . . . Bukovina."

Schulenburg hemmed and hawed, and then said, "I'll report to my government." He did, and Hitler agreed.

Chernovitsy, which had never belonged to Russia, became ours and still is. For the moment the Germans weren't out to spoil or sever relations with us. We were overwhelmed with joy and surprised with Chernovitsy.

I was told later by people who had visited Chernovitsy that there had been order there but now there was disorganization. . . . It turns out they had been using Ukrainians for all the hard work when Chernovitsy had been a part of Austria. Now that they had joined us, the Ukrainians didn't want to work. They became independent, not merely unskilled workers. They could not make it by themselves; they had no management experience and didn't want to be left behind.

The final agreement on borders took place after the war. Some were astonished: Why did they talk about Chernovitsy and Russia? There has never been such a thing!

We weren't fools. No one, at least among our enemies or supporters, considered us fools.

[4-25-75, 9-30-81]

■   Ribbentrop-Molotov   ■

Western broadcasters talk a lot about you, curse you and Stalin.
It would have been worse if they had praised us.
They say, "There are a few people in history whose names have been attached to border agreements." They have in mind the Ribbentrop-Molotov Line. And why were incendiary bottles called "Molotov cocktails" during the war? You had nothing to do with it?
They thought it up . . . a mixture. I mixed Russians and Germans.
You are considered one of the main instigators of the war because your treaty with Ribbentrop freed Hitler's hands. . . .
They'll go on saying that.

[8-1-84]

"Ribbentrop was a good champagne salesman," Shota added.
Certainly. He was a wine merchant. . . . Our men fired at his plane when he came to visit us. They all but shot him down. They didn't realize who was up there.
He was a lean, tall man. . . . The talks took place in the Kremlin. That's where we drank champagne.
Did he bring his own?
No, it was our treat.

[10-4-72]

When we received Ribbentrop, of course he toasted Stalin and me—on the whole he was my best friend. *Molotov's eyes twinkled.* Stalin unexpectedly suggested, "Let's drink to the new anti-Cominternist—Stalin!" He said this mockingly and winked at me. He had made a joke to see Ribbentrop's reaction. Ribbentrop rushed to phone Berlin and reported ecstatically to Hitler. Hitler replied, "My genius minister of foreign affairs!" Hitler never understood Marxists.

[7-9-71]

I had to toast Hitler as the leader of Germany.
Over there, in Germany?
Here, at dinner, they toasted Stalin, me, and Hitler, in our little company. That's diplomacy.
Molotov was at the head of the table during a reception in honor of Ribbentrop. When Stalin spoke, he offered a toast to "our people's

commissar of the railways, Lazar Kaganovich"—who was a Jew—who sat at the table one chair next to the fascist minister of foreign affairs. "And Ribbentrop had to drink to me." Kaganovich told me the story.

[3-12-82]

Talk is that you and Stalin decided, in order to gain Hitler's favor before the war, to give him the Baltic states. . . .

"This has nothing to do with reality. We realized very well that such a step would not only fail to stop Hitler but on the contrary would whet his appetite. And we ourselves needed space.

The writers say that . . .

Writers perhaps of philistine views. That's absolute nonsense. We ourselves needed the Baltic states.

[7-17-75]

They persistently write in the West that a secret agreement was signed together with the [German-Soviet] *nonaggression pact in 1939. . . .*

None whatever.

There wasn't?

There wasn't. No, that's absurd.

Surely we can talk about it now.

Of course, there is no secret here. In my view these rumors were deliberately spread to damage reputations. No, no, this matter is very clean. There could not have been any such secret agreement. I was very close to this matter, in fact I was involved in it, and I can assure you that this is unquestionably a fabrication.

[4-29-83]

This wasn't the first time I asked Molotov, "What was the secret protocol signed during talks with Ribbentrop in 1939?"

I don't remember.

Churchill writes that Hitler didn't want to cede south Bukovina to you, that this strongly affected Germany's interests and that it was not mentioned in the secret treaty.

Well, well.

And that Hitler urged you to join the Triple Alliance.

Yes, the scoundrel. That was just camouflage. A game, a game, and quite a primitive one at that.

But you told Hitler that you didn't know Stalin's opinion on this issue. You knew, didn't you?

Of course. With Hitler I couldn't wear my heart on my sleeve.

[3-9-86]

Molotov says the rumors are groundless that there was a secret correspondence between Stalin and Hitler, Molotov and Ribbentrop during the war, that one of the sides offered an armistice after the battle for Moscow, and that Stalin telephoned Hitler when the war started.

That's nonsense. They would do anything to stir up trouble. Stalin wouldn't dirty his hands. He wouldn't have benefited from it. I had to sound out...

[7-31-72]

Western sources say that during the war you met with Ribbentrop in Mogilev.

This story is going around. Apparently in 1943—I know about this—American radio broadcast this story. It's absurd, of course. I am only surprised they are still interested in broadcasting such trash, which is patent nonsense. But they keep printing it.

[4-25-75]

It seems to me that at times Stalin was impelled to hold your feet to the fire.

It happened. He was the leader and had to move matters forward. That was unavoidable, and there was nothing unusual about it.

[5-1-81]

■   In Berlin   ■

Hitler was an extreme nationalist. A blinded and stupid anticommunist.

Did Stalin meet him?

No, I was the only one to have such a pleasure. There are people of that kind now, too. That's why we must pursue a vigilant and firm policy.

[5-9-85]

Hitler. . . . There was nothing remarkable in his appearance. But he was a very smug, and, if I may say so, vain person. He wasn't at all the same as he is portrayed in movies and books. They focus attention on his appearance, depict him as a madman, a maniac, but that's not true. He was very smart, though narrow-minded and obtuse at the same time because of his egotism and the absurdity of his primordial idea. But he didn't behave like a madman with me. During our first conversation he spoke a monologue most of the time while I kept pushing him to go into greater detail. Our meetings were most accurately recorded by Berezhkov. Fiction based on this subject contains a good deal of made-up psychology.

Hitler said, "What's happening? An England, some miserable island, owns half the world and they want to grab it all—this cannot be tolerated! It's unjust!"

I answered that it surely was intolerable and unjust, and that I sympathized with him.

"This cannot be considered normal," I told him. He cheered up.

Hitler said, "You've got to have a warm-water port. Iran, India—that's your future." And I said, "Why, that's an interesting idea, how do you see it?" I drew him into the conversation, giving him an opportunity to speak out. For me this was not a serious conversation, but Hitler continued to expatiate bombastically on how England was to be liquidated and the USSR would thrust its way across Iran to India. He had little understanding of Soviet policy—a myopic man, he wanted to involve us in risky policy. And he'd be better off after we got stuck in the south. We'd depend upon him there when England went to war with us. You had to be too naive not to realize that.

But in our second conversation I switched to our concerns. Here, I said, you are offering us splendid countries. But when Ribbentrop visited us in 1939 we agreed that our common borders should remain calm and that there should be no foreign troops in Finland or Rumania. But you are stationing troops there! Hitler said, "That's a trifle!"

There's no need to speak roughly, I said, but if the socialist and capitalist states want to reach an agreement there must be a partition—this is your sphere of influence and this is ours. So Ribbentrop and I had agreed that the border with Poland would look this way, and there would be no foreign troops in Finland and Rumania. Why do you keep them there? "Trifles." "How can we talk about the big questions when we cannot agree to coordinate our actions on secondary matters?" He stuck to his story, and I to mine. He became agitated. I persisted. In sum, I wore him down.

[12-6-69, 7-9-71]

We had dinner after the talks. Hitler said, "The war is on, so I don't drink coffee now because my people don't drink coffee either. I don't eat meat, only vegetarian food. I don't smoke, don't drink liquor." I looked and it seemed a rabbit was sitting next to me eating grass—an idealistic man. It goes without saying that I was abstaining from nothing. Hitler's team drank and ate, too. It should be noted that they didn't appear insane.

[2-19-71]

"We had coffee and small talk as prescribed among diplomats. Ribbentrop, the former wine merchant, talked about wine labels and asked about Massandra.... Hitler played along and tried to impress me.

Hitler clasped me with one hand when our picture was being taken. I was asked in Canada in 1942 why I was smiling in that picture. Simply because they got nothing from us and never would!

Hitler was surprised that I persisted with the "trifles" that could easily be sorted out....

I said to him, "Let's sort them out!"

He answered with something vague.

He came out of his room when we were leaving and walked me to the coat rack. He told me while I put on my coat, "I am sure history will remember Stalin's name forever!" "I don't doubt it," I answered. "But I also hope it will remember me, too," Hitler said. "I don't doubt this either."

I sensed he was not only afraid of our power but that he also stood in awe of Stalin's personality.

[6-22-71]

"*I remember a film about your arrival in Berlin. It was a steam locomotive. Even the Germans didn't have electrically powered locomotives. Berlin station, soldiers, rifles,*" Shota said. "*And you were slowly getting off the train. You wore a hat.*"

Could be.

Yes, you wore a hat. You moved slowly. Ribbentrop greeted you in the SS manner, Goering, Goebbels... and in the Reichstag Hitler was embracing you.... Hitler welcomed you so.

No, no.

Wait a minute, Viacheslav Mikhailovich, I saw that, I remember how it was in the film: you were there, Hitler here. . . . So how was it then?

The devil knows how. . .

I can show you.

You can show me! You weren't even there!. . . Hitler was there, Ribbentrop, two interpreters. One of them, Hilger, lived his whole life in Russia alone in Moscow. He used to say he was our friend. And I was there, of course, with that group of four. Berezhkov was there, though I don't remember. Probably Pavlov was there. I suppose they both were there. Pavlov, not Berezhkov, actually made the translation. He was the chief interpreter. Our ambassador was there; I later appointed Dekanozov to the post. There was not much to choose from. We were in Hitler's office—a vast, lofty hall.

Hitler was of medium height, approximately as tall as I was. He certainly did the talking; the rest of us just added some remarks or explanations and asked questions. . . .

He wanted to win me over, and almost did. *Molotov smiled ironically.* Everyone kept urging me that we should be together, Germany and the Soviet Union, that we should combine our efforts against England. "England is all but smashed." "Smashed?" I said. "Not yet!" "We'll get rid of her soon and then you will turn to the south, to warm water and take India."

I listened to Hitler with great interest. He was using all his powers of persuasion. Was he persuasive? He had a very one-sided view—he was an extreme nationalist, a chauvinist, blinded by his own ideas. He wanted to aggrandize Germany, to squash the whole world under his heel.

He refrained from criticizing the Bolsheviks. Diplomacy, of course, but how could he negotiate otherwise? If you want to reach an agreement and you start spitting in the other person's face . . . We had to talk like humans. And we had to talk.

"And Churchill?" Shota asked.

With Churchill, too.

But Roosevelt was softer with you?

Yes, he was a wilier comrade. He drank with us, of course. Stalin nursed him along just right. He was very fond of Soviet champagne. He loved it. Like Stalin.

I wired Stalin after my talks with Hitler, quite lengthy telegrams every day—what I said, what Hitler said. Stalin asked me when we met, "How did he put up with you when you were telling him all this?"

Well, he had to put up with it. He spoke in a calm voice, he didn't curse. He just tried to persuade. "Would you like a conclusive agreement with us?" he asked.

We came to an agreement when Ribbentrop visited us in 1939. But in September-October we had already taken what was ours. And there was no other way. We didn't lose time. And we got an agreement that along our borders, especially in Finland, which is fifty kilometers from Leningrad, there would be no German troops. And in Rumania—along our borders—there would be no troops except Rumanians. "But you keep many troops in both places." Political questions. I had a lot to say.

"Great Britain is what we need to talk about," Hitler said to me. "We'll discuss this, too," I said. "What do you want? What are your proposals?" "Let's divide the whole world," he said. "You need the south, to get to the warm waters."

Then we had dinner. I dined at his place. Himmler, Goebbels, Goering were there. Only Hess wasn't there. I visited Hess in his office, too, in the central committee of the Nazi party. Hess appeared very modest. His office was a modest, hospital-like room. Goering's office was the opposite—filled with big paintings, Gobelin tapestries. . . . The dinner at Hitler's was attended by the whole company. They seemed to be at home there.

He went on, "Here are five countries. . . ." I said, "There is an agreement with Ribbentrop, made in 1939, saying that you would not station troops in Finland, but they are there; when is this going to end? You are also not supposed to have troops in Rumania. There should be only Rumanian troops there, but you have your troops on our border there. How can this be? It contradicts our agreement." "These are trifles. Let's negotiate the big question," he said.

We didn't settle anything with him, for I kept pressing him: "That's not an answer. I asked a question and you're not giving any clear answer to it. I request a clear response." We had to see if they really wanted to improve relations with us or whether we had run into a void, into empty talk. It became clear they didn't want to yield to us on anything. They pressed and pressed, but they were not dealing with cranks—Hitler realized this. For our part, we had to probe deeply as much as it was possible to speak seriously with them. We had agreed to observe the treaty—they were not doing so. We saw they didn't want to observe it. We had to draw our own conclusions, and they of course drew theirs.

"Yes. We defeated the biggest monster raised by imperialism," Shota *said.*

More exactly, England and France, too.

[11-16-73]

Was there any point for the Germans to meet with you in 1940?

They wanted to fool us and draw us into a war with England on the side of Germany. Hitler wished to see whether he could involve us in the adventure. They would remain Hitlerites, fascists, and we would help them. Could he involve us in that?

I said to him, "What about our immediate concerns? Do you agree to fulfill obligations you have pledged to fulfill?"

It became clear, of course, that he only wished to draw us into an adventure. But for our part I was unable to secure promises from him regarding Finland and Rumania.

[3-8-74]

We were seated at the table during negotiations with Hitler. There was a table for experts, a table for an interpreter. Hilger translated for Hitler. He was born in Odessa, his mother was Russian. His son was later killed near Moscow. Hilger disapproved of the war against us. He was frightened. His Russian was excellent, you couldn't tell him from a Russian.

Schulenburg understood Russian a little bit but spoke it badly. He had accompanied us from Moscow. He had forgotten his uniform. The train had already left the station, and he had had to catch up with us by car somewhere outside Moscow. A guard of honor stood along the rail line all the way from the border to Berlin.

Hitler did most of the talking during our first conversation. And I pressed him. I raised questions, cleared up some things. He described in detail what he considered necessary, and I listened. Then, in our second conversation, I had to talk.

In diplomacy you don't have to begin with abuse and name-calling—one can do without that. But you need to sort out the plans, the intentions, the moods. You have to think about these. Hitler was very correct with me.

[5-12-76]

"Diplomacy exists exactly for the ability to talk, to keep quiet, and to listen," Talleyrand taught.

A diplomat cannot use abusive language.

[7-24-78]

I changed our ambassador to Germany after my visit to Berlin in November 1940. He was out of his depth. I had appointed him myself, but it hadn't been successful. I was just getting down to business and had to replace the old hands and of course I made some mistakes. He was not a bad comrade but very weak and ineffective. His name? Like Shvarkov. Shkvartsev [Alexander A. Shkvartzev, Soviet ambassador in Germany, September 1939–November 1940]. He was a professor; he knew a bit of German. He had worked only a few months. When I came to the Ministry of Foreign Affairs in 1939 I had to change almost all its chiefs.

And I remained the Predsovnarkom [chairman of the Council of People's Commissars].

And Dekanozov became ambassador to Germany. Stalin nominated him. Apparently he was an Armenian but pretended to be a Georgian. Even Stalin argued with him, "You aren't a Georgian!"

He was not a bad worker, a very honest man.

[7-31-72]

"Do you have a party program?" I asked Hess. I knew they didn't. How could it be, a party without a program?

"Do you have party rules?" I knew they didn't have party rules. But I decided to feel him out anyway. Hess was Hitler's first party deputy, a party secretary. Bormann was his deputy.

I went on tripping him up. "And do you have a constitution?" They didn't have that either. What a high level of organization!

"Did you know that Hess was a pederast?" Shota asked.

I didn't know. I wasn't interested, but I knew he wasn't the only one of them like that.

[6-16-77]

Properly speaking, what was Hitler's aggression? Wasn't it class struggle? It was. And the fact that atomic war may break out, isn't that class struggle? There is no alternative to class struggle. This is a very serious question. The be-all and end-all is not peaceful coexistence, peaceful coexistence. After all, we have been holding on for some time, and under Stalin we held on to the point where the imperialists felt able to demand point blank: either surrender such and such positions, or it means war. So far the imperialists haven't renounced that.

[7-7-76]

■ The Send-off Was Worth It... ■

Stalin was the greatest tactician. Hitler, after all, signed the nonaggression pact with us without the acquiescence of Japan! Stalin made him do that. Japan was deeply resentful toward Germany and gained no benefit from their alliance. Our talks with the Japanese minister of foreign affairs, Matsuoka, had great significance. At the end of Matsuoka's visit Stalin made a gesture that caught the whole world's attention. He personally went to the station to see off the Japanese minister. No one had expected this; Stalin never met or saw off anyone. The Japanese and the Germans were stunned. The train was delayed for an hour. Stalin and I made Matsuoka drink a lot, and we almost carried him onto the train. Seeing him off was worth it because Japan refused to wage war on us. Matsuoka himself paid for his visit to us....

And in 1945 I declared war on Japan. I called the Japanese ambassador to the Kremlin and handed him the note.

What was their reaction?

Their reaction? They were delighted.

On TV they showed how you and Stalin hosted Matsuoka in 1941. Stalin drank champagne and watched him. And you were holding a glass and smiling. Matsuoka took Stalin's arm....

He had already drunk quite a bit. The journalists made him do it. It was in my office. There were a lot of people. Events were moving toward war....

[4-29-82]

They say you and Matsuoka sang, "The cane was rustling..." when you went to see him off in 1941.

That happened.... Why, he could barely stand up in the station....

[1-1-79, 3-9-79]

■ We Wanted to Delay the War ■

All the history books say that Stalin miscalculated the beginning of the war.

To some extent, but it was impossible not to miscalculate. How could you know when the enemy would attack? We knew we would have to deal with him, but on what day or even what month...

It is known there were fourteen dates.

We are blamed because we ignored our intelligence. Yes, they warned us. But if we had heeded them, had given Hitler the slightest excuse, he would have attacked us earlier.

We knew the war was coming soon, that we were weaker than Germany, that we would have to retreat. The question was, retreat to where—to Smolensk or to Moscow, that's what we discussed before the war.

We knew we would have to retreat, and we needed as much territory as possible. We did everything to postpone the war. And we succeeded— for a year and ten months. We wished it could have been longer, of course. Stalin reckoned before the war that only in 1943 would we be able to meet the Germans as equals.

But there were the intelligence reports...

What is written about this is contradictory. From my point of view, there couldn't have been another beginning for that war. We delayed it and, in the end, we were caught asleep; it turned out to be unexpected. I think we could not have relied on our intelligence. You have to listen to them, but you also have to verify their information. Intelligence agents could push you into such a dangerous position that you would never get out of it. Provocateurs everywhere are innumerable. That's why you can't trust intelligence without constant and scrupulous checking and rechecking.

Some naive people, philistines, have written in their reminiscences: the intelligence agents spoke out, deserters from the enemy crossed the border...

You couldn't trust such reports. But if you were too distrustful you could easily go to the other extreme.

When I was the Predsovnarkom I spent half a day reading intelligence reports. The only thing missing was the date of the invasion! And if we had trusted these reports [and gone on a war footing] the war could have started much earlier. The task of intelligence was to report in a timely manner.

On the whole, everyone expected the war would come and it would be difficult, impossible for us to avoid it. We delayed it for a year, for a year and a half. If Hitler had attacked us half a year earlier, you know, bearing in mind our situation then, it would have been very dangerous. So it was impossible to begin obvious preparations without revealing to

German intelligence that we were planning serious measures. We took many serious steps, but still not enough. We didn't have time to finish very much. Some think Stalin should have to answer for all this. But there was the people's commissar for defense, the chief of the general staff. . . . On the other hand . . .

Some people, Marshal Golovanov in particular, argue that the war caught the general staff asleep.

They were not asleep. But they had a directive ordering that the first reports not be trusted, that they must be verified. Time was lost.

But that's a failing of Stalin's.

You may think so, of course. He was in a difficult situation because he didn't want the war.

And maybe Stalin overestimated Hitler? Maybe he thought Hitler was smart enough not to attack us until he finished the war with England?

That's right, that's right. Not only Stalin had this feeling but I and others did, too. On the other hand, there was nothing left for Hitler to do but attack us. He would never have finished his war with England— you just try to finish a war with England!

A writer described the beginning of the war this way: "Stalin cursed the ambassador to Germany Dekanozov and Molotov as well, who had boasted that now we would be friends with Germany."

He is spitting on and smearing me, knowing that now I can't publicly defend myself. . . .

They write now that Stalin trusted Hitler, that Hitler deceived him with the pact of 1939, lulled his vigilance. Stalin trusted him. . . .

Such a naive Stalin. No. Stalin saw through it all. Stalin trusted Hitler? He didn't trust all his own people! And there were reasons for that. Hitler fooled Stalin? As a result of such deception Hitler had to poison himself, and Stalin became the head of half the world!

We had to delay Germany's aggression, that's why we tried to deal with them on an economic level—export-import.

No one trusted Hitler, but Stalin was so credulous! . . . He wanted to delay the war for at least another half a year, or longer. Everyone wanted this delay, everyone who was close to the concerns of the time. No one as close to the situation as Stalin could have avoided miscalculation. But in fact there was such a man who managed to find the way out, and not only to find the way out but to win!

A mistake was made, but of minor importance, I would say, because we were afraid to get ourselves drawn into the war, to give the Germans a pretext for attack. That's how everything got started, I assure you.

To me, these were not our mistakes but our weaknesses. Weaknesses because I think psychologically it was almost impossible for us to be completely ready for war. We felt we were not yet ready, so it was quite natural for us to overdo it. But there is also no way to justify that. I personally don't see any mistakes in that. In order to delay the war everything was done to avoid giving the Germans a pretext to start it.

But Hitler had already made up his mind. It would have been hard to make him change it. . . .

We weren't inside his mind, anyway. He was out to unleash the war in 1939. But when? We wanted a delay for a year or several months. Of course we knew we had to be ready for war at any moment, but how do you do that in practice? It was very difficult.

So many times we talked about this subject, and each time I tried to clear it up. After five, ten, fifteen years Viacheslav Mikhailovich made the same statements. And it was not an attempt to justify himself but an unshakable conviction. We were at the dacha in Zhukovka; Ivan Stadniuk, a writer, was visiting. Molotov had followed the publication of his novel The War. *He liked it, gave some advice. After reading the third book of the novel he reproached the author for writing that Stalin had assumed the Germans would not attack us until 1942. Stadniuk had relied on memoirs of Marshal K. Meretskov.*

But I consider that wrong. To slander a dead man, Stalin, as if he had said this. In the first place, Meretskov is inaccurate, you can't trust him on this. Stalin called him "Yaroslavets." Why "Yaroslavets"? People in Yaroslavl were so shifty, he said, that there were almost no Jews. Russians themselves played such roles and one of them was Meretskov. I doubt Meretskov's accuracy when he wrote this! I was close to Stalin and I don't remember anything like that, and no one who saw him every day would say that. I admit I could have forgotten something. Maybe he did say something of that sort, but with the word "probably." . . . You [Stadniuk] have written this to justify Timoshenko who in your book reflects upon the beginning of the war. Timoshenko wasn't a low-ranking officer—he was people's commissar for defense! But did he measure up? So why slander Stalin?

I take a very critical view of your work. As you would have it, there appeared a man Timoshenko—who spoke more truthfully, and suddenly he is against Stalin! The point is not that we didn't divine the exact date of the attack; the point is that we didn't let Hitler into Moscow,

Leningrad, or Stalingrad—that's the point! The crux, after all, is our final brilliant victory! And you cast doubt on Stalin now, when he is no longer alive. . . .

"I proceeded from the assumption that this would justify Stalin," Stadniuk said. *"Why weren't we prepared? Because we supposed . . ."*

But we were prepared! How is that—weren't prepared? That is wrong, that we weren't prepared. Unprepared for what?

For the day of the attack, for the hour of the attack—that's what we weren't prepared for.

Oh, but no one could have been ready for the hour of the attack, even God himself! We'd been expecting the attack and we had a main goal—not to give Hitler a pretext for it. He would have said, "Soviet troops are assembling at the border. They are forcing me to take action!"

Of course that was a slip-up, a shortcoming. And of course there were other slip-ups. You just try to find a way to avoid mistakes on such a question. But if you focus on them, it casts a shadow on the main point, on what decided the matter. Stalin was still irreplaceable. I am a critic of Stalin; on certain questions I did not agree with him, and I think he made some major, fundamental mistakes. But no one talks about these mistakes; instead they keep criticizing things on which Stalin was right, and they talk endlessly as if they were negative.

In essence we were largely ready for war. The five-year plans, the industrial capacity we had created—that's what helped us to endure, otherwise we wouldn't have won out. The growth of our military industry in the years before the war could not have been greater!

The people went through a colossal strain before the war. "Hurry, hurry!" And if they didn't they were expelled from the party, arrested. Is it possible to keep the people or the party or the army or even your near and dear ones under such strain for a year or two years?

No. And still there were things that cannot be justified.

There were mistakes, but the point is how to understand them. First, whose mistakes were they? Second, how could they have been avoided? There are at least two questions there.

The tension was palpable in 1939 and 1940. Tension ran very high; that's why there was so little good cheer about and why everyone longed for a respite. Recently someone asked me reproachfully, "And where was [Politburo member] Zhdanov?" He was vacationing in Sochi when the war broke out. Well, it was certainly possible not to go to Sochi in 1939 or 1940 and even in 1941, but after all you had to give a sick man a rest. They taunt us: "What were they thinking about? About the war? No, they were in Sochi!" The members of the Politburo, it is said, were optimists.

To keep every member of the Politburo, healthy or sick, under pressure every day. . . . And think of all the people, all the personnel. We even abolished the seven-hour working day two years before the war! We abolished the right of workers to move from one enterprise to another in search of better conditions, even though many of them lived poorly and were looking for better places to live—but we abolished this. We built no apartment houses, but there was great construction of factories, the creation of new army units armed with tanks, aircraft. . . . We drove all the designers—"Faster, faster!"—they couldn't finish in time, they were all young designers!

I knew Pavlov rather well—the commander-in-chief of the Belorussian district. He was a tank man, a brawny fellow and, of course, utterly loyal to the party. He was executed because he had panicked. He was ready to sacrifice his life on a battlefield or anywhere else for our country. Well, let's admit, he was a bit of a blockhead—that's more the man's misfortune than his fault. Although he couldn't have been that stupid if he managed to become a commander-in-chief! Not smart enough, a bit stupid, but he became the commander in honest fashion, as a communist. As it turned out, he went to the theatre on the 21st of June. He was informed that not everything was quiet on the border, but he said, "Never mind, we'll sort it out after the performance." Could we have told him not to attend the theatre in 1939, 1940, and 1941?—that's also wrong. It's not that the man didn't understand; he was tired and wanted a respite.

. . . I told Molotov that Marshal Golovanov had recounted to me that he had personally witnessed a telephone conversation between Pavlov and Stalin in Pavlov's study only a few weeks before the war. Stalin had warned him about a possible attack, but judging by the talk it seemed that Pavlov, who was almost on the border, did not take the warning seriously.

"The thing is," I told Molotov, "now some think you appointed such untrained people as Pavlov, but if it had been Tukhachevsky. . ."

Take someone like Tukhachevsky. If trouble started, which side would he have been on? He was a rather dangerous man. I doubted he would have been fully on our side when things got tough, because he was a right-winger. The right-wing danger was the main danger at the time. And many right-wingers didn't realize they were right-wingers, and were right-wingers in spite of themselves. Trotskyites, those loudmouths, shouted, "We won't be able to hold out! We'll be defeated!" They damned themselves out of their own mouths, so to speak. And these defenders of the kulaks were deep-rooted. They were more cautious; they had lots of supporters around—peasants and the lower middle classes. There was only a thin layer of party leadership in the 1920s, and there were always fissures in this thin layer—now right-wingers, then nationalists, then workers' opposition. . . . How Lenin managed to bear this is amazing. Lenin died, but they all lived on, and Stalin had to pass through very tough times. Khrushchev is proof of that. He turned out to be a right-winger, though he was pretending to be for Stalin, for Lenin. "Father Stalin! We are ready to give our lives for you, we'll wipe out everyone!" Only when Stalin's power weakened did the conspirator in him surface. . . .

We demanded great sacrifices from workers and peasants before the war. We paid little to peasants for bread or cotton or their labor—we simply had nothing to pay with! What to pay? We are reproached—we didn't think of the material interests of the peasants. Well, if we had, we would have wound up in a dead end. We didn't have enough money for cannons!

We delayed the war. This calmed the people a little. If we managed to delay it for a year and ten months, we could probably have delayed it for a month or so more. Anyway, I have been thinking about it ever since. We should have kept in mind that the best time for an attack on Russia was June. It wasn't fully taken into consideration in any quarter, to my mind. Napoleon attacked Russia in June, too. Summer months are very dangerous. But the Soviet Union heroically found the way out of that situation.

That was a mistake.

Yes, a mistake. But one June had already passed. June of 1940 had passed, and that suggested that June 1941 would pass, too. This was a miscalculation, I suppose. We were under great pressure to prepare better, which I thought was impossible. Well, perhaps we could have been 5 percent better prepared. But no more than 5 percent. We were going all out to get our country ready for defense. We inspired the people—if war comes tomorrow, if tomorrow they take to the field, we shall be ready to march today! We didn't let the people oversleep, but we encouraged them and cheered them up all the time. If everyone was under such a strain, some kind of respite was needed. . . .

But the time for a respite was poorly chosen.

No. The need for a respite was continuous—in January, in February, in March, and so on. But when would they attack? We could be blamed for not taking June into more consideration than May. But you would have to be a pedant to blame us for this, knowing all the measures that were being taken. If you blame us for this you are, if not a bureaucrat, a pedant. Of course we should have been somewhat more alert in June than in May. But already in May we had been under colossal pressure with no chance to let off steam. Even if a higher alert had been ordered in June, there would still have been need for a respite. Why was Zhdanov in Sochi, why were officers on leave, why was Pavlov at the theatre? My God! Of course, we might have done without these niceties; just the same, they were not decisive!

Why did you destroy the old line of fortifications before you managed to build a new line?

That's simple—we didn't have the opportunity. We didn't have the time not only to destroy what we needed to destroy but also to replace it with something new—that's a fact. Maybe there was haste; I don't exclude that possibility.

But anyway, objectively, it turned out that Hitler outwitted you.

No. No, I don't agree with this. Yes, he had his own calculations. There couldn't have been a better time chosen for the attack. But to demand a greater effort from us than in May... there was the danger of a breakdown. Everything was stretched, stretched to the limit, and there wasn't all that much to eat. A mistake in timing is an unjust accusation, quite wrong. There was a miscalculation of some sort, certainly. But this was more a misfortune than a mistake or a fault.

Khrushchev used Churchill's words saying that he had warned Stalin. Stalin said later, "I didn't need any warnings at the time. I knew the war was coming, but I thought I could gain another half a year." That is why Stalin is blamed. He relied upon himself and thought he could delay the war.

That's stupid. Stalin couldn't rely upon himself; in this case he had to rely upon the whole country. He thought not about himself but about the whole country. That was our main interest, that of a whole people—to delay the war for a few weeks more.

But Churchill didn't have anything against us at that period....

Yes, but could Churchill be trusted in this matter? He was interested in pushing us into a conflict with the Germans as quickly as possible, how could it be otherwise?

Ambassador Schulenburg warned Dekanozov about the beginning of the war.

He didn't warn, he just hinted at it. Many people hinted at it to speed up the conflict. But to trust Schulenburg . . . so many rumors, so many assumptions made the rounds! It was also wrong not to pay attention to them.

But if you had ordered the army . . .

That's what a provocation is.

Why would it be a provocation? Better to let them attack the unarmed? To give military men leave? . . .

We were not unarmed, we were on alert. And no one would work for a year without a vacation. To my mind it was impossible to ensure against a surprise attack in our condition. But we should have been preparing for it anyway. We march to heroic deeds, but we often lack endurance. It's hard to blame the people for this, though there were culprits. The Germans were more disciplined. You tell them what to do, and that's it. Ours would do the same—with much pressure. But we still didn't have enough perseverance, or enough methodicalness. Our peasant's nature showed itself here. They would work, then drink themselves half-dead, then harvest. . . . Surprise, of course, played its part. I am sure there are intelligence reports coming in even now that something may begin somewhere. It's the nature of intelligence. And Marxism-Leninism doesn't have anything to do with it. Our ideology stands for offensive operations when possible, and if not, we wait.

While we are gathering strength, they peck at us.

True, that's not excluded. And not because we are gathering strength but because we do not know how fully to utilize our talent. This takes time, and we didn't have much of that.

Stalin is portrayed as vain and willful, as though everything would be as he wished. . . . This is wrong and slanderous. But as to the surprise that unfortunately happened, it couldn't have happened differently. You probably won't find such know-it-alls who could predict exactly such things about their enemy.

People write that faith in Stalin was based in part on his own self-glorification and the cult of personality he created. Is that so?

A little bit. You see, a man is still a man. But he did a great deal, and that's the main thing. No one could have done more than Stalin in that situation—not only during the war but before the war and after it.

There are many questionable statements in Zhukov's book. And untruths, too. He describes how he reported to Stalin before the war (I was present, too) that the German maneuvers were creating a danger of war. Supposedly I asked him, "So, do you think we'll have to fight the

Germans?" Such a shameless thing. Supposedly I was the ultimate fool, so to speak. Everyone understood the situation, but I understood nothing. Zhukov writes that Stalin was sure he would manage to prevent war. But if Stalin is to blame for everything, then he built socialism alone and won the war alone. Even Lenin didn't rule alone, and Stalin wasn't the only one in the Politburo. Everyone bore responsibility. Of course, Stalin's situation then wasn't easy. It's not true that we didn't know. After all, Kirponos and Kuznetsov put their troops on alert but Pavlov didn't. . . . The military men, as always, turned out to be helpless. Well, of course we were then weaker than the Germans. Of course we should have deployed better. But we had our best officers working on that. Zhukov was considered a rather good commander; he worked in our general staff. Timoshenko, too, was a rather good military man; he was the people's commissar for defense.

But military men blame everything on Stalin—that he hobbled initiative, that they had to wait for his orders.

Everyone wants to pass responsibility to someone else. But Kuznetsov, a sailor, the navy minister, issued an order on the night of the 21st–22nd to expect an air raid. Zhukov didn't do this. Kuznetsov boasts that he did this on his initiative. In this case he proved to be more than right, because he was not asked to verify his reports. Such verification was demanded of the general staff, which was under standing orders not to rush but to check every report—even those just minutes before the war began—before accepting it as truth. We knew there was a delay there, but it didn't matter.

Nekrich writes, "Stalin thought that Hitler was playing a game to extort political and economic concessions."

And why not think so? Hitler was an extortionist, to be sure. He could have been extorting concessions. You could have counted on extortion. Around each issue there could have been extortion and deception and duplicity and flattery and . . . it's hard to say really. . . .

The main idea in the literature is that Stalin didn't think Hitler would start the war.

That's right, they write so. Vasilevsky writes a bit naively about the beginning of the war. I read the beginning of Berezhkov's book.

It's a good book.

Not on the whole.

But interesting.

Yes, interesting. I've read only the first hundred pages, and I've noticed two things with which I cannot agree. One is that Stalin thought that Hitler wouldn't attack the USSR that year. How could he put such words into Stalin's mouth, especially now when you can accuse him of anything? And he cannot defend himself, and no one can do it for him. All the more, "Stalin believed, Stalin thought..." As if anyone knew exactly what Stalin thought of the war! Of course some people were inclined to believe that the war would not start that year. If it should come, it would be later. I consider this normal, but in my opinion there are no grounds to assert that Stalin believed the war wouldn't come that year. No one can say that about another person. That's the first thing.

Second, he mentions a TASS report. A week or so before the war it was announced in a TASS bulletin that the Germans were taking no actions against us, that we were maintaining normal relations. It was, I think, Stalin's idea. Berezhkov reproaches Stalin, saying there was no ground for such a report. This was a diplomatic game. A game, of course. And it didn't work. Not every attempt yields good results, but the attempt itself was not a bad idea. Berezhkov writes that it was patently naive. It wasn't naiveté but a diplomatic move, a political move. In this case it didn't work, but there was nothing unacceptable or impermissible about it. And it wasn't stupid but, so to speak, an attempt to clear up the situation. The Germans' refusal to respond to it simply showed they were pursuing a treacherous policy toward us. They tried to show the whole world that they were taking legitimate measures. In my view it is wrong to condemn and ridicule the TASS report. But Berezhkov describes it as an obviously wrong move, as naive. There was nothing naive about it. It was a highly responsible action. The move was aimed at depriving the Germans of any excuse for an attack. If we had moved our troops out just a bit, Hitler would have declared, "You see, over there they have moved their troops forward! Here are the photographs, here are the activities!" They say we had insufficient troop strength at the border, but had we started moving troops to the border, we would have given Hitler an excuse! Meanwhile, we were preparing at full speed.

We had no other way out. So I consider it vile to reproach us for this. The TASS bulletin was necessary as a last resort. If we had managed to delay the war for the summer, it would have been very difficult to start it in the fall. Up to the last moment we were successfully delaying the war by diplomatic means, and no one could have predicted when we would fail. And keeping silent meant inviting the attack. It turned out that on June 22 Hitler became an aggressor in the eyes of the world. And we gained allies.

Nekrich suggests Stalin hoped to pull Hitler into negotiations.

Yes. That's right. We had to test them! Of course, in dealing with such beastly people you might get tricked, and not everything might work, but essentially no concessions were made, and testing them was quite legitimate.

In a way, Stalin distinguished Hitler from the German military, believing that the war might begin as a result of their provocations, but that Hitler himself wouldn't have broken the pact. I don't think Stalin believed that.

I don't think so either. These are very wild speculations aimed to cast doubt upon Stalin. He wasn't a naive person, he wasn't such a good-natured simpleton that everyone could . . . But we had to try, we had to find ways to get to Hitler.

■   **Stalin's Attitude Toward Hitler**   ■

I read to Molotov the so-called "Hitler's will," as noted by Bormann on February 14, 1945. "The critical factor of the war was that for Germany it started too soon and at the same time too late. From a purely military point of view we should have started the war earlier. I should have taken the initiative in 1938 instead of allowing myself to be drawn into war in 1939. . . ."

No doubt!

". . . For the war was inevitable anyway. Nevertheless, I am hardly likely to be blamed, for England and France agreed with all my claims in Munich!"

"From the present-day point of view, the war came too late. But from the point of view of our moral preparation, it started much earlier than it should have. My disciples had not yet reached their full maturity. . . ."

Well, did he say that?

". . . I needed, in essence, another twenty years to make that new elite ripe, an elite of youth, immersed from its earliest childhood in the philosophy of National Socialism. Our tragedy as Germans is that we never have enough time. Circumstances always were such that we were forced to hurry, and if we don't have time now, that is mainly explained by our lack of space. Russians with their huge spaces can afford the luxury of time. Time works in their favor and against us. . . ."

But Russians found themselves in such a situation long before 1941, and Hitler could have understood this, but he didn't. That's his failing.

"... *Why just 1941? Because, considering the constantly growing power of our western enemies, if we were destined to take action at all, we should have done it with minimal delay. And note: Stalin wasn't idly sitting by, hands folded....*"

That's for sure!

"... *Time was against us on both fronts. Actually the question was not why June 22, 1941, but why not earlier?*"

That's right, that's right.

"... *If it weren't for the difficulties caused us by the Italians and their idiotic campaign in Greece, I would have attacked Russia a few weeks earlier....*"

Well, probably.

"... *Our main problem became how to delay Russia from attacking us as long as possible. I had a never-ending nightmare that Stalin could take the initiative earlier than I....*"

Of course, it was a well-known question.

"... *We can foresee with confidence that no matter the outcome of the war the British Empire has come to an end. It is mortally wounded. The future of the British people is to die of hunger and consumption on their accursed island....*"

Yes. He himself told me that. He said it like this: "some accursed island ..."

And did you assume that if not they, we would start the war first?

We didn't work out such a plan. We had five-year plans. We didn't have allies. They would have combined with Germany against us then. America was against us then. England against, France not far behind.

But official doctrine at the time was that the war would be fought on foreign soil, to spill little of our blood.

Who could draft such a doctrine—if you please, invade our territory, and, if you please, fight here?! Of course the minister of war would say, "Little of our blood will be spilled, and the war will be fought on foreign territory!" That's just propaganda. Such sloganeering prevailed over our real policy. This too was necessary and indispensable.

Hitler said, "We need only one thing—not to admit defeat, for the fact of our independence, of our existence, is already a victory for the German people. This is enough to justify the war, which will not be in vain. It could not be avoided in any case. Enemies of German National Socialism pressed it on me as long ago as January 1933....

"*If I am fated to perish, let the German people perish too, because they turned out to be unworthy of me.*" That's how he began.

This phrase of his is famous. Quite a stupid one.

What did Stalin think of Hitler as a personality? How did he evaluate him?

It would be incorrect to say that he underestimated him. He saw that Hitler had organized Germany in a short period of time. There had been a huge Communist party and it had disappeared, wiped out! And Hitler led the people and the Germans fought hard during the war. Stalin, as a cool-headed man, took these facts seriously when discussing grand strategy.

[12-6-69, 6-16-83]

■   **Receiving Schulenburg**   ■

I was rereading Zhukov's Memoirs and Reflections, *and the situation on June 22, 1941, is still not completely clear to me. He says, "The commander-in-chief of the Kiev military district, General Kirponos, reported at approximately midnight that yet another German deserter informed him that the German troops would go on the offensive at 4 a.m.*

"Everything pointed to the fact that," Zhukov writes, "German troops were moving closer to the border. We reported this to Stalin at half past midnight. Stalin asked whether the instructions had been passed to the military districts. I gave an affirmative answer.

"Versions that appeared after Stalin's death claimed that some commanders and their staffs, suspecting nothing, slept peacefully or were heedlessly having a good time on the night of June 22.

"That doesn't correspond to the facts. . . . The commander-in-chief of the Black Sea fleet, Admiral F. Oktiabrsky, called me on a high-frequency communication (used only by high-ranking officers) at 3:07 a.m. and informed me, 'Fleet observation reports an approach from the sea of unidentified aircraft in large numbers. . . .' I asked the admiral, 'What's your opinion?' 'There is only one answer—to meet the planes with anti-aircraft fire from the fleet.'

"The chief of staff of the Western district, General V. Klimovsky, reported at 3:30 a.m. a German air raid on Belorussian cities. . . . The narkom [people's commissar] ordered me to call Stalin. No one answered the telephone there. I kept calling. . . ."

"That means it was close to four in the morning," I said to Molotov, looking up from the book.

Oh, but we met earlier! Zhukov wants to show himself in the best light. He believes he understood the situation correctly, but he too hardly understood it at all.

I went on reading Zhukov's book.

"Finally I heard the sleepy voice of the duty officer, a general of the security service. I asked him to call Stalin to the phone.

"Three minutes later Stalin was on the phone.

"I reported the situation to him and asked permission to commence military countermeasures. Stalin remained silent. I heard only his breathing.

" 'Did you understand me?'

"Silence again.

"At last Stalin asked, 'Where is the narkom?'

" 'He is talking on high-frequency with the Kiev district.'

" 'Come with Timoshenko to the Kremlin. Tell Poskrebyshev to summon all the members of the Politburo.' "

This was earlier.

I went on reading Zhukov's book.

"I was talking again with F. Oktiabrsky at 4 a.m. He reported with a calm voice, 'The enemy's raid was repulsed. The attempted air strike on the ships was foiled. But there was some destruction in the city.'

". . . All members of the Politburo were assembled by 4:30 a.m."

Earlier.

"The narkom and I were invited into the office. A pale Stalin was seated at the table, a pipe in his hand stubbed with tobacco. 'We have to call the German embassy immediately,' he said.

"At the embassy they replied that Ambassador Count von Schulenburg requested that he be received to transmit an urgent communication.

"Molotov was instructed to receive the ambassador.

"Meanwhile, the first deputy chief of the general staff, General N. Vatutin, reported that after heavy artillery fire on a number of sectors in northwestern and western theatres, German ground forces had attacked.

"Shortly after, Molotov entered the office. 'The German government has declared war on us.'

"Stalin sank into the chair and plunged into deep thought."

"And this seems to be around 5 a.m.," I said.

Oh, but that's incorrect, wrong.

Zhukov does not mention here that Stalin ordered us to keep our eyes open and report on everything, but it should be understood that surely there would be all kinds of provocative communications. You couldn't take their word for it. . . .

Either Zhukov is mistaken, or I have lost track of something. Zhukov called. He didn't tell me the attack had begun but that there was danger at the border. It was either bombing or some other alarming information. It's quite possible that the real war hadn't begun, but there was such tension that the staff realized the need to meet. We assembled at Stalin's in the Kremlin around 2 a.m. If you came from the dacha it took you thirty to thirty-five minutes.

But Zhukov writes that he woke Stalin and informed him of the bombing. That means they were already bombing at 1 a.m., doesn't it?

Wait a second. . . . He may be in error here. Zhukov and Timoshenko awakened us: something alarming had already begun at the border. Perhaps someone had earlier reported a separate bombing, and that two had been carried out. By now this was a secondary question. We met at Comrade Stalin's in the Kremlin around 2 a.m. All members of the Politburo were summoned. It was an official session. Before that, on June 21, we stayed until 11 or 12 p.m. at Stalin's dacha. Maybe we had even watched a movie. We used to do this often—watch a movie after dinner. Then we parted and met again later. But between two and three in the morning a phone message came from Schulenburg to my secretariat, and from Poskrebyshev, saying that German ambassador Schulenburg wished to see the minister of foreign affairs, Molotov. I started from Stalin's office up the stairs to my own office. We were in the same building but in different parts of it. One corner of my office faced the statue of Ivan the Great. The other members remained at Stalin's, and I went to my office to receive Schulenburg. It was a two- or three-minute walk. Otherwise I would have had to phone Stalin had I been called at the dacha with Schulenburg's request for a reception. Ambassadors don't make night calls to ministers of foreign affairs. I wouldn't have gone to meet Schulenburg without of course informing Stalin. I don't remember phoning Stalin from the dacha. And I would have remembered, because I thought of nothing else except that the war was beginning, or something like that. It was not Schulenburg who called me but a KGB officer connected to Poskrebyshev—Stalin ordered us to meet. I received Schulenburg between 2:30 and 3 a.m. I think it was not later than three o'clock. The German ambassador handed me a note timed to coincide with the attack. They had everything coordinated, and apparently the ambassador had instructions to present himself at the appointed hour. He knew when it would start. We of course couldn't know it.

But even at three o'clock the Germans hadn't attacked us yet. . . .

Everywhere it was different. We beat off an air raid in Sebastopol. They attacked between 2 and 3 a.m. Why do you stick to such a minor point? Everything is interesting, of course. We can iron out the details to the minute by looking through documents and inquiries. But they aren't important. Malenkov and Kaganovich ought to remember when they were summoned. To my mind, it was not later than half past two. And Zhukov arrived with Timoshenko no later than 3 a.m. And Zhukov sets the time after four o'clock—on purpose, to match his own timetable. The events occurred earlier.

It's known that Stalin usually worked at night. Somehow he happened to be asleep that night, and Zhukov woke him up. . . .

Why, Zhukov wants to prove himself. That's not quite correct.

I don't know whether it's true or not, but who can I ask but you? Allegedly you said to the ambassador, "How did we deserve this?"

That's an invented story if you got it from Werth's book. He wasn't there, so how was he to know? That's pure fabrication. I surely couldn't have said such a stupid thing. Nonsense. Absurd. Who could he have gotten it from? There were two Germans and my interpreter. . . . There is also a lot of farfetched psychology in Chakovsky's book when he describes that episode. But it was I who received Schulenburg anyway, not Chakovsky. . . .

It's known that Count Schulenburg opposed the war with the Soviet Union. He even sent a memorandum to Hitler to that effect before the war. Apart from his official message, did he say anything personal?

It wasn't a time for personal talk. Schulenburg was calm. Of course he couldn't say anything. He was later shot.

Did he inform Hitler poorly about Russia?

Well, probably, that goes without saying. But he joined in a conspiracy against Hitler. And as for his interpreter, a counselor at the German embassy, Hilger, he shed a few tears when they were delivering the note.

Schulenburg was old then, wasn't he?

What do you mean 'old'? He was younger than I am now. And I don't consider myself an old man.

[12-6-69, 7-31-72, 8-15-72, 5-21-74]

■   **Did Stalin Lose His Head?**   ■

Zhukov shirks responsibility for the beginning of the war. But that is
naive. He is not only evasive, he gets confused. On June 21 we sent out
a directive alerting the troops to prepare for action. In his book he
equivocates. He doesn't say whether he thinks Stalin put things right or
wrong. But of course Stalin did put things right. So they prepared in
some military districts but not in the Belorussian. . . .

[3-8-74]

Stalin and I went to the ministry of defense when the war started.
Malenkov and someone else was with us. Stalin was quite rude with
Timoshenko and Zhukov.

He rarely lost his temper.

*Then Molotov told how with Stalin they wrote an address to the
people which Molotov broadcast from the Central Telegraph at noon on
June 22.*

Why me and not Stalin? He didn't want to be the first to speak. He
needed a clearer picture in order to choose the proper tone and correct
approach. He couldn't respond like an automaton to everything. That
was impossible. He was a human being, after all.

Not only a human being—that's not quite correct. He was both a
human being and a politician. As a politician he had to wait and see
what was happening. For he had a very precise style of speech, and it
was impossible immediately to get oriented and give an exact answer. He
said he would wait a few days, and when the situation on the front was
sorted out he would make a speech.

*Your words, "Our cause is just. The enemy will be smashed, victory will
be ours," became one of the main slogans of the war.*

That was an official speech. I wrote it. But it was edited by all the
members of the Politburo. That's why I cannot say these were only my
words. There were corrections and additions, of course.

Did Stalin take part in this?

Of course! Such a speech couldn't be delivered without his approval.
He was a rigorous editor. I can't tell you which words he added, the
first or the last ones. But he too was responsible for the editing of the
speech.

And was it he or the Politburo who wrote the speech on July 3?

It was he. You didn't work that way with him. You didn't write for him. It was not our wording. He made certain speeches without prior editing. In 1945 or in 1946, when I delivered my report on the anniversary of the November Revolution, or spoke at the UN, the words were mine—no one else edited these speeches. I spoke not from prepared text but more or less extemporaneously.

I knew, of course, that Stalin planned to address the parade on November 7, 1941. He told me this. I don't remember whether he gave me the speech to read—probably he did. He usually gave them to me to read. His speech at the November 7 parade wasn't recorded; he recorded it afterward.

At the start of the war Stalin, Beria, Malenkov, and I went to the ministry of defense. Beria and I went from there to Stalin's dacha. It was the second or the third day. It seems to me that Malenkov was with us, too. I don't remember who else. I remember Malenkov.

Stalin was in a very agitated state. He didn't curse, but he wasn't quite himself.

It is written that he lost his head and lost the ability to speak in the first days of the war.

I wouldn't say he lost his head. He suffered, but he didn't show any signs of this. Undoubtedly he had his rough moments. It's nonsense to say he didn't suffer. But he is not portrayed as he really was. They show him as a repenting sinner! Well, that's absurd, of course. As usual, he worked day and night and never lost his head or his gift of speech.

How was he behaving?

How did he comport himself? As Stalin was supposed to, firmly.

But Chakovsky writes that he . . .

I don't remember what Chakovsky wrote about that, but we were talking about a completely different matter. Stalin said, "We blew it." This referred to all of us. I remember it well; he simply said, "We blew it." Yes, we blew it. Such a troubled state Stalin was in then. I tried to cheer him up a bit.

"It grieves me that an army was lost," said Shota Ivanovich, "but suppose the Germans had not broken through our defenses and we had gone on the offensive and advanced successfully in Poland. Would England, America, and other countries have allowed us to crush Germany in 1941? Would they have been on our side?"

Of course we still didn't know.

How much it meant for the Soviet state that we had England and America as allies!

That's right. That's right.

[7-31-72, 1-13-84]

■   We Fought for This Land   ■

*I visited Molotov with Shota Kvantaliani and guests from Georgia—
Indiko Antelava and Meliton Kantareia, who had hoisted the banner of
victory over the Reichstag.*

*It was a lovely early spring day. We went for a walk in the forest. There
were many people around and everyone kept turning and gazing at
Molotov.*

We sat at a table after our walk.

*"Now look here, our Meliton and his friend Egorov hoisted that
banner," Shota said. "How did you start to climb and find the dome? The
Reichstag was unfamiliar to you, wasn't it?"*

"A soldier's sixth sense," Kantareia replied.

"It was a good idea," Molotov said.

"You made it in time, weren't late. Our troops got there before the
others—that was right."

*At the end of the conversation Kantareia said, "I am not well
educated, but I love my country. I'll always defend Soviet power if need
be. I love my country. . . ."*

"Georgia?" Molotov asked.

*"No. The Soviet Motherland. It doesn't matter where I was born. The
Motherland is the heart; this is the land we fought for. For Stalin and for
the Motherland. For the multinational Soviet Union we stood shoulder to
shoulder and won. And we will win again if need be."*

*"Tell us the good news from Georgia," Shota told him, "how the
Georgian republic is building communism. Viacheslav Mikhailovich likes
that."*

"Even if it is only socialism," Molotov said.

[3-17-74]

■   At the Front   ■

When did you go to the front?

I went to Leningrad in 1941. I dismissed Konev, then I went to
spur on Zhukov. That was probably 1942 or 1943. These are the trips
I made.

[6-13-74]

October 1941 I went to the front to dismiss Konev. He wasn't doing well. I had to explain to Konev why he should be replaced by Zhukov. Zhukov mended things.

It seems Zhukov stood up for him.

Yes. I had to dismiss Voroshilov in Leningrad, too.

He couldn't handle the job?

He could—he spent all his time in the trenches!

[1-14-75]

I happened to be in Leningrad in the last days before the siege finally closed. We flew there. Malenkov was with me. Kuznetsov from the navy, and Voronov, an artillery man. It was a large group. They all were military people. It was probably in August 1941. Yes, in summer. We took a plane to Cherepovets and then went to Leningrad by train. It was not far, but we couldn't get to Leningrad even by train because the rail lines were already cut. We used a section of car from the Mga station to go to Leningrad. But I couldn't get back by train—the ring was closed. So after four or five days I flew over Lake Ladoga. That was the toughest time.

Zhdanov was in Leningrad. He was a very good comrade, a very good man. But he was very dejected then. Everything was going badly. The Germans were surrounding the city and finally locked them in.

I arrived there under Stalin's instructions at this very moment. And Zhukov was sent to Leningrad soon after my return.

Zhdanov—how should I say this—was good but a bit spineless.

[4-13-72]

Zhukov reproached Stalin. I don't believe Stalin thought, as Zhukov claims, that the main German thrust would be in the Ukraine. I don't think so. I also don't think Zhukov's reference to Stalin is correct. For I knew, no less than Zhukov, what Stalin said, and I don't remember him saying this. I don't remember it. I can't prove it, but the fact is that the Germans moved first of all toward Moscow. They stumbled at Smolensk and, like it or not, had to turn to the Ukraine. . . .

The main concern was Moscow, not the Ukraine. But Stalin also took into consideration not giving them an opportunity to head for Donbass and Dnepropetrovsk.

Zhukov writes that Donbass and Kiev delayed the Moscow battle for three months.

Because the Germans were set on Moscow. They failed. One must take this into account. . . . Therefore you must cite Zhukov more cautiously. . . . You can say now what you like, but I was a bit closer to that scene than you. But you think I've forgotten everything. . . .

                                                                    [1-14-75, 10-4-85]

I asked if Stalin, in October 1944, had thought about leaving Moscow.

That's nonsense. He had no doubts. He wasn't going to leave Moscow. I went for just two or three days to Kuibishev and left Voznesensky in charge there. Stalin told me, "See how they are settling in there and come back right away."

Molotov appreciated Zhukov as a soldier.

Rokossovsky was not as firm and persistent; Zhukov bawled out his orders. I became convinced of Zhukov's abilities when Stalin invited Vasilevsky, near the end of the war, and asked him how long it would take to seize Koenigsberg. "Two or three weeks," he replied.

Then Zhukov was summoned. He gave a realistic appraisal of the assault and said it was not a simple matter, that it would take two or three months. It turned out to be so.

                                                                    [5-7-75, 7-16-78]

Marshal Shaposhnikov was a good person. Stalin treated him well. He was an officer of the tsar. But thanks only to a Leninist understanding of history do we now hold such positions which would otherwise be beyond anyone's forces, any Shaposhnikov. But he had no political ambitions. He was good at his profession.

And Zhukov would have failed in politics, though he had ambitions for it. I know Vasilevsky well. He was a very good general staff officer. And as for the commanders-in-chief, Zhukov was in the top three. Zhukov undoubtedly; Rokossovsky is also there. Who's the third one—I have to think. Rokossovsky was a very nice person. Golovanov was right; for many people Rokossovsky's personal qualities overshadowed his outstanding abilities as a general.

                                                                    [4-2-78]

■   **Stalin's Postwar Toast**   ■

General Ivan Ryshkov, who had served on the general staff during the war, told Molotov how they had written an order for the first salute to mark the liberation of Orel and Belgorod, but had forgotten to mention those who had fallen. Stalin reminded them of this.

"I added to it," Ivan Nikolaevich recalled, 'May the memory of the heroes who fell in battle live forever. . . .'

"Stalin read it and said, 'Not the memory, you know, but the glory. The 'memory' has a gospel sound. Eternal glory to the heroes who fell in battle for the honor and independence of the Motherland!'"

[3-9-79]

We were celebrating the thirty-ninth anniversary of the victory. Ryshkov was talking about Molotov's role in the war, about diplomacy. Viacheslav Mikhailovich interrupted him: "Let's postpone the second part of your speech until tomorrow. Our army had been a great help to our diplomats. If not for the army's help, none of the diplomats could have managed! We've had even tougher times than the war. There were days when things hung by a thread. The 1920s were more difficult. But we had been preparing for the war and were ready for it!"

Molotov was ninety-four years old, blood pressure 120/80.

[5-9-84]

You said that Stalin's first postwar toast was "To our Viacheslav!"
He apparently wanted to emphasize the role of our diplomacy in the war. Stalin said publicly, "Let's drink to our Viacheslav." I don't remember exactly, but it was something like that—that the diplomacy sometimes played a larger role than one or two armies. I can't quote it exactly, but it was in that spirit.

[8-18-71, 6-6-73]

They say now that the main result of the victory is that we live in peace.
That's just some kind of peace-lovingness.
The main achievement is the socialist system?
That's right. An international one.
We celebrated the fortieth anniversary of the victory.

[5-9-85]

■   The Eternal Flame   ■

I consider this wrong—the Eternal Flame. Why wrong? We followed the bourgeois way, we copied them. We should not have made a Tomb of the Unknown Soldier but a Tomb of the Antifascist.

We are the only country in the world which has a Tomb of the Unknown Soldier and a Tomb of the Unknown Supreme Commander-in-Chief. We should probably have built a monument to the Soviet soldier in Moscow. . . .

Right you are. They should remember this. It's normal for the bourgeoisie to have some unknown soldier. For us it's not every soldier but only those who helped in the struggle against fascism, against imperialism. These are the soldiers we should glorify. The others are fit for whom—Egypt, Iran?

[4-13-72]

■   Allies   ■

Admiral Kuznetsov writes that on May 1, 1945, Stalin read a telegram from Molotov, congratulations from San Francisco.

Yes, I was in America in May. . . . I wanted to send Gromyko there, but the Americans asked me to come for the first UN assembly. . . . Harriman sent a plane and I flew with their pilots over Yakutia. . . .

On May 9, 1945, I was in San Francisco. I made a speech on the radio on Victory Day. They asked me to do it on the 8th. I said I couldn't, we were celebrating on the 9th. They were on the 8th and we were on the 9th. Many celebrate it on the 8th, but we consider that incorrect. I think Stalin worried about being duped or disappointed by our allies. Or that they might involve us in something nasty.

Stalin was wary. . . .

The Allies had talks with the Germans through Allen Dulles beginning in March 1945. And they did not let us in on them. Of course we showed great distrust until it was all resolved. We waited. That was the right thing to do, to my mind.

Churchill gave Montgomery instructions to save the German arms because they might turn out to be useful against the Soviet Union. They feared we would go further. . . .

On May 8 they congratulated me. But the party was small. A moment of silence, of course. But I didn't feel . . . Not that it wasn't a concern, but they were guarded with us. And we were even more apprehensive about them. . . .

[5-9-72, 5-11-78]

We asked for troops from our allies, proposed they send forces to our western front. But they didn't. They told us to shift our troops from the Caucasus and they would provide protection for our oil fields. They also wanted to stand guard over Murmansk.

And Roosevelt [wanted to establish air bases against Japan in the Soviet] Far East. He wanted to occupy certain parts of the Soviet Union instead of fighting. Afterward it wouldn't have been easy to get them out of there. . . .

I knew them all, the capitalists, but Churchill was the strongest, the smartest among them. Of course he was a 100 percent imperialist. But he admired Stalin. . . . Clever. He said, "Let us establish our airfield at Murmansk, for you're in a difficult situation." "Yes," we said, "it's a hard time for us, so send these forces to the front. We'll guard Murmansk ourselves." He backed down after that.

[12-6-69, 4-10-72]

We didn't let the Germans destroy our allies when Hitler was smashing them in the Ardennes. It was not to our advantage. In 1942 I took part in all the negotiations for a second front in Europe. From the first I didn't believe they would do it. I remained calm and realized this was a completely impossible operation for them. But our demand was politically necessary, and we had to press them for everything. I don't doubt that Stalin too believed they would not carry it out. But we had to demand it! For the sake of our people. They were waiting for some kind of Allied military aid. For us that piece of paper had vast political significance. It raised our spirits, and in those days this meant a lot.

Churchill flew to Moscow and insisted they couldn't open a second front in Europe in 1942. I saw that Stalin accepted this calmly. He understood it was impossible. But he needed that paper agreement. It was of great importance for the people, for politics, and for future pressure on the Allies.

To pressure them?

Of course. Well, if you can't help us with a second front, help us with arms, help us with aircraft. If they had opened the second front in 1942 or 1943 instead of 1944 it would have gone very hard for them, but it would have helped us immensely!

Could they have done it in 1943?

Yes, but they didn't! They started in Italy. Even this was helpful to us. In the end, we fought not for England but for socialism. That's the point. To expect help from them in defense of socialism? The Bolsheviks would have been idiots! But in order to pressure them, we said: What knaves! You say one thing but do another. This also put them in an embarrassing position in the eyes of their own people. For the people sensed that the Russians were fighting and they were not. Not only were the Allies not fighting, but they were writing and saying one thing while doing another. This unmasked them in the eyes of their people. Why are you cheating? This undermined faith in the imperialists. All this was very important to us.

I believed that my journey in 1942 [to London and Washington] and its results were a great victory for us. We knew they couldn't dare mount a second front, but we made them agree to it in writing. Stalin also instructed me to demand they draw off thirty to forty enemy divisions from the Russian front. When I met with Roosevelt I had to hide my astonishment when I told him that and he replied, "A legitimate, reasonable demand." He was probably thinking only of dollars and thought, "You'll have to come begging, anyway. Of course we have to help you, but it's in our best interests that you fight a bit longer. And that's why we're ready to support you." He agreed without changes to the communiqué I drafted, saying that a second front would be opened in 1942. That disgraced him in the eyes of his own people. Most people are honest, and when the government promised on the people's behalf to open the second front, and then didn't, the people realized they couldn't trust such leaders. And such a disappointment with the imperialists was to our benefit. All this had to be taken in consideration. I had no doubts on this score, and Stalin trusted them even less. Of course. But we reproved them! And rightly so.

Roosevelt believed in dollars. Not that he believed in nothing else, but he considered America to be so rich, and we so poor and worn out, that we would surely come begging. "Then we'll kick their ass, but for now we have to help them keep going."

That's where they miscalculated. They weren't Marxists, and we were. They woke up only when half of Europe had passed from them. Then

Churchill, of course, found himself in a quandary. To my mind, Churchill, as an imperialist, was the cleverest among them. He sensed that if we smashed the Germans, little by little feathers would fly in England. That's the way he felt. But Roosevelt thought, they will come groveling to us. A poor country with no industry, no bread—they will come begging. They will have nowhere else to go.

But we viewed the situation quite differently. All our people were prepared for sacrifice and struggle. We didn't believe in a second front, of course, but we had to try for it. We took them in: You can't? But you promised.... That was the way.

We had no other way to help our army and speed our victory. And we needed great patience. The fact is, even before the war we were dragging the people forward under complex, severe conditions. I can only wonder how they stood it! There were colossal hardships.

I heard that during the civil war there were stacks of corpses around the train stations in the Urals! Stacks of corpses! We had always done everything with enormous sacrifices. But people trusted the Bolsheviks! And the Bolsheviks turned out to be right, expressing the real feelings of the people, which wasn't always to be expected. Because their patience would be exhausted, they would run out of energy, we simply would lack...

That's what Lenin said in 1919 or in 1920—we've done so much that even if we are smashed, everything will have been worth it. If not today, then tomorrow.

[6-9-76]

A. Golovanov was in charge of arranging flights for Molotov to London and Washington in 1942. The idea for the trip occurred to Stalin at the end of 1941, after the battle for Moscow. Stalin considered the success of the Red Army short-term. He wanted Molotov to see Churchill in London and then Roosevelt in Washington in order to press the Allies to open a second front in 1942—or at least to get a commitment on paper. Stalin ordered General Golovanov to work out an air route. Later he was appointed commander of long-range aviation.

"Stalin was a great conspirator," Golovanov told me. "The journey was planned in total secrecy. I had to hide a map of the route in my desk, even when my assistant entered my office. Stalin had told me, 'Only the three of us know about this—you, Molotov, and me.'"

Stalin wanted to go himself. But in 1942 the situation at the front

grew complicated, and he couldn't leave the captain's bridge. Stalin said,
"Viacheslav Mikhailovich will go."

So on May 8, 1942, Molotov flew overnight in a four-engine bomber to
London, over German-occupied territory and then over the ocean, and
then to Washington. Churchill refused to sign the necessary papers for
Molotov. He managed to persuade Roosevelt, though. Then Molotov flew
back to London, instead of returning to Moscow, and showed Churchill
what the president had signed. . . .

The flight was a tough one because of weather conditions and battle
situations. The bomber was attacked by enemy fighters, and approaching
Moscow it was even shot at by one of our fighters. But God and the skills
of Golovanov's aces were on our side.

I signed a treaty in London with Churchill present, before going to
America. Eden and I signed it—about an alliance, about organizing a
union of countries to prepare for peace, that we should finish the war
together and together organize the peace. . . . We stayed at Checquers,
about forty miles from London. I arranged a dinner there on the first day
of the visit; Churchill and Eden were invited. Some sort of a small
garden. Not a fancy old building. Apparently some nobleman had given
it to the government to use as a residence for the prime minister. There
was a bathroom but with no shower. I've been to Roosevelt's place, I've
stayed overnight in the White House. Everything there was as it should
be. He had a bathroom with a shower, too.

[8-15-75]

We insisted on a document defining our postwar boundaries. I don't
remember the details, but the essence I remember, of course. I pressed
for it, Stalin in 1941 too, then I arrived in London in 1942 with a
draft. . . . Churchill said, "There's no way we can accept this."

I dodged this way and that. I cabled Stalin. He replied: Agree without
this [recognition of the USSR's borders as of June 1941]. But I am
getting ahead of the story. Everything hinged on their recognizing
the Baltic states as ours. They refused to agree. But when we dropped
our demand—this was of course necessary at the time—they were
astonished. Churchill was stunned. Eden was elated that we had agreed
to their terms.

When Eden visited us Stalin constantly wounded his vanity, taunting
him that he could not resolve the territorial question on his own.

[6-30-76]

We had to give in, to leave the question open. Open. Only now have England and America for the first time officially recognized our borders, including the Baltics. Late, but they have recognized. . . .

President Ford said, "It's a scandal that the Baltic states have not won their independence, but politics prevents us from intervening."

The fact that the Americans have recognized the Baltics as ours is a big step in our favor.

Churchill wrote about your meeting in London: "Only once did I seem to get a natural, human reaction. This was in the spring of 1942, when he alighted in England on his way back from the United States. We had signed the Anglo-Soviet Treaty, and he was about to make his dangerous flight home. At the garden gate of Downing Street, which we used for secrecy, I gripped his arm and we looked each other in the face. Suddenly he appeared deeply moved. Inside the image there appeared the man. He responded with an equal pressure. Silently we wrung each other's hands. But then we were all together, and it was life or death for the lot."

[8-15-75]

Churchill said as early as 1918 that Soviet power should be strangled in its infancy. But at our intimate dinners with Roosevelt in Teheran and Yalta, he said, "I get up in the morning and pray that Stalin is alive and well. Only Stalin can save the peace!" He was confident that Stalin would play that exceptional role which he had assumed in the war. His cheeks were wet with tears. Either he was a great actor or he spoke sincerely.

Not without reason did England lose a little more than 200,000 people while we had more than twenty million victims. That's why they needed us. That man hated us and tried to use us. But we used him, too. We made him work with us. Otherwise it would have been very hard for us.

[6-16-77]

Comments on the foreign edition of Khrushchev's memoirs state: "Unfortunately, in the entire book (except for a few passages) there is no profound analysis of Stalin's qualities that enabled him to stand firmly on his own and to negotiate knowledgeably and persuasively with Churchill and Roosevelt. Probably only Molotov could speak authoritatively about that."

It's a difficult story, but the mere fact that Stalin forced the capitalists Roosevelt and Churchill to war against Hitler says much.

[5-9-85]

In 1943 in Teheran, Stalin went to a reception given by the young shah of Iran. Even the shah was surprised. Beria was against such a visit.

Stalin and I were together with the shah. He didn't understand the shah altogether and got into a bit of an awkward situation. He tried to make an ally of the shah right there, but that didn't work. Stalin thought he could impress him, but it didn't work. The shah felt, of course, that we couldn't give orders there. The English and the Americans were nearby and weren't about to give the shah away to Stalin. They gave him advice, no doubt about that. They constantly kept tabs on him.

[11-1-77]

I told Molotov an anecdote he didn't know. At the Teheran conference Roosevelt and Churchill got tired of Stalin constantly pressing them about his proposals. They decided to trick him. In the morning before the regular session Churchill said, "I had a dream that I became ruler of the world!" "And I dreamt," Roosevelt said, "that I became Master of the Universe! And what did you dream of, Marshal Stalin?" "I dreamt," Stalin casually replied, "that I didn't confirm either of you."

They really did indulge in such banter at the meetings of the Big Three, and Stalin in fact always found a way out of a seemingly hopeless situation.

[6-11-70]

Ernest Bevin was a Churchill man. Hostile. And Eden, Churchill's assistant, was spineless, too delicate, quite helpless. I certainly liked Eden more. I could deal with him. It was impossible to deal with Bevin. One evening Bevin came to our reception in London. Well, our people like to entertain. My lads gave him a drink, and they did their best with him. When I went to see him off, he had already left the house. He was with his wife, a respectable older lady. She got into the car first, and he followed her. But getting into the car he threw up on his wife's skirt. What kind of a man was he, what kind of a diplomat, if he couldn't take care of himself? He was given to drink, he enjoyed it. And Russians like to make people drunk.

[3-9-79]

Molotov went to look for Clementine Churchill's letter of condolence on Polina Zhemchuzhina's death.

She still writes to me: "Molotov. The Kremlin, Moscow." Stalin had given her a present through Polina, a signet ring, but it was stolen in her country. She advertised in the papers for its return, for a considerably large reward. But apparently it never turned up.

Molotov couldn't find the letter, but he brought a portrait of Roosevelt presented to him at the talks in Washington in 1942—a large photograph of a handsome man in a splendid frame, covered with green silk, with an inscription in English in a violet ink, "To my friend Viacheslav Molotov from Franklin Roosevelt. May 30, 1942."

[6-11-70]

Roosevelt was an imperialist who would grab anyone by the throat.

As a comrade has noted, to be paralyzed and yet to become president of the United States, and for three terms, what a rascal you had to be!

Well said.

[2-5-82]

We signed a very important declaration at the Yalta conference in 1945, on the liberation of the peoples of Europe. A magnificent declaration. Stalin treated it warily from the outset. The Americans submitted a draft. I brought it to Stalin and said, "This is going too far!" "Don't worry," he said, "work it out. We can deal with it in our own way later. The point is the correlation of forces."

It was to our benefit to stay allied with America. It was important.

[8-15-75]

In 1945 Molotov was aboard a train in the United States when he learned of Roosevelt's death.

We had dinner in the dining car. It was my next-to-last visit to America. We had to prepare for the UN assembly and to provide leadership for it.

The dining car was crowded. Someone came in and said, "It's just been broadcast that Roosevelt is dead." No one paid attention. No reaction at all. The president was supported by most Americans. Can you imagine how we felt, can you picture that no one would pay any attention to this news?

We took it more to heart than they did.

Of course, Americans are thick-skinned that way. As long as it doesn't affect them personally, in their pocketbook, they don't pay attention to it. . . . Roosevelt knew how to conceal his attitude toward us, but Truman —he didn't know how to do that at all. He had an openly hostile attitude.

They had even planned how they would occupy the Soviet Union: they would infiltrate us with emigrés from America—arm them, give them troops. They would form their own government, wipe out the communists, break up the Soviet Union, separate all the nationalities. . . .

Sure. They're dreaming! But in recent years they sensed they were losing ground. That's why they elected Reagan, an openly rabid anticommunist.

[6-16-83]

Eisenhower used to say that peaceful coexistence meant existence in a concentration camp. I met with Eisenhower. And with Dulles, too. Eisenhower was so good-natured. Dulles was such a pettifogger that one had to keep this in mind all the time. His brother was in intelligence, too. These were brothers who would pick your pocket and cut your head off at the same time.

[1-14-75]

John Foster Dulles was a typical imperialist. And narrow-minded at that. Case-hardened, zealous. Very much like Churchill. Once we negotiated a whole week in Paris and couldn't even agree on an agenda, and returned home.

[7-30-70]

■   **At the Talks**   ■

Did the Americans propose breaking up Germany into small areas?
Into small states. A stupid idea. There were such proposals. To my mind American politicians are obtuse anyhow. That's nonsense.

[1-1-85]

There is a story that Zhukov suggested going farther, capturing Paris, not stopping at Berlin. . . .
I don't remember this. Some people have a poor knowledge of geography.

[3-8-74]

We were looking at a photograph of the Potsdam conference. I asked Molotov to show me who was who.

This is Vyshinsky, Gromyko, Nicholas Kuznetsov. That's the head of security Vlasik, Maisky. . . this one—Gerashchenko, director of the Economic Department.

That one is Stalin, this is Molotov.

That's right, Stalin, Molotov. This is my assistant Podtserob, there is Tsarapkin, a certain Novikov, Silin, my second assistant Potrubach, these were my lads. . . .

And who's sitting next to Stalin?

That's Golunsky, director of the Legal Department of the Ministry of Foreign Affairs. He did the translation. He not only knew languages but was also good at law, and that's why Stalin had him seated beside himself, so that we wouldn't be cheated. Stalin often said that Russia wins wars but doesn't know how to avail itself of the fruits of victory. Russians fight magnificently but don't know how to conclude a peace; they are always passed by, never get their due. But we did well after this war because we strengthened the Soviet state. It was my main task as minister of foreign affairs to see that we would not be cheated. In that sense we did our best, and to my mind our results were not bad.

We were very worried about the Polish question and the question of reparations. We got what we needed, though they tried in every way to encroach on our interests—to impose a bourgeois government in Poland that would certainly have been an agent of imperialism. But we, Stalin and I, insisted on having at our border an independent but not hostile Poland. At the negotiations and even before, disputes raged over borders—the Curzon Line, the Ribbentrop-Molotov Line. Stalin said, "Call it what you please, but our border will be here!" Churchill objected, "But Lvov was never a Russian city!" "But Warsaw was," Stalin calmly replied.

[7-9-71]

Regarding Polish borders at Potsdam . . . Stalin said about the Curzon Line, "Do you want us to be less Russian than Curzon and Clemenceau? What will Ukrainians say if we accept your proposal? They will probably say that Stalin and Molotov turned out to be less reliable protectors of Russians and Ukrainians than Curzon and Clemenceau.

The main question at Potsdam was about reparations, but the Polish question was also of great importance. The Americans offered us a way out of the situation that reduced friction between us and our Western allies. What was agreed on the Polish question had been discussed at length beforehand. Poland should not be hostile toward the Soviet

Union. Independent but not hostile. But they tried in every way to impose a bourgeois government, which naturally would have been an agent of imperialism and hostile to the Soviet Union. As early as the Yalta conference in February 1945 the Polish question had been discussed in that spirit, but a clear decision had not been made. A commission was established which worked in Moscow. I was on it with Harriman and Clark-Kerr. . . .

[7-9-71]

The Poles are interested in the fate of the Polish officers we held prisoner. This is a painful question. . . . They say we shot . . .

They may have. A special report was made by the Soviet government. And I stick to it. There was a commission after that. Rudenko was on it.

And how much grief the Poles have caused the Ukraine and Belorussia. I. F. Stadniuk, a writer, said, "By the way, the Poles were most dreadful to the Ukrainians during the First World War. They were very cruel. They did not single out individuals but punished entire villages at a stroke."

The Poles, the Russians, the Ukrainians, the Rumanians—they are all the most awful nationalists. They would do anything.

[6-13-74]

Before appointing Rokossovsky to Poland I went there and told the Poles we would give them one of our experienced generals as minister of defense. And we decided to give them one of the best—Rokossovsky. He was good-natured, polite, a tiny bit Polish, and a talented general. True, he spoke Polish badly, stressing the wrong syllables. He wasn't happy about going there, but it was very important for us that he be there, that he put everything in order. After all, we knew nothing about them.

[7-16-78]

Reagan has proclaimed that Poland marks the beginning of the end of communism. Poland has always been in a difficult situation. We had many conversations about Poland with Truman, Harriman. . . . We cannot lose Poland. If this line is crossed they will grab us, too. We have to be ready for this as well.

[12-4-81]

The Poles never calm down and are never at peace. They are irrational. They are always on one's neck. Obviously there will still be serious events. . . .

[12-9-82]

The question of dividing Berlin had already been resolved in London. We had agreed to divide both Germany and its capital into three parts. Then, when the Allies suggested giving a zone to France, we said, "Give it to them from your share—they didn't take part in the fighting." Well, they allotted it, but our zone remained untouched. The thing is, if it hadn't been Berlin there would have been another snag somewhere else. We had different goals and positions, and the snag came up in Berlin. How could we refuse them on Berlin if they said, "We are fighting together, aren't we?!"

[8-24-70]

Their anti-Soviet crusade failed—we split the imperialist camp.

We fooled them, and no one considered us fools. Some tried. . . .

Roosevelt died. At our first meeting with Truman, he began talking to me in such an imperious tone! Just before that I had had a discussion on the Polish question with Harriman and the British ambassador Clark-Kerr in Moscow—how to form a government there. We wanted it formed by the National Committee of Poland. They pressed Mikolajczyk on us in every possible way. And Truman said, "Why do you frame the question in such a way that we cannot agree with you? It's intolerable!" I thought, what kind of president is he? I said, "I cannot talk with you if you take such a tone." He stopped short a bit. Rather stupid, to my mind. And he had a very anti-Soviet mind-set. That's why he began in that tone; he wanted to show who was boss. Then he began to talk with us more respectfully and calmly. He talked modestly about himself: "There are millions like me in America, but I am the president." He played the piano. Nothing special, of course, but not badly. He was far from having Roosevelt's intellect. A big difference. They had only one thing in common—Roosevelt had been an inveterate imperialist, too.

[7-9-71]

■ Truman Decided to Surprise Us ■

At Potsdam Truman decided to surprise us. As far as I recall, after a dinner given by the American delegation Truman took Stalin and me aside with a secretive look and told us they had a special weapon that had never existed before, a very extraordinary weapon. . . . It's hard to say what he himself thought, but it seemed to me he wanted to shock us.

Stalin reacted very calmly, so Truman thought he didn't understand. Truman didn't say "an atomic bomb," but we got the point at once. We realized they couldn't yet unleash a war, that they had only one or two atomic bombs, which they exploded later over Hiroshima and Nagasaki. But even if they had had some bombs left, they could not have played a significant role. We had been doing research in that area since 1943. I was in charge of it. I had to find a scientist who would be able to create an A-bomb. The Chekists gave me a list of names of trustworthy physicists, and I began choosing. I summoned Kapitsa, an Academician. He said we were not ready, that it was a matter for the future. We asked Yoffe. He too showed no clear interest. To make a long story short, I was left with the youngest and least-known scientist of the lot, Kurchatov; they had been holding him back. I summoned him, we chatted, and he impressed me. But he said he still had a lot to clear up. I decided then to provide him with our intelligence data. Our intelligence agents had done very important work. Kurchatov spent several days in my Kremlin office looking through this data. Sometime after the battle of Stalingrad in 1943 I asked him, "So what do you think of this?" I myself understood none of it, but I knew the materials had come from good, reliable sources. He said, "The materials are magnificent. They add exactly what we have been missing."

It was a very good intelligence operation by our Chekists. They neatly stole just what we needed. And just at the right moment, when we were beginning this work.

The Rosenberg couple... I refrained from asking about that, but I think they were connected with our intelligence effort.... Someone helped us mightily with the A-bomb. Intelligence played a great role. In America the Rosenbergs were punished. There is a chance they were helping us. But we shouldn't talk about that. We may have use for it in the future.

These materials were American, not German?

Oh yes, for the most part. Before and during the war our intelligence worked quite well. We had a fine group in America. Even old "moles." Beria also kept it up after the war.

I presented Kurchatov to Stalin. We supported him in every way and began to find our bearings with him. He organized a group and everything worked well.

Of course, relatively little of this was done by the time of Potsdam.

[7-9-71, 12-28-77, 8-28-81]

We relied on no one but ourselves. As for the might of the state, and increasing our defensive capacity, Stalin strove not only to eliminate our backwardness but to be in the vanguard. He understood that we had advanced in the face of our colossal domestic backwardness—a peasant country! But we had begun serious research into rockets during the war. Could we have launched the first satellite in the world in 1957 and the first man in space in 1961 if we hadn't started on this much earlier?

Academician Vasili Mishin told me about that. He was Korolev's assistant for a long time and then his successor as chief designer. "The Soviet future in space," he said, "began at the end of the war with an exchange of messages between Stalin and Churchill."

There were some interesting messages. Stalin and I drafted many of them together. Everything was done through me. It couldn't have been any other way.

Mishin writes: "I read without paying much attention to it a cable from Churchill, top secret as always, which said that Soviet troops would soon capture a Polish city, Debice, where the Germans were conducting missile tests. '. . . I should be grateful, therefore, Marshal Stalin,' Churchill wrote, 'if you could give appropriate instructions for the preservation of such apparatus and installations at Debice as your armies can ensure after the area has been taken, and that afterward you would afford our experts an opportunity to study this experimental station. July 13, 1944.'

"Stalin replied that he didn't know which Debice Churchill was talking about, 'since there are several places in Poland by that name.'

"The British prime minister sent a new, more anxious message giving the exact whereabouts of the Debice he wanted.

"Stalin replied shortly that he had issued appropriate instructions on the matter. '. . . I promise you I will see to this matter myself in order to make sure everything is done according to your wish.'

"And he really took it under his personal supervision.

"The very same day, Sergei [S. Korolev] and I were on the carpet before Stalin. He instructed us to fly immediately to Debice, gather information on the missiles, and bring everything to Moscow, lest the British get anything—their intelligence had long been at work there.

"And so we did. Following the blueprints and fragments we found there, we sketched a winged missile and produced a metal prototype in Czechoslovakia. Our intelligence found a certain Kozak, an assistant to the chief German rocket scientist Werner von Braun, a Czech by nationality. He began helping us. I recall Korolev and I visiting him. We were

dressed in the military uniforms of lieutenant colonels, but his wife glanced at us and said, 'You are not in the army. Your boots are different and your foreheads are too high.' She had our number, as they say.

"For the October holidays we sent to Moscow by rail, a finished winged missile, a Tatra car, and a case of Czech beer, and wrote, 'A present to Stalin.' That's how the Soviet space program started."

Stalin very attentively followed such matters. They write that he didn't know about cybernetics. . . .

As a student I was honored to attend lectures given by Aksel Berg himself. He was an authority on rocket science!

It was Berg whom Stalin appointed vice-chairman of the state committee on this project. That's the level on which the matter was considered! Of course we didn't shout about that to the whole world. Stalin was a great conspirator."

The UN, in 1946. I remember your speech . . . *"We must not forget that an atomic bomb made by one country can also be made by another [Molotov commented, "That's right!"] and then the final failure of the calculations cherished by some smug people, not far from here, will become obvious."*

It was my own idea. I thought there was nothing dangerous in it. I very carefully considered it. At the same time I had to say that the bombs dropped on Japan were not aimed at Japan but rather at the Soviet Union. They said, bear in mind you don't have an atomic bomb and we do, and this is what the consequences will be like if you make a wrong move!

We had to set a tone, to reply in a way that would make our people feel more or less confident.

To tell you the truth, I didn't have a prepared text. People asked me later, "And what are these 'other things'? You said we would have an atomic bomb and 'other things.'"

Afterward Stalin said to me, "Well, that was strong stuff!"

We still had nothing, but I was up to date on the matter.

And this is also from your UN speech in 1946: "The delegate from the Philippines has tried to show that a vote on the Soviet proposal is impossible because it allegedly contradicts parliamentary rules. . . . I thank the delegate of the Philippines for this useful lesson on parliamentary rules. I think this will be useful particularly in the Philippines when they have a parliament (general laughter), and in other places where they already have parliaments."

Yes, of course, that's the way it was.

[7-1-79]

No one instructed me to speak about the "other things." Afterward Stalin used this to cut off talk about our being weak when we still had nothing. We had nothing. But it wasn't trickery, because generally I knew what was being done. That's why what I said didn't contradict the facts. But still we had nothing. We had just started. It was justified because we would have an atomic bomb, and we were even the first to explode a hydrogen bomb, but this was later.

[11-1-77]

When I said in the UN that we would have "other things," I was asked later, "What did you mean?" I meant, of course, rockets. We visited Korolev's lab after the war.

Stalin also went with you?

I think so, yes.

■　　The Cold War　　■

Churchill was one of the leaders of victory. And to this day I cannot understand how he lost the elections in 1945! I need to know English life better. The talks in Potsdam had begun with him and then . . . He had been very active. And he never forgot to write things down. Keep in mind that he stated the facts in his own way. You need to check them against other sources. He stated them very artfully. He was an imperialist to the core.

[7-31-72]

The cold war—I don't like the expression. It sounds like Khrushchev's. It was used in the Western press in Stalin's time, and then it passed to us. Goebbels was the first one to use the "iron curtain." It was often used by Churchill, that's for sure. But what does the "cold war" mean? Strained relations. It was entirely their doing or because we were on the offensive. They certainly hardened their line against us, but we had to consolidate our conquests. We made our own socialist Germany out of our part of Germany, and restored order in Czechoslovakia, Poland, Hungary, and Yugoslavia, where the situations were fluid. To squeeze out the capitalist order. This was the cold war. Of course, you had to know when and where to stop. I believe in this respect Stalin kept well within the limits.

[11-28-74]

Churchill's speech at Fulton, Missouri, began the so-called cold war. Stalin couldn't retire though he had intended to after the war. . . . "Let Viacheslav do some work!"

One of our writers has suggested that Stalin would have been crowned if he had lasted ten more years. Everything was moving that way—people loved him, enemies feared and respected him, he had vast authority. The tsar's double-eagles had already been brought to the Kremlin, a throne was installed. . . .

A monarch does everything for the sake of the empire. Here everything was done for the sake of the proletariat, of the workers.

Did you know Adenauer?

Yes. I even put him in an embarrassing position when he visited us. We were seated next to each other and he whispered in my ear, "I would have strangled Hitler if I had had the chance under fascism!" At the time they were covering it all up, but in fact Adenauer himself continued many of Hitler's deeds, suppressing communists, blessing the Nazis. So I simply repeated, in my speech at this dinner, what he had just whispered to me. And it was published. I decided, let him remember his being an unreliable friend, and let people regard him as two-faced.

[8-24-75]

■   **Reparations**   ■

We took reparations after the war, but these were trifles. Our state was huge. And these reparations were of old, obsolete equipment. But there was no other way out. Even if it offered only minor alleviation, it had to be used. But in pulling it out, with whom did we have to reckon? Bit by bit we were creating the German Democratic Republic, our Germany. What would these people think of us if we had pulled everything out of the country? America, England, and France were helping West Germany. After all, we were taking from the Germans who wanted to work with us. It had to be done very carefully. We didn't work out everything completely. But this was helpful, too: the Germans renewed their capital equipment and switched to new technology. We couldn't do that at once in our country. But we sent some part of the equipment to China.

[5-12-76]

■ Lend-Lease ■

... About negotiations on Lend-Lease.

I participated in them from the beginning. The Lend-Lease agreement was signed in my presence when I visited America in 1942.

And did you have talks after the war?

Yes, quite often. I had to sign notes, too. Disagreements over Lend-Lease arose after the war. We hadn't had them before. We didn't repudiate our debt. We returned some things.

They set up a press to crush flat those Studebaker trucks we returned to them, and threw them into the sea.

Quite possible.

You said, we will return them—but did you set any deadline?

There were all kinds of controversial questions. I can't recall, but there was no refusal. We were not repaying in full. But we did not renege. We did not default.

[7-31-72]

■ The Marshall Plan ■

In the West they write that Soviet diplomacy made a big mistake in not accepting the Marshall Plan.

Precisely the opposite. Our withdrawal was correct. At first I agreed to participate and, among other things, proposed to the Central Committee that not only we but the Czechs and Poles, too, take part in the conference in Paris. Then I came to my senses and sent a second memorandum the same day: let's refuse. We would go, but we would advise the Czechs and the others to refuse to participate in the conference, for we still could not count on them. So we passed the resolution and distributed it right away. We advised them not to consent. They had prepared to take part, especially the Czechs. The Czech minister was rather shady. I've forgotten his name—Clementis, I think. After receiving our instructions not to participate, they didn't go.

The meeting at Paris was such that we couldn't count on any honest attitudes. I answered back, invective for invective. I had no assistants who might confuse matters. The Czech Clementis had right-wing views that made him dangerous. This was in 1948, already after Benes.

There was much turmoil. But if Western writers believe we were wrong to refuse the Marshall Plan, we must have done the right thing. Absolutely. We can prove it now as easily as two times two is four. At first we decided in the Ministry of Foreign Affairs to propose to all the socialist countries that they participate; but we quickly realized that was wrong. The imperialists were drawing us into their company, but as subordinates. We would have been absolutely dependent on them without getting anything useful in return. What's more, the Czechs and the Poles were in dire straits as it was. . . .

[3-9-79]

After the war the Czechs used to take bread from us and feed it to their livestock. And we were starving.

[9-30-81]

It was right that we moved troops into Czechoslovakia in 1968. Many supported this from a great-power position while I supported it from a communist position.

[7-24-78]

■   **The Two Most Difficult Countries**   ■

The book Andropov *was just published in America. It's written there that Malenkov promoted him and introduced him to Stalin. He made a good impression on Stalin, who appointed him second secretary to Kuusinen in the Karelo-Finnish SSR for the purpose of becoming head of Finland in due course. But Stalin lost interest in Kuusinen and Andropov when his plans in Finland failed. That's how they interpret this.*

In my opinion Andropov is running things quite well so far. He speaks ably and firmly, without boasting. Quite the contrary, one can't help noticing that he engages in self-criticism about past and present short-comings, and that's good. He is not being pulled to the right. And he is more authoritative than his two predecessors.

He was sent to me from the Central Committee, the personnel department or one of its secretaries. He made quite a good impression. He came to me at the Ministry of Foreign Affairs and said, "I was assigned to the diplomatic service." I don't remember who in the Central Committee told me I could use him for diplomatic work. I suggested Hungary; it was agreed. And he worked well in Hungary. The appointment, I think, was successful, because at the time he was appointed ambassador nothing untoward or unexpected was occurring in Hungary. It was calm there.

Epishev passed through a Rumanian school—it was my doing. Yes, yes, I sent him as an ambassador to Rumania. He too had found his niche.

These were two of the most difficult countries for us.

I took an active part in forming the first government of Hungary in 1945. We formed it quickly enough.

I was recently in Hungary and was told that no one there believes in communism.

The Hungarians? They are deeply petty bourgeois. Russians have a kind of instinct—they like a broad sweep. If there is a fight, it's a real fight; if socialism, then socialism on a world scale. . . . A special mission? In this case, yes.

As Dostoevsky used to say, the God-bearing people.

God-bearing, yes. In their own way. . . . They made their decision, were not afraid of hardships, cleared the way for other peoples. . . . Here different peoples live side by side and lead diverse lives. For some, socialism is the great goal; for others, it's acceptable and they are not overly concerned about it.

[12-9-82, 6-16-83, 10-14-83]

Stalin led the cause for the downfall of imperialism and the advent of communism. We needed peace. But according to American plans, two hundred of our cities would be subject to simultaneous atomic bombing.

Stalin looked at it this way: World War I has wrested one country from capitalist slavery; World War II has created a socialist system; and the third will finish off imperialism forever.

[7-30-70, 12-2-71]

■   On the World Scale   ■

I was reading Molotov's speech at the XVth Party Congress in 1926. ". . . The policy of our party is and remains the policy of the final triumph of socialism on a world scale. . . ."

See, forty-nine years have passed, and I don't take back my words even now. The idea is correct. We must hold on. I sent this speech to Stalin before publishing it. "Do you have any comments?" He wrote to me in response—I saved that note—he wrote, "You're killing me with your modesty. You are asking me to comment on your speech, but you put me in a difficult situation. I didn't send you my own report for you to look at. That's why I am not going to write any comment on your speech." I think he was unwilling to answer.

But he said, "So, do you want to take a position between me and Trotsky? To be middle of the road?" He understood correctly. My point of view differed somewhat from Stalin's. He also said, "Yours contains a prophecy." And I thought, how could we not prophesy if we supported the international revolution? That was my opinion, not prophecy. But Stalin believed it was possible to build communism in one country, and said so at the XVIIIth Party Congress. Furthermore, under communism the state would exist as long as capitalist encirclement existed. But this is untrue, and I challenged him on this issue. He and I were very close; nevertheless, as far back as 1926 we had a dispute over this question, because our training was nonbureaucratic. We grew up in the spirit of bolshevism, in the spirit of truth.

[1-14-75]

It is said in Khrushchev's program that communism should be estab-lished first in our country, then in others. Have you read it? That is nationalist character, a Soviet nationalist's character. A kind of a na-tional avarice. All nationalists are avaricious. By the way, Stalin said, "Nationalists are like this, they are ready for anything."

Any form of nationalism is dangerous, isn't it?

No, not any. If it is against imperialism and colonialism, then we support it. But sometimes when nationalists seize power, it acquires other forms.

I think we were not wrong in renouncing the word "Finnish" in the name of our Karelian republic, or that we refused the name Buriato-Mongolia, calling it instead the Buriat Autonomous Republic. Even though the Mongolians wanted admission to the USSR during the war, we rejected their proposal. And the Bulgarians, too, wanted admission.

[1-14-75]

■   **Desirable, but Not the Right Time**   ■

The Bulgarians often ask why after the war we didn't let them annex a part of Greece, a maritime province.

Comrade Kolarov, who worked with Dimitrov, used to urge that. It was impossible. Why didn't we manage to get all of Berlin? It would have been better. But you had to stay within limits. Raising this issue would have caused trouble right at the beginning of the peace. The English and French would have been opposed. I consulted with the Central Committee and was told not to bring it up, that the time was not right. We had to remain silent on the issue. But Kolarov was urging it. It was desirable but not timely.

[11-4-78]

■   **A Vagueness**   ■

Viacheslav Mikhailovich, one point is not clear to me. . . .
Only one? I have more.
In the formation of the state of Israel, the Americans were opposed.
Everyone objected but us—me and Stalin. Some asked me why we favored it. We are supporters of international freedom. Why should we be opposed if, strictly speaking, that meant pursuing a hostile nationalist policy? In our time, it's true, the Bolsheviks were and remained anti-Zionist. We were even against the Bund, though it was considered to be a socialist organization. Yet it's one thing to be anti-Zionist and antibourgeois, and quite another to be against the Jewish people. We proposed, however, an Arab-Israeli union, for both nations to live there together. We would have supported this version if it could have been arranged. Otherwise we favored a separate Israeli state. But we remained anti-Zionist.
After all, you had to realize it would be bourgeois.
Oh, Lord!
Why didn't you make it [Israel] socialist?
Why? Why? If we had, we would have had to fight England. And America, too. . . . You might say we should have made Finland socialist, it would have been a simpler matter. We did not, and I believe we acted correctly. If we had crossed a certain line we would have gotten mixed

up in utter adventurism. Adventurism. That is why we ourselves gave way in Austria.

The Jews had long struggled for their own state under a Zionist flag. We, of course, were against Zionism. But to refuse a people the right to statehood would mean oppressing them.

Israel has turned out badly. But Lord Almighty! That's American imperialism for you.

[10-4-72]

■   A Vulgar Point of View   ■

Many people are displeased that we help others too much. They say it's time to take care of ourselves. . . .

In Stalin's time we helped, too, though we had less wherewithal. Then people grumbled, too. Now our bonds are stronger, of course, and the scale is greater, but in general, from my point of view, it is necessary. All of this is necessary not just for those whom we are helping but first for us. . . . The Vietnamese fight for us even more than we do for ourselves—they get killed. And from the point of view of weakening imperialism, our most dangerous enemy, they do a colossal job. Every step that weakens imperialism is absolutely great. Otherwise it will become more difficult for us after a number of years or maybe even tomorrow or the day after.

Otherwise we can isolate ourselves, can't we?

That's the point. It's more that we could make plenty of trouble for ourselves. And very many people, including communists, think this way—peace, no matter what, only peace! That's right, but it has to be ensured. We are not given this for nothing. Or else we have to give up. The Vietnamese don't want to give up. Tiny Vietnam is fighting imperialism with unbelievable heroism! Why should we fear imperialism? . . .

The people say now, if only there won't be a war.

This is Khrushchev's shortsighted view. It is very dangerous. We need to think about preparing for new wars. Events are moving in that direction. Yes, we must be ready. Then they will be more careful. And if they go to extremes, we will be strong. Vietnam sets an example for the whole world. If tiny Vietnam, with help from friends, can stand up to American imperialism, what does the Soviet Union have to fear? Only its own helplessness, faintheartedness, slackness of discipline.

[5-9-72]

■   **Centralized Diplomacy**   ■

In most cases ambassadors just transmit what they are told to pass on. They operate only within these limits. When I had to serve as minister of foreign affairs, especially after Stalin's death, I saw how many were surprised that I behaved so independently. But I was independent only within the limits of my instructions. I was trying to show in this way that we had agreed arrangements for everything. That's how a diplomat should act.

With Brezhnev, in my opinion, the direction is fundamentally weak. Everything is staked on peaceful coexistence. Of course we need peaceful coexistence, but you have to remember that is not guaranteed us.

[12-7-76]

I was reading to Molotov some notes from Churchill's memoirs.

He gave his book about World War II to my secretary. Not without purpose, I suppose. I had to contend with him so much!

He writes, "Litvinov's dismissal meant the end of a whole epoch. It meant the abandonment by the Kremlin of all faith in a security treaty with the Western powers. . . ." He believed Litvinov to be in favor of an alliance with the West.

That's correct.

He writes that Western papers reported Litvinov had resigned after a bitter quarrel with Marshal Voroshilov, "the party boy," as daring and cheeky Russians called him in candid moments. Was Voroshilov called "the party boy"?

First time I have heard of it.

Litvinov was kept on as ambassador to the United States only because he was known worldwide. He turned out to be very rotten.

We left him out of negotiations during the whole war. And now they talk about his role—that we couldn't make an agreement without him! Roosevelt invited me for talks without him, aware of my attitude toward him.

Litvinov was utterly hostile to us. We bugged his talk with an American correspondent, an obvious spy, who wrote that he met Litvinov—Litvinov was my assistant in the ministry at the time—in 1944.

The correspondent wrote only what was passed for publication at that time and not what was in fact. We got an entire recording of the talk—in the usual way. What did Litvinov say?

He said, "You Americans won't be able to deal with this Soviet government. Their positions preclude any serious agreement with you. Do you think this government, these hard-liners will meet you halfway in any sense? Nothing will come of your dealings with them.

"What can be done about it now? Domestic forces for change are nonexistent. For the people have no tanks, but the government has. The people have no aviation, but the government has. The people have no artillery, but the government has. The government has party officers in such numbers that the people cannot exert their own will to change things. Only external pressure can help, that is, a military campaign. Only Western intervention can change the situation in the country."

That's how Litvinov appraised the situation. He deserved the highest measure of punishment at the hands of the proletariat. Every punishment.

He said nothing to me personally. That too was unconscionable. Utter treason.

How could Stalin forgive him?

How could he forgive him? It had to be done circumspectly, observing formalities. Our intelligence monitored the conversation, but we had stopped trusting him even before that. This conversation took place in Moscow. I didn't take Litvinov along when I went to America in 1942 to negotiate with Roosevelt and Hull. Hopkins was at Roosevelt's side, and I had only an interpreter, even though Litvinov was the ambassador. . . . He was at our general meeting when Roosevelt said to me, "Introduce me to your delegation." I had Chekists and everyone from the ministry with me, and even a pilot. So Roosevelt greeted everyone. He was a very affable person, deft and good-natured—all this was splendid. Litvinov was there, too. But I didn't take him with me when we got down to brass tacks. Pavlov did the interpreting.

And when you left Litvinov behind he probably took it to heart, didn't he?

Sure. I couldn't take him. We didn't trust him. I didn't take him to the negotiations. He might say many nasty things. He was intelligent, first rate, but we didn't trust him. And after I returned we kept him in

Washington for a while and then recalled him and appointed this Umansky. He was lightweight, of course, but we had no alternative.

Then I appointed Gromyko—also a very young and inexperienced diplomat. Honest, though. We knew he wouldn't let us down. So it went. And there was nothing to do with this, with Litvinov.

Surits was his pal. He was less independent, I suppose. He was a former Menshevik, but Litvinov was an old Bolshevik.

He was a Bolshevik?!

People change! Yes, yes, they change! Litvinov remained among the living only by chance.

[4-25-75, 5-7-75, 7-16-78, 1-1-86]

They write a lot about Litvinov these days. I remember you saying you didn't trust him.

He was, of course, not a bad diplomat—a good one. But at heart he was quite an opportunist. He greatly sympathized with Trotsky, Zinoviev, and Kamenev, and thus couldn't enjoy our absolute confidence.

How could we trust him when he was in fact betraying us right then and there? But he was intelligent, worldly wise, and knowledgeable about foreign affairs. He had a good attitude toward Stalin, though I think he didn't always privately agree with resolutions we passed. I believe at the end of his life he turned rotten politically. That's why [Ilya] Ehrenburg's lament over Stalin's removal of Litvinov is pointless.

[10-4-85]

Whom do you consider to be our ablest diplomat at the time you were working?

Who was a diplomat? An able one? We had a centralized diplomacy. Ambassadors had no independence. And they could not have had any because the situation was so complicated. It was impossible for the ambassador to take any initiative. This was unpleasant for competent ambassadors, but we couldn't do it any other way. Except for Chicherin and Litvinov, who were at the top, the role of our diplomats and ambassadors was deliberately limited, for we had no experienced diplomats. But we had honest, prudent, competent, and well-read diplomats. I think it was hard to fool us because Stalin and I kept a tight hold on everything—we couldn't do it any other way at the time. On the whole we quite confidently directed our centralized diplomacy. "Centralized" meant dependent on the center, on Moscow, for everything. We didn't take risks; we had to have trustworthy people, competent and familiar with foreign diplomats and diplomacy—German, French, British. American diplomacy didn't play an active role. Not until the beginning of World War II did it begin to play a strong role.

I don't recall our ever being cheated by foreign diplomacy. Of course, in some cases we acted more skillfully, in others less. We were always careful and didn't pull any big blunders, to my mind. But there were small mistakes, of course. And middling blunders and failings. Ambassadors from other countries who worked here couldn't spread their wings either, for it was necessary to be very careful in such complicated, tense situations. I think we got what we needed.

Our diplomacy was not bad. But it was Stalin, not some diplomat, who played the decisive role in it.

And Stalin apparently was a diplomat too, wasn't he?

Of course. And how! Very much so. . . . I emphasize that our diplomacy in the thirties, forties, and fifties was very centralized. The ambassadors were merely executors of specific instructions. That kind of diplomacy was necessary in our situation, and it achieved positive results.

But much depends on an ambassador. . . .

Much. But not all our ambassadors knew a foreign language well. Nonetheless we knew how to maintain good relations with those whom we needed, and within acceptable limits.

[1-16-73, 10-4-85]

■   **The Country for Socialism**   ■

I told Molotov about my recent trip to Kolyma, about a meeting with Vadim Kozin in Magadan. He thought highly of Stalin.

The man was given a good lesson. He began to understand politics. I suppose Voroshilov was the first one to speak about Kolyma. He visited the Far East, Kamchatka. Someone pumped him up with stories and he came back talking, "Kolyma! Kolyma!" We had no knowledge of any Kolyma. And so it went, so it went!

A geologist Bilibin landed there in 1929 and discovered a vast gold field.

That's when they began to talk.

Ordinary people went there first, members of the Komsomol, and later it was turned into a place of exile. Korolev was exiled there, too—to

Susuman. He was taken for someone else and was mistakenly sent to Kolyma instead of to the Tushinsky factory.

I didn't know that Korolev was imprisoned there.

I am talking about the mineral wealth of Kolyma—they were prospecting for gold but discovered mercury. . . .

We have such vast territory that you can't cover it all. You can't research everything, the distances are too great. We are quite fortunate people in that sense. We found just the country for socialism. Everything is here, you just have to look for it! And you can find whatever you want.

I recounted how General I. G. Pavlovsky, a former commander-in-chief of ground forces, and I went to Chukotka. Still standing there are the barracks where in 1946 the 14th Landing Army had a strategic mission: if the Americans carried out an atomic attack on us, this army would land in Alaska, move down the coast, and develop an offensive against the United States. Stalin had ordered this mission to be set up.

Yes, I wouldn't mind getting Alaska back.

Had you thought of it?

We had, of course. Just thoughts and nothing more. To my mind, the time hadn't arrived for such tasks.

A large political map of the world faced the table. Molotov said that after the war he had gone to the UN session in the United States. He had flown over Chukotka and landed in Anadir.

The U.S.A. is the most suitable country for socialism. Communism will come there sooner than in other countries.

[5-1-81, 6-3-81]

■   Mao Tse-tung Held Up One Finger. . .   ■

Khrushchev told me that when he left China, at the farewell Mao Tse-tung held up one finger: one question remained unsolved—Mongolia. Mao considered it Chinese territory. A large proportion of the Mongols live in China. In its time this territory was called Outer Mongolia—the part that became an independent state. It separated itself from the Chinese area. So it had been considered Outer Mongolia and not simply Mongolia. In China they do not stand on ceremony with the Mongols who live there. But there is a monument to Ghengis-Khan. The Chinese erected it in honor of the Mongols.

We couldn't take Manchuria. It was impossible. It contradicted our policy.

We took a lot. But that's another matter.

[8-28-81]

■   Friends with the Bourgeoisie...   ■

Did you drink with Hitler? He was a teetotaler, wasn't he?

I drank instead of him! And what do you think? We didn't let him visit us, though he wanted to come. Why did he encircle Moscow?

And Churchill treated you well in London, didn't he?

Well, we drank a glass or two.

Did you talk with him?

We talked a whole night long.

And did he promise to help you?

No. He asked us to help him.

And what do you think of Roosevelt as a person?

Reasonable enough.

So nice, and sociable, yes?

Sociable, yes, a nice person. I have a portrait from Roosevelt—"To my friend Molotov. . . ." So I came to be friends with the bourgeoisie.

Was there at least a little help?

They thanked *us* for the help. We didn't thank them—there was no reason to. We did more for them.

Mankind would have perished if not for us, right?

It wouldn't have perished. To my mind, humanity cannot perish. But Hitler would have done a lot along that line. And he had already systematically done so. Yes.

[11-7-79]

■   The Bosporus, the Dardanelles   ■

It is said you put the question of the straits to Hitler and he agreed with you.

No, no, there was no such thing.

I felt I had touched a sore subject. Molotov grew animated and he began to stutter.

At the end of the war we raised the question of control over the Dardanelles with the Turks. They would not agree, and our allies didn't support us. This was our mistake. Stalin wanted to accomplish this legally, through the UN. When our ships entered the straits the British were already there, and ready. Of course, this was our mistake.

[7-31-72, 8-15-75]

I raised the question of control over the straits by us and the Turks. I think this formulation of the question was not quite correct, but I had to carry out my instructions. I raised the question in 1945 after the war was over: the straits should be under the protection of the Soviet Union and Turkey. It was an inopportune, impossible affair. I consider Stalin an outstanding politician, but he too made mistakes.

We proposed this control in honor of the victory gained by Soviet forces. But it couldn't be accepted, I knew that. In essence it was the wrong thing for us to do. We could have talked about it if Turkey had been a socialist state.

[7-24-78]

We had claims on Turkish lands. The Georgian scholars were for that. . . . It was awkward. To stand guard together with the Turks over the Bosporus. . . .

Miliukov talked about the Bosporus all the time. Russian generals talked about it all the time . . . an exit from the Black Sea!

It didn't work. If we had gone ahead, everyone would have come down on us.

[8-28-82]

In his last years Stalin got puffed up a bit. In foreign affairs I had to demand exactly what Miliukov had demanded—the Dardanelles! Stalin said, "Go ahead, press them for joint possession!" Me: "They won't allow it." "Demand it!"

[9-30-81]

They say Harriman asked Stalin whether he was pleased: the Germans had been outside Moscow itself, and now he was sharing Berlin. Stalin responded, "Tsar Alexander made it to Paris."

That's right.

■   **It Was Hard to Argue**   ■

We had a need for Libya after the war. Stalin said, "Go ahead, push for it!"

And what were your arguments?

That's the point, it was a difficult argument. I stated in one of the sessions of the conference of foreign ministers that a national liberation movement had arisen in Libya. It was still weak, but we wanted to support it and to build our own military base there. Bevin became ill. They even had to give him an injection.

The refusal then came. Bevin jumped up and shouted, "It's a shock, shock! Shock, shock! You've never been there!"

And how did you respond to that?

It was very difficult to ground the argument. It was not clear. Something like, we were for independence, and we wanted to protect this independence. . . . That didn't work.

Earlier we hadn't paid much attention to the unstable borders in Africa. So I was instructed to raise the question about Libya being placed under our control. To leave the population there but under our control, immediately after the war ended.

And we had to solve the question of the Dardanelles. It was good that we backed down in time. Otherwise it would have led to joint aggression against us.

At the same time Azerbaijan laid a claim to almost double the size of their republic at the expense of Iran. We sounded out some people about this—no one supported us. Besides that we tried to demand an area bordering on Batum, because there had once been a Georgian population in that Turkish area. The Azerbaijanians wanted to occupy the Azerbaijanian part and the Georgians their own. And we wanted to turn Ararat over to the Armenians. It was very difficult then to raise such demands. The tsar's government had gathered many areas around Russia. We should have been very careful. But we threw a bad scare into them.

[7-31-72, 9-30-81]

■   **"I Am Not a Real Diplomat"**   ■

I was sent back to the Ministry of Foreign Affairs after Stalin's death. In the first year we decided to work out a proposal to stop the Korean

War. The situation was developing in a way not in our interests. It was pressed on us by the Koreans themselves. Stalin said it was impossible to avoid the question of a united Korea.

We prepared a draft proposal on the German question, and besides that I raised the Korean question.

[10-21-82]

The Voice of America calls the idea of an all-European conference "an old Molotov idea."

That's right.

"We know Molotov's 'salami tactics'—cutting from Europe pieces for the Soviet Union."

That's right. This is also politics. And we still haven't thought of a better policy. Just words are not enough. . . . Salami is a sausage made with lard. I liked it until I found out this was what they were calling my policy. It turned out it didn't taste bad. I was treated to salami quite often at the Hungarian embassy. I liked it. Delicious, it was very tasty. I have a kind of old-fashioned taste. . . . And as yet there are no better politics.

[8-15-75]

I learned from a Yugoslavian poet, Yole Stanishich, a song which Serbian communists sang during their underground activity:

"Molotov, live, live

And create new states!"

My regards to him. I didn't think I'd live so long, but I have to hang on now.

[6-16-83]

I go quite often by train to Moscow. Workers recognize me and sit near me. We chat. "Who is our deputy minister of foreign affairs? What kind of deputy is he? We don't know him. What does he understand about that? Everyone knew you when you were there."

[12-18-70]

I saw pictures in old newspapers—you wore a military uniform. Was it a Ministry of Foreign Affairs uniform? And why?

Yes, it was. There was some reason in it. What reason? You don't have to wear evening dress—a dinner jacket and all that stuff—when you have a uniform on. A uniform for all occasions. It was a good uniform. And supposedly Stalin had an idea to tighten up discipline. A uniform helps. . . . But, of course, it didn't last long. We even had dress swords. I wore a dress sword, too.

I saw Molotov's full uniform in his apartment on Granovsky Street— an impressive black uniform with gilt embroidery and stars.

[12-30-73]

Did you see on television yesterday the meeting of Kirilenko with foreign correspondents?

I saw it. Of course, he hasn't had many experiences like that. I had myself been in such situations. Not very pleasant sometimes. You always have to laugh the matter off.

Once I was asked to give a press conference in America, in New York—no, in San Francisco. "What is the correct way in Russian to pronounce it—'vo-o-o-dka' or 'vodka'?" I said, "I like your pronunciation!" Everyone laughed and the question was forgotten.

Another time in San Francisco, well, how should I say, not admirers, but former Russians who had been living in America for quite some time had organized a party in honor of the Russian representative. 6ey spoke only American, that is, English. An elderly man, apparently their chairman, asked me, "What has impressed you most about America?" "What has impressed me? Most of all I am impressed by how poorly they know Russia in America. They know very little about Russia." They were taken aback, for they were all Russians. But I thought, why should I stand on ceremony with them? You come across such rubbish at times. . . .

But it seems that diplomats need special training. They're not just party workers.

I personally was never specially trained. My experience was party work and party polemics. Quite often I had to give speeches at big party meetings—against the Trotskyists, against right-wingers—in a situation when you were told at noon that you were to give a speech at 6:30. You couldn't read the speech. No one would rewrite and edit for you. This kind of experience was highly useful for diplomacy because you had to deal with such serious opponents, politically sophisticated, like the Trotskyists and the right-wingers. It was a good school, so to speak.

Party workers don't have such experience nowadays.

No, they don't. They would prefer to argue about how much production has increased, or the productivity of collective farmers. This too is important and interesting, but it is not polemics, not fighting with the opposition.

And there are no disputes at plenary sessions.

Right, at plenary sessions as well. Anyplace. Everything is smooth. It's different now, of course. That's a great loss.

I gave a speech at a plenum of the Central Committee of the Young Communists League. My speech was sent to the Central Committee of the party three months in advance. They read it, checked everything. . . .

So you see, we were trained under different conditions.

[4-25-75]

In my time I organized the Institute of International Relations at one time in order to train staff. It's my creation. But there is little of the party spirit there now.

[7-16-78]

What kind of a diplomat am I? I know not a single foreign language.

I had a smattering of the basic languages, but I didn't have a real knowledge of them. I always went to the UN with an interpreter. I couldn't thoroughly study a single language. That's why I was not a real diplomat.

But I remember that you corrected an interpreter at the UN when he mistranslated your thought. . . .

Here I was foreign minister, yet I had no command of foreign languages. I could read and understand a bit of conversation in German and French, but it was difficult for me to reply. English came into use only in recent decades. This was my main shortcoming in diplomacy.

Didn't you translate for Stalin Hitler's speech after the Japanese attack on Pearl Harbor? Stalin had asked you to listen to it and report to him. Wasn't that so?

Yes, that's the way it was.

[7-17-75]

And Stalin had no one else to whom he could entrust foreign policy.

That's another matter. I've been abroad a few times and in various situations. I have been written about not only by my supporters but by my opponents as well. They have not taken me for a fool.

As you say, you reserve the right to return to this question. Diplomats say that.

I am not a real diplomat.

You are the only one among the Soviet people to think that. The Soviet

*people consider you Diplomat Number One. And not just the Soviet
people—Churchill, too!*

He has a right to think so, and you don't. I think of myself first of all
as a politician, not a diplomat.

And what good diplomat is not a politician?

Your reasoning is wrong, because a politician is often higher than a
diplomat. That's why I cannot be called a diplomat. It doesn't fit.

Dulles called you the greatest diplomat of the twentieth century. . . .

That had to do with Port Arthur.

Churchill ranks you among the greatest diplomats of all time!

No, I don't consider myself a diplomat. A politician, yes. And that
name is no small one, of course.

[7-30-70, 5-7-75, 3-8-85, 5-9-85]

■   **We Dropped Our Pants in Front of the West**   ■

We have now dropped our pants in front of the West. It turns out that
the main goal is not a struggle against imperialism but a struggle for
peace. No doubt one should always fight for peace. But words and
wishes achieve nothing; you need strength.

[6-30-76]

*Take Portugal, Viacheslav Mikhailovich. We don't even know what's
happened there. . . . After fascism—Leninism.*

This is temporary. It can't last long. But I consider that also very good.
It's remarkable in Portugal. Cunhal is a fine fellow! The whole system of
capitalism is cracking up. For the present we can't touch it. This will
happen over time. There will be results, but not right away. It's a small
country surrounded by imperialism.

It turned out badly in Chile.

Bear in mind this is temporary. We also had a defeat in 1905 but we
triumphed in 1917. We wouldn't have won in 1917 if it hadn't been for
1905. This should be taken into consideration. This should be understood. Some say, give us victory now! If not, it's no good. Tea drinkers.
They want everything handed to them in a tea saucer.

Unfortunately there are many such people.

Many, and for a long time.

And they grow in number.

No, you must also realize that alongside them the new is being born.

[5-21-74, 7-28-76]

How long should we continue the war in Afghanistan? Is it time to finish it, to come to a solution?

It doesn't depend upon us. Don't oversimplify. In Afghanistan and in other countries we are training people who can help us in diplomacy. There is no other way. They border with us and we train our people there. They are a backward people, but they support us.

Not yet.

They will. To my mind you oversimplify the matter, and you're impatient. Of course landlords and prosperous farmers aren't on our side and can't be. But we must not lose Afghanistan. . . .

[10-4-85]

■   **Foreign Figures**   ■

Ernst Thaelmann

Thaelmann was remarkably good, from a family of workers. Very firm. But not sufficiently cultured. This fellow Neumann used to help him write his speeches, to ground them theoretically. Neumann was a Trotsky type, but cultured, quick, and well read, and cultivated. Thaelmann would roar the moment Neumann included any vague words or passages that were not revolutionary enough! He didn't like that. . . . He was a tall, strong man. I met him. But apparently he lacked education, and it was hard for him to explain communism and Marxism to the German people. A lot of passion and revolutionary character; he had a strong commitment but lacked education. He had a sharp mind, was flexible, quickly grasped an idea or a matter of principle—this should be done so and so, right away! He made a very good impression. He treated us well. Loyal, a good speaker. His personality could win you over, and how!

Bela Kun

Bela Kun was hardly a Trotskyist. What caused his death? I think he was unstable. He was very good in the midst of revolutionary enthusiasm. In the 1930s... he was the representative of the Hungarian Communist party in Moscow. Then something happened, and he was taken away. Many were taken away at the time—old Social Democrats. Many of the Poles were taken away. . . .

Shota Ivanovich said, "The struggle was bloody and cruel. Who would come out on top? You can't make an omelet without breaking eggs. Stalin was engaged in a bloody struggle for life and death. One blunder and everything would have been lost! I'll never forget your words: Yes, there were victims, but there would have been more! At that time, what else could Stalin have done?"

Correct. But there were also mistakes and victims.

[6-9-76]

Matyas Rákosi

Rákosi was good, but he had shortcomings, too: he pretended to be Stalin in Hungary. That was too much, way too much. But he had his good points. He had been imprisoned by the Horthy government. We exchanged him for Hungarian banners seized by tsarist armies in 1849.

Wladislaw Gomulka

Gomulka was a nationalist, right-wing deviationist. As I recall, he was put under house arrest. Perhaps he was imprisoned, but I never heard of it. When we came to Warsaw he refused to let us into the plenary session of the Central Committee. There were three of us—Nikita, me, and who was the third? Malenkov or Kaganovich? We had sent Rokossovsky there as a defense minister. Stalin sent him, of course.

Gomulka welcomed us. He provided us with comfortable accommodations and with everything else we needed, but he wouldn't let us into the plenum.

But in Potsdam you won powerfully on Poland.

That's right. We clashed there with Truman over the Polish question.

[8-18-76]

Georgi Dimitrov

Dimitrov was a good person and a heroic revolutionary. But he showed his best a little too late. He lived briefly but left a mark. He swatted the Germans really hard.

I suppose he was too big for Bulgaria. He needed a larger arena.
You might say so. He was suited for a big country.
Was he a leader of the international movement anyhow?
He had not busied himself with international affairs until forced to do so by fascism.

[3-11-83]

Ruth Fischer

Do you remember Ruth Fischer?
Who wouldn't? An original personality. She scarcely looked like a communist, but she found herself among leaders. She came to Russia from Germany.
They say she was one of the characters in Manuilsky's amusing stories. . . .
Because both Manuilsky and Ruth Fischer worked in the Comintern. He made up a story about himself, that when he died no one from the government came to his funeral except Ruth Fischer, who followed the coffin while she was reading a newspaper. . . .

Mao and Chou

The Chinese repaid all their debts to us. They paid us with precious metals just after the war. They were quite honest in that regard.
How did you like Mao Tse-tung?
He offered us tea. And he talked about meeting Stalin and when it would be convenient. . . . Stalin hadn't received him for some days after he arrived. Stalin told me, "Go and see what sort of fellow he is." He stayed at Stalin's dacha Blizhniya.
I talked with Mao and then suggested to Stalin that he receive him. He was a clever man, a peasant leader, a kind of Chinese Pugachev. He was far from a Marxist, of course—he confessed to me that he had never read Marx's *Das Kapital.*
Only heroes could read *Das Kapital.* When I was in Mongolia talking with the Chinese ambassador—he was nice to me—I said, "You want to create a metals industry quickly, but the measures you have planned— backyard blast furnaces—are improbable and won't work." I criticized the Chinese, and our people reproved me later. But it was such obvious stupidity! . . . Backyard blast furnaces to produce worthless metals—nonsense.

[7-28-71, 12-4-73]

I had to deal with Chou En-lai. He was a courteous, well-read man, a practical worker rather than a theorist. But very clever. He wasn't very smart to walk out of our XXIInd Congress, but . . . A diplomat, without a doubt. I got to know him better at the conferences in Geneva in 1954.

[4-28-76]

Maurice Thorez

Thorez was a very good man—a Stalinist, but he followed Khrushchev. Actually it wasn't Khrushchev he followed but the Soviet Union, the CPSU.

[4-19-77]

The Mongolian Leaders

I visited all the districts except two, and stayed in the yurts [nomadic tents] when Khrushchev sent me to Mongolia as ambassador. Portraits of Stalin, Voroshilov, me, Kalinin hung there. I didn't mind the climate, but Polina Semenovna didn't feel good there. I wasn't ill there but suffered health problems later in Vienna, where I spent a year and a half. I had pneumonia a few times, but since then my lungs have been in good shape.

I remember Choibalsan. He had little culture but was loyal to the USSR. After his death a successor had to be appointed. Damba was nominated. I examined this Damba and decided to appoint Tsedenbal instead. He had a good attitude toward us.

[4-13-72, 5-9-75]

I visited Tsedenbal quite often when I was ambassador to Mongolia. And Polina Semenovna liked to come along. They spoke nothing else but Russian, that's why. His wife was from Riazin. A woman who put on no airs.

It wasn't wise to speak only Russian; the Mongols didn't like it.

I knew Damba well. He was a man who was simply left behind. At one time he was a first secretary. He was pushed aside by Tsedenbal.

When I arrived Tsedenbal was chairman of the council of ministers and Damba was nominated to be first secretary. He was a sly Mongol, cautious, and he spoke no Russian. This alone disqualified him for leadership—one had to read *Pravda* and *Kommunist*. Tsedenbal had studied at the Irkutsk College of Finance and had married a Russian there. He had a library at home. He liked to drink—hard. He never refused a drink.

[12-7-76]

Klement Gotvald

Gotvald—a good fellow, very good, but he drank. . . .

He had no decisive role in our victory, of course, but he had a positive influence on the building of socialism and the transition from capitalism in Czechoslovakia. A fine fellow, Gotvald.

Willy Brandt

Willy Brandt headed the Socialist International. I consider this a most decent political distinction. It seems he is doing well. His son is a communist. Anyway, he made an important agreement—with the Soviet Union on the borders of the two Germanies. That's a great accomplishment, not a small one.

[12-7-76]

Tito

In 1953–1954 I spoke out [against reconciliation with Tito's] Yugoslavia at the Politburo. No one supported me, neither Malenkov nor even Kaganovich, though he was a Stalinist! Khrushchev was not alone. There were hundreds and thousands like him, otherwise on his own he would not have gotten very far. He simply pandered to the state of mind of the people. But where did that lead? Even now there are lots of Khrushchevs. . . .

Tito is now [1970s] in a difficult situation. His republic is going under, and he will have to grab onto the USSR for dear life. Then we shall be able to deal with him more firmly.

There are many people worse than Tito.

Nationalism is causing him to howl in pain, yet he himself is a nationalist, and that is his main defect as a communist. He is a nationalist; that is, he is infected with the bourgeois spirit. He is now cursing and criticizing his own people for nationalism. This means that the Yugoslav multinational state is breaking up along national lines. It is composed of Serbs, Croatians, Slovenes, and so forth.

When Tito visited us for the first time, I liked his appearance. We didn't know everything about him at the time. You couldn't understand Tito on first meeting. I liked him, but at the same time there was something different about him. . . . I was reminded of the provocateur Malinovsky.

Tito is not an imperialist, he is a petty bourgeois, an opponent of socialism. Imperialism is something else again.

[6-21-72, 7-31-72, 6-16-77]

Two

WITH
LENIN

H ERE Molotov offers interesting information on Lenin's personality, work methods, and relations with leading Bolshevik personalities—Trotsky, Stalin, Bukharin, Zinoviev, and Kamenev, as well as Molotov himself.

Most significant is Molotov's account of how Stalin came to the newly created post of general secretary of the Central Committee of the Communist party in April 1922. Previous accounts report that Stalin was "elected" or "appointed" or "designated" or "accorded" the title by the Central Committee. In fact all of these terms apply. According to Molotov, Lenin engineered the whole thing in an effort to get around oppositionists within the Central Committee. Lenin had presented his faction within the CC a list bearing the names of ten members he wanted elected to the Politburo, to the exclusion of oppositionists. Alongside the name of Stalin, Lenin had written in "general secretary." This slate, with Lenin's annotation attached to Stalin's name, was elected to the Politburo as a bloc by the CC plenum. In short, Lenin insisted on Stalin's election to this office. And despite Lenin's opposition to "factionalism" within the party, Molotov shows that Lenin had no compunctions about organizing a faction to overcome oppositionists. Thus for Molotov "factionalism," formally banned within the party since 1921, was permissible for Lenin and Stalin. Indeed, they were permitted everything in their efforts to persuade the party to adopt and implement the "correct" line, which they always propounded on major questions. It was "factionalism" by oppositionists—to counterpose "incorrect" policies—which must be banned.

This section also contains two other highly intriguing bits of information. Molotov has no doubt that despite denials by most biographers of Lenin, Inessa Armand was Lenin's mistress. It should be noted, however, that Molotov got this information second- or thirdhand, from Bukharin.

Finally, Molotov offers a novel twist to a hypothesis offered by some historians. They hold that Stalin, who was charged by the Politburo with supervising Lenin's medical care, might have poisoned Lenin because the Soviet leader in his last days sought to have Stalin removed from the position of general secretary. According to Molotov, in February 1923 Lenin took a turn for the worse and asked Stalin to bring him some poison. Although Stalin promised to do so, he did not. Whether or not this story is apocryphal can only be cleared up by examining records of the Politburo which, according to Molotov, had discussed Lenin's request.

■ Early Days ■

At the end of 1916 and in early 1917 none of the top Bolshevik leaders, members of the Central Committee, were present in Petrograd. Lenin had found asylum in Switzerland; Stalin and Sverdlov were exiles somewhere in Siberia. Of the leaders, only the Russian bureau of the Central Committee, the body acting as deputy for the Central Committee of the party, was on the spot in Petrograd. The bureau consisted of three of us, a troika: Alexander Shliapnikov, P. A. Zalutsky, and myself. In the land of the blind the one-eyed man is king. That was the Russian bureau of the CC. For despite our youth, inexperience, and junior status in the party, we were in charge of party work in the capital.

Although in February 1917 I lived in Piter [Saint Petersburg] in underground status and was a member of the Russian bureau of the CC, I was not up on things, not even where an "illegal" could best hide to avoid arrest. All the same, we prepared the February Revolution.

Did you put out a newspaper?

A newspaper—then? Everything was shut down. Only illegal papers were circulated. We overthrew tsarism. We did quite well, quite well.

When the events of February 26 unfolded, Zalutsky and I—we had the closest possible personal association—went to our secret meeting place on the Vyborg side to find out how things were going. But our other companion, Shliapnikov, was not there. We were told he was probably at Gorky's place. We set off to Gorky's. It was late, probably already the morning of February 27.

There was shooting on the streets, from all directions. Zalutsky and I stood in the entryway at Gorky's. He came out. This was the first time I saw him.

I said, "What have you heard? Isn't Shliapnikov with you?"

He replied, "The Petrograd Soviet of Workers' Deputies is already in session."

"Where is it sitting?"

"At the Tauride Palace. Shliapnikov is probably there now. He dropped in to see me and then left."

89

Well, we went to the Tauride Palace, summoned Kerensky—he was chairman of the soviet—and introduced ourselves: "We are from the CC of the Bolsheviks and we wish to participate in the session." He escorted us to the presidium and introduced me to the Petrograd Soviet, which had just been formed. Bolsheviks there were few in number.

All of this took place in the Tauride Palace, the seat of the Imperial State Duma. Kerensky was *au courant* with all its affairs, all the revolutionary events. As the leader of a peasant group, he was in touch with all the other deputies. During the Revolution every liberal wanted to have some kind of link with the peasant group. He was highly influential.

Our Russian intelligentsia was closely associated with the peasantry, especially with the kulaks, the well-to-do peasants. Thus began our participation in the session of the Petrograd Soviet of Workers' Deputies. The session in all probability had just opened. It was chaired by Chkheidze, the leader of a Menshevik Social Democratic group. An orator? I did not hear much of his oratory. At this session he delivered few speeches. He was an obliging man—bearded, respectable.

"Do you know how Chkheidze's life ended? In Paris, with a bread knife," said Shota Ivanovich.

I know.... Anyway, we proposed the slogan "No support to the Provisional Government!" No support. My formulation was that this was a bourgeois government of capitalists and landowners, and that was why it was pursuing a counterrevolutionary line. My analysis was somewhat imprecise, nevertheless it was later approved in the main by Lenin.

So I took a seat at the presidium table. What else could I do? We had to join the soviet.

At the presidium I found myself sitting almost side-by-side with Yordansky, at that time publisher and editor of *Sovremennyi Mir* [*Contemporary World*] where I, under the name Alexei Petrovich Karpov, used to work as bookkeeper and secretary to the editorial staff. This Yordansky was a big drinker and later was our ambassador to Italy. All his business was managed by a woman, Maria Karlovna, who lived with him.

So here he sat by my side. I was known to him as Karpov, but now I was speaking as Molotov. How he glared at me! I had spoken in favor of a proposal that would permit publication only of those newspapers supporting the Revolution. Those that were not would be barred. The proposal failed; apparently I argued poorly. In essence I think I was right. But I had to hurry to our secret meeting place to edit a manifesto composed by a worker, Kaiurov. I edited and amended it; the finished product was quite good. Afterward Lenin approved it, and the same day we published it. I walked, now openly, to the printing shop where the first issues of the *Izvestia of Workers' Deputies* were printed. An extra had come out in the evening before I had arrived, but in the morning the first regular issue of *Izvestia* was to be published. I spent the whole night at the print shop. Among the editors, Steklov, Sukhanov, and Serebrov were there, all quite well known. I cajoled them into running our manifesto in that first issue of *Izvestia* and in the morning returned to the Tauride Palace by automobile. We got no sleep those days.

You had automobiles?

Automobiles? In revolutionary days we seized them and, as commanders, utilized them.

At 5 or 6 a.m. I again went to the Tauride Palace and from the automobile scattered copies of *Izvestia* carrying our manifesto. That's how we did it.

"We were born too soon," Steklov had said to me. Later, for a long time under Lenin, he was editor of *Izvestia*. He was an old Bolshevik, but then he turned himself into a Menshevik troubadour and left our party. At the second session at the Tauride Palace I put forward a motion which was not supported. I had to speak out against Kerensky.

I was a direct participant in these events. Lenin was not there, so we had to fend for ourselves. There were no directives from him, and there couldn't be any. After all, not only for Lenin but for those of us in Piter, the day of the Revolution arrived unexpectedly. It is impossible to foresee everything.

You once recounted how when you were at Pravda *in the July days of 1917, Stalin and Kamenev discharged you from the editorial staff.*

Before Stalin's return I had revived *Pravda*. The first issues appeared while Stalin and Kamenev were not yet back in Petrograd, but then Stalin and Kamenev turned me out of *Pravda* in 1917. . . .

While we opposed Kerensky's bourgeois government as counterrevolutionary, we had not yet arrived at the conclusion drawn by Lenin: a *soviet* government, *soviet* power based on the soviets. Nothing of the kind. I defended the democratic revolution and did not dream of a socialist revolution.

When Stalin and Kamenev returned to Petrograd I was turned out of the Petersburg Committee, then removed from the editorial staff—delicately, without any fuss, undoubtedly because they held higher rank. Also they had ten years' seniority on me. I did not resist—what was the use when I had no support? I had expressed my opinion, had an aim, but ended in the minority. It was after I had been removed from the editorial staff that the notorious editorial "A Bullet for a Bullet!" written by Kamenev appeared in *Pravda*. Answer the Germans bullet for bullet, he wrote. This was the defensist line. Yet Stalin was on the editorial board at the time. Herein lies the source of the error. As long as I was on the board, such things did not happen.

This was Stalin's mistake. And here is another one of his mistakes from this period—an article later printed in his collected works. I am still surprised that he included it there. Take 1917. There is an article on the question of the war. It follows the line of reasoning that held it necessary to struggle for peace and take advantage of whatever the Provisional Government was doing for peace. This, of course, was not at all the essence of Lenin's line. But this article was published. It is precisely analogous with Kamenev's editorial "A Bullet for a Bullet!" because it too held that the Provisional Government must be supported "to the extent and so long as" it seeks peace. Perhaps I am exaggerating, but just read it. Why did Stalin include it in his collected works? After all, Stalin mastered the exceptional language of the propagandist—classical language, precise, terse, and clear. Yet he got this notion into his head. But he made a mistake.

As I recall, I have not yet spoken to you about this. Perhaps I had not reread this article, but later when I began to have more free time I got around to reading it to see what had been incomprehensible to me. But why? Because not everything had been clear to Stalin. . . .

Now about the prosecutor's writ ordering Lenin's arrest and trial on conspiracy charges in July 1917. I know that Stalin's critics accuse him of opposing Lenin's appearance in court. But it's possible that Stalin held a more circumspect position on this matter. Critics say it was not necessary to oppose every order of the Provisional Government. But Lenin's nonappearance in court could have been a means, so to speak, of again discrediting the government, using it to demonstrate that it could not guarantee Lenin's safety. I think that is most likely. I know they accuse Stalin of badly advising Lenin in this matter, but I have not had an opportunity to reread the documents.

But the position of Stalin on the question of Lenin's court appearance is, it seems to me, distorted. This is what it boils down to.

Back then, Stalin and I lived in the same apartment. He was a bachelor, I was a bachelor. There were such big apartments on the Petrograd side. I lived in one room with Zalutsky, a member of the bureau of the Central Committee, later a Zinovievite. Smilga lived in the apartment with his wife. Stalin joined us, so that we were five people in the same apartment. We had a kind of commune. Three or four rooms . . .

Later, during the July Days, Stalin said to me, "You were closer to Lenin than all of us at the initial stage in April." He had had certain doubts, and he did not immediately support Lenin's April Theses. Stalin held out, thought more carefully. As for me, I was younger, approached the matter more simplistically, supported Lenin without any hesitation, and firmly followed his course.

Something bothered Stalin. He had ideas on the question of peace; he mulled it over and sought answers to questions early in March, around the 8th or 10th, but Lenin did not arrive until April 3. During the first days Stalin, of course, gave Kamenev too much leeway and let his article be printed.

Sometimes Lenin was not all that easy to understand.

When you met Lenin at the Finland Station in Petrograd in April 1917, were there as many people as films would have it?

It's difficult to say; it was nighttime. As I recall, a pair of tanks was standing by.

"Armored cars"—the correction came from a guest at the table.

Yes, armored cars.

I first saw Lenin in April 1917 at the Finland Station and became acquainted with him there. He emerged from the railway car together with Stalin who had met him several stations before Petrograd. Lenin mounted an armored car and proclaimed, "Long live the socialist revolution!"

We Bolsheviks were suddenly confronted with a different direction. Later Lenin spoke to a very small group, about forty-five persons, no more. . . .

In Petrograd I sat at the presidium of a party conference while Lenin took the floor and said: The danger to us now comes from the old Bolsheviks who do not understand that we have entered a new stage. They think we have a democratic revolution. But we should move to socialist revolution! Suddenly everyone was dumbfounded. What!—to socialist revolution?

I had never opposed Lenin, but neither I nor any of those who were always with Lenin immediately grasped the sense of his message. All Bolsheviks spoke about democratic revolution, now behold—socialist revolution!

Well, after all, Kamenev was a Bolshevik, Rykov was a Bolshevik—yet they did not understand matters Lenin's way. They asserted, as usual, that we were still at the stage of democratic revolution. They were very prominent Bolsheviks. In their speeches they affirmed the democratic revolution, Lenin the socialist revolution. Even when the old Bolsheviks said "socialist revolution," it was a matter of the future. Lenin replied: No, even now we must remake ourselves for the socialist revolution, and anyone who says "democratic" revolution is one of those old Bolsheviks who are getting in the way. The main danger lies within the party. Not because they are bad people but because their minds have not made a U-turn. I was ready to lay down my very life for certain goals, but the goals had suddenly changed; one needed to think things over again, and that was not so simple. Lenin had opened our eyes.

■   **A Member of the Military Revolutionary Committee**   ■

Shortly before the October insurrection, a party center was formed which included Stalin. But I was a member of the Military Revolutionary Committee (MRC) which had been formed by the Petrograd Soviet. The chairman of the Petrograd Soviet was Trotsky. He acquitted himself quite well back then.

About ten days earlier a session of the Central Committee had been held, which of course was illegal. Lenin came to Petrograd, and at this secret session five persons had been assigned to a kind of party general staff, which maintained liaison with individual troop units and of course with the Petrograd Committee. As a member of the bureau of the Petrograd Committee of the party, I was sent to be a member of the MRC, the official body under the Soviet of Workers' and Soldiers' Deputies. Our MRC sat at Smolny, which was also the seat of the party center, and where Lenin and especially our committee, starting with the October days and over the course of five, perhaps even ten weeks, carried out all the practical work connected with the insurrection. Formally the MRC headed the insurrection, but standing behind it was the Central Committee, the party group that exercised leadership over the MRC. Today there is not a single person alive who was with the MRC. I am probably the only one of those who was at Smolny from the very first days.

How do you remember the day of October 25, 1917?

Difficult to say. The main thing is that we sensed we had achieved something great and important.

I retain no overall picture of the day. Back then I was a bachelor, twenty-five or twenty-six years old, did not go home, spent the night at Smolny.

Did you have a staff there?

Staff?—I can't say. I was a member of the MRC, and for that reason things were arranged more or less normally so that we could take our meals and sleep there. The committee included among its members Stalin, Sverdlov, Trotsky... Bubnov, too. Many prominent leaders were members. . . .

Did Trotsky play a large role?

Big, but only as an agitator. He took only a small part in matters of organization; apparently he was not invited. . . .

We ourselves did not think we were ready for the Revolution, but it came. To Lenin! Yes, how steadfast he was. . . .

During the first days of the October Revolution I saw him frequently but did not chat with him. He knew me in my capacity as secretary and member of the *Pravda* editorial staff.

I was present—but no more than present—at a discussion at Smolny on the night of October 25, maybe even October 24, on the question of the formation of a new government. I remember that Lenin was there, and for some reason Sokolnikov sticks in my memory. Apparently because he reported some sort of factual information. Also a group of Central Committee members connected with Lenin. I was not a member of the Central Committee but was a kind of elder representing the Petrograd Committee. We discussed the question of how to open the Second All-Russian Congress of Soviets. It was obvious that Lenin had to open it. He did.

"What shall we call the government?" Lenin asked us. It was decided that "Council of Ministers" smacked bourgeois. Someone proposed "Council of People's Commissars." In France the term "commissar" was widely used. Commissars of police, municipal, and so forth. At the time France was closer to us in spirit than Germany, say, where there was more regimentation. . . . In the army we borrowed "marshal" as being closer to France, but not field marshal. We tried mightily not to borrow from Germany. . . .

As a member of the MRC I was appointed head of the agitation department of this committee. What were its main functions? Workers, young people, and workers of Piter were flocking to the MRC: "I am going home to my native province. What shall I say? Where can I get literature?" We had to brief them, answer their questions, and provide literature. I busied myself with this, enlisted workers from various factories and from the army, issued orders concerning who was to get pamphlets and leaflets. On the night of October 25 or thereabouts I was ordered to arrest and sequester the editors of the Socialist Revolutionaries' *Peasants Newspaper*. It was headed by Argunov, an old, prominent Socialist Revolutionary. I took a detachment of Red Guards with me to the editorial office: "You are closed down!" "Well, we knew it would happen. Could anyone expect anything good of you people?" "Close it down, there is nothing more for you to do here!"

We ejected the editor and his staff members and sealed the premises. It must have been the night of October 25.

A day or two later a watchman from the Most Holy Synod came to us and asked, "Whom can I speak with?" Various members of the committee rotated as duty officer. As one went to bed or another was sent on a mission, he was replaced. The watchman said, "A strike committee is being formed near the Most Holy Synod." More precisely, he did not say "strike committee" but "Some suspicious people are gathering and are up to something."

I was then assigned a detachment of Red Guards, well disciplined, about twenty to thirty strong.

Did you have automobiles and trucks?

Come now, we had seized power and still did not have automobiles or trucks? We rode there. Behind a capital letter "P," sitting at a table were the conspirators—the "Strike Committee of Saboteurs," so to speak, representatives of various ministries, about forty to fifty persons.

"Hands up!"—the usual procedure. "Search them!"

We searched them and took them all away. It turned out they were Mensheviks and Socialist Revolutionaries.

"We shall lodge a complaint with the Petrograd Soviet!"

"Good." I took two of the bellowing protesters with me to the Petrograd Soviet. The MRC was there too. I do not know the arrestees' subsequent fate. My task was to take them away. . . .

Even now engraved on my mind there is, of course, the scene of Lenin proclaiming Soviet power. I was seated above and behind the lectern where the presidium was located. Lenin is at the lectern, here is the presidium, and I am sitting there, off to one side. For some reason I remember that Lenin, while addressing the audience, stood with one foot slightly raised as was his style when delivering a speech. The sole of his shoe was visible, and I noticed a hole in it. The shape of the hole is imprinted in my mind. [He draws the shape of the hole in Lenin's high shoe.] But there was an insole. It was still intact, but the sole had a hole in it.

This was the only time Trotsky acquitted himself quite well. He was an excellent speaker, and oratorical skill is important in holding an audience. And he had that skill. He was a spellbinder, and that is why later on the fight against him was difficult. I was close to Arosev. He hated Trotsky passionately, even overdoing it. Trotsky conjured up figures of speech of the kind one finds in the works of belletrists. . . .

I was at Smolny from the very first moment and did not leave it for three days. It was the former Institute for Daughters of the Nobility, the gymnasium for girls of the nobility, so to speak.

We sat side by side—Zinoviev, Trotsky, and I; opposite were Stalin and Kamenev. At the chairman's place sat Lenin. Thank God, I personally knew each of them very well. I knew Zinoviev especially well because I later worked with him in Leningrad. He did not quite take to me, indeed he wasn't overly fond of me.

After the Revolution I was chairman of the Council of the National Economy [Sovnarkhoz] of the Northern Region.

The Encyclopedia *states: "After the overthrow . . . V. M. Molotov became one of the leaders of the Petrograd Soviet of Workers' and Soldiers' Deputies."*

That was the first period. I don't really know how this turned out; in fact I can't remember this period precisely. I stayed on as a member of the MRC of the Petrograd Soviet, which existed for about two months after the Revolution. But early in 1918 I organized and became chairman of the Sovnarkhoz of the Northern Region, which comprised five provinces with Petrograd at the head. It included Novgorod, Pskov, Olentsk [now Karelia] . . . I don't remember whether it included Murmansk or not. Industry had to be developed, and I was in the chief industrial center, Petrograd. But then for fear of a German onslaught we had to move to Moscow. At that time I was a member of the bureau of the Petrograd Committee of the party and carried out a good deal of party work, delivering speeches at factories and all kinds of conferences. But I also had to work in the Petrograd Soviet to maintain liaison with the factories. All this up to the end of 1917. It was in the Petrograd Committee that I greeted the New Year, 1918.

Lenin and Stalin were not on the committee, neither was Trotsky, and neither perhaps was Zinoviev. Sverdlov was, also Sokolnikov, Dzerzhinsky. . . .

During the first days of October, how did you imagine the new life, socialism?

We had only the vaguest notion. We did not have a full picture. Much turned out differently from what we had sought. Lenin, for example, believed that our first order of business would be the elimination of three main enemies: oppression by money, oppression by capital, and oppression by exploitation. There was serious talk about doing away with money by the 1920s.

Many difficulties and unresolved problems lay ahead, but we began 1917 quite well, and things moved forward. Not everything we had dreamed about turned out, but much did.

You undertook so much in 1917. Surely you believed it would all be over shortly. . . .

A very great cause. They said we would hold on for two weeks at most.

I had something else in mind: Does a man switch to a new psychology so rapidly?

Not all the way, and not everyone. . . .

In March 1921 I began to work in the Central Committee.

When did you become acquainted with Polina Semenovna Zhemchuzhina?

In 1921 during an international conference of women at a palace which had passed from tsarist authority into the hands of the Bolsheviks, in Piter.

Polina Semenovna worked in the underground in the Ukraine. She was from Zaporozhe. . . .

We married in 1921. Before this I had little time for personal life. I was a bachelor. My suitcase was always with me and I traveled. . . .

■   **First Alternate to the Politburo**   ■

At the Xth Party Congress in the spring of 1921, I was elected a member of the Central Committee of the party and then, at the Central Committee plenum, as an alternate member of the Politburo. At the time the Politburo of the Central Committee consisted of five members—Lenin, Stalin, Trotsky, Kamenev, and Zinoviev—and three alternates—myself, Kalinin, and Bukharin. As a first alternate I often had a vote in the Politburo's deliberations when one of the members was unable to be present. At the same time I was elected one of the secretaries of the Central Committee, which made me responsible for a great many organizational matters.

Several weeks after I had begun my work in the central party apparatus, I asked Vladimir Ilyich to receive me to take up certain problems. In the course of our conversation we touched upon several important questions concerning political cadres—for example, strengthening the leadership in the Tula Provincial Committee, and putting an end to the attempts of the Socialist Revolutionaries to use peasant dissatisfaction to develop an anti-Soviet uprising in the Tambov Province. Lenin emphasized the complexity of the country's political situation. He suggested that improvements required fundamental reforms in financial affairs, but that the slightest haste could provoke an eruption of discontent, especially among the peasants, which could threaten the still feeble soviet system. . . .

According to Molotov, Lenin had selected him to have a voice ahead of that of Kalinin or Bukharin.

I was chosen as the first alternate to the Politburo so that I could replace the first absent member of the body. Kalinin was second, and Bukharin was third. Since there were five members, Bukharin never actually had the opportunity to replace anyone. Lenin had decided this.

His association with Lenin began through correspondence, with a note written in 1912 when Molotov was working at the newspaper Pravda, *organizing its first issues. Ilyich directed the newspaper from exile and each day sent letters and articles to Molotov's address in Petersburg.*

It happened quite often that as packages from Lenin and Zinoviev were arriving from abroad, the situation in Russia would change, and we would have to edit Lenin's articles or compose something ourselves. Some of his articles simply could not be used. Sometimes Lenin criticized my articles, but there were no better ones. From the time it took for our Petersburg newspapers to reach Austria, where Lenin and Zinoviev lived—almost on the border of Austria—to the time they sent an article, a good many days passed. But we had to publish something anyway. The editorial staff would compose something. In such a small newspaper it was awkward to publish two articles on exactly the same subject. *Pravda* was a small paper then.

In 1921, of course, we had more difficulties than, say, in 1941, when we had a monolithic socialist state. Once during the civil war, when Denikin was approaching Moscow, Makhno [the anarchist leader] unexpectedly saved the Soviet republic by attacking Denikin's flank. Denikin called back his corps to repulse Makhno's attack. We saw that even Makhno could be useful. The situation was such that Lenin called us together and said, "It's all over. Soviet power has ceased to exist. The party will go underground." Documents and secret addresses were prepared for us. . . .

I often had opportunities to communicate with Lenin unofficially. He said to me after work one evening, "Come over to my place, Comrade Molotov." We had tea with blackcurrant jam. "Our country is so peasant in character," Lenin said, "that in order to accomplish anything we must first move strongly in one direction and then slowly correct our course. And we are still far from having learned how to do everything correctly the first time. But if the party of the Bolsheviks were replaced with, say, the party of Lev Nikolaevich Tolstoy, we might be delayed a century."

I visited Lenin's home in 1919 or early in 1920. He lived in the Kremlin. I came from Nizhny Novgorod. Before this he had talked with me on the telephone and had sent me a message. I was chairman of the Nizhny Novgorod Provincial Executive Committee. We had held a congress there, our first regional congress of radio engineers. Bonch-Bruevich was the leader there. He was a relative of V. D. Bonch-Bruevich, chief of staff of the Council of People's Commissars. He was a rich man and a publisher. He wrote some books on the sectarian movements. He knew the subject well. A highly cultured man, he helped Lenin. That relative of his was, I believe, the best radio technician in our country. Lenin used to say that we had to support his experiments and help him in his work.

Then there was the timber cutting. I reported to Lenin on the timber cutting.

We were alone at Lenin's place. We talked probably for an hour. I don't remember the details. We drank tea.

Was Lenin fond of tea?

Well, how to say. . .

And did he drink wine?

A bit. That sort of thing didn't particularly attract him. He was a companionable man.

And what did Lenin tell you?

There was nothing extraordinary in our conversation. He was interested in the local mood in Nizhegorod. He wanted to know about the condition of the local workers.

Lenin was gradually drawing Molotov's attention to foreign affairs, too.

G. V. Chicherin, commissar for foreign affairs, 1918–1930. . . . Chicherin was from the old nobility. He had lived abroad for a long time, knew foreign languages, and, of course, was very useful to Lenin. Years later I worked for a long time as minister of foreign affairs.

When you read our contemporary economists and philosophers . . . it is evident they are spinning incredible tales as regards foreign policy. The main error, of course, is that they do not understand the kernel, so to speak, of the Leninist approach. Lenin consistently and pointedly undermines capitalism and bourgeois ideology from the most diverse angles. Take Lenin—his every work, every line is a bomb thrown at imperialism. That's the main thing in Lenin. In our country they are moving away from this and beginning to skirt the issue. When you think about how this situation is to be overcome, the answer is that only the young will be able to manage it.

[1-8-74, 4-27-78, 3-10-77]

■ Lenin Led Everyone onto the Correct Path ■

While there is imperialism, while classes exist, imperialists will spare no expense to undermine our society. And some people can always be bribed. When Malinovsky—a deputy of the state Duma, a Bolshevik, a member of the central committee of the Russian Social-Democratic Labor party, the best Bolshevik speaker—was exposed as a police agent, Lenin did not believe it. Malinovsky was a lively, resourceful fellow. He could behave boldly when required and with silence when necessary. He was a metal worker, a deputy from Moscow. I had met him quite often and remember him well. He looked something like Tito. Handsome, quite attractive, especially when you were in rapport with him. But he became unpleasant when you discovered he was a scum. The Mensheviks informed us that he was an agent. We didn't believe it and decided they were trying to defame a Bolshevik. Lenin said later, "He has done more for us than for the police, even if he was an agent. In the end, he's done what we've told him." We not only had him deliver speeches in the Duma; we also planted him in workers' organizations. Just you try to give the wrong sort of speech there; the workers would tell you where to go right away! And Malinovsky fulfilled all the instructions of the Bolsheviks—yet he was at the same time an agent of the tsarist secret police. He ruined organizations and betrayed Bolsheviks to the police. Malinovsky was shot after the Revolution, in 1918 I think.

Shurkanov—or Shingarev—a deputy to the Duma from Petrograd, was also a provocateur. In 1914 he betrayed an antiwar conference. Our deputies—there were five of them—were condemned to penal servitude. But Kamenev was exiled, for he confessed before the court that he did not support the Bolshevik point of view but merely participated in the conference.

A Bolshevik deputy, Badaev, was a lightweight. Most of the elected deputies were from bourgeois and landed-gentry backgrounds, and the Bolsheviks needed a deputy who clearly came from among the workers. So they began to look around for the least offensive man, someone who had participated only slightly in revolutionary actions. That was Badaev, so let's vote for him. He turned out to be an honest man, though poorly educated and not very active. But he had a capacity for work. After he'd been elected he came to see us at *Pravda* and said, "I'm not very educated. It will be difficult for me to work in the Duma. Can't you give me a book where I can read what I am supposed to do, and what Bolshevism is? I'll read this book, remember it, and then follow it."

But no matter, he then improved.

Lenin made do. All the Bolsheviks languished in prisons and in penal servitude. Take me, for example. I was twenty-two years old and publishing *Pravda*. What training did I have? A superficial, juvenile knowledge. What did I understand, though I had already been twice in exile? I had to work. And these old Bolsheviks, where were they? No one really wanted to take risks. Krzhizhanovsky had a job, Krasin too. Both were good electrical engineers. Tsiurupa managed an estate. Kirov, who wasn't with us at the time, was a journalist for a small provincial newspaper. And I haven't mentioned Khrushchev. He was always active, but he joined the party only in 1918, by which time everything had become clear.

When it became necessary for us to run things, Lenin led everyone to the field. He wasn't one to be downcast, and he knew how to make use of everyone—Bolsheviks, half-Bolsheviks, and quarter-Bolsheviks alike, but only literate ones. They were few. In the Politburo, three of five spoke against Lenin. And he had to work with them. They were good speakers—they could write articles, make speeches. They were capable people and sympathetic to socialism, but they were confused. But there was no one else. So you made your choice.

[8-15-75]

■ I Did Not Consider Myself an Old Bolshevik ■

People were different then. . . . I was walking at the Novodevichy cemetery. On one grave was the following inscription: "A warrior of the old Leninist guard, V. I. Ivanov," and in brackets "Dawdler." That was his nickname. For some reason they called him that, but they didn't have to inscribe it on his headstone! What's more, they wrote, "from his friends."

Oh, those old Bolsheviks. . . . By the way, I never considered myself an old Bolshevik until recent times. Why? The old Bolsheviks were those who joined before 1905.

And you were still a boy in 1906. You became a party member when you were sixteen.

So what? What kind of old Bolshevik does that make me?

You took part in publishing Pravda *in 1912.*

Well, I could consider myself an old Bolshevik during the Revolution or after it. But beside me were bearded men who had already been at the helm in 1905. . . . We respected them as fathers, of course. I listened to them though I held a high post alongside them at the same time. I took an active part in the Revolution. Still, I am not one of the old Leninist guard of 1903–1904. But I am very close to them. That's a fact. Because of my age, I couldn't have been there in 1903. But at age sixteen I managed to join the party. Yes, I did it. These days sixteen-year-olds are in high school. Take my grandson. He is sixteen. But what does he understand? He is a very good boy. He leads an hour of political discussion for his pals at school. And what does he tell them about the newspapers? If you are clever enough to repeat what's in the newspaper, you'll get Bolshevik propaganda. We had no newspapers of this kind, only bourgeois ones. . . .

We are walking in the settlement.

Here is the village store where we buy our bread. There are two or three stores not far away. But the main one is the village general store. On the whole, this district is well supplied with food. They take into account that a number of bosses live here. Many come here from the city, too. So the supply is fairly good here.

We walked almost three miles. We approached the house. You planted lilacs, I observed.

We're doing our best. I had nothing to do with it. Tania tries hard. She was born in a village.

"The best occupation is to work on the land," said Shota Ivanovich.

To each his own, of course. I wouldn't say that it's the best, but it's one of the good ones.

[4-25-75]

■   How Stalin Became General Secretary   ■

Unexpectedly I became a secretary of the Central Committee in 1921. The secretariat consisted of three secretaries: myself, Yaroslavsky, and Mikhailov. As it was published, I was the secretary-in-chief. At the time there was no first or general secretary but rather a secretary-in-chief. Reception hours were announced. I met with Lenin. We discussed a number of issues, then went for a walk in the Kremlin. He said, "I will give you only this advice: as secretary of the Central Committee you must occupy yourself with political matters and let your deputies and assistants take care of the technical work. Until now Krestinsky has been secretary of the Central Committee. He has been more of a manager than a Central Committee secretary! He has busied himself with all sorts of nonsense, and never politics!"

This happened after the Xth Party Congress. But at the XIth Congress there appeared a "list of ten," the names of the members of the Central Committee, backers of Lenin, slated for election to the Politburo as members and candidate members. And alongside Stalin's name "General Secretary" was written, in Lenin's handwriting. Lenin had organized a factional meeting of "the ten." He had found a room somewhere near Sverdlov Hall in the Kremlin. It had been agreed that this was to be a factional meeting, that the Trotskyists, the Workers' Opposition, and the Democratic Centralists should not be invited. Only the supporters of "the ten," the Leninists, were to be present. Before the voting Lenin had assembled, as I recall, some twenty people from the larger organization. Stalin, it is said, even reproached Lenin for holding a secret or semisecret conference during the congress, because it looked like a faction. And Lenin responded, "Comrade Stalin, you are an old, experienced factionist yourself! Don't worry. At present we cannot do this any other way. I want everyone to be well prepared for the vote, and the comrades must be told that they are to vote firmly for the list without any amendments! This list, as it stands, must be passed as a bloc. There is a great danger that, once they start voting for each person, they will add more—'we need him, he's a good writer'; 'we need him, he's a good speaker'—and they will thin out the list and once again we won't have a majority. And how shall we direct this?"

But Lenin, after all, at the Xth Congress had prohibited factionalism.

And we voted with that note on Stalin in brackets. He became general secretary. This cost Lenin a great deal of effort. But of course he had considered the problem thoroughly and made it clear whom he regarded as an equal. Lenin apparently reckoned that I wasn't enough of a politician, but he left me in the secretariat and in the Politburo, and made Stalin general secretary. Lenin was, of course, making preparations, for he sensed his ill health. Did he perhaps see in Stalin his successor? I think one can allow for that. And what was the general secretary needed for? There had never been one before. But gradually Stalin's authority rose and grew much greater than what Lenin had proposed or even considered desirable. It is, of course, impossible to foresee everything. And under the conditions of intense struggle an ever more active group closed ranks around Stalin: Dzerzhinsky, Kuibishev, Frunze, and diverse others.

■ Contenders for Leadership ■

Lenin realized that Trotsky had a very deleterious effect by complicating affairs of party and state. He was a dangerous figure. It seemed that Lenin would have been glad to get rid of him, but he couldn't. Trotsky had strong, devoted supporters, and there were also those who were neutral but recognized his great authority. Trotsky was a quite clever and capable man, and he had wielded enormous influence. Even Lenin, who had waged an irreconcilable struggle with Trotsky, was impelled to write in *Pravda* that he had no disagreements with him on the peasant question. I remember that Stalin was indignant about this as not corresponding with reality, and he went to Lenin. Lenin replied, "What can I do? Trotsky has the army at his disposal, and it is full of peasants. Our country is in ruins. Are we going to show the people that there is squabbling even at the top?"

Lenin no less than Stalin understood what Trotsky was and reckoned that the time would come to get rid of him.

Zinoviev also was in contention for leadership, real leadership. He often gave speeches. He loved to speak and did it well, got applause. But

Zinoviev wasn't as deep as, say, Stalin or even Kamenev. As it turns out, the names of Zinoviev and Kamenev stand alongside each other in the literature. But they were completely different people, though Kamenev pumped up Zinoviev ideologically. Zinoviev was a scribbler and a windbag, and had a loose tongue, as they say. Kamenev was more reliable, more thoughtful, and a consistent opportunist. Zinoviev sang Kamenev's tune, so to speak. He *spoke* in a revolutionary manner, but Kamenev had already entered the fray. Zinoviev was cowardly; Kamenev had character. He actually guided Zinoviev. But Zinoviev was considered superior to Kamenev, who was merely his assistant or adviser. Zinoviev was the chief.

A theoretician?

Not a theoretician but a politician. He wasn't especially adept in theory and was, I think, superficial. He had a good command of language. Lenin knew him quite well. They had lived together abroad. Lenin appreciated him as a journalist. Grisha this, Grisha that. . . . He valued him because he often needed someone who could write quickly and capture his ideas. At one moment Zinoviev would follow Kamenev, at another Lenin. More often he inclined toward Kamenev. Kamenev was a rightist, a typical 100 percent rightist. Sometimes he concealed this, but most of the time he spoke quite openly. And against Lenin, too.

Kamenev valued Lenin highly and could see that he was a genius. Kamenev himself was a very intelligent man, but he was alien to Lenin. Zinoviev was adaptable and adroit. He could write an article at a moment's notice. Although it might not be of the highest quality, it more or less correctly expressed what Lenin had said. Plain words. They discussed many issues together. But Lenin never trusted Zinoviev.

Lenin liked Kamenev better. During World War I, Kamenev was in exile and Zinoviev lived abroad, in Switzerland, where Lenin was. Judging by the Lenin-Zinoviev correspondence, you can see that Lenin was not really pleased with Zinoviev because Zinoviev vacillated, though he posed as a Leninist. He was not up to Kamenev's level, and he was extremely unsteady. Lenin kept correcting him, putting him in his place. . . . Finally Zinoviev contended for leadership, for Lenin's role. He made his bid when he delivered the political report to the XIIth Party Congress in 1923, while Lenin was still alive. At the same time he was starting an intrigue against Stalin and our entire group which had formed around Stalin.

Soon Zinoviev and Kamenev, who were both vacationing in Kislovodsk, summoned Rudzutak and then Voroshilov. Together they went for a walk in a cave and argued that the secretariat should be politicized. It seemed that the only real politician at the time was Stalin. The following secretariat should be formed: Stalin was to remain, of course, but Zinoviev, Trotsky, and Kamenev—though I can't say for sure—were to be added. Of course, Stalin immediately understood what was at issue: they wanted to place him in the minority. This was the so-called "cave platform." Later Zinoviev wrote a famous article, "The Philosophy of the Epoch," and came out with his own formulations and claims to leadership. He dashed off a feuilleton in *Pravda* on the peasant question. He sank so low as to write that we must not only bow to but even fall to our knees before the middle peasant. Fall to our knees? The party of the working class? Certainly we had to be sensitive and attentive to the middle peasants. In the Leninist group we discussed the article, criticized it, and forced Zinoviev to correct it. At the time Stalin was on vacation in Sochi. When we sent our critique to him, he responded, "The critique is correct!"

The rift had not yet occurred, but it was already apparent and was deepening. Bukharin and Rykov then supported Lenin and Stalin. Rykov became a member of the Politburo at the XIth Congress. But Lenin did not admit Dzerzhinsky into the Politburo. Lenin could not forgive Dzerzhinsky for his lack of support in the Brest peace talks and in the trade union discussions. He had lost his old confidence in him. Lenin was quite strict in this respect.

■ Who Was More Severe? ■

Who was more severe, Lenin or Stalin?

Lenin, of course. He was severe. In some cases he was harsher than Stalin. Read his messages to Dzerzhinsky. He often resorted to extreme measures when necessary. He ordered the suppression of the Tambov uprising, that everything be burned to the ground. I was present at the discussion. He would not have tolerated any opposition, even had it appeared. I recall how he reproached Stalin for his softness and liberalism. "What kind of a dictatorship do we have? We have a milk-and-honey power, and not a dictatorship!"

Where is it written that he reproached Stalin?

It was in a small circle among us.

Here is a telegram from Lenin to a provincial food commissar in his native Simbirsk in 1919: "The starving workers of Petrograd and Moscow are complaining about your inefficient management. . . . I demand from you maximum energy, a no-holds-barred attitude to the job, and thorough assistance to the starving workers. If you fail, I will be forced to arrest the entire staff of your institutions and to bring them to trial. . . . You must immediately load and send off two trains of thirty cars each. Send a telegram when this is complete. If it is confirmed that, by four o'clock, you did not send the grain and made the peasants wait until morning, you will be shot. Sovnarkom Chairman, Lenin."

I remember another case. Lenin had received a letter from a poor peasant of Rostov province saying that things were bad with them, that no one paid any attention to them, the poor peasants, that there was no help for them and that, on the contrary, they were oppressed. Lenin proposed the formation of a group of "Sverdlovers." There was the Sverdlov University for adults who were untrained for ministerial work and hadn't attended high school but wished to improve their knowledge. Malashkin had studied there. Lenin directed this group to go to the place in question and, if the report was confirmed, to shoot guilty parties right then and there and to rectify the situation.

What could be more concrete? Shoot on the spot and that's that! Such things happened. It was outside the law, but we had to do it. It was a dictatorship, a superdictatorship.

[2-29-80, 1-9-81, 2-5-82, 10-14-83, 2-16-85]

Lenin was a man of strong character. If necessary, he seized people by the scruff of their necks.

[6-30-76]

They say that Lenin had nothing to do with the execution of the tsar's family in 1918, that it was a decision of the local authorities following Kolchak's attack. . . . But some people say it was revenge for Lenin's brother.

They make Lenin out to be a crank. They are small-fry philistines who think this. Don't be naive.

I think that, without Lenin, no one would have dared to make such a decision. Lenin was implacable when the Revolution, Soviet power, and communism were at stake. Indeed, had we implemented democratic solutions to all problems, this would surely have damaged the state and the party. Issues would have dragged on for too long and nothing good would have come of this sort of formal democracy. Lenin often resolved critical problems by himself, on his own authority.

[11-23-71, 2-3-72]

■ **All Power to the Soviets** ■

Lenin used to advise that, if you go to your boss with a request, make sure you take some paper with you so that he can write a resolution on it. Otherwise it will be forgotten.

[6-16-77]

Lenin said: All power to the soviets and not to the party. Doesn't it seem to you that the role of the soviets has declined significantly?

Actually, it had declined under Lenin. Power should be concentrated in one pair of hands.

[7-9-71]

■ **Chicherin** ■

We had a few educated people, and Lenin tried to use every one of them. Lenin didn't consider Chicherin a true Bolshevik, but he valued him as a worker. He was the people's commissar of foreign affairs—and not a member of the Central Committee!

. . . Lenin's note on Chicherin's letter from January 20, 1922, has been preserved:

"To Comrade Molotov for all the members of the Politburo: This and the following letter from Chicherin clearly prove that he is seriously ill. We would be stupid if we did not dispatch him immediately and by force to a sanatorium.

1-24-22. Lenin"

You read this and you remember Lenin's concern for people. It turns out that earlier Chicherin had written to Lenin to suggest that "it would be possible to introduce a minor amendment to our constitution in exchange for due compensation." He wanted NEPmen, priests, and the like to be represented in the soviets. This would have pleased the

Americans. Lenin underlined the words "would be possible" and wrote, "Insanity."

Types like Chicherin could always be found in politics, but at the same time they were capable. Otherwise Lenin wouldn't have bothered to criticize him. . . . Chicherin worked for a long time under Stalin despite the fact that he was a very sick man with high blood sugar—diabetes was treated badly then. I remember he wrote a letter saying, "What's going on? The Commissariat of Foreign Affairs is being prostituted! The Comintern is being vandalized! The Zinovievists are in charge of everything!"

It seemed to him that everything was being done wrong. Litvinov was already commissar for foreign affairs.

Didn't he criticize the Central Committee?

No. He wouldn't dare! How could things go on without the Central Committee? The Commissariat of Foreign Affairs reported only to the Central Committee and no one else. All the business of the Commissariat of Foreign Affairs was forwarded only to the Politburo.

Chicherin was stronger in the beginning. He was from the ranks of the Bolsheviks, but he degenerated.

[6-21-72]

Chicherin wrote letters to the Central Committee in abusive numbers. Every day he sent three or four letters about Ethiopia, France, America, whatever. Lenin called him a graphomaniac because of this. He worked at night, writing. That was his problem. He wrote letters quickly and easily. He was very cultivated, very educated. He knew languages superbly and wrote letters about everything. All of them went direct to the Politburo. But the departments to respond to them did not exist. It was necessary to be familiar with international affairs and to read encoded documents. And no one read them except me.

[1-14-75]

■   **What Is Your Reason?**   ■

I recall a deputy chairman of the People's Commissariat of Georgia, Mdivani, an opportunist. He allowed the import of foreign goods to Batumi. I was present at the Politburo when Lenin asked him, "What is your reason?" Mdivani answered, "My reason is cheap goods." Some Marxist—"for cheap goods"!

Lenin was opposed to any weakening of the monopoly on foreign trade. In the first years of the Revolution the arrival of foreign ships was allowed. They could flood us with goods. That's where the argument lay. Lenin was an ardent supporter of the unconditional closing of such "foreign trade." It might be done privately, but it was necessary to adhere firmly to the monopoly of foreign trade. But the Georgians, for example Mdivani, were exporting black and pressed caviar. . . . He obviously was an opportunist. He was considered to be an old communist, a Bolshevik, but a rotten one.

[12-9-82]

■   Not the First People   ■

"Kollontai, along with Shliapnikov, spoke in opposition to Lenin and really made his life miserable," Shota Ivanovich remarked.

At any rate, she was an outstanding person. Yes, without doubt. She was interesting. She went through many admirers. . . .

What did you think of the film about Kollontai—"The Ambassador of the Soviet Union"?

Kollontai won the war? That's naive. She was an ambassador and implemented our instructions, as an ambassador ought. I knew her well. We had rather good relations, but she was not a true revolutionary. She came from the margin. But an honest person. A beautiful woman. She was with one man, then with another. . . . Dybenko was her husband and, before that, Shliapnikov. That sort of company didn't inspire much confidence. But she herself was a very skillful writer. And a good speaker, especially in a women's forum. She spoke beautifully, with great feeling and sincerity. She made an impression. Polina Semenovna worshiped her. Very courageous, very free in her words and gestures. She lived for a long time in Europe and spoke there. She knew foreign languages and was a highly cultivated person. A general's daughter. Lenin really took her down a peg. Read his speech at the Xth Party Congress, where he speaks against the workers' opposition. An opposition of Shliapnikov and Kollontai, as Lenin derided it, embraced "class-welded followers."

Who had been before Shliapnikov? There was one main husband.

She was the wife of a certain officer, a member of the gentry. But she broke up with him on principle and ideals and became a revolutionary. She joined the Bolsheviks during World War I. Lenin corresponded with her. She was not part of the old *Pravda*.

[1-25-75, 4-28-76]

Manuilsky, a member of the Central Committee, was an old Bolshevik, but confused! He became mixed up with the Trotskyists. He had a spirit of conciliation and thought it was possible to come to an agreement with Trotsky. This Manuilsky was a great storyteller, always amusing us with jokes that he made up for the most part. . . . He was minister of foreign affairs in the Ukraine after the war. He asked me, "Do you consider me a diplomat?" I told him, "There are different kinds of diplomats, but mainly two: stupid or false." He laughed, "Does that make me a false one?"

[11-28-74]

Lozovsky was my deputy. He also was arrested for connections with American Jews. He gave no evidence against Polina Semenovna.*

Lozovsky knew how to talk for a long time. Because of this, Lenin called him a cart-horse. He aspired to wit. "De Gole [a pun: *Gole* means "the poor" in Russian] is sly at invention?" That was his expression.

Manuilsky spread a story that I died. Lozovsky volunteered to speak at the funeral and spoke for so long that I couldn't stand it. I vomited and came back to life.

[4-10-79]

■ "I Propose to Pay Homage to . . ."   ■

Of course, Lenin was superior to Stalin. I always thought so. He was superior in the theoretical sense, superior in his personal qualities. But no one could surpass Stalin as a practical worker.

*Alexander Lozovsky, deputy minister of foreign affairs 1939–1946, and Polina Semenovna (Zhemchuzhina), Molotov's wife since 1921, were both of Jewish origin. They were arrested in 1948 during the "anti-Zionist" campaign. Lozovsky's torturers failed to extract from him false evidence against Zhemchuzhina. Accused of "anti-Soviet" collusion with foreign Jews, he was among more than two hundred prominent Soviet Jews executed in Stalin's last year. Lozovsky was posthumously rehabilitated. Zhemchuzhina survived exile and was released after Stalin's death. She died in 1970.—ED.

Molotov refused to celebrate his ninetieth birthday.

I told everyone that I would not be there. We would get together some other time. . . . This is difficult for many people. They cannot scold—it's not in the regulations. . . .

In 1920 Lenin was forced to celebrate his birthday. He said the main thing was for communists not to become conceited. Revolutionaries could win if they did not put on airs.

A curious episode happened at the celebration of Lenin's fiftieth birthday in 1920. Preobrazhensky ended his congratulatory speech with these words, "I propose to pay homage to . . ." The audience was laughing. Lenin waved to him. To whom would he pay homage? One can pay homage only to a memory.

Preobrazhensky was later among the opposition, a Trotskyist. He proposed that Stalin be dismissed from the position of general secretary on grounds that he held too many offices. At the time Lenin strongly defended Stalin. . . ."

[2-29-80]

■   **Why Did Ordzhonikidze Shoot Himself?**   ■

Sergo Ordzhonikidze was a good and doubtlessly worthy member of the Central Committee. But at the Xth Congress speeches were made opposing his election to the Central Committee: he was rude, he was impossible to work with, and so forth. Lenin spoke in his defense: "I know him as a man devoted to the party. I know this from personal experience, as he stayed with me abroad. . . ." Someone from the audience asked why Ordzhonikidze manhandled people, and Lenin responded, "What do you want from him? He is hot-tempered, and, if you have noticed, he is hard of hearing in one ear." What did his hearing have to do with it? But Lenin had to defend a good man, for Sergo really was a good man. That was in 1921. Sergo was always at the front. The times were frantic and he was hot-tempered. I guess he might have cuffed somebody.

Zinoviev's book, *Leninism*, was published. Sergo was ecstatic about it, but I said I disagreed with Zinoviev. "How could you disagree?" Sergo fumed. "Isn't he a Leninist? Why don't you think he's a Leninist?" "No. It's not a Leninist book." "What do you know?!"

So he got excited, I cursed him, he jumped on me. Kirov separated us . . . then Bukharin reconciled us. Sergo went to Stalin to complain about me. It was in my presence, too. And Stalin said, "Molotov's right." "How could he be right?" "Because it is not really a Leninist book." And Stalin explained in detail to Sergo that Leninism à la Zinoviev held that Leninism was applicable only in a backward country such as Russia, where the peasantry predominated.

[7-28-71, 5-24-75]

Who were your friends, Viacheslav Mikhailovich?

Sergo. He was a good comrade. We became acquainted in 1917 and always had good relations. . . . We cursed each other out only once, over Zinoviev's book. Sergo was a good man but politically shortsighted. He was a person of strong feelings and passions. Stalin often said this wasn't the way to be. Sergo drew people to himself who were guided only by emotions. He had a brother in Georgia, a railroader. Is it possible for a good Central Committee member to have a bad brother? This brother had spoken against Soviet power, and there was solid evidence against him. Stalin ordered his arrest. Sergo was outraged. Afterward he committed suicide at his home. He found an easy way out. He thought only about himself. What kind of a leader is that? He left Stalin in a very difficult situation. And he had been such a loyal Stalinist, and had defended Stalin in every way. He had served time at hard labor, and this too had enhanced his authority.

You can find a range of opinions about Ordzhonikidze. But I think the intellectuals praised him too highly. By his last act he proved that ultimately he was unstable. He had opposed Stalin, of course, and the party line. Yes, the party line. This was such a very bad step. It couldn't be interpreted any other way.

Ordzhonikidze's family considers Stalin responsible for his death.

They will always say that. If the final push toward his suicide was the repression of his brother, they can say this. They can heap blame on Stalin. But if my brother was to conduct anti-Soviet agitation, what could I say if he was arrested? I could say nothing.

After Sergo shot himself, was Stalin very angry with him?

Certainly.

And could they have expelled Sergo from the Politburo? Could it have come to this?

Hardly. . . . Sergo didn't understand everything. A good person. A sincere man. Tricksters like Radek and Zinoviev adroitly adapted themselves to him.

[12-6-69, 4-13-72, 3-8-74, 12-9-82, 1-26-86]

Sergo was a good Bolshevik but spineless, especially in matters of principle. But he was no Mikoyan. Our friend Andreev was a Politburo member under Stalin for quite a long time, but he had joined a Trotskyist group. Yes, he erred. He was a Trotskyist. He came from the workers, a Bolshevik. He was among the more prominent Bolsheviks before the Revolution.

More prominent than Rudzutak?

Rudzutak was stronger before the Revolution. It's hard to compare. You might say they were roughly equal.

"They remember Rudzutak in Georgia," Shota Ivanovich said. "They think Stalin had no use for him. . . ."

How can one say that one has a use for someone or not? People are reliable sometimes and unreliable at others.

"Kuibishev and others were not superior to Molotov or Sergo, were they?" Shota Ivanovich asked.

They were a bit, of course. Kuibishev was more educated. He read extensively. He was an excellent organizer. But he joined the Trotskyists. Because he didn't understand, he didn't attach any importance to it. You see, Trotskyists were good people. It is unfortunate there were differences of opinion. Some corrected themselves, others were for the time being irreplaceable. We had to use everyone. If Trotsky said something good, then Kuibishev thought Trotsky himself was good. That was his fundamental weakness.

I did not know Kuibishev before the Revolution. But he had passed through a certain village on the Lena before I was exiled to it. He had escaped from exile. And then I escaped too and went through Samara, where he had his main base.

[1-16-73, 4-27-73]

Dzerzhinsky was a more straightforward fellow, but even he followed Trotsky in 1920. And earlier, on the issue of the Brest Peace . . .

But at any rate he was a true Bolshevik.

Real! Without a doubt. He followed Trotsky because of his desire to be a Bolshevik. Trotsky was very left-wing then.

They read Trotsky in the West and don't see anything wrong with his work.

Over there, of course, they won't find anything bad in Trotsky.

[4-19-77]

■   "He Saved Us All"   ■

Lenin had no friends in the Politburo. But he saved us all, various and sundry. Many were drifting away from him to various factions, yet there was no one else! And it was not clear when others would arrive. That's where Lenin's strength lay. Otherwise he could not have maintained his position, and the whole cause would have failed. The times were not as they are now. Frequently we view those times in light of our own and apply today's standards.

Lenin's relations with Stalin were close, but they were mainly businesslike. He elevated Stalin far higher than Bukharin! And he didn't simply elevate him but made him his mainstay in the Central Committee. He trusted him.

They were very close in Lenin's final days. Probably it was only Stalin's apartment that Lenin visited. Several times Stalin sought to resign from the post of general secretary, but each time his request was denied by the Central Committee of the party. The struggle raged, and it was necessary that Stalin remain in that position.

It was a difficult time for Lenin, and he was moving up the younger ones.

Lenin was close to Bukharin in his last years. No, I think they were closer in the early years. Without ceremony he often visited Lenin in Gorky, dining together with the family. He was the most skilled theoretician, more so than Zinoviev, for the latter was rather a public speaker and journalist. But both were arrogant. Bukharin comported himself with great self-confidence, though he was extremely unstable politically. Lenin called him "the favorite of the whole party" but said at the same time that "his theoretical views can be classified as fully Marxist only with great reserve...." That's some kind of favorite! Lenin criticized him relentlessly before that, too. But Bukharin was a pleasant, good-natured man.

Lenin related to him well. Of course, he couldn't be Bukharin's close friend, for he clearly understood Bukharin's philosophical and political ideas. Lenin valued Bukharin, but he placed him last among the three candidates to the Politburo, after me and Kalinin. Lenin was very careful about the Politburo. He didn't enhance one's authority but rather drew one in. He didn't spurn a person, but he might show that a certain person could not be trusted. This shows in his choice of candidates to the Politburo. I have said that Bukharin was very muddleheaded. Not only Lenin but others too recognized this. People sensed that Lenin sympathized with him but could yield no ground to him in the field of ideas.

Bukharin was looking for a union with the Socialist Revolutionaries. He was drawn in this direction. He maintained personal contacts with them after the Revolution.

Bukharin was more serious than Zinoviev. "Grisha . . ." He liked fancy words.

I found a volume of Lenin, third edition, under the editorship of Bukharin, Molotov, and Skvortsov-Stepanov, from 1931.

Yes, I had a part in that. The Politburo assigned me to it, on orders from Stalin, so that I would keep an eye on Bukharin.

Skvortsov-Stepanov was a very good, educated person. He was better than me in certain respects. He was an old Bolshevik, a Russian. A little bit bookish. Not a bad speaker. He was the editor of *Izvestia*. A translator of *Capital*. That's no small thing—to translate correctly.

Bukharin was a scholar, a writer. He would speak more or less confidently on any subject. He was an authority, to be sure. The address of the Central Committee of the party upon Lenin's death is really well written, and Bukharin wrote it.

He is popular now, too.

Now, too, of course. He was the best trained in matters of theory. But he was drawn in the wrong ideological direction. All this had to be taken into consideration.

In Lenin's time, Bukharin and Dzerzhinsky were quite popular. Dzerzhinsky wasn't in the Politburo but as a person capable of a certain kind of work for the party, he was necessary to Lenin. He took on the most difficult and unpleasant duties from which the party received all the gains, so to speak, and none of the losses. And Lenin recognized and appreciated him. Of course, Lenin couldn't always take Dzerzhinsky's side in economic problems. But in general Dzerzhinsky was close to Lenin's position. . . . History, especially the history of communism, cannot be trusted to people who are indifferent or unfavoraby disposed.

[2-18-73, 1-1-79, 3-9-85]

You put Bukharin above all the pleiades of oppositionists, don't you?

On the theoretical level, yes. He was more knowledgeable. Zinoviev tried but in a very superficial way. When he was already in the opposition, in 1925–1926, Zinoviev said, "I stand for Engels's principles of communism." "I don't know," Stalin responded, "whether Comrade

Zinoviev has read them. I'm afraid he hasn't. And even if he has, it's
evident he hasn't understood them."

How unexpected! Stalin immediately put his opponent in this sort of
situation: had he read them or not, and if he had, then he hadn't
understood them. And if not, I will read them to you again and then
you will see.

Was Stalin cunning?

Oh yes, very cunning.

[7-9-71]

*Shota Ivanovich Kvantaliani said, "The last time I went to the
countryside, everyone was talking about Bukharin. Bukharin, Bukharin!
My uncle said, 'Write to Bukharin on any issue!' Bukharin's portraits . . ."*

He was editor of *Pravda*, and then he became the actual editor of
Kommunist, then called *Bolshevik*. Certain circles sympathized with
him.

And what was Bukharin like as a person?

A very good man, very kind. A decent person, undoubtedly. A man of
ideas.

He died for his ideas.

Yes, because he moved against the party line.

Does he deserve respect?

As a person, yes. But he was dangerous in politics. He ran to extremes
in life. I can't say that it has been fully proven, at least to my satisfaction,
but he joined in a conspiracy with the Socialist Revolutionaries to
assassinate Lenin. He supported arresting Lenin. When these two
opposing groups were facing each other, the situation was so tense that
Lenin could have been executed.

Could these charges against Bukharin have been fabricated?

I don't think so.

To make the case more convincing?

You have to realize that in political struggle anything is possible if you
support the other power. Bukharin spoke against Lenin more than once.
He called him a utopian. What's more, he called him a traitor!

The right-wingers were also communists, weren't they?

They just called themselves communists. Social Democrats were both
Mensheviks and Bolsheviks. Some were on one side of the barricades,
some on the other. The Socialist Revolutionaries said we were not far
enough to the left. Then they turned out to be with the kulaks and
against the Bolsheviks. A name is a secondary concern for a politician,

and it's often used to deceive. There has always been a bourgeois party of radical socialists. Radicals were extreme, but the party was purely bourgeois.

Bukharin was a left-winger during the Brest peace and afterward turned to the right. In 1929 he talked about the military-feudal exploitation of the peasants. . . .

[11-28-74]

"Did Bukharin like to drink?" asked Shota Ivanovich.

No. Rykov did. Rykov always had a bottle of Starka. There was "Rykovskaya vodka"—he was famous for that. Well, we all drank in company, so to speak, among comrades. I could drink very hard when I was young. Stalin—no need to say more. Kuibishev liked it! He wrote poetry. He was a good man, a very good man. And Kirov was a wonderful person!

Zinoviev was a better theoretician than Sergo, wasn't he?

Yes, he was better.

And Bukharin, was he better than Kirov?

And Kamenev was better, as was Bukharin.

Kamenev was competent, wasn't he?

Very much so. But Bukharin had the best training. A long struggle was on. Right before everyone's eyes, in the pages of the press. Bukharin was at our side until the XVIth Congress. The three of us—Bukharin, Stalin, and I—wrote documents together all the time. He was the main writer.

When their relations were good, Stalin affectionately called Bukharin "Bukharchik." I am trying to recall something, but it's escaping me. They had had good relations.

Was Tomsky weaker?

He wasn't very good at theory. . . . Tomsky was good at leading the masses. He could talk with the workers.

[7-28-71]

Rykov and I came from the same village of free peasants. The same village, yes. He was smart, but I would say that his mind . . . Rykov was always an opportunist, and Lenin would say, "Here is a consistent opportunist but a very clever person!" A prominent Bolshevik. Lenin knew him very well and appreciated him as a good organizer. But Rykov often opposed Lenin, even before the Revolution. Yet Lenin made him his deputy in Sovnarkom. Tsiurupa was the first deputy. An outstanding agronomist. He worked actively in the party until 1905, then stepped aside. Lenin considered him to be knowledgeable in agriculture, but not much of a party man. Lenin appointed him commissar of food supply, then his first deputy, but never admitted him to the Central Committee.

One Sunday in 1921 Lenin phoned me from Gorky: "Go to Rykov and tell him that I propose to raise at the Central Committee his appointment as my first deputy chairman of the Council of People's Commissars and his release from duties as chairman of the V.S.N.Kh. [Supreme Council of the National Economy]. Lenin knew that Rykov was a right-winger and not very reliable with respect to the party. But he was a good economist, and Lenin had promoted him to the position of chairman of our main economic center, the V.S.N.Kh.

So he called: "Go see Rykov, talk to him. I plan to put an engineer on the Economic Council, a technically trained man. Rykov does not have this training."

After Lenin's death, when three of his assistants—Tsiurupa, Rykov, and Kamenev—remained, we discussed the question of whom to appoint as chairman of Sovnarkom. There was support for Kamenev, but Stalin preferred Rykov. Although Rykov was in favor of including the Mensheviks and the Socialist Revolutionaries in the government, he had never openly opposed the October Revolution, as Kamenev had. Another consideration was that a Russian be the head of the government. At that time Jews occupied many leading positions, though they made up only a small percentage of the country's population.

[5-9-72]

Zinoviev came from somewhere in Ukraine. Radomyslsky was his real name. He had a great head of hair. At any rate, he was a magnificent speaker. Well, perhaps not magnificent, but good.

Kamenev was physically stronger. He had quite Russian handwriting. He didn't even look like a Jew except when you were looking into his eyes.

[4-13-72]

There were many dubious people in the guise of Leninists. There was a sort of joke about this: Lenin regained consciousness, opened his eyes, looked around, and then closed them again. The surrounding company was either unfriendly or simply hostile. Lenin had many opponents, of course. I remember when I worked at *Pravda* in 1912, we received a letter from Krestinsky. He wrote that Lenin was an anti-Semite because he abusively cursed out those Menshevik liquidators who supported questionable people. So Krestinsky accused Lenin of anti-Semitism. The letter wasn't published, so Lenin didn't have to respond to it. Almost all the Mensheviks were Jews. Even among the Bolsheviks, among the leaders, there were many Jews. Generally, Jews are the most oppositional nation. But they were inclined to support the Mensheviks. No wonder! They understood that if you followed the Bolshevik way you might lose your head! And the other way—you get what you get. A bird in Menshevik hands was worth two birds in the Bolshevik bush. Lenin criticized the main Menshevik theoreticians, and they were Jews without exception. That's why Krestinsky portrayed him as an anti-Semite.

Krestinsky was not much of a Bolshevik. In fact, he wasn't one at all. He was radically inclined in his youth and fell in with the Bolsheviks. He was, of course, more of a Trotskyist. He tried to show his revolutionary character in meaningless situations. Apparently he was a former Jew, but he was probably baptized, and thus he had the name Krestinsky. Perhaps I am wrong. A *barin* [of the landed gentry], surely a *barin*.

And Tukhachevsky?

He was more of an aristocrat, but Krestinsky was even more of a *barin*, a very active *barin*. He even looked like a Russian. He was the first secretary of the Central Committee. A rather malicious man, though; he was considered to have been a Bolshevik before the Revolution. Then he worked in the People's Commissariat of Foreign Affairs. We didn't know where to put him until we arrested him. . . . I wouldn't say that Krestinsky was slippery, but he was a lawyer. he knew how to please both sides. He equivocated. He helped Trotsky, that's for sure!

[12-18-70, 1-14-75, 5-24-75, 6-16-83]

Trotsky spoke eloquently with fine diction. It turns out that he had studied the art of speaking. If you listened closely you could sense a Jewish accent, but it was not very noticeable. He was a better speaker than Bukharin. First class, of course. . . . He could influence politically naive people. Bukharin was an effective speaker. Lenin was a bit weaker. As a speaker Stalin was unique. He spoke in a low voice, but people always listened to him, even before the Revolution.

The polemics between Lenin and Trotsky were ceaseless after 1902. After the Revolution Lenin knew Trotsky had split off but still kept him in the Politburo, along with Zinoviev and Kamenev. The people he had to work with! Lenin took to anyone who supported him in the slightest.

As far as I know, no one has written about this, but in fact each

member of the Politburo was backed by his own coterie. Even under Lenin. Lenin suggested convening Politburo meetings without
Trotsky. We reached an agreement against Trotsky. And a year or two
later we were meeting without Zinoviev and Kamenev. Later without
Bukharin, Tomsky, and Rykov. They remained in the Politburo, but we
didn't keep them informed, of course.

[5-9-72, 8-14-73]

Did Trotsky have much power during the civil war?
He wasn't given great power. Lenin and Stalin played a large role.
[1-14-75]

Stalin used to joke that he had sailed a cutter, the *Trotsky*, from Yalta
to Sochi in the Caucasus. Someone had asked him, "Are you going to
travel for a long time on *Trotsky?*" He told me about that in the thirties.
By an ironic twist of fate, Trotsky left the Soviet Union on the cruiser
Ilyich.
Really? He was carried out of his apartment. Two men carried him
out. One was chief of my security, Pogudin. He died long ago. "Pitukh,"
Pogudin, was strong.

[7-25-75]

■   **"Speak as Sharply as Possible"**   ■

Many followed Lenin until the New Economic Policy, but when we
made this transition a lot of these people were displeased and could no
longer be relied on. They used to say, "Communism is due tomorrow,
but we have switched to capitalism and private enterprises!" They were
disillusioned and were giving back their party cards; they turned to
drink. . . . But Lenin was always an optimist. He said, "Now we are
retreating to retrench, but then we will mount a still greater offensive!"
Of course, Lenin was not always understood.
I was a bit younger and followed him right away. In April 1917 Stalin
and I discussed at length what Lenin meant by the socialist revolution.
We lived in the same apartment on the Petrogradskaya side. Zalutsky and
Smilga, along with his wife, also lived in the same apartment.
Smilga was later shot, wasn't he?
Certainly, that goes without saying. He was a Trotskyist.

In 1921, when the NEP began, some theses were proposed at the preparations for the Central Committee plenum—two proposals on the problems of economic reconstruction. One of these proposals belonged to the Trotskyist Smilga, a deputy chairman of the Supreme Council of the National Economy. In the Politburo I was replacing an absent member, Stalin. He had undergone an operation, an appendectomy. It was a serious thing then. As the first candidate I had the right to a full vote. I took part in the discussion and spoke against Smilga's theses. They were quite contradictory. Then the discussion ensued. Lenin was the last to speak. "I propose that Smilga's theses be adopted as the basis!" No one expected that, least of all me.

Then Lenin added, "I propose a commission to study the theses more carefully, to take the criticisms into account. . . ." A commission was set up and it reworked the theses, under Lenin's direction, of course, and then the plenum was convened. The plenum wasn't as large as it is now, about twenty-five people. Smilga's theses were discussed and ratified by the commission. We were at a big table. Lenin was seated at the narrow end of it, and I was next to him on the right, because as secretary of the Central Committee I was responsible for editing all the resolutions. From the beginning of the NEP I sat next to Lenin. A stenographer recorded the resolutions, then I edited them and passed them to Lenin for confirmation. He did the final editing, revised them, and then I signed them as secretary of the Central Committee. Opposite me, a few people over, sat Trotsky. I saw him very clearly, and he also saw me. Lenin wrote me a note. "When you speak, speak as sharply as possible against Trotsky! Tear up this note." When it was my turn to speak, I began to revile Trotsky to the utmost. I likened him to Vandervelde, a Social Democrat and a leader of the Second International. I was criticizing not the theses but rather Trotsky's speech. He had spoken before me. The speech was economically illiterate, without any basis in fact. I was criticizing him sharply. Well, Lenin knew my negative attitude toward Trotsky, and he apparently wanted to provoke a reaction from Trotsky. And Trotsky, of course, saw our exchange of notes at the table and took the floor again: "There is a Molotov for every occasion!" And he started to have at me with great anger and malice. That was what Lenin needed. He made a speech, supported Smilga, routed Trotsky, and drove a wedge into the Trotskyists' camp.

Such was the situation.

Smilga did not yet adhere firmly to Trotskyist positions, and Lenin needed to win him over from Trotsky. . . .

It's obvious that this memory is dear to Molotov. More than once he has cheered up in telling the story.

[7-5-80, 7-22-81]

Is Fotieva alive? How old is she?

She's alive. She is probably 175. *Molotov smiled.* Fotieva is an old party member. Back in Switzerland she had already been acquainted with Lenin.

I have read an interesting passage that she wrote. Lenin greatly disliked—I remember this, too, but she emphasizes this—Lenin disliked conversations during meetings. The men were under stress and worried, though Lenin himself managed to work on translations with an English dictionary while the debate was on. Yes, yes. And Trotsky, for example, read some book or another during Politburo sessions. But Lenin very much disliked it when people whispered during the sessions. He could not stand smoking at all. He himself didn't smoke. He was annoyed by whispering, all kinds of talking. This was quite understandable. Fotieva wrote in her memoirs: At one of the Sovnarkom sessions, I, as always, was in charge of recording the proceedings of the session and signing the resolutions. A participant of the session came up to ask me something. Lenin sent me a note: "I will send you out of here if you continue to talk during the session." Send her out! No more or less. Such a sharp tone! Lenin was exasperated, of course.

Fotieva was a technical secretary during Lenin's last years. She recorded proceedings and sat not far from Lenin, so if necessary she could pass things to Lenin to read. The commissars sometimes came to her, looked at the record, and whispered something. Lenin usually used small pieces of paper for his notes—sometimes to a Politburo member, other times to a commissar, other times to a visitor. He asked questions and demanded a response by note! But in general he knew how to comport himself well. He didn't take advantage of his position. Rudeness cannot be justified. It cannot be turned into a special issue, but it also cannot be justified. If you get to the top, you must behave properly. You must be patient. Otherwise, what kind of a leader are you? That's an elementary obligation. As for a subordinate, if you abuse him, it's no life: it's prison. It's already hard enough for him without that. . . .

[6-6-73, 11-28-74, 6-16-77]

■ Impossible to Work with Trotsky... ■

I recently read some memoirs about Lenin. Krupskaya writes that, before the Revolution, Lenin used to ask her, "Will we live to see it?" He too had doubts.

And in January 1917 he spoke before Swiss youth: "We are old men...." The old man was forty-six! We, the old men—as if we probably will not live to see a revolution, but you, the young ones...

Swiss youth remains under capitalism, but in those same years Lenin became the head of a socialist state.

The Russian character can be clearly seen in this. Once Russians get to work, they can accomplish a great deal, but they must have leaders. If leadership is insufficient, this hinders the cause.

In 1917 Lenin did not yet know how things would turn out. It is impossible for a person even of his stature to judge historic events in precise detail. It is impossible. In a series of speeches he said we must either follow this course or perish.... We either pass to the NEP or perish. That is how he put the question. He wanted us to gather strength.

"How were his relations with Trotsky at this first stage?" Sevastianov asked.

I didn't take part in the early years, but after 1921, after the transition to the NEP, I sat almost next to Trotsky at the Politburo. I sat next to Lenin, with Trotsky in front of me. Trotsky was the first and constant opponent of Lenin. But he was flexible at that time and worked as part of the team. That's why Lenin still valued him. But after Lenin, of the four Politburo members only Stalin remained. Trotsky, Kamenev, and Zinoviev deviated. And Bukharin, the third candidate to the Politburo, also deviated. Lenin wanted to draw him in, to involve him more deeply in the common cause. You see, he used to say that Bukharin was a wonderful person, the party favorite, but he was devilishly unstable in politics. In politics! And politics was the most important thing! Struggle was everywhere, relentless struggle. We were pressed first from one side, then from another. Factions were very well developed.

Didn't they lean for support on those elements of the Jewish Labor Bund who, after unification with us, joined the party?

The Bund played no special role. Bundists had important connections with some Bolsheviks of Jewish origin. In fact there was not a single prominent intellectual remaining who firmly took up Leninist positions.

The Jews, I think, are the most active people. You see, Lenin assembled the Politburo: he was a Russian himself, Stalin was a Georgian, and there were three Jews—Trotsky, Zinoviev, and Kamenev. Furthermore, Trotsky was a continual opponent of Lenin on all major issues both before and after the Revolution. Still, Lenin included him in the Politburo. He was such a figure. . . .

Already in 1921 it had become impossible to work with Trotsky. He had vast authority, he was a commissar, he had been through the entire civil war. Well, the army would not have followed him, but still it was hard to make top personnel changes at the time. Devastation was everywhere. It was a highly complicated situation. Industrial production was lower than prewar. We gave the peasants a chance to revive, but they had possessive instincts.

At a Politburo meeting Trotsky declared—this was in my presence—that our time was up, that we could no longer retain state power. But if he were removed for this, how could it be explained to the army and the people? They'd say, where were you earlier if you see Trotsky as a bad man now? We believed you when you said he was so useful, so necessary. It was one of the most critical moments in our history. It was a turning point. We somehow had to make the transition to a new policy, but how were we to do it? We had little economic experience. And the political enemy was within the party. There was not simply one faction, there was Trotskyism, the Workers' Opposition, Democratic Centralism, and all kinds of national groupings. Stalin played an outstanding role in their defeat.

Lenin was still able to work. He went to Gorky only on Sundays. Work proceeded at a full pace. He did a colossal amount of work in 1921. He fell ill in 1922.

A dangerous situation was developing in the party. There were two extremes: Trotsky at one end and right-wingers at the other. Bukharin even ended up among the opposition three or four years after the NEP began, when he declared in a report addressed to peasants, "Enrich yourselves!"

Certainly a handful could do this, but how could our whole peasantry enrich itself? Could the middle peasant or, what's more, the poor peasant?

Bukharin was promoting a different ideology, one that had nothing to do with looking after the people. He thought that since we had given land to the kulaks, if we now gave land to the middle peasants they too would be revived. But with what could we revive them? They had no implements, no education, and, most important, no organization. "Enrich yourselves!"

Trotsky put it more slyly, more cautiously. His purport was: our time is up. I have always opposed you Bolsheviks but joined you, changed to the Bolshevik party before the Revolution. But nothing came of it. The international proletariat did not support us. This means you have failed, you have no future!

And Bukharin said, "Enrich yourselves!" He did not see that the way out of the situation lay with the people. He was just a windbag. According to him, the people were in a situation in which they could do nothing without cooperatives, without collective farms, without industry. How could collective farms operate without machinery and without tractors? Where were the means to enable us to take the levers in hand and raise up the people? There was no machinery; factories had to be built. For some time they would turn out a small number of machines. Many people would lose faith, nothing would come of it! Bukharin said that in one way, and Trotsky said it in another. As for talks with imperialists, I think it was proven beyond a doubt that these occurred. It certainly looked that way. Maybe the documents I read were forged and cannot be believed. But there is nothing to refute those documents!

Trotsky himself was making speeches saying, "Nothing is working!" I really wondered, how could Lenin endure it? Lenin, however, saw through Trotsky.

Then Lenin said, "Let's go to Zinoviev and decide what to do." The three of us, Lenin, Kamenev, and I—two Politburo members and I, an alternate—went to Zinoviev. He wasn't feeling well and lived in a dacha at Morozovskaya, near Moscow. He had been given a brief leave of absence. He was chairman of the Petrograd Soviet and chairman of the Comintern [Communist International, the headquarters of the world communist movement], and he often had to be in Moscow.

So we went. A Chekist was sitting beside the driver, and the three of us were sitting in the back.

Do you remember what you talked about in the car?

About some book we had read. . . . A tire blew on the highway near Vsekhsviatskoe. We got out of the car at a village. A few peasants came over. They recognized Kamenev, since he was the chairman of the Moscow Soviet and some of them probably had been to Moscow meetings. They began to talk with him. They paid no attention to Lenin and me. In those days there were few photographs, so they didn't recognize him. Lenin and I stepped aside, and he began to ask me questions: "When do you get up? When do you go to bed? Do you stay up late?" "I stay up late." "How old are you?" "Thirty-one." "You're practically a Komsomolets," Lenin said thoughtfully and patted me on the shoulder. He was fifty then.

The tire was changed and we headed off to Zinoviev's. At this time Zinoviev opposed Trotsky. When he spoke about relations with the peasantry, he bowed down to them. But only three years later he joined Trotsky.

So we went to Zinoviev to discuss what to do with Trotsky. He had to be dismissed from his position as commissar of the navy. We appointed him chairman of the Moscow Trust of State Farms. Yet another job piled on! Lenin shook hands all round! He said, "Just try to accomplish something in agriculture in one year! Impossible!" Indeed, no one could have done it.

Trotsky hired a former Socialist Revolutionary to be his deputy, one who had been appointed commissar of agriculture in 1918—or perhaps it was the Commissariat of Land Affairs. There were several Socialist Revolutionary ministers then. He was a rather prominent Socialist Revolutionary. By 1921 he had, of course, long since been dismissed from the post, but still he was considered to be a member of our party. Trotsky made him his deputy, for this Socialist Revolutionary was familiar with the village. Trotsky himself, of course, did not seriously work on such issues. We also piled on him the committee on concessions. We tried every which way to shut him out of military affairs. It was impossible to do this all at once. He was well known among the people, and he was a fine orator. When he made speeches he received thunderous applause. He could not be pushed out easily. We had trouble with him for a long time. Several years. . . .

We began criticizing him openly, in front of everyone. There was no other way. He gave speeches, too. He appeared less frequently in the press, but he continued to publish his polemical works. We had to isolate him ideologically. The groundwork for this was laid and, as far as I remember, he was dismissed no later than 1925 and Frunze was appointed in his place as commissar of war. Frunze did not last long, though. He died after an operation. Then a writer, Pilniak, wrote a tale in which he hinted that Frunze was murdered and that this had been plotted by the party leadership. It was indirect, but he hinted at it. . . . In fact our attitude toward Frunze was very positive, though he was rather confused. . . .

Lenin! You had to have his stamina, the devil knows how! He was a man of colossal character and persistence. . . .

In practical work Stalin was not so much stronger as he was more persistent. That could be a disadvantage. He was a great specialist on the national question. But during the formation of the Union of Soviet Socialist Republics, he stuck to the old Leninist line and followed it persistently while Lenin took it a step further. Lenin proposed that a Union of Soviet Republics be created.

And meanwhile you all forgot to organize a Central Committee of the Party of the Russian Federation?

It's not that we forgot it, rather that there was no place for it. It would have diminished the role of the party. The present form, in which Russians do not have their own Central Committee, permits Russian affairs to be settled through the main apparatus, and this is a very powerful force. . . . Then there was the secretariat of the Central Committee and the Organizational Bureau. In the Orgburo all kinds of organizational questions were resolved. Each republican committee had its own bureau. Only then it was called neither the Politburo nor the Orgburo. Ukrainians were the only ones to have a Politburo. There was a Bureau of Russia under Khrushchev and at some time before. As I recall, Zhdanov was the chairman. But this didn't work out. Russia is such a large part of the USSR that any decision it makes will surely be accepted everywhere.

All republics have their own academies of science and authors, but Russia does not. Because, thank goodness, Russia already has a major influence, provided the central apparatus directs affairs intelligently and competently. Yes, on that condition. The party would fall apart without it.

[5-7-80]

■ The NEP—A Temporary Retreat ■

The NEP was, of course, an idea of the people. A peasant directed Lenin to the idea. And Lenin formulated it as would a scientist and a politician. Its roots were of the people, but it had to be given a scientific, Marxist direction. Only Lenin could do this.

[5-12-76]

Lenin had proposed the continuation of the NEP for a longer period of time. Did he not say that the NEP was to be pursued seriously and for a long time?

No. Lenin planned the NEP as a temporary retreat. Only one year later, in 1922, in a speech he said it was time to end the NEP. He said we had been retreating for a whole year. On the party's behalf we could now say, "That's enough . . ." The period of the NEP had ended, or was coming to an end.

What is the most prominent of Lenin's traits that you can recall?

His purposefulness. And his ability to fight for his cause. You see, almost everyone in the Politburo was against him—Trotsky, Kamenev, Zinoviev, Bukharin. In the Politburo, Lenin was supported only by Stalin and me.

[5-9-85]

The situation was so difficult in Lenin's time. . . . But Lenin was a man who could see things from various perspectives and who could motivate people: "Bear in mind that death is threatening us!" Of course, he couldn't take everything into account, but he got everyone going: "Otherwise all of you will be torn to pieces!"

[6-9-76]

In 1921, at the beginning of the NEP, there was famine. People began saying that grain should be imported. We needed resources for this. Lenin said the churchmen must help. If we confiscate church valuables, the priests will acquiesce. If they start to resist, this too would benefit us. Clinging to their wealth while the people are starving will undermine their authority. In the struggle against religious sentiment, we would win either way.

[10-14-83]

■   **Uneasy Relations with Krupskaya**   ■

Trotsky wasn't a coward, was he?

No, he was courageous. He was in exile, then escaped, and then was sent to prison. He lived in America. In 1905 he became chairman of the first Soviet of Workers' Deputies in Petersburg. He left again in 1906 or at the beginning of 1907, and returned for the second time in 1917. He was a man of means. First, he published a newspaper. Second, he apparently was well off. I read his autobiography. He begins with his mother and himself going to visit a neighboring landlord in Khersonchshina. He was about five years old, and he played with a girl of the same age there and peed in his pants. To describe that! What a vain man!

When the book came out, Demian Bedny lashed out against him. Stalin read it as well. Trotsky was a scribbler.

Krupskaya criticized you at the congress after Lenin's death: "And so I see in Comrade Molotov's report the same kind of optimism about the state apparatus. You know, I felt great satisfaction listening to Comrade Molotov's report about how quickly we're growing and how everything is proceeding smoothly and well. . . . "

Certainly it was a weak report. Secondary concerns. Well, it was deficient and there is nothing to be done about that!

She says further on: "The point is how together we can find the right policy. It seems to me that there was nothing of this in Comrade Molotov's report. He simply fell for an illusion, as did Comrade Bukharin. . . . We cannot simply satisfy ourselves by thinking that the majority is always right. There have been congresses in the history of our party when the majority was wrong. Remember, for example, the Stockholm Congress. (Voices: 'Platitudes!') The majority should not revel in its majority but should impartially seek the correct decision, one that will turn out to be right. (A voice: 'Lev Davidovich [Trotsky], you have new comrades-in-arms!')"

These remarks were made from the floor. Krupskaya was becoming Trotsky's comrade-in-arms; she was switching to Trotskyist rails. . . . After Lenin's death she in fact spoke out briefly against him. But later she began supporting the party line and the trials of the Trotskyists and right-wingers as well. Krupskaya followed Lenin all her life, before and after the Revolution. But she understood nothing about politics. Nothing. In 1925 she became confused and followed Zinoviev. And Zinoviev took an anti-Leninist position. Bear in mind that it was not so simple to be a Leninist!

Maria Ilyinichna, Lenin's sister, sympathized with Bukharin. She was completely under Bukharin's spell and was closer to him than to Lenin. And if it were not for Lenin, she probably would have crossed over to the right wing. But she did not follow them though she was a Bukharinist in her soul. And Lenin's sister, you know, was a devoted Bolshevik. This pull to the right was so strong! But Lenin didn't follow philistines. Just as German philistines could do nothing about Marx and Engels, so Russian and Soviet philistines couldn't manage to attract Lenin.

Maria Ilyinichna, and Krupskaya as well, lived alongside Lenin through all the last years and yet trailed along after Bukharin. They didn't see that he was cut from different cloth.

Anna Ilyinichna was perhaps the best of Lenin's relatives.

But Dmitri Ilyich [Lenin's brother] was shortsighted. He was a good drinker. He liked to drink.

[11-28-74, 11-1-77]

Have you seen the movie Nadezhda, *about Krupskaya?*

It doesn't hold much interest for me. My attitude toward Krupskaya was more or less positive in our personal relations. But Stalin regarded her unfavorably.

He had reasons. She made a poor showing at the XIVth Party Congress.

Very bad. She turned out to be a bad communist. She didn't know what the devil she was doing.

[4-25-75]

Anyway, what caused the conflict between Stalin and Krupskaya?

Krupskaya acted badly after Lenin's death. She supported Zinoviev and obviously was confused by Zinoviev's line. And she was not alone. There were Politburo members who were confused as well. In fact they were deviating from Lenin, though they thought this was Lenin's position.

[1-1-83]

Doctors forbade visits to Lenin during his illness, once his condition grew worse. But Krupskaya allowed them. And this brought on the conflict between Krupskaya and Stalin. Stalin supported the Central Committee's decision not to let any visitors see Lenin. Stalin was right in this case. If the Central Committee, and even the Politburo, decided to entrust Stalin to supervise the implementation of this resolution...

[10-21-82]

What Lenin wrote about Stalin's rudeness was not without Krupskaya's influence. She disliked Stalin because he had treated her quite tactlessly. Stalin implemented the decision of the secretariat and did not permit Zinoviev and Kamenev to visit Lenin once this was prohibited by the doctors. Zinoviev and Kamenev complained to Krupskaya. Outraged, she told off Stalin. He responded, "Lenin should not have visitors." "But Lenin himself wants it!" Stalin: "If the Central Committee says so, we might not let you see him either."

Stalin was irritated: "Why should I get up on my hind legs for her? To sleep with Lenin does not necessarily mean to understand Leninism!"

Stalin told me something like this: "Just because she uses the same bathroom as Lenin, do I have to appreciate and respect her as if she were Lenin?"

He was too coarse and rude.

[12-11-72]

Krupskaya played no special role in the party. She was friendly with Zinoviev. This was bad, of course. But remember that even Dzerzhinsky voted for Trotsky. With this view, no one would be left. This must be understood.

Gorky also made mistakes. He came out against the October Revolution. In the last analysis no one understood Leninism better than Stalin.

[1-8-74, 4-28-76]

■ The Sealed Railway Car ■

A book, The C.P.S.U. in Power *by N. Rutich, has been published in the West. Rutich writes that Lenin was getting German money for the Bolsheviks, that he came back to Russia in April* 1917 . . .

That's pure provocation. Everything about Lenin was spotless. He thundered against German imperialism openly, unceasingly, mercilessly.

But perhaps it was to the Germans' advantage to support Lenin at the time?

Lenin might not have received a cent of this money, but, on the other hand, he might have gotten some of it. . . . But Lenin's power was exactly that he could make use of anything.

Talks about Lenin's sealed car. . . . What Kerensky was talking about . . .

We put an end to that! You'd be walking down the street and start propagandizing. You'd give a speech, a group of people would gather around. The crowd would grow and grow. . . . The people were active then. For the first time they had freedom in the full sense of the word. The press was buzzing. Plekhanov published a book opposing Lenin. He charged that Lenin had availed himself of the services of a German consul: thus Lenin is helping the Germans! Alexenko, a former Bolshevik and a deputy of the state Duma, had been one of the Bolshevik leaders at the Duma. Later he lived abroad and distanced himself from the Bolsheviks, vilified Lenin. He sold some of Lenin's letters. He excoriated Lenin for helping the Germans, for speaking against the allies. All of this helped Kerensky.

[12-12-72]

Lenin was transported through Switzerland and Finland in a sealed car. It was agreed that there would be no conversation or contact with the German authorities or the German people. Zinoviev traveled in this car with Lenin.

But the Kaiser still had plans for Lenin...

Of course, he had his own advantage in mind. The money was entrusted to a Swiss bank, to the socialist Platten.

[1-14-75]

■   **Inessa**   ■

They say that Armand was Lenin's mistress.

So they say. Lenin writes, "Dear, sweet friend! Hello, dear friend!" I remember Inessa Armand well. A non-Russian type. A nice lady. To my mind there was nothing special about her. . . . Lenin treated her very affectionately.

Bukharin told me bluntly that she was Lenin's passion. He was very close with Lenin, and he probably knew Inessa very well. I remember that Bukharin and I shared a room in the Hotel European in Petersburg. We went to a conference there. It was when we were still together and had sacked Zinoviev at the conference, before we had sent Kirov off to Leningrad. Bukharin chatted about various things. . . . He was jolly, witty, joked a lot. A leader of the rightists. He had the soul of a peasant.

A pity about Bukharin.

"You may choose or not choose to be a poet, but you must be a citizen." Very well said, wonderful words. Many repeated them then. . . .

Inessa Armand had a French husband. I think he was a manufacturer. She lived abroad a long time, and that's where Lenin met her. She was preparing some sort of speech and told Lenin her thesis. She had made critical remarks about one of Engels's phrases. Lenin clarified things for her and wrote: I am against such a critique of Engels. Keep in mind that I regard with extreme caution any attempts to criticize Marx and Engels. These were real people, and there is much to learn from them. That was the essence of it. He corrected Armand so that she would not waste her time. As if all this was the result of a misunderstanding.

[4-27-73]

They say that Krupskaya insisted that Inessa Armand be removed from Moscow. . . .

That's possible. It was an unusual situation. Lenin, to put it bluntly, had a mistress. And Krupskaya was a sick person.

[2-16-85]

■ Temporarily, at a Certain Stage ■

Krupskaya had a big grudge against Stalin. But he had a grudge against her, too, because Lenin's signature to his testament was supposedly affixed under Krupskaya's influence. Or so Stalin believed. Perhaps it's true to some extent. But it is inconceivable to regard Lenin as being under Krupskaya's thumb. . . .

Krupskaya supported Zinoviev at the XIVth Party Congress. He spoke then from a left-wing position, criticizing Stalin for not applying sufficient energy to industrialization, and not caring enough for the working class, all of which meant that Stalin was deviating from Lenin's bequest. She did not come out openly against Stalin but favored Zinoviev. Later she offered her apologies and renounced her views.

There was an open discussion in the press, and it demanded a response. It was impossible to remain silent. Trotsky was publishing his collected works. He had to be dethroned ideologically. Everyone was extremely erudite: everyone was for Lenin, for Marx. If you allowed your attention to wander, you would be left behind and out of it! Stalin achieved colossal results. If not for him, the cadres would not have pulled together. The Bolshevik cadres would not simply obey orders at the wave of a wand. They had to be convinced. The same applied to the old Bolsheviks. Habitually they deferred to no authority or command. They regarded themselves as the equal of an ideological leader. Stalin led, but around him rallied both firm supporters and some not so firm but talented. In 1924 discussion against Trotsky was proceeding full tilt.

Suddenly a statement bearing all our signatures—Stalin, Zinoviev, Kamenev, Rykov, Bukharin, and mine too was published to the effect that we could not conceive of the Politburo without Trotsky! Everyone had signed. It was as if, despite our quarrels with him, he was such a figure that we could not imagine the Politburo without him. It was politics, the times, whatever you will. We were engaged in a very serious ideological struggle yet, at one and the same time, we valued Trotsky so highly!

The time was not yet ripe for an open break. It couldn't be done. Once the ideological fight was in the open, it was possible to consider how to get rid of Trotsky.

We sent him into exile. And even then we had a lot of trouble with him. While living abroad he actually called for terror. . . . As long as imperialism's alive, there will be many such swine.

"We shouldn't have any!" Shota Ivanovich exclaimed.

What do you mean, we shouldn't have any? It's absolutely unavoidable, inescapable.

Well then, we are fighting badly against them.

That's true.

And you are not guilty for having fought against them.

We should be considered guilty insofar as we fought badly. You see, we didn't put an end to all these swine.

But you cannot be reproached, for you were strengthening the socialist system.

We were not only strengthening the system, but we occasionally bashed some heads.

[8-17-71]

John Reed rather glorified Trotsky in his book *Ten Days That Shook the World*. But Trotsky must be given his due, for he was good in those days. He behaved badly in Brest, of course. And in the civil war he displayed good and bad qualities. Without a doubt he fought for Soviet power. How else could he have become head of the Red Army? He relied too much on professional military experts, and Lenin mentioned this. On the other hand, we couldn't have gotten by without the experts. In this respect, Voroshilov acted excessively against the experts. That was bad. They had a different outlook, but they were essential.

[8-24-71]

Trotsky had planted his people everywhere, especially in the army. Gamarnik was head of the political department. Skliansky was his first deputy. I knew him. The devil only knows where he came from! Where Trotsky found him I don't know.

[8-15-75]

To this day I recall the first party congress in Petrograd in April, after the February Revolution, when Rykov expressed his rightist sentiments. Kamenev, too, showed his true colors. Zinoviev was still considered to be close to Lenin. Before the elections of members to the Central Committee, Lenin spoke for Stalin's candidacy. He said Stalin had to be in the Central Committee without fail. He spoke up for Stalin in particular, saying he was such a fine party member, such a commanding figure, and you could assign him any task. He was the most trustworthy in adhering to the party line. That's the sort of speech it was. Of course, we voted in concord. So that's how it went. But Lenin criticized him, too. Just take the whole history of Lenin. Now Lenin is portrayed as a monster, evil and so forth. This is because he was like a rock, armed with knowledge, science, and a colossal mind. . . . He had vision. Perhaps he didn't see everything, but he saw the main thing.

Many talented people were drawn to Lenin, but that's not the important thing. He picked and chose. In the 1890s and even after 1900 Lenin believed in Plekhanov. But soon he was lashing out at Plekhanov, and rightly so. After Plekhanov, Bogdanov was closest to Lenin among the prominent Marxists. Malinovsky was his surname, yes. He was a great authority in political economy. In 1897 Lenin reviewed Bogdanov's first book, *Political Economy*. But then he drubbed him. Even Stalin played the liberal toward Bogdanov. In particular Bukharin supported Bogdanov. Bogdanov became the head of a laboratory where Lenin's brain was deposited for research. Bogdanov, as director, had requested this. He was a nonparty man, alien to all our revolutionary policies. They gave him the brain nonetheless, and he studied something or other. . . .

Then take Trotsky. At first Lenin was favorably disposed toward him. Take Zinoviev, Bukharin, Kamenev—they were closest to Lenin. Temporarily, at a certain stage, they supported him, but they lacked consistency, so to speak, sufficient revolutionary character. So who's to blame? That's history. That's life.

With Marx, only Engels remained faithful. Marx assailed the others on the right and on the left. He taught and taught, but those who resisted had to be hit hard. But that was another sphere, so to speak, a more theoretical one. They had less political activity. We had to deal with practical politics.

■   **"A Topsy-turvy Library"**   ■

Marx was merciless toward Lassalle. No sooner did Lassalle begin to set forth his wisdom than Marx attacked him. It could not be otherwise— that's science. One cannot somehow combine philistinism and science. That would be highly dangerous.

[11-23-71]

I recall a Marxist and a party figure called David Riazanov. I forget his full name, but he was well known for he was the director of the Institute of Marxism. He was its first head, and he was director even in Lenin's time, as I recall. The institute was named after Marx, but later it was called the Institute of Marx, Engels, and Lenin. And now there is a museum of Marx and Engels where the institute used to be. I was a member of its board and sometimes sat with this Riazanov. Rarely, but occasionally. He was knowledgeable and well read. But, as Lenin used to say about him, "This man is a topsy-turvy library." Everything was mixed up in his head, everything was a muddle. He could not sort things out. What use could he be?

He wore a beard and bore some resemblance to Marx. "The topsy-turvy library." I didn't hear this directly from Lenin, but I was told he said this. But what I really heard Lenin say was, "With this ulcer we'll surely die!" Riazanov criticized everything constantly, but he was confused and always in a muddle. He was neither a Trotskyist nor a rightist, but with all his knowledge he was just muddleheaded. As far as I remember, he was exiled to Saratov much earlier than 1937. Lenin thought it was hardly worth punishing him, that we would likely live and die with that ulcer. In Saratov he used to say, "I would like to live to see how socialism is going to be made in one apartment, in one town, in one township." He was mocking. He was an active fellow. He wrote a lot about Marx, and the first edition of the Marx-Engels works was published under his editorship. He was considered to be a great savant, though his usefulness . . .

[6-21-72]

◼ Whom to Forgive and for What ◼

At different times it was difficult to adhere to correct Bolshevik policy. If some policies were mistaken their advocates should be dropped, but whom could you turn to next? Infallible people do not exist, Lenin used to say. It depends, first, on the kind of error and, second, how long it persisted. And whether there was willingness to pursue the line considered correct. If there was such willingness, certain errors had to be passed over.

In 1917 Lenin called Zinoviev and Kamenev prostitutes for their treachery in the October Revolution. And not only prostitutes but strikebreakers as well. They were impeding us and directly helping the enemy.

Zinoviev and Kamenev committed an act of betrayal yet remained in the party, and they were even admitted into the Politburo.

Certainly. Stalin helped Zinoviev and Kamenev. Why? Because there were very few trained people. They could not be trusted, but it was very difficult to do without them. Politics is a complicated matter. At that time Lenin demanded their expulsion from the party, but Stalin and Sverdlov objected. We had to wait a while. And then Zinoviev and Kamenev repeated their errors. . . . When we no longer relied on them for anything, we got rid of them!

Zinoviev and Kamenev remained in the Politburo for several years following their treachery. There were only five members—Lenin, Stalin, Zinoviev, Kamenev, and Trotsky. Two of the five Lenin had called prostitutes, and before that he had often called Trotsky "Little Judas." He had also called him an irreconcilable enemy, and so forth. But Trotsky remained in the Politburo and was head of the army during the civil war. So Lenin made use of him. Mistakes should be evaluated correctly but not to overdo it. Nor can one completely trust people who have made flagrant mistakes. Lenin wrote in his so-called letter of farewell that Zinoviev's and Kamenev's mistakes were not accidental.

You're saying that Lenin forgave Kamenev, Zinoviev, and Trotsky. But Stalin forgave no one and even innocent people perished.

At first Tsiurupa was Lenin's only deputy, the vice-chairman of the Council of People's Commissars. But he was not a member of the Central Committee. Stalin brought him in later. Krzhizhanovsky was chairman of Gosplan and Lenin's personal friend. They had been good friends since the nineties and later were exiled together. Krzhizhanovsky was the head of GOELRO [State Commission for Electrification of Russia] and Gosplan [the State Planning Commission], but he was not on the Central Committee. Only Stalin let him into the Central Committee. Take the third figure—Krasin, also an old friend and comrade of Lenin. He played a large part in the IInd Party Congress, where bolshevism was formed. He was the people's commissar of foreign trade under Lenin. But Lenin didn't let him, a party worker, into the Central Committee.... Chicherin was commissar of foreign affairs under Lenin. Lenin quite often praised him as an outstanding figure of Soviet power, and yet he didn't admit him to the Central Committee. But Stalin let him in. It was a different time. Stalin knew how to choose people; he even advanced those whom Lenin did not allow inside. But they were closer to Stalin, and he brought them directly into the Central Committee. Two different periods. In the one period Lenin considered it unwise to appoint certain people, even those he knew well, to leading positions in the political work of the party. But when the situation changed slightly, these less reliable types could do no harm politically. They had been good people in their youth, and it became possible to admit them to the Central Committee and to work with them. Everything depends on the combination of circumstances.

[1-16-73, 4-28-76]

Kirov had been in Leningrad since January 1926, after Zinoviev was removed. Bukharin and I went to a conference and put Kirov in as the secretary. It had been done democratically. At that time Bukharin supported the Central Committee line. Then he left a dirty trail, saying that our policy was the policy of military-feudal exploitation of the peasantry. Bukharin supported us from the right.

[4-27-73]

■ "Tea Drinkers" ■

I'm from the Petersburg school and Piatakov was from Moscow. He was a bit older than I, almost of Stalin's generation, from a rich family, as far as I know. He had been to the Ukraine.

It seems to me Lenin sympathized more strongly with the Saint Petersburg workers than with the Muscovites.

Of course, he worked very closely with the Saint Petersburg workers.

He considered Muscovites to be petty bourgeois, part of a merchant environment. They had no patience. Lenin quite often called the Moscow communist leadership "the Moscow tea drinkers." He used to say, "These are not workers but tea drinkers!"

[5-7-75, 4-29-80]

■ "Comrades!!!" ■

"Did Lenin praise Sverdlov on the day of his funeral?" asked Shota Ivanovich.

Yes, far too much. He was an organizer, a party man, but he left nothing to distinguish himself. Nothing. I don't remember a single article by him.

They say that Kirov left nothing either.

Kirov left many articles and speeches. People like Sverdlov appeared earlier; Kirov arrived on the scene when everything was already in place.

Sverdlov was a short man. He wore a leather coat. He had a thunderous voice. The devil knows how that monstrous voice could come from such a small man. A Jericho trumpet! He used to yell at the meetings, "Comrades!!!" Everyone would immediately wonder about the noise and would shut up. He was useful to Lenin. Everyone knew he would say whatever Lenin instructed him to say. He was a good organizer. He would make a short speech at large conferences to maintain order. . . .

Sverdlov had a brother named Peshkov, whose godfather was Gorky. He left for Paris and denounced Soviet power. He used to be the French military attaché in Japan. I knew Sverdlov's family well and his wife, Klavdia Andreevna. She was Russian.

What caused Sverdlov's death? Do you remember?

It seems to me that he went to Kharkov and caught cold. What is it called? "Spanish influenza." The phrase is out of use now. "Flu."

There are rumors that he was attacked somewhere, was beaten and died after that.

That's possible. Lenin valued him greatly and regretted his loss. He carried out Lenin's organizational instructions. That was important to Lenin. Sverdlov wasn't very curious and didn't show initiative. He was an honest person, though, and devoted to the party. But these were not great credentials for a leading figure. Lenin praised Sverdlov excessively.

He died young, at age thirty-four. And there was nothing to criticize him
for.

[7-28-71, 12-4-73, 11-1-77, 1-26-86]

■ Lenin's Theoretical Innovation ■

To Trotsky it seemed that the only way out of our plight was the
establishment of a bourgeois republic, because we were not supported by
the working class of the West, and our alliance with the peasantry wasn't
working. That was his chief shortcoming. Listen, unity of the proletariat
alone is insufficient according to any theory of Marxism. But Lenin—
and herein lies his strength—was able to find an approach to the
peasantry. He criticized the petty bourgeois essence of the peasantry but
also discerned its toiling side. If a correct approach to the peasantry were
applied, they would support us. This is Lenin's innovation in Marxist
theory, and in practice he proved to be right.

Trotsky was cunning. During the vote on whether to accept the Brest
peace treaty, he said he would adhere to his own opinion, nonaccep-
tance. But Lenin said he would resign from the Central Committee and
go to the masses to struggle against the Central Committee if it should
vote to reject signing the peace. Trotsky said that inasmuch as this would
lead to a split in the party, he would abstain. Lenin then got a majority
by one vote.

[1-8-74]

■ Lenin Was Displeased ■

In 1921, after the Xth Congress, there were all of nineteen members
on the Central Committee. (Now there are sixteen members just on the
Politburo.) Back then, of the nineteen, five were members of the
Politburo and three were alternates. The remaining eleven were from
the provinces and some were people's commissars. The last time I read
today's list I was astounded: some sixteen full members of the Politburo
and six alternates. That makes a total of twenty-two persons. In 1922,
when it was proposed to Lenin to add Rykov and Tomsky to the
Politburo, he was hardly pleased. It was a rather awkward situation.

Frunze came out with this proposal. It was not inappropriate, but it was a political move by the right-wingers. Frunze raised this question at the Central Committee plenum, after the congress had ended. Of course, it was not his proposal. The right-wingers made use of the poor man. He wasn't pushed into this; rather, they convinced him that the Politburo had to be renewed. A new plenum convened after the XIth Congress and elected members to the leading bodies and the Politburo. Whom? Frunze rose and suggested a figure: "Seven persons." Lenin said, "Why seven? It's always been five!" "Who's for it?" There was a slight hesitation, then they voted for seven. "Who?" Frunze got up again and said, "Rykov and Tomsky." This was obviously at the suggestion of Zinoviev and Trotsky. Rykov and Tomsky were themselves vacillating, but the others wanted to use them. Lenin was displeased. He did not want to admit them to the Politburo, but he had to agree. He could not turn them away.

Trotsky was in the Politburo, but in fact everyone had united around Stalin, including the right wing—Bukharin and Rykov. We called ourselves "the majority" against Trotsky. He surely sensed, of course, this collusion against him. He had his supporters and we had ours. But he did not have many in the Politburo or in the Central Committee, only two or three. There was Shliapnikov from the Workers' Opposition and Krestinsky from the Democratic Centralists.

Then we held a factional meeting. I remember it took place in the Central Committee. Dzerzhinsky had certainly become a member of our group, and said, "Zinoviev and Kamenev, where are you leading us? You are just Kronstadtsy!" He reminded them that they had set a course on an uprising against Soviet power! "You are Kronstadtsy!" He was outraged. Dzerzhinsky had a sincere, expansive nature, but he was hot-blooded. Already in 1925 he called Zinoviev and Kamenev "Kronstadtsy." . . .

Both Zinoviev and Bukharin were certainly against Lenin, but they could not be dealt with at once. Everything depends on stages. . . .

Dzerzhinsky died while he was giving a speech against Piatakov. Piatakov was a Trotskyist, one of those closest to Trotsky. He strongly believed in Trotsky.

[4-28-76]

■   **Only Once Against Lenin**   ■

Did Lenin make any mistakes?

Certainly. As the first candidate in the Central Committee I was a full and equal member of the five during the voting, and only once did I vote against Lenin. It was in Lenin's presence.

In the summer of 1921 Lenin suggested closing the Bolshoi Theatre. He said there was famine in the country and the situation was very grave. The Bolshoi Theatre was inherited from the nobility. In order to economize, we could do without it for the time being. Lenin was defeated. A majority voted against. Stalin was absent. I remember that I voted with those who disagreed. Not much harm came from it. Lenin was rather too edgy in this case: "Why the devil do we need it!" This was the time of transition to the NEP, and one of the most difficult years.

Did Lenin use strong language?

Lenin did not use foul language. Voroshilov, however, liked to swear. And Stalin wasn't opposed to it—he swore in certain situations. Zhdanov would swear sometimes, when he was in a good mood, from the heart. People ease their moods this way. It's not harmful.

[6-9-76]

■   **Lenin Writes to Molotov**   ■

Among Lenin's works are many letters addressed to you . . . even more letters than were addressed to Stalin.

Of course. You see, I held the position of first secretary of the Central Committee for an entire year, the senior secretary. There was no one else. Stalin became general secretary later.

[8-16-77]

We worked nights, but this was more common under Stalin. We worked on Sundays sometimes too, of course. Sometimes we would stay up all night in order to finish a task. We were served tea. As I recall, Lenin did not hold all-night sessions.

One evening I was working in my office as secretary of the Central Committee. There were no visiting hours at the time. I was busy with current affairs, doing some kind of paperwork, when suddenly I received a note from Lenin. I suppose there had been a Sovnarkom meeting. I published the note in my book, *On the Leninist Enrollment.*

Lenin writes, "Comrade Molotov, does the Central Committee investigate the points of view of different party groups? In particular, are we studying the opinions of people who do not work in any single department of our shitty apparatus? If not, would it be possible to organize the investigation of this matter?"

In my book I dropped the word "shitty" and used three dots in its place. Evidently Lenin was sick of all this. I imagined him writing this note to me. He sensed what the influence of the bureaucratic apparatus was, that it hindered a person's understanding of the whole situation. People were mired in their narrow departmental points of view, with all kinds of personal interests which no one was studying. I responded to him with a note of my own.

[6-30-76]

■ They Deviated from Lenin ■

In 1922 Polina Semenovna was undergoing medical treatment in Czechoslovakia. I visited her and decided to take advantage of my being abroad to go on to Italy. I wanted to take a look at fascism on the rise. It was hard to predict. But the bourgeoisie is always seeking such forms. Strictly speaking, Hitler wasn't a fascist. He was a National Socialist, although the two were essentially the same.

At that time a discussion was held in the Central Committee. In 1922, at the October anniversary, Lenin said that NEP Russia would be transformed into a socialist Russia. And Kamenev made a similar speech at some workers' or trade union meeting or other, to the effect that Nepman Russia would be transformed into a socialist Russia. Lenin referred to Russia as "a country of the NEP," while Kamenev called it "a country of NEPmen." A country of NEPmen is bourgeois, but a country of the NEP is completely different. The NEP embraced both positive and negative: the dictatorship of the proletariat ruled, but the bourgeoisie still remained.

Stalin resolutely opposed Kamenev's formulation, and an argument was joined in the Politburo. Zinoviev and Kamenev, two members of the Politburo, formed a coalition. Zinoviev was chairman of the Petrograd Soviet and the Comintern, and Kamenev was chairman of the Moscow

Soviet and deputy chairman of Sovnarkom. Both claimed we did not have a dictatorship of the proletariat but a dictatorship of the party. That's how the Mensheviks reasoned: you Bolsheviks are well organized, you seized power, and you are cut off from the people. . . . But Lenin said, "No, we have a dictatorship of a class, a dictatorship of the proletariat headed by communists. We are not cut off from the people, from the working class, we are part of it, the leading, guiding, directing force."

And so the fight started. I arrived right at that time. Stalin then began to pile it on, very tellingly and brilliantly, I think.

Rykov straddled the fence, as did Bukharin. I don't remember the details of everyone's position. I noticed that Mikoyan was supporting Zinoviev. Mikoyan carried on ignobly. He supported Zinoviev on such a fundamental matter. The dispute raged on. Violent disagreements broke out. I said: "I am in complete disagreement. We must defend the dictatorship of the proletariat, as Lenin said, and as Stalin explained so well."

In capitalist countries the bourgeoisie leads. So long as imperialism and socialism are locked in struggle with each other, it's either a dictatorship of the bourgeoisie or a dictatorship of the working class.

[8-18-76, 7-29-81]

Zinoviev deviated from Lenin after 1925. Krupskaya also moved away from Lenin, but in truth she didn't meddle in big politics.

So Lenin lived in such circumstances. And he was, after all, a man who could cut right through any obstacle. How irreconcilable he was with the right and the left! Bukharin and Zinoviev were closest to him, but he criticized them too, especially in the end.

In 1921 I participated in Lenin's coalition against Trotsky.

Lenin didn't know what to do. Whatever blow he struck first could have recoiled on him, and it was impossible to strike hard at the left and the right simultaneously.

Stalin was in a very difficult situation then. Lenin probably wasn't as harsh as Stalin, but he had vast authority!

They say Lenin would have accomplished collectivization with fewer victims. But how could it have been done any other way? I renounce none of it. We carried out collectivization relentlessly; our measures were absolutely correct.

[3-4-78]

There's a story in *Iunost* magazine to the effect that Lenin promoted workers from peasant backgrounds. We had to appoint a people's commissar of agriculture. A Ukrainian name . . . Lenin found him.

Iakovenko. I trained him. He was from western Siberia. Later he turned out to be a right-winger. I chose him. It was part of my duty as secretary of the Central Committee.

We counted on him. He was a partisan and had fought against Kolchak. You see, he could fight against Kolchak, but he left us when it came to building socialism. He didn't work on collectivization. He was purely of the peasantry: quite a capable man, but without vision.

Was he repressed?

I don't remember. Who cares? . . . You can't remember everything.

[8-26-79]

■   **Lunacharsky Was Dazzling**   ■

Lunacharsky was very talented. He wrote well, made speeches with ease. He knew several languages. German and French at least, and perhaps English, Italian . . .

[10-9-75]

He wasn't especially scientific but was highly cultivated and educated. His wife Rosenelle was an artiste, and she was successful with men.

Lunacharsky helped Lenin a good deal before the Revolution, especially by publishing party literature abroad. I am not sure how much he did on *Iskra*, but his work ran in later Bolshevik publications from 1906 to 1908, in the *Proletariat* and in the *Vpered*. He deviated from the party and joined the so-called Interregional Organization. Trotsky and Manuilsky were in it. . . .

Lunacharsky's plays are on the whole hard to read. But one must read some of them. His speeches were interesting. He was a talented speaker. But sometimes the word was in command of him, rather than the other way around. One could sense his foppishness. He was dazzling in this respect. He could speak knowledgeably on any subject. Lenin valued him. There were few people like him.

[10-9-75, 12-7-76, 5-19-80]

■   **One Person Gets Trousers, Another Gets Shoes...**   ■

Viacheslav Mikhailovich, Lenin attributed such dreadful qualities to everyone, without exception!

Certainly. But he gave very accurate descriptions. He could not come to run-of-the-mill conclusions. It was not without reason that Lenin distinguished Stalin and Trotsky as leaders, as the two who stood apart from the rest, as the most talented.

But he criticized everyone in his testament, even those he regarded as outstanding.

Yes, he criticized everyone. I suppose he realized there was not enough time left for him to set everything right. And he had to say something so that people would have some idea of the direction to take. In 1921 Zinoviev was still supporting Lenin, but there were quite a few people on the Central Committee who wavered. And you see, the Xth Party Congress took place before that. It was the beginning of the NEP. Lenin's secretariat was formed—three secretaries, and all three were Trotskyists! Devil take it, all three—Krestinsky, Serebriakov, and Preobrazhensky. They formed a tight ring around Lenin. All of them were kicked out at the XIth Congress. I became first secretary and Yaroslavsky and Mikhailov became secretaries. Mikhailov was a mediocrity on a provincial scale. No better than this, just a provincial apparatchik. True, he had been chairman of the Moscow Council of Trade Unions, but he had no stature politically.

After some time I begged, entreated Lenin to receive me. I said, "I have some questions to discuss with you." He agreed and set a day. One moment Yaroslavsky would request trousers for one person, another time it would be shoes for someone else. Trifles. True, the times were such that people were in need of everything. But attention had to be focused on major problems. Yet there were endless requests: someone or other needed food supplies, they couldn't get them, and so we had to discuss who should get food and who should not. We were busy with nonsense. I said, "It's impossible to work, Vladimir Ilyich. We're wasting our time on rubbish." Lenin remained silent.

And did you call Lenin "Vladimir Ilyich"?

No, Comrade Lenin. We rarely called him Vladimir Ilyich. Only friends closest to him, those from the early years, like Krzhizhanovsky, called him Vladimir Ilyich. All the rest—Lenin, Lenin. . . . Maybe Tsiurupa called him Vladimir Ilyich.

And then Stalin became Comrade Stalin, didn't he?

Yes. It was a tradition—Comrade Lenin, Comrade Stalin. Given name and patronymic were not used in party circles. Vladimir Ilyich, Josif Vissarionovich—it didn't suit them. It would conform with current attitudes and manners, but then it did not.

So, in August, after the plenum and Yaroslavsky's report, Lenin said, "I have one more question." He suddenly announced, "It concerns Comrade Yaroslavsky. I move that we send him to Siberia. We can replace him with a Central Committee member here, but there are too few people in Siberia, and they need a helping hand. Any opposed? None. The motion is adopted."

I went to work after the plenum. At the time we were across from what is now Voentorg. So I went to my office, and Yaroslavsky suddenly rushed after me and started to assail me—"You careerist! Your hands are all over this affair! You are a schemer!" and so forth. What was I to do?

"What are you scolding me for?" I said. "I just want you to work somewhere else."

He cursed me, but it was already too late. Lenin passed the resolution right away. The plenum approved it. Of course it was my doing, but I don't regret that he was sent to Siberia. He worked there for two or three years.

And this occurred more than two months after my talk with Lenin.

Yaroslavsky thought I had been severely demoted when Stalin replaced me as chairman of the Sovnarkom on the eve of the war in May 1941. But that was just not so. Power had to be concentrated in one pair of hands before the war. He wrote an insulting letter about me for *Pravda*. But Stalin read it in galleys and said, "What's this? An allegation that under Molotov there was no Soviet power in our country?"

[3-8-74, 6-9-76, 8-28-81, 4-29-82]

■   The Intellectuals Have a Worldview, but . . .   ■

Molotov and I were watching a documentary about Lenin on television. It showed Simbirsk. "Kerensky was also born there," I said.

Kerensky was a man of ability, a good speaker. I listened to him quite often and spoke against him early on. He became the leader of the Russian state when he was thirty-five. His father had signed Lenin's diploma. Surely their families were acquainted, for they lived in the same town and the town wasn't very big.

Do you remember Lenin's mother?

I think I met her in Saint Petersburg in 1916.

I told Molotov that Marshal Golovanov was the grandson of Nikolai Kibalchik, but it was not good form to talk about this, because Kibalchik's friends became Socialist Revolutionaries. A petty bourgeois party. . . .

A petty bourgeois revolutionary party, we should add. A revolutionary party. They advocated terror and the bombing of ministers! They stood for the peasants. It was a Peasant party. They were considered to be the main party of the peasants. But what distinguished the Bolsheviks from the peasants' party of Socialist Revolutionaries? A peasants' congress was held in Petrograd, probably in June 1917. Lenin spoke there, but the Socialist Revolutionaries formed the overwhelming majority of the congress, and they were the real leaders of it. The peasants' deputies worked out a mandate at the congress: to turn the land over to the peasants, to organize peasants' committees in the localities. The Socialist Revolutionaries helped to formulate this. The resolution passed. But land was still not being given to the peasants!

In the summer of 1917 the peasants were demanding fulfillment of the resolution. But Viktor Chernov, the head of the SRs, the minister of agriculture in the Kerensky government, said, "It's not yet time. The Constituent Assembly will convene and decide the question." They delayed action until the Constituent Assembly convened [January 1918]. But as soon as the October Revolution triumphed, Lenin proclaimed the decree on land—the peasants' mandate on land was to be implemented! Yes, the SR land program was to be implemented: take the land, immediately! He had utilized the peasants and explained: we are not in agreement in a number of respects, but as the peasants have drawn up the policy, let them become convinced by experience in implementing it that not everything is right with it, and they will begin to see things our way. But we must begin implementation of the decree, begin smashing the landlords to confiscate their land. In this struggle the peasants will find the right path.

And so it went. Courageously and wonderfully! Or take the NEP, for example. After all, it was the Mensheviks who demanded freedom of trade, to allow opportunities to sell, and so forth. So in 1921 Lenin took this Menshevik program and started implementing it, but under control of the workers' state. It was a measure forced on us by circumstances, but a necessary one.

There is a certain article of mine, "Lenin in the Years of the Revolution." I published it in the *Molodaya Gvardia* after Lenin's death. In it I showed that Lenin had "stolen" the program of the Socialist Revolutionaries. I wrote that they had adopted a resolution at the peasants' congress—not quite a correct one, but against landlords, in general. Lenin adopted it. And with it he won the October Revolution.

Further. The Mensheviks were continually talking about the kinds of trading relations we ought to have. Lenin criticized them: "You are counterrevolutionaries, scum, enemies of the working class." But then he introduced the NEP in 1921. This time he had "stolen" from the Mensheviks.

The civil war was preventing us from switching over to normal methods of work. That's why we had the so-called food requisitioning system. Balking at nothing, the state took from the peasants what it needed. If you had more, the state would take more from you; if someone else had a great deal, the state would take everything; if another had nothing, the state would take nothing. There was no other way out. We were a bit carried away with this policy. Peasants tolerated this for a while, but once the war was over, the uprisings began. . . . And not only in the Tambov province but in many other places. As early as January 1921, that is, two months before the NEP, Lenin announced "a crisis of the party." He wrote an article about it. Opposition was everywhere— Trotskyists and "workers' opposition" and Democratic Centralists and nationalist groups. Now somehow we must through party unity save the cause and carry out the reforms of the NEP, that is, make concessions to the peasantry that would enable them to engage in trade. The state was taking all the grain from them. There was no food for the army, and we had to feed the workers. The workers were few in number, but the army was large and we couldn't exist without it.

Lenin said we have reached the point with the peasants where if we do not make certain concessions to them, they will drive us from power. He pushed us: "Let's correct this quickly!" And he started to introduce the NEP into practice very rapidly: "Let's make some concessions, but under the control of the state and the party." Sure, there were limits. He wrote later that we had retreated but that it was an orderly retreat. At the time some said we had retreated to capitalism, that we were giving up everything! What had we been fighting for? Such feelings were evident at the time. Some of these critics dropped out of the party. They didn't understand. They thought all had been lost, that we were giving up and resorting to capitalism, which meant that it was all over. But Lenin said we must keep everything in our hands. At this time, by the way, before the XIth Party Congress in March 1922, he wrote to me about membership in the party. The letter is published in the complete collection of Lenin's works. Lenin wrote that now the orientation of our policy was determined not by the mass of party members but by an extremely small group, the old guard of the party. If a split should open there, everything would be ruined. That is why it was imperative with all our strength to preserve the unity of this group, which enjoyed vast, boundless authority among the people. The policy of the party, he said, was determined by this authority. If a split begins, we shall retain nothing. That is why he wrote with such bitterness and apprehension in those years, if only to preserve the party as a unified body under the leadership of this small group.

[8-14-73, 1-14-75, 3-11-76]

Intellectuals offer a worldview, but only the working class can achieve victory. I consider this to be Lenin's most important legacy.

[1-14-75]

Lenin's power resided in something that even Marx had not brought to light. Lenin knew how to lay hold of the peasantry. We achieved victory in a country of peasants. But if we, if the working class, had not captured the peasantry, we would have failed. We won over the peasants in order to beat the kulaks, the petty proprietors. . . .

[3-8-75]

■   Elections to the Constituent Assembly   ■

The elections to the Constituent Assembly took place in 1917. And in 1919 Lenin wrote a response to Kautsky, who had published a pamphlet. He landed a powerful blow to Kautsky's mug. Besides that he analyzed in detail the Constituent Assembly, on which Kautsky, as well as the Socialist Revolutionaries, pinned their hopes.

There was a certain Svetlovsky, a statistician, a splendid statistician. Kautsky quoted him. He was not an open anti-Sovieteer but was rather an SR type. In order to expose the Bolsheviks, Svetlovsky cited the elections to the Constituent Assembly. In fact the Bolsheviks turned out to have only a minority. He demonstrated with figures how this happened, and you were supposed to conclude from this that the Bolsheviks had grabbed power. But Lenin explained everything.

Yes, the Bolsheviks had received about 40 percent of the total vote, and the anti-Bolsheviks had more than 50 percent. Lenin admitted this, but he also observed that the Bolsheviks turned out to be in the majority at decisive times and in decisive places: in towns, in the army, at the front. They had triumphed. They were leading the country, though the majority remained an adversary turned bad. Lenin got very good results. And his article, "Will the Bolsheviks Retain State Power?"—oh, how he argued in it! A majority, indeed! On this question many Bolsheviks lacked faith. They were drawn to Lenin. They were afraid, nevertheless they were drawn to him.

But many fell into the ranks of Trotsky. Under later conditions, however, Bukharin, Rykov were more dangerous. . . .

[3-8-75]

■   "More Difficult but . . . More Profound Too"   ■

Lenin's books are now the most widely read in the world. Everyone studies them—both friends and foes. There was the president of Finland, Paasikivi, a bourgeois figure. I met him. At his home he had a large library that included Lenin's collected works. One had to know what the Bolsheviks were thinking about. . . .

It is astounding that they did not know and were not interested in what the Bolsheviks were thinking as the Bolsheviks triumphed.

Everyone, even those who do not sympathize with Lenin, is obliged to cite him.

[8-15-75]

I do not agree that Lenin is understandable to workers and peasants. Surely Lenin requires a trained reader.

I think he is quite understandable. For instance, in *State and Revolution* everything is clear. Just don't be lazy.

You have to read many other books in order to understand Lenin. I suppose you can learn from Stalin how to read Lenin. Stalin refers the reader to Lenin. And do you know why? Because Lenin is very cogent.

All of Stalin's works should have been published and circulated. Lenin is difficult, but he is also more profound.

Very true.

[4-27-73]

■   **"I Can See Him as If He Were Alive"**   ■

Was it right to put Lenin in the mausoleum?

At that time it was necessary. Krupskaya was opposed. It was done by decision of the Central Committee. Stalin insisted, and we supported it. It was necessary.

What color were Lenin's eyes?

I don't remember. This is a completely new question for me. Hazel, I think. I would have remembered had they been blue. Apparently they were ordinary. I remember him well, but the color of his eyes doesn't stick in my memory.

I can see Lenin now as if he were alive. By the way, he sometimes laughed merrily. Like a bell. Ha-ha-ha-ha-ha! A reverberating laugh. If he was in a good mood. . . . Yes, a reverberating laugh. He was not a jovial man, but neither was he sulky. He had a sense of humor. He was simply like a Russian in his relations with people. But I don't recall any idle conversations with him. He was like this in his personal life, too. At the same time he was a simple, sincere person. I had the chance to study him closely, of course. I can recall various moments, but it's hard to compose them systematically. At any rate, everything is clear now.

He always reminded us about danger. He assumed we could fall. Several times he wrote that even if we should fall, it could nonetheless be said that we had done everything possible. He was inspiring.

Stalin expressed himself more simply, you might say, more effectively. Suppose that the Entente was about to play some nasty tricks on us, that France was plotting. . . . Just wait until Stalin said something about that! From his pocket he would extract a letter from the Zaporozh Cossacks to the Turkish sultan. Stalin certainly was simpler and more closely connected with the upper echelon of the party. It was hard for Lenin, of course, mainly because he had unreliable friends and he was a different kind of personality. And his role, his place, and his situation were entirely different. You had to be very skillful in his situation. He was.

That's why he stood much higher than the rest of us, and in a different kind of situation . . .

An understanding of gaiety and even humor was characteristic of Lenin, rather than a sense of humor. He could react very irritably, to be sure. But the sound of his hearty laughter sticks in my memory. He was a man of colossal energy. He lived too briefly. There was not much of the German in him, but he was very meticulous and self-disciplined—devilishly self-disciplined! But he was of course rather more of a Russian.

Stalin used to say that if Lenin were alive today, surely he would speak differently—there is no doubt about that. He would surely think up something that has not yet occurred to us. But the fact that Stalin was his successor was very fortunate. Very fortunate indeed. Many revolutions have been crushed—in Germany, in Hungary . . . the Paris Commune in France. But we held on.

[12-7-76, 2-16-85]

■ The Last Years Were Complicated . . . ■

Stalin once took a dig at Lenin about his fanatical anti-liberalism. Lenin preferred to fight liberals rather than the Black Hundreds, the extreme reactionaries, about whom everything was clear. In a history of the party I too came across Lenin fulminating against Constitutional Democrats and "liquidators."

[2-29-80]

Is Lenin's testament his most important writing?
The testament is a secondary matter. Lenin had more important works.

[12-12-72]

The last years were distressing for Lenin. They were years of tremendous anxiety.

[5-9-85]

In February 1923 Lenin took a turn for the worse, and he asked Stalin to bring him some poison. Stalin didn't bring it, even though he had promised. He said later that Lenin probably bore a grudge toward him because of this. "Even if you insist, I cannot do it," Stalin said. The problem was discussed at the Politburo.

[12-12-72]

After Lenin, Stalin was the strongest politician. Lenin considered him the most reliable, the one whom you could count upon. But he criticized him, too.

[8-17-71]

Three

WITH STALIN

I n this section Molotov offers intimate details regarding Stalin and his entourage, collectivization, and the Great Terror (1936–1938) and repression that marked Stalin's reign.

The many authors of the "prison-camp literature"—Alexander Solzhenitsyn, Varlam Shalamov, Natalia Ginsberg, and Nadezhda Mandelstam, for example—have provided us with firsthand views from below, from the *Gulag* itself. Molotov, who directed the deportation of kulaks and with Stalin countersigned numerous, lengthy arrest and execution lists, gives us the picture from above. In a way it is no less horrifying. Under Stalin life at the top was nasty, brutish, and often short. The higher one rose in the Stalinist system, the higher the degree of insecurity and peril to one's life. No one was safe. Not even Molotov. Apparently not even Stalin.

Having attained absolute power, Stalin trusted no one. He saw enemies and conspiracies everywhere. He subjected Politburo members to a strange loyalty test: he made them accomplices in the liquidation, imprisonment, or exile of close friends, colleagues, and even of family members. Of the twelve men who had served on the Politburo in Lenin's time, only Stalin, Molotov, and Kalinin, the communists' token peasant and titular chief of state, died a natural death. Of the thirty-three men who served on the Politburo between 1919 and 1938, fifteen were shot or perished in prison; two committed suicide; two were assassinated. The survivors fared none too well. The wife of Kalinin was arrested and exiled. Kaganovich's elder brother avoided arrest by suicide. Two of Mikoyan's sons were arrested and not released until after the war. Khrushchev's eldest son, a fighter pilot, was lost in action in 1943. Stalin had his widow arrested. The wife of Poskrebyshev, Stalin's private secretary, was shot. The widower continued to serve his master faithfully.

Death brushed Molotov. In 1940 the Central Committee voted to remove Molotov's wife Polina Semenovna Zhemchuzhina from candidate membership. Molotov did not vote against but abstained. Stalin's doubts regarding Molotov's loyalty mounted. Stalin demanded that Molotov separate from his wife. He did. Stalin insisted that Molotov divorce her. Because the good of the cause demanded it, the Molotovs divorced in 1948. Nevertheless, in February 1949 she was arrested and exiled. One month later Stalin replaced Molotov with Andrei Vyshinsky in the office of foreign minister. By 1952 Stalin was muttering that Molotov was an American spy. Molotov was not included in the reorganized Politburo of 1952; in all likelihood his life was saved only by Stalin's death in March 1953. Molotov's wife was returned to him the day after Stalin's funeral. Molotov was reappointed foreign minister, a post he held until removed by Khrushchev in June 1956.

One might sympathize with Molotov (and his wife) except for their both having defended to their dying day Stalin's and, by indirection, Molotov's most murderous policies and actions. De-Stalinization under Khrushchev revealed that most of the so-called enemies of the people repressed in Stalin's day were in fact innocent of all charges. Rehabilitation of the repressed—many if not most of them posthumous —was one reason, among others, that brought Molotov into conflict with Khrushchev. For Molotov insisted that these people had been guilty. If not guilty of an overt treasonous act, they were "guilty" of what they might to do in a future crisis! For example, right-wingers such as Marshal Tukhachevsky, in spite of themselves, were likely to betray the Soviet Union in the event of war. (A propos, Hitler remarked in April 1939 that the USSR "had recently butchered four thousand high-ranking officers" and could not wage war. In fact, Hitler underestimated the number "butchered" by a factor of ten. Latest assessments hold that in 1937–1938 some 38,679 Red Armymen and more than 3,000 naval commanders were ordered shot.) While the purge of the military proved largely responsible for the USSR nearly losing the war in the first six months, Molotov claimed that repression, having eliminated a potential "fifth column," proved instrumental in the Soviet victory.

True, Molotov conceded that in the terror some mistakes and "excesses" had been committed owing to the haste required by the looming threat of war. But he also imputed the "abuses" to the nefarious work of enemies within the security agencies. Molotov defended the terror *en bloc*. He even defended the arrest and punishment of widows, wives, children, and other family members of the accused—they had to be put away lest they make trouble over the arrest of a loved one! Indeed, Molotov complained that the terror had not gone far enough. After all, it failed to purge incipient or covert right-wingers such as Khrushchev and Mikoyan.

And Stalin? Molotov concedes that Stalin in his final years was becoming "sickly suspicious," an understandable observation inasmuch as Molotov's master had turned against him and had set the stage for a new blood purge. Moreover, Molotov observes that Stalin, having borne the burden of power too long, was afflicted with a "persecution complex." Stalin feared that assassins would poison his food. Despite failing health, he refused medical care, fearing that doctors might poison him. Molotov wonders with good reason whether Stalin really died a natural death. Shortly before Beria was liquidated by his fearful colleagues, he took credit for Stalin's death. He confided to Molotov that he had "saved them all," implying that he had killed Stalin or at least seen to it that the stricken Stalin did not receive adequate and timely medical attention.

Chuev, who since childhood had idolized Stalin and Molotov, nevertheless put some probing and embarrassing questions to Molotov. Molotov complains that Lenin and Stalin were often confronted by oppositions that constituted a majority. Chuev asked, why should the majority submit to the minority? Molotov replied that the majority is not always right while Lenin and Stalin, as true Marxists, were virtually infallible. A Lenin or Stalin minority was "correct"; an opposition majority was "incorrect." When outnumbered in the Politburo or Central Committee, Lenin, by political maneuver, and Stalin, by terror, reduced or eliminated the errant majority piecemeal to create a "correct" majority. Chuev asked, is that why every Soviet head of government between Lenin and Kosygin had been shot (Rykov) or removed in disgrace (Malenkov, Bulganin, and Khrushchev) or subsequently disgraced (Stalin and Molotov)?

Molotov defended this political history: the obloquy heaped on Stalin and himself resulted from the triumph of a new majority of right-wingers exemplified by Khrushchev. Molotov derived the axiom of his political arithmetic from the two brief notes he received from Lenin in March 1922. Lenin contended that "the proletarian character" of the party was being endangered by the "small-proprietor elements" flooding into it. He admitted that "the proletarian policy of the party [was] not determined by the character of its membership, but by the enormous undivided prestige enjoyed by the small group which might be called the Old Guard of the party." In Molotov's interpretation of Lenin, only a "small group" of comrades around Lenin, and later around Stalin, were keepers of the flame, guardians of the true faith. And they were under constant danger of being swamped by comrades who reflected the class interests of the country's majority, the peasants and other small-holding proprietors. According to Molotov, this petty bourgeoisie animated every opposition group since Lenin and finally triumphed with Khrushchev.

Molotov in effect argued that by 1938, of Lenin's "Old Guard" only Stalin and he carried on the true Leninist proletarian faith; all except tried-and-true Stalinists—and many of these proved to be "double-dealers"—had turned into conduits of "petty bourgeois," "philistinic," "vulgar," peasant ideology and had to go. So much for the Trotskyist left wing and Bukharinist right wing, and all other oppositions. By eliminating these elements, Stalin's terror had saved the cause of "socialism." And Molotov called this "science."

The failure of socialist agriculture was a continuing problem for Lenin's heirs. They fought a life-and-death struggle over the ambiguous legacy of Lenin's last observations on the peasantry. Lenin had declared that the kulaks were the last exploiting class remaining in the country. But he also warned the party against employing violence to compel the mass of the peasantry to form and enter socialist farms. Four preconditions had to be fulfilled under the New Economic Policy to foster socialization of agriculture. First, return the market system to agriculture in order quickly to restore agricultural output to prewar levels. Second, make the country a mass producer of tractors and farm machinery, so as to switch the village to large-scale, mechanized, scientific, socialized farming. Third, create a network of highly productive model socialist farms throughout the country, whose successful example would inspire the peasantry to join up. And fourth, encourage the development of cooperatives as the peasants' stepping-stones to full socialist farming.

Bukharin, who was Stalin's idea man until 1928, elaborated on Lenin's "behests." Bukharin reasoned that in applying market and other economic levers, the Soviet government could edge the peasantry, gradually and peacefully, into socialist farms. Cooperatives were the key. The government would, by offering economic incentives, induce the peasantry to produce great surpluses on their puny plots (Bukharin to the peasants in 1925: "Enrich yourselves!"). Peasants would be encouraged to form elementary cooperatives: consumer, credit, seed, marketing, machine purchasing, and so forth, and move to joint tilling associations. Step by step the peasants would find it advantageous to move to ever higher degrees of cooperation until they reached the point where they would flock to socialist farms where all steps in the farming process would be carried out on a mechanized, scientific, large-scale production basis. Thus the peasantry would be weaned from their

primordial way of life to modern socialist farms without violence or
great shocks.

This was the agricultural policy the Stalin leadership pursued until
1928–1929, with strong support from Bukharin, which helped defeat
the Trotskyist "antipeasant" left-wing opposition. (Trotsky parried by
dubbing Stalin "king of the kulaks.") While the prewar level of grain
production had been attained by 1927, the major cities were beginning
to experience bread shortages. Peasants were withholding grain from
market in response to unfavorable terms of trade with the city. Stalin,
however, attributed the shortages to a conspiracy hatched by kulaks to
bring down the Soviet government. With Molotov in the lead, Stalin
launched a return to compulsory grain requisitioning, "extorting grain,"
to feed the cities and the army and to pay for imports of machinery
and equipment required for the crash program of industrialization.
Then in 1929, under the first Five-Year Plan, Stalin suddenly called
for "the liquidation of the kulaks as a class" and the total
collectivization of the peasantry, despite the shortage of tractors and
farm machines and a virtual absence of flourishing model socialist
farms. Stalinist propaganda had it that poor and even middle peasants
were rushing voluntarily into newly created socialist farms. In fact,
ordinary peasants joined the collective lest they be labeled "kulaks."

Bukharin, Rykov, and Tomsky broke with Stalin over his sudden
resort to massive violence against the peasantry. They denounced "total
collectivization" as an impermissible departure from the Leninist policy
of gradual, nonviolent collectivization of the peasantry. While Stalin
veered sharply to the left of the course he had held with Bukharin,
he now stigmatized the oppositionists, his former allies against Trotsky,
as "right-wing deviationists."

It can surely be argued that the position of the right, which Stalin
and Molotov professed until 1928–1929, was more consistent with
Lenin than the subsequent U-turn they took in peasant policy.
Moreover, as Chuev suggests, continuation of this policy could have
precluded collectivization's enormous toll on life and liberty—and
with much better economic results. Molotov and Chuev agreed only that
the contemporary collective farm system was in great trouble, but they
disagreed on what to do about it. Molotov offers his solution in
the next section containing his final thoughts on what constitutes
"socialism."

■ "The Caucasian Lenin" ■

I learned about Stalin in a letter from Surin in 1910. Surin was a Socialist Revolutionary provocateur killed in the Revolution. We roomed next to each other in exile in Sol-Vychegodsk, Vologodsa province. I read my books, he read his. . . . I went to Vologda for my technical high school examinations and spent approximately a year in Vologda until the end of my exile. It was at this time that Surin, a man of worker origins, wrote to me from Sol-Vychegodsk: "Stalin has arrived here. He is a 'Caucasian Lenin.'" "A Caucasian Lenin"! He was famous even then, in 1910, as Stalin. One of his brochures, "Marxism and the National Question," is signed simply "Stalin."

Many people wonder who gave him this name.

No one. That's what he called himself. And I called myself Molotov. The same with Lenin. You assume an alias, you change an alias. Stalin is an industrial name, apparently chosen for the same reasons as mine—Bolshevik reasons.

[12-4-72]

When I left, Stalin took my place in exile. Our paths didn't cross, but we started a correspondence. We didn't become acquainted until we lived in the same flat. Then he won over a girlfriend of mine. Marusia made off with him.

[6-11-70]

Lenin was no taller than Stalin, but he was stockier. Later Stalin developed a slight paunch. . . .

[8-17-71]

What kind of eyes did Stalin have?
I think they were beautiful. They were dark brown.

[5-7-75]

There is a portrait in which you can see the pockmarks on Stalin's face. Supposedly Stalin said of this, "Artists are too observant."

Stalin used to say that local peasants had called him "Pockmarked Joe" when he was in exile in a Siberian village. He had pockmarks on his face, but you could barely notice them. You had to look closely. . . . Now that you mention it, I remember.

[8-24-71, 4-13-72, 11-4-78]

Recently I gave to the archives seventy-five of Stalin's letters to me during the twenties and thirties. They gave me photocopies. . . .

[6-11-70]

I first met Stalin in 1912, before the publication of *Pravda*. We spoke about some basic problems. He couldn't work on the newspaper because he had gone underground while I had legal status.

We met at a dentist, at a secret address in Porokhovoi. There was a Porokhovoi district in Saint Petersburg, on the Neva, where a gunpowder mill was located. Sverdlov and Stalin were at a meeting there. In 1911, after my first exile, I arrived in Petersburg. I visited Moscow for the first time the same year in December and stayed at a comrade's place for about a week. . . .

[7-9-71]

And how did Stalin rise so high?

"Thank God. It was the whole story of his life, the Revolution, the Civil War. . . . Of course, he deserved it.

At the VIth Party Congress he substituted for Lenin and delivered the political report. This was early August 1917, as I recall, before the October Revolution. The Central Committee had assigned him to deliver this report, but obviously under Lenin's orders. Stalin was the rapporteur at the congress that decided on armed uprising.

How did he work his way up? Look, he wrote a very good book on the national question. . . . He edited the first issue of *Pravda*. He published commentary in it, and later several articles.

[8-24-71]

Twice in my life I called Stalin a genius. Once it was in some sort of a welcoming speech which I didn't write, and it was signed by a group of us. Stalin got angry, ordered that it be deleted, and said, "How did you end up in this?" "I was supposed to be in it," I replied. "Are you following everyone else, too?"

The second time was at his funeral.

I don't consider him a genius, but I think he was a great person.
I called him great at his seventieth birthday. He was close to a genius in
tactics; in theory and strategy he was weaker. In our party I consider
Lenin alone to be a genius. Stalin used to say, "Molotov can still restrain
himself, so can Malenkov, but others, Socialist Revolutionaries, cry
openly: 'Stalin, Stalin!' You see, only Socialist Revolutionaries talk this
way!"

Did he speak like that?

Sure he did.

Then why didn't he do anything about it? If he had wanted to . . .

He certainly didn't want to quash it completely. He couldn't. It could
have created problems at the time. Stalin did not entirely like this
adulation, but finally he came to enjoy it a bit.

[2-3-72, 6-16-77]

*At the office of the Central Committee of the Communist party, I was
told that Lenin did not nominate Stalin to the post of general secretary.
Rather, Kamenev did, and Lenin approved it. The comrade with whom I
chatted said that Stalin's election to the post is a mystery, a great secret
known only to one person—but he won't tell anyone. That person is
Molotov.*

Well, well. I know for sure that Lenin nominated him.

[12-4-73]

*The talk switched to Trotsky, and about Stalin's assessment of his
activity in the article "The October Revolution." It turned out that a
whole paragraph had been omitted from Stalin's collected works. Molotov
brought his own volume, in which he had written in the margin what had
appeared in Stalin's original version—how Trotsky managed to win over
the Petrograd garrison. It appears sometimes they also edited Stalin.*

*That Stalin himself had been a very skillful editor I determined after
leafing through a volume of* The History of the Civil War *containing
Stalin's marginal notes. He had sometimes replaced entire paragraphs
with a telling phrase. . . .*

[12-6-69]

*They say that Stalin replaced the Central Committee with a bureau-
cratic apparatus, and that after Lenin's death he won power with the help
of this apparatus.*

But who would have led better?

*They say that Stalin deprived the worker of participation in govern-
ment, liquidated the Workers' and Peasants' Inspectorate, eliminated
party oversight, and reduced the working class to drunkenness.*

Well, this is simply stupid. About the Workers' and Peasants' Inspectorate, did it do anything special? No. It wasn't dissolved, it passed
through all kinds of reorganization. We tried to adapt it to new
conditions, but nothing effective came of it then just as nothing comes
of it even now. At first it was the Workers' and Peasants' Inspectorate. It
was not liquidated, it was modified and later improved. Sergo headed it
up. Kuibishev was involved. They tried in every way to improve it. But
the best workers could not be channeled into it because we needed them
at other assignments. They would get one or two first-rate workers, but
the rest, like it or not, were picked from second-raters, because people
closest to the party had to be appointed to leadership positions in the
party and state. But what could these second-raters do that was special?
Nothing more than what the main party organizations were already
doing. They just helped a little.

So we searched for new strategies. As I recall, the Workers' and
Peasants' Inspectorate was renamed the Commission of Party and Soviet
Control sometime in the early 1930s. Then it became just the Commission of Soviet Control. Then a ministry was formed. All of this was
an attempt to better it. At one time it was still party and state
control.

One time you were also the head of . . .

I was the head of Soviet Control. There was no Party Control at the
time. All these efforts were aimed at somehow forming a more effective
party organization. Lenin attached great importance to it, but it didn't
work. Why? I suppose Lenin thought that in those difficult days, when
the party was falling apart, the Workers' and Peasants' Inspectorate would
consist of devoted workers who would react properly in case of a
split. . . . None of these reorganizations worked. Meanwhile the party
matured and gained strength.

■ Stalin Wrote Everything Himself ■

Stalin had a very good knowledge of antiquity and mythology. It was a
strong point of his. He worked very hard to improve himself. . . . Politics?
He worked on politics all his life. . . . He spoke in a rather quiet voice,

but if there were acoustical problems... He didn't like to speak fast. He spoke deliberately but at the same time quite artfully.

Sometimes he accented the wrong syllable, but very rarely.

[8-15-72]

Stalin spoke good Russian, didn't he?

Yes. He gave very good speeches. He read a great deal and had an artistic sense....

He wrote everything himself. The staff never wrote for him. This was a Leninist tradition. Zinoviev wrote for himself, Kamenev too, not to mention Trotsky.

Molotov wrote for himself.

He has seen everything and there's nothing for him to learn in this regard. Sometimes I dream that tomorrow I must make a report but I'm not prepared. Back then we all did our own writing.

[7-28-71, 8-17-71, 6-16-77]

I have heard it said that the History of the Communist Party of the Soviet Union (Bolsheviks): Short Course *was written by Yaroslavsky....*

That can't be. But it wasn't written by Stalin. And he didn't say that he wrote it. He read to us only one chapter, the one on philosophy....

[10-16-80]

Stalin himself admits that he made a mistake in advocating that land be divided among the peasants rather than nationalized. He told Lenin we were not ready for nationalization....

He meant that land had not yet been nationalized in a single country in the world....

[10-4-72]

■   Trotskyist Tricks   ■

This is what they write about Stalin in the West...

Go ahead, read it.

In 1928–1929 Stalin took up the Trotskyist program of superindustrialization....

These are typical Trotskyist tricks. The right accused us of supporting Trotskyist positions. They distorted the truth: "You accuse us of being right-wingers because you're Trotskyists." We were accused of Trotskyism.

Trotsky and Piatakov, his representative for economic affairs, and later Zinoviev, who in this matter joined with Trotsky, raised this objection: what kind of socialism is possible with the middle peasants? This is petty bourgeois socialism. But Lenin used to say that we should deal cautiously and patiently with the peasants. He taught that we must preserve the worker-peasant alliance as the only way out of the impasse. There was no support from abroad, no international revolution. The workers in the West were weak, communistically speaking. They could not play a large role. They could stay the hand of the imperialists but could render us no direct help. In that period the only ones we could rely on were the peasants.

Under Lenin and in the first years after Lenin, I was entrusted with the commission on work in the village. There I maneuvered with the peasants so that they would live in keeping with the interests of the New Economic Policy. Since they had been given an opportunity to trade, we wanted them to go ahead and trade. That began to reassure them. At the same time you had to squeeze the kulaks, to take everything possible from them in order to feed the working class. "Your policy is oriented on the middle peasant," Trotskyists would say. We should be aiming at industrialization. More means must be allocated to industry. At whose expense? Take it from the peasants. . . . As though we had no Marxist, proletarian policy but rather a pro-muzhik, pro-kulak one. They accused us, and Stalin above all, as responsible for this: "You are pursuing an irresponsible policy rather than an industrialization policy. Accelerated industrialization is imperative, but you tell us to wait." During all of 1923 and early 1924 the Trotskyists kept up the pressure. They claimed we devoted too little attention to industrialization, and that we needed to industrialize as rapidly as possible or perish.

We said, no, we will not perish! We will not perish if we don't fall out with the peasant. But we had to tighten our grip on the kulak. We clamped down on the kulak and the NEPman; at the same time we tightened labor discipline and slashed administrative costs. We squeezed out monies wherever we could—every ruble and kopek—to fund the revival of industry, even if only modestly. Yet the Trotskyists said, "This is intolerable! We are driving the cause of socialism to ruin!"

The point was to lay the foundation for industrialization. The Trotskyists had earlier proposed industrialization, but only in words. It was still impossible to get funds from the muzhik [peasant]. The muzhik had not yet recovered economically.

But in fact you took the same route, only later, didn't you?

In fact we did not take this route. They only babbled about industrialization, but we laid the foundation and began to carry it out with due care. This, it seems to me, distinguishes our industrialization from Trotskyist "superindustrialization," babbling about industrialization which accomplishes nothing.

Only after we had laid the foundation did we step up the pace of industrialization. Lenin directed our policy in the same way. He used to say that Trotsky held an absurd position—without a tsar and under a workers' government. What kind of revolution was this? To overthrow tsarism and shift immediately to a proletarian revolution? To Lenin that was nonsense and sure to fail. Instead we had to pass through all the stages of the democratic path to arrive at socialist revolution. He proposed that we form a revolutionary democratic government with the participation of the peasantry, and only when it no longer moved forward, had exhausted its revolutionary potential, would we move on to proletarian revolution.

Stalin proceeded in just that way. He believed that if you began instant industrialization without preparations, it would fail. Superindustrialization is just babbling. In fact you, the Trotskyist, are not for industrialization because you do not believe in the possibility of alliance with the peasantry. You believe only in the revolutionary potential of the Western worker; but he is in no hurry. You do not believe in the revolutionary potential of our people and so push us into risky adventurism, the pernicious policy of superindustrialization.

But when we prepared and got started, they found themselves overtaken by events: ah, you're doing it the wrong way, making mistakes, you're pushing too hard. Then right-wingers began to accuse us of following a policy of superindustrialization. Both Trotskyists and right-wingers were of course wrong. They were engaged only in word play—verbal industrialization. When we were duly prepared, we set about industrialization in a way the Trotskyists could not.

Preobrazhensky, an eminent Trotskyist, after he was readmitted to the party, confessed in *Pravda* that Stalin and his group had so successfully pursued the industrialization policy that the Trotskyists had been shaking in their boots. None of them could have done it this way. They spoke for industrialization but in fact were against using the support of the muzhik to prepare for it. "We may fail, but still we are for world revolution!" These were empty words. I don't know whether I have made this clear to you.

Still, was the Trotsky plan used?

No, by no means. The point is that he lacked faith in our people. He said, "We'd rather go down with revolutionary colors flying. We shall be true revolutionaries!" This was only a verbal smokescreen.

This debate was held on a razor's edge—you had to walk on it without falling to the left or the right, and you had to gain time and not lose your way. But Trotsky was incapable of this. He did not believe in it because his adventurism was dearer to him than the tried-and-true Leninist course. Nothing will come of it, he used to say.

In any case, it was impossible to accomplish anything without the peasants. But Trotsky did not simply propose to build socialism at the expense of the peasant. The essence of his view is that he did not believe in the possibility of an alliance with the peasantry, a worker-peasant alliance, for the building of socialism. That's the main thing. At the expense of the peasant—all of us agreed on that, because the workers were already giving everything they had. We had already taken everything from the bourgeoisie. The workers found themselves in very difficult straits and yet worked well, fulfilled their duty. There was no longer a bourgeoisie or landlord class. Only the peasantry remained from whom we could take something so as to move forward. The point, then, is not whether we should move forward at the expense of the peasant, but in the fact that Trotsky did not believe in the possibility of a worker-peasant alliance in order to move forward. But we believed in it.

[12-12-72]

Trotsky said that a socialist revolution is a workers' revolution. Every Marxist says that. Trotsky was not so foolish as to put himself in a highly vulnerable position. So he would say: all of you recognize that socialism can be built only by the working class. What role will the peasantry play? If the peasantry would follow the working class . . . But it can't because its majority is petty bourgeois! That is why we must set a course on socialism as far as the working class will be able to support us. But since the way is blocked by a peasantry that does not understand socialism, we cannot triumph in Russia under those circumstances unless we are supported by the workers in the West. They in fact will begin the building of socialism there while we trail along behind them.

According to this line, we had nowhere to turn. We had to give up, because we could not win without the peasantry—but they were against socialism. And there was no revolution in the West.

Lenin was right. We couldn't do without the peasant. We had to adapt our policy toward the peasantry. But within the peasantry the kulak, the well-to-do, too, were the strongest. What could the poor peasantry give? That meant we had to make concessions in some measure to the well-to-do peasantry. Lenin says it all clearly and well—there's no tripping him up: we understand an alliance with the peasants in the sense that the peasants support a dictatorship of the proletariat. At the time the middle peasant was to some extent neutral. But the poor peasantry, Lenin believed, could for the most part follow the working class. Herein lies Lenin's strength. It's no good waiting for the West.

At first socialism in one country, taken separately, but this does not mean this is sufficient to enable it to hold out. But if you proceed so: socialism at first in one country, followed by the building of socialism in other countries...

Trotsky's denial of this was chicanery. Had we followed him we would have had to stand by helplessly. Lenin had been reproached for, and Trotsky himself wrote that Lenin was in fact, pursuing Trotsky's policy of "permanent revolution." Actually, according to Lenin, the February Revolution triumphed, and the next one would be the socialist revolution. All of us were taken aback at that time when, as it were, events unfolded as Trotsky had projected. But Lenin's view, by its very nature, was quite different from Trotsky's. Lenin relied on the peasantry, lending the idea of revolutionary stages a different meaning. Stalin too had this difference with Trotsky.

The difference is that Trotsky did not believe in the cause of socialism. He said, let's try it, but we will fail. If we are not supported by revolution in the Western countries, nothing will come of it in our country.

But Stalin set about the task and boldly brought the idea to life!

Stalin, by and large, knew how to utilize both Trotskyists and rightists; nevertheless, when necessary he made the chips fly. . . .

From many persons. . . .

[7-28-71, 4-27-73]

■   **Allilueva's Death**   ■

What kind of person was Allilueva? They say she was not quite normal.

She looked sane enough. Nerves and so forth—that could be. But you couldn't consider her abnormal. Needless to say, her suicide had a bad effect.

Why did she shoot herself? Was Stalin treating her that badly?
He wasn't treating her badly, but there may have been some jealousy.
Was he unfaithful to her? Someone at work . . .
He wasn't unfaithful, but a person like her could be influenced. . . .
People keep talking about a letter she left. They say that besides Stalin, only Molotov read it.
A letter she left? First I've heard about it. Mmm, what things people think up.

[7-17-75]

Jealousy is the most probable cause of Allilueva's death.
Of course, jealousy. But to me, she had no reason for it. There was a lady barber to whom he used to go for a shave. That displeased his wife. A very jealous person. Why? She was so young. . . .

We had a big party at Voroshilov's place after the November 7 celebration in 1932. Stalin made a tiny ball of bread and, in front of everyone, threw it at Egorov's wife. I saw this but paid no attention to it. Perhaps this played a part.

I think Allilueva was a bit psychopathic at the time. This had such an effect on her that she couldn't control herself. She left the party with my wife, Polina Semenovna. They took a walk around the Kremlin. It was late at night, and she complained to my wife that she didn't like this, didn't like that. . . . About the lady barber. . . . Why Stalin had flirted at the party. . . . In fact he had drunk a bit, it was simply a joke, nothing special. But this troubled her.

She was jealous of him. Gypsy blood. She shot herself that night. Polina Semenovna condemned her act. She would say, "Nadia was wrong. She left him at such a difficult time!"

What do I remember? Stalin picked up the pistol she had used and said it was a toy, that it was fired only once a year. It was a gift. I think a brother-in-law gave it to her. . . .

"I was a bad husband. I had no time to take her to the movies," Stalin said.

People started a rumor that he had killed her. I had never seen him cry, but at Allilueva's coffin I saw tears running down his cheeks. . . .

[7-9-71, 11-4-78]

Stalin had a dacha called Blizhniya. There was also Dalniya, which we rarely visited. There was a third one too, which had belonged to a prerevolutionary engineer—it was on a lake and was called Sokolovka.

Bukharin would visit Stalin and Allilueva, that's certain. He was a very sociable, intellectual, and kind person. But I doubt she would have been attracted to Bukharin rather than Stalin. It's unlikely. She loved Stalin very much. That's a fact. But the truth is that she wasn't quite balanced.

Svetlana Allilueva writes that Beria came to Stalin in 1942 and insisted on the execution of Alesha Svanidze, who had earlier been convicted and imprisoned for five years. And Stalin airily agreed. Why was it necessary?

This was unfortunate.... Alesha Svanidze was quite a liberal, a European. He doted on the West. Stalin sensed this, and when the occasion arose (Alesha had passed some remark), Stalin made a harsh decision. Beria might have played up to him....

Svetlana writes that Nadezhda Sergeevna had left a letter which said, "Father might think that Mother had been with him only for show!"

She was, of course, easily swayed. She was influenced by Bukharin to some extent. Abel Enukidze... he had a brother. I have forgotten his name. He was a swarthy one. He was called Cain.... Enukidze was a right-winger, a Bukharinist. It's unlikely that he understood much, because he held on to superficial ideas for quite a long time.

She writes, "Father approached the coffin for a minute, then he suddenly turned away and left. And he didn't attend the funeral."

No, nothing of the kind occurred, nothing. I remember this well. Stalin approached her coffin at the moment of farewell, his eyes filled with tears. And he said so sadly, "I didn't save her." I heard that and remembered it: "I didn't save her."

Stalin was quite handsome. Women must have been enamored with him. He was successful.

Svetlana writes that he hated tears and didn't like cologne and perfume.

This could be. He was simple and liked cleanliness.

She writes that her father was loved by everyone—servants, body-guards. He treated people straightforwardly, demanded nothing special from the servants, always answered requests, helped people....

Yes, that's right. He arranged to have a lemon shrub [*citrus medica*] planted at his dacha. A big lemon shrub with a greenhouse especially built for it.... I never saw him digging around it. Everyone oohed and aahed at it. Frankly, I oohed and aahed less than others. I wondered, why the hell does he need that lemon shrub? A lemon shrub in Moscow! I do not understand the usefulness or interest it held for him. Was he conducting some kind of experiment? In the first place, expertise is required for that. Trying out some kinds of new methods?—for what? Relaxation? He suggested, "Let's build a second story on the dacha." I never visited it. I think Svetlana lived or visited there. Why the hell...

Akaki Ivanovich Mgeladze, former first secretary of the Central Committee of Georgia, told me about the lemon shrub. Stalin invited him to the dacha, cut a slice of lemon, and offered it to him. "Is it a good lemon?" "Very good, Comrade Stalin." "I grew it myself."

"We walked and talked. Stalin cut another slice. 'Here, try one more.' I had to eat it, to satisfy him. 'I grew it myself and, would you believe it, in Moscow!' Stalin said. We walked for a while and he offered another slice: 'Look, it grows even in Moscow!'"

When he couldn't eat any more lemons Mgeladze had an inspiration: "Comrade Stalin, I pledge that Georgia will provide the whole country with lemons!" And he set the deadline. "You've got it at last!" Stalin remarked.

[6-6-73, 10-21-82]

They say Stalin married Kaganovich's daughter?
This is from the White Guard newspapers. No, this is nonsense, of course, obvious nonsense.

[11-1-77]

■　　**He Regretted That He Had Agreed**　　■

Stalin regretted that he had agreed to become Generalissimo. He always regretted it. And that was right. Kaganovich and Beria overdid it. . . . Well, the commanders also insisted on it.

Kuznetsov writes . . .

He doesn't know the whole story. Stalin was opposed to it. He regretted it. "What do I need all this for?" Why would he need visible distinctions when he was famous in all respects! The military was one thing, but Stalin was a politician, the leader of the state. You see, Suvorov was neither a state nor a party figure! He needed that title. Stalin was the leader of the communist movement, of the building of socialism. He had no need for that title. No, he regretted this very much.

[12-30-73]

You have to keep in mind that there were many generals, but Stalin was the only generalissimo. Thereafter he would curse, "Why did I agree to that?" The leader of the party, the Soviet people, and the international communist movement, and only a generalissimo. This reduced rather than elevated his rank. He ranked much higher than that! A generalissimo is a specialist in military affairs. But he was a specialist in military *and* party matters *and* foreign affairs. Twice they tried to give him that rank. He rejected the first attempt, then agreed and came to regret it.

[5-7-75, 6-16-77]

A writer, V. V. Karpov, begged me to arrange a meeting with Molotov, and he agreed. Karpov said he was about to write a novel, "Generalissimo Stalin." "I want to write truthfully about Stalin. And to write truthfully about him means to write positively."

Bear in mind that Stalin was a very complicated figure. Sympathy is not enough. It's useful, of course, and you cannot write without it, but he had personal characteristics that require an understanding of the times. And in any event, you can't show him only as a military leader. He was mainly a politician. He played a great historic role in the affairs of the nation. It's being hushed up now. The riffraff do their job, that's for sure.

The conversation turned to the award to Stalin, after the war, of the title of Hero of the Soviet Union. Stalin said he didn't deserve the title. It was conferred only on those who showed personal courage.

"I didn't display such courage," Stalin said.

He didn't take the medal. He was only pictured in portraits with it. The head of decorations presented a Gold Star of the Hero of the Soviet Union when Stalin died. It was placed on a cushion and carried at his funeral.

Stalin wore only one small star—the Hero of Socialist Labor. Sometimes I wore the Order of Lenin.

At one time there were persistent suggestions that Moscow be renamed the city of Stalin. Very persistent! I objected. Kaganovich proposed it. He said, "There's not only Leninism, there's Stalinism too!"

Stalin was outraged.

[6-16-77]

■ "I Knew Him Well" ■

What kind of person was Stalin socially?

A simple, very sociable person. He was a good comrade. I knew him well.

Did he like champagne?

Yes, he liked champagne. It was his favorite drink. He started with champagne. . . .

What wines did you drink with Stalin? Kindzmarauli?

Very rarely Kindzmarauli. That was . . .

Tsinandali?

No-o-o, red wines. I drank Tsigistavi. And when I didn't refill my glass, Beria would say, "Come on, drink like everyone does."

It was a dry wine, and everyone drank sweet wines. . . . What was it called? . . .

Khvanchkara?

No, we drank it rarely. We drank Odahaleshi quite often before the war.

"Tsolikauri?" Shota prompted.

Tsolikauri! Stalin drank little wine. He preferred a bit of brandy. With tea. . . .

Is it true that Stalin had wine labels typewritten, as Shtemenko alleges?

No, nothing of the kind. Perhaps something was accidentally. . .

Kalinin used to be a light drinker. But he was rarely in our company.

Khrushchev began drinking hard later. And Bulganin couldn't abstain from it at all. He was inclined toward alcoholism.

People say Beria never drank vodka.

Are you serious?! He always drank with us, for he always wanted to make a show in front of Stalin. He would never lag behind if Stalin said something. . . . He was a talented organizer but a cruel, merciless man. Malenkov was his friend, and Khrushchev stuck to them later. They were distinctive personalities, but they had something in common.

It seems to me that Beria didn't like to drink, though he had to do it quite often. Malenkov didn't like it either. Voroshilov—he liked it. Voroshilov always served pepper vodka.

Stalin didn't drink much, although he pushed others to do it. Apparently he considered it a useful way to test people, so that they would speak more frankly. He himself liked to drink only moderately. He got drunk very rarely, but when it happened he was merry and would always turn on the record player. He would put on various records. He had many. First of all, he liked Russian folk songs very much, then he used to put on some comic stuff, Georgian songs. . . . Very good records.

[4-13-72, 10-4-72, 1-8-74, 7-28-76, 10-14-83]

Did Stalin go to bed late?
Too late, I'd say. He worked long hours.
Neither you nor he had a private life.
We had one, but of course it was limited.

[1-8-74]

We ate Siberian fish rather often at Stalin's place. White salmon. They would cut it in slices, like cheese. It was a very nice fish, tasty.

There was something of the Siberian left in Stalin. He used to fish when he lived in Siberia, but generally he wasn't fond of it.

We ate fish a la Siberian—frozen, with garlic and vodka, and raw. No matter, it turned out very well, and we ate with pleasure. . . . We often ate turbots. Beria used to bring them.

Beria would also bring grits, corn, and, in particular, certain kinds of cheese. The cheese was very good, and we all would pounce on it. We were hungry. . . . There was no time for lunch, and you never knew whether you'd eat later or not. . . .

[5-12-76, 6-9-76]

Stalin wrote poetry. I translated a few verses of his. Here is one. I'll
read you my translation:
"He strolled from house to house,
 Like an aloof demon,
 And in a thoughtful song
 He conveyed the prophetic truth.
 Many were inspired
 By this golden melody,
 And people sighed,
 Thanking the singer.
 But then they came to their senses, staggered,
 Overcome with fear,
 They lifted a cup filled with poison
 Over the land
 And said, "Drink, damned one,

An undiluted fate,
We don't want the heavens' truth,
An earthly lie is easier for us."
This was written in 1896. He hadn't turned seventeen yet.

Stalin wrote poetry until he turned seventeen. That's when everyone writes poetry—it's traditional. He wrote good poetry.

Did Stalin know some German?

He had been to Europe. He understood it.

Did he understand what Ribbentrop was saying?

No, that he didn't understand. I didn't understand it either. In different conversations I am often asked, "How many languages do you speak?" I always reply, "Russian."

[1-8-74]

Stalin will be rehabilitated, needless to say.

[3-17-74]

Stalin had a great flair for technology, though he never made a special study of it. I never saw him with a technical book. But he delved into the reports he received from designers and from industrial plants. He read them attentively, compared them, and immediately detected their weak points and how to correct them.

Of course, Stalin was inclined to certain excesses. . . . But he had a flair for the new. And he was on good terms with designers: Ilyushin, Yakovlev. . . . I wouldn't say he had much aptitude for economics. For military science, yes. I too was on good terms with the army, air force, and navy ministers. Only Khrushchev experienced hostility. . . .

Stalin had an astounding capacity for work. . . . I know this for a fact. He had a thorough knowledge of what he needed and stuck to the point. And he considered a question in all its aspects. This was politically important. If the subject was cannons—then cannons; if tanks—then tanks; if the situation in Siberia—then the situation in Siberia; if British policy—then British policy. In short, all that a leader should keep within his ken.

On the other hand, it's worth remembering how he handled resolutions of the Council of Ministers and the Central Committee. The Council of Ministers sometimes passed a hundred resolutions a week. Poskrebyshev had all of them sent in a big package to the dacha for Stalin to sign. Packages would lie unopened at the dacha for months. But then they'd all be published over Stalin's signature. In our meetings he would inquire about these resolutions, what the problems had been. We'd have dinner, talk, argue, and compare notes. If they were not clear, the problems got sorted out. It was senseless for him to read all those resolutions. He simply would have become a bureaucrat. He wasn't in a position to read all that. And you know what questions were discussed—economic, military, political, cultural, and the devil knows what else. . . . All this came out in the name of the Council of Ministers, of which he was chairman. Everything was promulgated over his signature, yet all these packages of resolutions were thrown in a corner, unopened. You would go to the dacha and they would have been lying there for a month, and now there is a new pile. Lenin used to say, "This is published"—and he said this when there was ten times less paperwork. He would sign resolutions that he had not yet managed to read. "I don't read everything I sign. You must have confidence in your staff."

Stalin would ask, "Is it an important question?" "Yes, it's important." Then he would pore over it to the last comma. But it was, of course, impossible to know everything in order to approve a resolution on how much to give whom for this or that. So he had to trust his deputies, or the people's commissars and members of the Central Committee.

[11-23-71, 3-8-74, 1-14-75, 8-1-84]

Now the role of chairman of the Council of Ministers has been reduced, hasn't it?

Yes, it has. Under Stalin it wasn't so. It was written thus: "Chairman of the Council of Ministers and Secretary of the Central Committee of the CPSU, Stalin." For a time, when decrees were issued jointly by the Council of Ministers and the Central Committee, it was written this way: "Chairman of the Soviet of Peoples' Commissars (Sovnarkom) Molotov, Secretary of the Central Committee Stalin." That's the way it was printed. This is a Leninist rule. The result was somewhat embarrassing, because the decrees were usually signed this way: chairman, then secretary. Secretary was misinterpreted as indicating a kind of office manager, which was certainly awkward. As a solution, we began to sign on the same line: Chairman of Sovnarkom and Secretary of the Central Committee.

When I was appointed chairman of Sovnarkom, I asked to be released from the post of secretary of the Central Committee. Why? First, it was a burden. Second, new people ought to be promoted.

Stalin said, "All right." And Kaganovich was appointed second secretary. He was Stalin's deputy in the Central Committee. All in all, he was then the most prominent person in the Central Committee after Stalin and myself in Sovnarkom. Before Sovnarkom I was secretary of the Central Committee and of the Moscow City Committee at the same time.

Stalin was a very talented person, very resourceful. No one has proved better. We were like teenagers. I am of the old revolutionary school and came to bolshevism intellectually. He relied on me to a considerable degree. I studied everything, bore every burden laid upon me, and had no interests outside the cause. I was well trained but so overburdened with work! But I work rather slowly. Why slowly? Because I am apparently insufficiently prepared for a profound consideration of all these questions. That's why when I begin work I need a lot of time to really think things through. I don't commit big blunders, but this eats up time. Everything is clear, yet one must push on further, further, further.

But now I have time. I dig into everything from dawn to dusk. I now see things which began, unfortunately, back in Stalin's time and mine.

You said there was a vast distance between you and Stalin.

Of course.

After all, he was ten years older than you. . . .

Not only that. His role was different from mine. Stalin played a great, an extraordinary role. He guided, he was *the* leader. At first he resisted the cult of personality, but then he came to like it a bit. . . .

You can't compare me with him. After Lenin, no one person, not me, or Kalinin, or Dzerzhinsky, or anyone else could manage to do even a tenth of what Stalin accomplished. That's a fact. I criticize Stalin on certain questions of a quite significant theoretical character, but as a political leader he fulfilled a role which no one else could undertake.

But none of the members of the Politburo can be compared with you either.

Perhaps. All the same, one must conduct oneself properly, without conceit.

Of course, Stalin did not work alone. Around him he had gathered a rather strong group. Others would have messed up. Many of them were, of course, very able people, but at the pinnacle Stalin alone stood out. As regards personal qualities, he had a very strong character, dogged determination, clarity of mind that most lacked. There were some very good people, highly competent workers, but they lacked clarity. Dzerzhinsky was the best known. He, it would seem, was irreproachable. But at the time of the Brest treaty negotiations even Dzerzhinsky voted against Lenin when Lenin was in a tight spot. True, Lenin called the

treaty obscene, but without it we could not stand. Dzerzhinsky underestimated the situation. In 1921 Lenin spoke out on questions of the trade
union discussion.... Dzerzhinsky did not support him. In January 1921
Pravda published Lenin's article "The Crisis in the Party." A crisis in the
party, no less!... Lenin wrote that we had reached the point where we
had lost the confidence of the peasant, and without the peasantry the
country could not succeed. Lenin put the question point-blank. Even
then Dzerzhinsky, despite all his good, indeed remarkable qualities—he
is sometimes depicted as sickly sweet but I knew him very well personally
as did Stalin—and despite his boundless fidelity to the party, despite all
of his passion, did not quite understand the policy of the party.

In Stalin there were no such vacillations.

XVIIth Congress. Debates after Molotov's report...

Yes. This was the main question. The second five-year plan.... A
resolution was worked out at my dacha—we spent all night working,
Kuibishev, Mezhlauk, and me. Mezhlauk was then chairman of state
planning, and Kuibishev was people's commissar of heavy machine
building. Councils of the National Economy had already been abolished.

Mezhlauk was arrested in 1937.

Yes.

And Kuibishev is an honored man.

Well, Kalinin usually held a special position. He did not go out on a
limb but stuck with us. He always took the side of the Politburo.
Naturally that meant Stalin, above all, and me. All of us together—
including Mikoyan with certain reservations—were as one.

The most frenzied opposition came from the right, of whom the most
effective, of course, was Bukharin. Tomsky was venomous, I should say,
in certain questions, venomous. In matters of theory he was weak....

Anyway, I delivered the report. We worked out the appropriate
resolution. Stalin read it; then he summoned us and introduced some
amendments. The final text asserted: the main political task of the
second five-year plan was to carry out the liquidation of capitalist
elements in the country. The kulak class, it goes without saying, was
included among capitalist elements. The kulak class was referred to in
particular and the elimination of classes in general.

You went too far.

It was adopted, no one objected.

*"You did everything right," said Shota Ivanovich, "a bit prematurely,
but good. Well done, except for the premature death sentences on classes."*

About classes we were wrong. It could not be done! People were confused and did not focus on this.

I noted that all our prime ministers proved to be either enemies of the people, or antipartyists, or deviationists—all except Lenin.

Of course.

Lenin. Lenin was succeeded by Rykov. They shot him [1938]. You succeeded Rykov. They expelled you from the party [1957]. Then Stalin— the Cult of the Personality [1956]. Malenkov. Expelled, like you. After Malenkov, Bulganin. He too fell into your group.

Right.

After Bulganin—Khrushchev, voluntarism, subjectivism [1964]. After Khrushchev we now have Kosygin. We shall see, let us see. I have omitted none. But the state continued to develop, to proceed on the correct path?

Yes, the true, the correct path. . . . I was removed from the chairmanship in 1939 without any accusations. Stalin died, after which they accused me.

Stalin! The more they assail him, the higher he rises. A struggle is going on. They fail to see the greatness in Stalin. After Lenin there was no more persevering, more talented, greater man than Stalin! After the death of Lenin, no one understood the situation better than Stalin. I was always of that opinion and said so. To speak about him in such exaggerated language as did Kirov, I believe is incorrect: "There is not a single problem in our country that is resolved by anyone other than Stalin." This cannot be said even about Lenin. Stalin fulfilled his role, an exceptionally important, very difficult role.

Let us assume he made mistakes. But name someone who made fewer mistakes. Of all the people involved in historic events, who held the most correct position? Given all the shortcomings of the leadership of that time, he alone coped with the tasks then confronting the country.

I believe they do not comprehend what is positive in Stalin, and instead they stress what is negative. They don't want to correct Stalin's mistakes; instead they exploit these mistakes in order to discredit the entire party line.

Despite Stalin's mistakes, I see in him a great, an indispensable man! In his time there was no equal!

Stalin was probably aware of my critical opinion. True, I did not state it bluntly, but I did express some critical remarks that did not always please him. All the same, I do not know who was closer to Stalin than I. Khrushchev? Malenkov?

[2-3-72, 12-12-72, 7-17-75, 6-16-77, 7-22-81]

Marshal Vasilevsky said he never met anyone with as good a memory as Stalin's.

He had an exceptional memory.

[3-11-76]

You have been in the leadership all your life. . . .

I was very close to it. . . .

Did you know what the poverty line was? Sixty rubles a month was not enough for a worker. Did you know this?

Yes, I did. But what was the solution? We knew about it. We didn't need police spies, everyone knew. You would have had to be deaf not to know about it. We knew, but we were unable to do what should have been done. We knew, but the question of how to rectify the situation was very complex. It seems to me, however, that we knew by and large how to rectify the problem. We just didn't have the opportunity.

In my opinion, not everyone has yet found the way. But I think we found a quite promising way. Much remains to be fulfilled, but the imperialists still block us. As long as imperialism exists it will be very difficult for people to improve their lives. Defense capability and much else are needed. A lot has to be built. We are not guaranteed against a third world war, though it is not unavoidable. As long as imperialism exists, however, it is difficult to expect improvement. That's my opinion.

■ The Church of Christ ■

Many historical monuments were razed during the reconstruction of Moscow.

Which, for example?

The Church of Christ the Savior.

Oh.

It's a much-talked-about question now.

Really?

They say Kaganovich organized it.

They blame him? Really? This is too much. I don't recall whether I was chairman or just a member of this commission—a member surely. A decision was taken to replace the Church of Christ the Savior with a Palace of Soviets. I voted for it. But when Yofan, the architect—he was not a distinguished architect, but he managed to win the competition—showed us the design of the colossal edifice he had planned, I rejected it. I said, "I won't sign it." They began pressing me. Stalin said, "You have to sign." I knew that the very idea was nonsensical. I looked into certain criticisms of the project. It became clear to me that if the Palace of Soviets were located on the site of the church and topped off with a colossal statue of Lenin, the feet would be visible but not the head. How absurd! A statue of Lenin whose head and body would be invisible! Besides, there are frequent fogs. It was just stupidity on the part of the architect to set about such a project. I said, "I won't sign." Then Stalin and Voroshilov, who were members of the commission, insisted that I sign. I did.

But why was the church blown up? Couldn't you have found another place for the palace?

It was destroyed on purpose. Objections were raised. I, personally, did not object. . . . Why preserve a church in the center of the city? It wasn't a rare antiquity, we rationalized. A church in the very center of the city—that wasn't right for Soviet power.

You could have turned it into a museum.

That's right. But instead there's a swimming pool. It's nonsense! They say the church contained many real masterpieces.

Yes, it did. Individual articles, it appears, are still preserved. They are now scattered around, but in the church they had all been kept as a single collection. The names of Cavaliers of St. George had been inscribed. This was a glory of Russian arms.

We don't need churches in the center of Moscow. It's wrong.

But why blow it up? It was there, let it stand!

We did not hit upon an ideal solution. We couldn't leave it there, but blowing it up was not a good idea either. It wasn't worth it. I too believe this. And I took part in the discussion of this question. . . .

Why do they say it was Kaganovich who blew it up?

Kaganovich? . . . that's the anti-Semitic mind.

Then who . . . Stalin? He gave the order?

No. The Politburo adopted the resolution, and our commission approved it.

To blow it up?

Not to blow it up, but to remove it. Not to leave it there.

And why was it blown up?

I don't know. At the time, after all, it was all the same whether it was blown up or not.

It was so firm, so solid. Afterward they tried to lay the foundation of the palace, but it didn't work because of underground water.

I lose little sleep over that. I see no special value in it. There will be talk. Let them prattle on. Talk can't be avoided. The church had to be removed.

At that time many churches were destroyed. . . . The church could have been closed down. It's a pity they blew it up. They say it was beautiful. I never saw it.

You didn't?

It was before I was born. I was born in 1941, before the war.

Before the war? I don't recall. Surely not everything was right in this matter, but in my opinion resentments are not in order.

But why was it blown up?

What significance does blowing it up have? All the same, the church had to be removed from there.

There were works by Vasnetsov, frescoes . . .

That's fine for a museum, but in my opinion the church could not be preserved for that purpose.

The church was a work of art in itself.

Devil take it. . . .

No praying went on there. . . .

Well then, what was the church good for?

It could have been left standing like the Church of Vassily the Blessed. After all, Stalin saved it!

True enough. That church dated from a much earlier period while the other came from the nineteenth century. . . . Many years have passed, and of course some poor decisions were made. Today they appear to be mistakes, but they did not always look that way.

[12-9-82]

I read an article about Masons, their role and charter. I hadn't paid much attention to them before. Not only do they exist, they are very dangerous. We pay no attention to them and they grow stronger. They are adamantly against communism and for capitalism and religion. They have long existed in intelligentsia circles under various names. They sink rather deep roots among the masses of philistines and the petty bourgeoisie, and pull them into their ranks. . . . They operate quite flexibly and are very malicious, anticommunist. But they keep a low profile, otherwise it would be dangerous for them. Much about them is enigmatic.

There's a lot of talk about the Masons now. People say you can find Masons even in the Soviet Union.

Surely you can. Underground.

They say you too are a Mason.

I have been one for a long time, since 1906. *Molotov smiled.*

You joined the party in 1906. You were sixteen years old. In what month?

I don't recall. On my vacation I came to see my parents. It was summer.

Some think there are Masons even among communists.

This may be.

And they say Molotov was the chief Mason in the Politburo.

The chief Mason? Well, well, so I remained a communist but at the same time managed to be a Mason. Where do you dig up such "truths"?

Several of the presidents of France, the USA, and other countries were Masons. By analogy some people cite the names of certain of our former leaders. Khrushchev was not accepted, they say, because he was too dull-witted.

No, Khrushchev wasn't such a dullard. He was culturally deprived.

And they accepted you?

The things they think of! Our enemies often dreamed that World War II would find us unable to cope. We would lose without fail and communism would cease to exist, but it did not turn out that way. We strengthened our position and created a socialist camp. Herein lies Stalin's vast contribution.

Certain writers reason as follows: Russia is the kind of country that would have endured even if it had fallen under the Germans. What kind of victory is it when we lost 35 million people! Did we really win?

It is just that kind of talk that made victory difficult to achieve. The people who talk that way are animated by prejudice. Have they forgotten that Rus lay under the Tatar-Mongol yoke for three hundred years? And were it not for Stalin . . . Unthinking people speak this way. They are parroting someone else's words.

Furthermore: Molotov will have nothing new to tell you because he is impelled to justify his false point of view. By and large, you won't be able to draw anything out of him.

I do not believe that everything we did under Stalin was right. But the main thing we achieved gives us justifiable pride. Had we been conquered, we would have had to wait a long time for liberation.

Our system passed the test of war, as did our party and our peoples, above all the Russian people, whom Stalin called the most outstanding of all the nations making up the Soviet Union. This was not a manifestation of Great Russian chauvinism but an historical truth. Stalin had mastered the national question. He was correct in calling the Russian people the decisive force that broke the back of fascism. Like no one else, Stalin understood the great historical destiny and fateful mission of the Russian people—the destiny about which Dostoevsky wrote: the heart of Russia, more than that of any other nation, is predestined to be the universal, all-embracing humanitarian union of nations.

Marshal Golovanov told me that he had never met anyone who rooted more for the Russian people than Stalin.

There will be a Russia, and there will be a Soviet Union, and everything will turn out well. Not for nothing did Stalin study questions of linguistics. He believed that once the world-wide communist system had triumphed—and he did everything possible to bring this about—the world's main language, the language of international communication, would be the language of Pushkin and Lenin. . . . Do you read history books?

I have read Karamzin's History of the Russian State, published before the Revolution. Unfortunately it's out of print.

It's interesting, of course. But to know history solely à la Karamzin is bad. Diverse points of view are needed. But Karamzin loves only one, the Orthodox.

Yes. Nevertheless, Orthodoxy did serve Russia in a positive way.

Absolutely. I once had to speak before my staff at the Ministry of Foreign Affairs concerning an article or fable by Demian Bedny on this question. He contended that the Slavs had mindlessly been thrown into the Dnieper to be forcibly converted to Orthodoxy. He had to be cooled off, persuaded that Christianity had not been mindlessly imposed. It was a step taken toward the West, a step on our part, toward people we most needed in order to avoid making a lot of mistakes in relations with our neighbors. This move was useful for Russia, and it is pointless to maintain that it was stupid. Not all our pure communists, our Bolsheviks, understood this. Adoption of Orthodoxy was a political as well as a spiritual step in the interests of developing our country and our people. . . .

For that reason we turned to the West. The culture there was more highly developed, it seemed, the only one that could raise us up. Hence the turn to the West.

It must be noted that Stalin was not a member of the "League of

Militant Atheists." He was, of course, first and foremost a revolutionary, and he continued Lenin's anticlerical line.

Our generals have told me that before a battle Stalin's usual parting words were, "May God grant us victory!" or "May the Lord help us!" Moreover, the writer Vladimir Soloukhov, who served in the Kremlin during the war, said, "Josif Vissarionovich [Stalin] once appeared on the Church porch. At his left was the Patriarch Alexei, at the right..." "Surely, Molotov?" I asked. "The Metropolitan Krutitsky and Kolomensky," Soloukhov replied without batting an eye. Why are you laughing? Stalin respected priests. It was the influence of his seminary education....

Well, Soloukhov is exaggerating. True, we sometimes sang church songs, after dinner. Sometimes even White Guard songs. Stalin had a pleasing voice....

We have survived many vicissitudes. But now we stand on firm ground. Our historians and those who share their views commit certain stupidities. The main thing is that we passed the test of war, and victory has made us strong.

Of course, now and then we will still have to suffer hard times.

■   **Let Viacheslav Go to Work...**   ■

Recently we went to Stalin's former dacha, Blizhniya. We had a talk with the bodyguard who was on duty there the night Stalin fell ill. He told us: "Stalin went for a walk that evening. He asked a servant, 'Well, what's for dinner tonight?'"

Yes, yes.

"He entered his room and never came out."

Never came out.... I lived with Stalin in the same flat in the Kremlin, in the building that used to be where the new Palace of Congresses was erected. On rare occasions we visited one another of an evening. Years passed this way. I usually visited him at one of his dachas, more often, Blizhniya. Dalniya was out in Domodedovo district.

"What will become of you without me if there is a war?" he asked just after the war. "You take no interest in military affairs. No one takes such an interest or knows military affairs. What will become of you? The imperialists will strangle you."

There was a grain of truth in this reproach. Military affairs were of little interest to me. It should be said that in the 1930s and during the war Stalin was very much abreast of military affairs. Because one must not only know military affairs, one must also have a taste for them. He had that taste.

After the war Stalin intended to retire on pension. At table he said, "Let Viacheslav go to work now. He is younger."

He indulged in that kind of talk in small gatherings at his dacha. He said it without proposing a toast.

[10-1-72, 6-6-73]

Do you think Stalin ought to have retired after the war?

No, I do not. But he was, in my opinion, overexhausted. Some took advantage of this. They slipped things over on him and buttered him up. That's why he trusted Khrushchev and distrusted me.

Perhaps the post of honorary chairman of the party could have been reserved for him?

Perhaps, but not just honorary. . . .

But was he still capable of work?

Less and less, you see. He was chairman of the Council of Ministers of the USSR, and at the meetings of the council, Voznesensky, not he, chaired. After Voznesensky, Malenkov chaired inasmuch as I was busy with foreign affairs and in addition was not one of the first deputies. Or if I was, it was only on paper.

■   "We Are Russians..."   ■

"He loved Russia very much," said Shota Ivanovich. "I think I know why. He lived in Russia, in Siberia, he studied the civil war, visited farmsteads everywhere. He understood and loved the Russian people very much."

True, very much.

To rule Russia and not to love the Russian people...

The Germans do not.

We are Russians... Stalin spoke in the name of the Soviet people.

We, the Russians, are preeminent, but everything cannot be reduced to Russianness. Reality is more complex. One cannot regard only Russians as being good. Your poem about Stalin reads, "A Great Russian was this Georgian." This is a rather scathing phrase, and in my view it requires that something be added about internationalism and that Russianness not be emphasized. Russians alone would have done nothing, because Russians too have many defects. It cannot be otherwise.

But no one else thought up the socialist revolution. The Russians were the first ones to do so. Q.E.D.

They say the Jews made the Revolution, not the Russians.

Well, hardly anyone believes that. True, in the first Soviet government and in the Politburo, Jews constituted the majority.

Russians bestir themselves when Jews rouse them into action or an enemy attacks, then they close ranks.

[12-9-82]

After his expulsion, Bukharin changed families. He married a very beautiful young Jewish girl. (He was not allowed to live a high life.) His first wife was a Russian. Many of Stalin's men had Jewish wives: Voroshilov, Andreev, Rykov, Kirov, Kalinin.... There is an explanation. Oppositionist and revolutionary elements formed a higher percentage among Jews than among Russians. Insulted, injured, and oppressed, they were more versatile. They penetrated everywhere, so to speak. ...They were urban people; for centuries they had lived in cities. Life schooled them to become very active, unlike the typical Russian who first has to scratch his head....

Biding their time, they sniff around, stir things up, but are always prepared.

[4-13-72, 8-15-72, 4-27-73, 8-15-75]

Even earlier, the Americans stood at a higher level than we. They had no need to take a giant leap forward, but we did. And we were scarcely capable of this. We even had a shortage of manpower because we had to build so much more. Consequently the state took everything upon itself; there was no concern for the individual.

[9-30-81]

In 1918 Lenin wrote that the Russian is a poor worker. He called the country a small-holding, peasant country. To advance from an abysmally low level to a higher one we would need many more years than the more developed countries.

For us, ten or twenty years appeared an eternity. And how to rise from such a low base? The typical Russian—at first he is at the heights of enthusiasm, the next thing you know he is lying satisfied on the oven. Just try!

In 1918 we were in dire straits, but Lenin drew the right conclusions. We would have had sufficient manpower if it had been well organized. But good organization is precisely what we lacked.

The Japanese were well trained, but in our country insufficiently developed capitalism adversely affected socialism.

[9-30-81]

Stalin was people's commissar of nationalities and at the same time commissar of Rabkrin, the Workers' and Peasants' Inspectorate. Lenin instructed Rabkrin to investigate some mess. Stalin recounted that he went to Lenin and said, "I am setting up a commission of inquiry. I am appointing so and so to it." Lenin said to him, "Not a single Jew? No, nothing will come of it!"

How offensive to us Russians! To Lenin, too! Lenin used to say, "Russians are lazy!" and one sensed that he was terribly hurt by the fact that Russians actually *were* lazy. They don't finish what they start. "They are masters at chattering, at babbling. How to organize such . . . ?" "Idle chatter," was a favorite phrase of Lenin's.

[4-29-80]

In 1939, when Litvinov was dismissed, I began to work on foreign affairs. Stalin said to me, "Purge the ministry of Jews." Thank God for these words! Jews formed an absolute majority in the leadership and among the ambassadors. It wasn't good. Latvians and Jews . . . And each one drew a whole crowd of his people along with him. Moreover, they regarded my arrival in office with condescension and jeered at the measures I began to implement. . . .

Of course, Stalin was guarded where Jews were concerned. Nevertheless, the person most devoted to him was Kaganovich. Behind Kaganovich's back, Beria used to say, "Lazar, that Israelite . . ."

Stalin was not an anti-Semite, as he is sometimes portrayed. He appreciated many qualities in the Jewish people: capacity for hard work, group solidarity, and political activeness. Their political activeness is unquestionably higher than average. That's why they are passionate advocates at either extreme. Under conditions obtaining during the Khrushchev years, the second group came to the top. They bitterly hated Stalin.

All the same, in Russia there were Bolsheviks of a kind not to be found elsewhere in the country. One can be proud of them. One may spit on Russians when they behave badly, but there is something there to be proud of.

Russia saved the world several times, in spite of everything. . . .
And Russia robbed and strangled and was the jailhouse of peoples.

[11-23-71, 1-14-75, 7-17,75, 3-10-77]

Lenin saw Great Russian chauvinism as the main danger. I regard it as a great service on his part that he made communists aware of it.

The Russian people helped other peoples. That's true, but only half true. Other peoples were unable to begin to develop their capabilities until after the liquidation of Russian despotism and tsarism. Failure to see this means failure to see the main point. It must not be glossed over. If we, the Russians, do not talk about this, we shall forever have half-friends at our back.

After victory in 1945, Stalin said in his toast that the Russian people were the leading and directing force in the war.

No one can deny this; I too regard it as correct. He spoke about mind, patience, and character, but also about our mistakes. His approach was not uncritical. But, you see, the point is that this was a speech suited to a definite period. Overall it was inadequate.

For in order to achieve the Revolution, the Russians had to have a lasting alliance with other nations.

[12-12-72]

It is the USSR that runs things, not the RSFSR [Russian Soviet Federative Socialist Republic]. It began with the RSFSR, but to begin was not enough; the Revolution had to be broadened, made worldwide. Was this possible only by relying on the RSFSR? Without the world revolution, no victory. But it has been delayed.

The greatest pride of the Russian people is that it rose to head not only the USSR but worldwide development as well. This role must not be belittled; quite the contrary, we must show that we are struggling for the very greatest, world-historical goals. Without this, communism is impossible. We must consider this seriously.

The Russian communist cannot stand on the sidelines of the world revolution. He must take a broader view, fight for the world revolution. This must be explained, not concealed.

This does not diminish but heightens the significance of Russian socialism. Otherwise we will end up in the hands of swindlers.

[3-12-82]

After the Revolution the Bolsheviks succeeded in preserving a vast empire on the basis of the union.

Of course. This was an extremely complex task. . . . If a Leninist nationalities policy is not pursued now, republics might secede from us. We have colossal experience in this regard. Despite all difficulties, none has seceded, apart from those whom we permitted to secede, for example Poland, Finland, and—temporarily—the Baltic states. And this occurred thanks only to the fact that we pursued a policy that Lenin had thoroughly worked out and firmly implemented while criticizing those on the right and on the left, levelers and nihilists on the nationalities question. Piatakov, Bukharin, and others said that the national question no longer had significance. This was just a myopic, petty bourgeois, devil-may-care attitude. They believed that all problems boiled down to a question of social class, and that was it. But Lenin and Stalin understood perfectly well. It was none other than Lenin who made the appointment to one of the most important posts of the time, people's commissar of nationalities. He appointed Stalin to head up this ministry!

[12-12-72, 4-27-73]

Lenin strongly praised Stalin for his writings on the nationalities question and entrusted him with these difficult tasks. But at times Lenin also criticized him. Regarding Stalin and Dzerzhinsky, he said non-Russians are often more Russian than the Russians themselves. This was especially true of Stalin in his last years. Lenin didn't like it when non-Russians took Russian surnames. He used to say about such a person, "Won't he desert the Russian nation?" He thought that Russians, Ukrainians, and Belorussians should for the most part be entrusted to fill the highest positions.

[5-7-75, 7-17-75]

One must take into account the complexity of Stalin's character. . . . Concerning Russianness, he held that the government should be headed by a Russian. For a long time he refused to become chairman of Sovnarkom. At the end of the 1920s, just before I became head of Sovnarkom, I wrote to him the following, *inter alia*: it would be better if it were you. Rykov could no longer be left in that position; we want to appoint you. I was then working as secretary of the Central Committee. He was on vacation at Sochi. He answered by letter, saying that I must be appointed. I replied to him that, of course, it was not by chance that I was a member of the Politburo. If I am up to the position, if the people find me qualified, let it be so; but it would be better if you accepted this position. So it was in Lenin's day. Lenin in reality was both leader of the party and chairman of Sovnarkom. I was a kind of first secretary. Back then, however, this position exercised far less power than it later acquired. But under Lenin, after the Xth Congress when I became first secretary, Stalin was not in the Secretariat. He was a member of the Politburo and a member of the Orgburo. I also chaired in the Orgburo.

The letters between us were secret, conveyed by couriers and delivered by Cheka agents. When he was on vacation and I deputized for him and prepared materials for the Politburo, our correspondence was both personal and semiofficial.

Stalin used to say, "The horse thief does not say that I stole the horse but that the horse carried me off!"

[6-6-73]

In July 1978 we spoke about the unrest in Abkhazia and about the demands of the Abkhazians on the Georgians.

After the Revolution a definite part of the population there favored adopting English as the official state language.

[7-16-78]

How do you explain the forced resettlement of entire ethnic groups during the war?

Oh, so we have become wise after the event, have we? Now we know everything, anachronistically mix up events, squeeze time into a single point. Everything has its history. The fact is that during the war we received reports about mass treason. Battalions of Caucasians opposed us at the fronts and attacked us from the rear. It was a matter of life and death; there was no time to investigate the details. Of course innocents suffered. But I hold that given the circumstances, we acted correctly.

[4-22-70]

Why were the Kalmyks deported during the war?
They helped the Germans.
One writer told me you said that by 1943 Stalin had ceased to be a communist.
Nonsense! I wouldn't even think that, let alone say it about Stalin!
Stalin proposed in 1922 that all republics become part of the RSFSR on the basis of autonomy, which Lenin opposed. But then Stalin admitted his mistake and agreed to Lenin's proposal to form the USSR with all Soviet republics having equality.
The point is that Stalin in this instance continued Lenin's line. But

Lenin had moved beyond the solution he had advocated earlier and which Stalin knew well. Lenin then moved the question to a higher plane.

Lenin had opposed the federal principle, federalism, because he favored centralism. All the reins, everything must be held in the hands of the working class so as to strengthen the state. Just read his article on the national question. Autonomy within a unitary state, yes.

But Lenin suddenly dropped this unitary principle for a federal solution: "Let us create the Union of Soviet Socialist Republics!"

But Stalin did not know this at the outset.

[6-21-72]

The question of cosmopolitanism.... A group of writers with noms de plume were called "cosmopolitans." All of them were of Jewish origin. Rather harsh measures ensued. Many people ask about this....

The question is, of course, inescapable. Probably not everything about it was handled correctly. But there were also quite serious grounds for action.

In a number of republics, rather large groups of enemies of the Soviet state were revealed. Securing victory and minimizing casualties among those peoples who had already suffered colossal losses made ruthlessness a necessity. There is no contradiction here. No one mastered the national question, no one organized our national republics more sagaciously than Stalin. The formation of the Central Asian Republics was entirely his doing, a Stalinist cause! He skillfully mastered the matter of borders and the very discovery of entire nations. No one at the center had been interested in or really knew anything about these peoples, because all of us, including Lenin, had not gone into this matter and lacked the time. After all, a violent struggle was raging. The Kazaks, for example—their upper crust fought for Tashkent and wanted to make it their capital. Stalin gathered them together, discussed the matter, examined the borders, and declared, "Tashkent to the Uzbeks, Alma-Ata to the Kazaks."

He stood his ground, unshakable. Of course, Stalin took upon himself a burden that left him burned out in his last years. He seldom underwent medical treatment; he had his reasons for this. He had enemies more than enough. If anyone had poured oil onto the flames ... I think that if he had remained alive another year, I would not have survived. Nevertheless I regarded and still regard him as having accomplished colossal and difficult tasks that were beyond every one of us in the party at that time.

■   And Under Communism?   ■

Under communism will national characteristics remain?
No. They'll disappear.
That's too bad.
Why? We will enrich ourselves. You think the Germans or the French have no good qualities?
Then we will never have a new Pushkin, Tchaikovsky, or Surikov. It will be one international culture.
You can't limit your vision to what has already been created. It's time you learned to be more broad-minded. If you don't understand this you'll remain a narrow-minded, semicommunist Russian and nothing more. No one wants to take away your national identity, but you will advance to a higher stage. If you remain where you are you'll become a good poet of the Russian Federation but not of the USSR. Tvardovsky fights for Russian poetry, and he is the best Russian poet now. I remember him. He is very talented but narrow-minded. Like many of us he is limited to the Russian horizon where peasant life prevails—which Marx called the idiocy of the village. The peasants' limitations shade into idiocy. The peasant likes narrow horizons, be he Russian, Georgian, or German. I had a little book which I picked up somewhere after the war. It was the correspondence between Tchaikovsky and Taneev. Taneev admired Tchaikovsky's music and was proud of Russian culture. That's fine, said Tchaikovsky, but I also admire German, Italian, and French music. Wasn't he a nationalist? Very much so. But one doesn't limit oneself only to Russian. The most talented people never limit their field of vision. They add useful aspects from their neighbors' work. This is what's truly wonderful.

[12-12-72]

■   Merits and Demerits   ■

Does Stalin appear in your dreams?

Sometimes. In extraordinary situations. . . . In a destroyed city. . . I can't find a way out, and I meet him. In a word, very strange, confusing dreams.

[7-17-75, 6-30-76]

Stalin was not only an effective popularizer of Lenin's ideas. No, he introduced something new in Leninist theory, no question about that.

First, it should not be forgotten that even before the Revolution Lenin praised Stalin for his work on the national question and called him "the wonderful Georgian." In my time I read Stalin's booklet, a splendid booklet. It played, of course, an exceptional role in elucidating Marxist theory on the national question, which is of colossal significance.

In the later period I believe his greatest accomplishment was in collectivization. What kind of role? A very important one as concerns theory. Only Stalin, in contrast to Lenin, said, "Our way passes through the kolkhoz, the artel." Lenin did not and could not see this. You won't find it in Lenin. He wrote about TOZs [Associations for Joint Tilling of the Soil], artels [cooperatives], and agricultural communes, but mostly about the latter.

Stalin used to speak very amusingly about the time he spent in the Transcaucasus at the beginning of collectivization, when Sergo was still in the Transcaucasus Regional Committee—sometime in the late 1920s or perhaps the mid-1920s, I could be mistaken.

Sergo led Stalin to a commune: "Come on, I will show you how we manage things."

Stalin then quite artfully and kindheartedly recounted: "Sergo was ecstatic over the fact that he had a good commune. It really was good—strong. We visited it, and individual members of the commune told us how things were going with them, how their life was improving, and so forth. Then Sergo said to me, 'Don't ask about details, because you might uncover something. If you begin to delve, the commune may collapse.' 'But how can such a good commune collapse?' 'No, don't interfere,' he implored me. I examined the chairman, a very strong muzhik, an intelligent person, with a highly distinctive character. He was well organized, controlled everything himself. One sensed that with the slightest diminution of his authority, the commune would fly to pieces."

Stalin related how Sergo trembled for this chairman of the commune, how he did not want Stalin to ask questions. In fact, everything depended on this one person—the good organizer, the rugged, devoted comrade. In my opinion, this was for Stalin one of those important occasions when he saw for himself what a commune was really like. It apparently made a very deep impression on him. He issued a decree—and everyone supported it—which held that we now need artels, individual incentives, and mechanization. The principle of individual incentive—of course, only on a base of modern technology and supported by large-scale state power—could help.

Communes had been started in Siberia, primarily in the initial period of collectivization, in the late 1920s. In many large agricultural regions the secretaries of local party organizations thought that communes were the main hope for us. They drove the peasants into communes. That's why Rykov thought we had failed.

You see, communes were in Siberia and in certain of the large agricultural regions. Good leaders were there, devoted Bolsheviks; they strove to support communes.

I visited a commune in the Kursk region in 1924. They pooled their sheepskin coats in the same closet. They took turns wearing them.

In the West they raised a howl over communal practices [the rumor that women were common property].

The devil take the West. Stalin, just in time, grasped that we must set a course on artels and through the artels gradually move forward. I still think about this, and lately I think about it a lot, because I took a very active part in collectivization. Because of famine we tried to rally the peasant poor and the small-holding middle peasants, and thought the commune indispensable for this. Then, in the early 1930s, Stalin set a firm course on kolkhozes [collective farms] and, of course, on mechanization—mechanization at any cost. It was the correct solution.

But Lenin had said, "Create TOZs and communes." That was our theoretical preparation. Just examine Lenin's works. He speaks about uniting peasants, he speaks about communes which would benefit nearby peasants so they would come to believe in communes.

Rykov held to that position. He thought collectivization would fail.

That's right. But there was also the Bukharin point of view. It was allegedly based on Lenin's last articles on cooperatives. But the articles say nothing about communes, or artels, only about consumers' cooperatives!—so-called supply-purchasing cooperatives. Collectivization was a very big step forward for our work and for Marxism, because Lenin did not see this as the end but the starting point, while Bukharin charted a course that would pass through trade and through consumers' coopera- tives as the be-all and end-all. Stalin was right, because Lenin pro- pounded only the most general principles of cooperation—how we had to begin, and what was the clearest, simplest, and most accessible path for the peasant. Actually this was so. You see, for ten years we encouraged consumers' and supply-purchasing cooperatives. In the mat- ter of collectivization this question was of colossal difficulty and impor- tance. None of us had any experience with the muzhik; we were not closely linked with the muzhik. Communists were always closer to the workers, while the Socialist Revolutionaries were entrenched in the peasants. The SRs considered the peasant as strictly their affair. All the same, Stalin fixed the correct orientation on this question and carried it through well.

But this is just what they accuse Stalin of: Lenin, they say, would have carried it through more democratically. . . .

Well, the fact is that in Lenin the commune formulation was harsher, yes, harsher.

In his article "On Cooperation" (1923) he utters not a word about communes, not a word about artels; instead we must have cooperative trade. Of course we could not get along without that. But Lenin focused on the initial stage, pending world revolution. . . . The Bukharinists stopped there, at the starting point; Lenin regarded it as only the initial stage, the starting point. Lenin did not renounce the commune; he did not advance beyond it, but Stalin did. He boldly embarked on the path of artels. Lenin resolved the question as it stood at the first stage: by means of consumers' and supply-purchasing cooperatives, trading coop- eratives. On one hand they deal in consumer goods and on the other in machines; they sell the peasants' produce to the city, and purchase machines from the city for the peasants. But in the commune everything is lumped together in common. Stalin had stated in a report: our task is to make every peasant well off from the socialist point of view. Every family should have a cow; pigs and goats are permitted, but in limited quantity.

Furthermore, industrialization was Stalin's contribution. It began as early as 1924–1925. How? Stalin formulated the question correctly: industrialization by our own means, our own manpower. We could not rely on foreign loans. He charted a course on industrialization. But how to implement it? At the end of the 1920s and early 1930s his slogan was: technology is paramount, technology decides everything. After we had acquired technology—cadres decide everything. That was the second task. These were the stages of industrialization.

At the first stage, technology is decisive; at the second, it is cadres. We have only ourselves to rely on; let us with our own forces proceed. And Stalin inspired faith: faith is extremely valuable. By what means? Industrialization, come what may. In the first place, heavy industry and self-restriction on consumption.

Kirov once told how he was somewhere in the Saratov region at a meeting of a collective farm. One woman said, "Why did they bring us this tractor? It sputters and sputters and does nothing." Stalin was right, saying that we are fifty to a hundred years behind Western Europe, and if we do not close this gap in five to ten years we shall perish.

So there was the nationalities question, industrialization, collectivization, the war. One can include the war, for it's not theory but practice. Of course it's not only practice. Stalin made a profound study even of this field and synthesized a good deal. For example, he said, why have the Germans had the edge in this war? Because they are more advanced in their cadres, in culture, and have paid much attention to advanced artillery, the god of war. With regard to artillery, the Russians strove not to lag behind. They attached great significance to it but nonetheless did lag behind. In this war Hitler did not have really good artillery; he counted on blitzkrieg for victory. But Stalin had thoroughly worked out an analysis which concluded, no, you won't take Russia by blitzkrieg. The Soviet Union is a big country, the Soviet people are a big people. The Germans counted on a short war since they were well armed and well prepared. That's why they had not prepared powerful heavy artillery. They had the necessary tanks and airplanes. The Hitlerites thought that tanks and planes plus good infantry, which they had, would guarantee them victory. And maneuverability, of course. That's why they availed themselves of strike groups, especially tanks. They were skilled in striking concentrated blows. Wedge-shaped, powerful blows by tanks punched holes into our front through which they poured infantry.

Stalin transcended that. He not only employed all of this, he was also creating artillery armies. How to begin an offensive? First, start with a thorough aerial bombardment. Next, the artillery, long-range artillery, continues. Only after this come the tanks, and after the tanks, the infantry. Stalin profoundly worked out the four stages in the development of an offensive. I don't know whether the Germans had artillery armies. Such massing of artillery will break through any front. We applied it, in any case, at division strength. Massed artillery at army strength was still at the talking stage. But it was under way.

In the first months of the war—and in my opinion even before the war—Stalin noted that our commanders did not know how to command all types of troops simultaneously. I do not see this denied anywhere by our military.

He set about training a new type of commander who mastered the command of all types of troops. As far back as the early 1930s he said to Marshal Budenny, "Isn't it time to consign the *tachanka* [wheeled machine gun] to the museum?" The cavalry had to be utilized effectively, with minimum losses and maximum results. Our commanders did not understand this. Not to mention people's commissar of defense Marshal Voroshilov.

Stalin was not a military man. Nevertheless he coped ably with the leadership of the armed forces. Ably. There was no people's commissar heading the air force but Stalin. The navy, led by Stalin, and the artillery, led by Stalin. Mistakes were committed, that's inevitable, but everything moved forward. The forging of a new military technology proceeded at his initiative. Scarcely anyone knows this.

[11-4-76]

Golovanov, in his memoirs, writes that Stalin, and not the marshal of artillery Voronov, determined the main thrust of artillery at Stalingrad.

That's right. Golovanov couldn't know everything, but this is correct.

[2-18-77]

■   **About the Constitution**   ■

The constitution of the USSR [1936] was entirely the creation of Stalin. He supervised and directed the drafting. It was worked out according to his plan under his direct, continuous leadership.

[5-7-75]

I think he made some errors in theory, some of which matter even today. The principle of socialism was not formulated clearly and understandably. But who remembers it?

From each according to his ability, to each according to his work.

That's right, but not quite right.

[6-16-74]

All of Khrushchev's errors flowed from this mistake. Marx raised this question, and Lenin confirmed it in his essay "State and Revolution." I know it well. There he wrote that at the final stage of communism the principle will be: "From each according to his ability, to each according to his needs." The later formulation has only part of this phrase: "from each according to his ability." But the second part, "to each according to his needs," was replaced by "to each according to his work." Our press follows this line like a law, but it's not correct from a Marxist perspective. Why? First, Marx wrote that only at the final stage of communism could the principle "from each according to his ability, to each according to his needs" be fulfilled. It's logically connected. Why? You can't demand the best from the common laborer under our conditions. But the constitution was written in 1936, when it was impossible to take "from each according to his ability." They didn't even have housing. Only at a higher stage could you talk about it. Could one demand this of a collective farmer? After all, we have established that he must work a certain minimum number of labor-days. But he is paid only a pittance for these labor-days. If he does not fulfill his quota of labor-days, the kolkhoz has the right to exclude him from membership. So what kind of "according to his ability" is that? It's nothing but window dressing. But window dressing is intolerable in Marxism. Marxism is an objective science; it views things soberly. It calls bad things bad and good things good. It demands genuine, uncompromising struggle for the good. Window dressing is not allowed.

Marx argued, and Lenin confirmed, that the rights of man cannot exceed his economic potential. You can demand that a communist work "according to his ability," and it doesn't matter what his working conditions are. But you can't demand this from the people. How can we have the same demands under socialism as under communism? Do we create some kind of fiction about something that still does not exist? I wrote a letter to the Central Committee when I was in Mongolia. I said we weren't even demanding this of communists, even though they acknowledged their duty to struggle for communism irrespective of conditions. Revolutionaries must destroy what is bad and sacrifice themselves if necessary. Workers scrape by and receive their crusts of bread—what more can we demand of them? Meet your quota! That's it. God grant that everyone conscientiously fulfill his norm. We would lead a much richer life. Better yet—exceed one's norm. This applies all the more to communists; a communist must work better. This means that contrary to "from each according to his ability" we must inscribe:

fulfillment of the norms established by society. Fulfill what is demanded of you by the state, by society; conscientiously fulfill the norms prescribed by the factory, the workshop, the kolkhoz. This applies especially to white-collar workers. They are so many idlers. As they gossip and smoke in corridors, do you believe they are actually working "according to their ability"? Why do we put up with it? Lenin used to say, we must have factory-style discipline in our workplace. It's not very pleasant, but it's necessary. Factory discipline is not our ideal, but for the present it is indispensable. Honestly, conscientiously, with all your heart, fulfill the norm established by the state. If you exceed your norm, you will be thanked.

Second, "To each according to his work." This is especially popular. All of our books go on about it. Some people interpret it as follows: If I work in a factory, I am paid according to my work. But if you are a boss, you have no work-norm to fulfill. In a word, you can take all kinds of liberties. Thanks to this scandalous situation, under the guise of "according to one's work," loafers—and they are numerous—get money for nothing. But the most important thing is this.

Marx and Engels said, to each according to his work, but in an economy that has abolished money-commodity relations. In our country they say, on the contrary, money-commodity relations are indispensable, they are the main thing. Why do we write that way? We should say, according to one's work but with the gradual abolition of money-commodity relations. We preach the opposite. Our 1961 program states: money-commodity relations are to be retained through the entire period of socialism. It has things turned around. Stalin said, "I acknowledge theory, I interpret it as follows: 'Life is one thing, theory another.'" That is why I sit, write, and pore over mountains of material. After all, it is horrible—what they write is confused beyond all bounds. Here I look at these Academicians—economists, philosophers—after all, they know they are lying day after day! Those Academicians and professors—no one raises a voice against them. Marx and Lenin said exactly the opposite. In Lenin's *State and Revolution* the words "commodity" and "money" are not even mentioned. Why? Everything was already based on them. But these are vestiges of capitalism. It's not a simple question but a complex and very serious one. Here we see young people growing up; honestly they say: this is stupid. What our elders babbled to us does not correspond to reality.

How to handle this is another matter. I will not lie to you and will never lie. I can remain silent. Back in 1936 I said this twice to Stalin.

He understood everything, of course, but waved me off: "You have communism in mind. But your position is false, does not correspond to science. Science holds..."

But did the Revolution in Russia correspond to science according to Marx?

It did. Lenin proved that.

Apart from this point, everything in the constitution of 1936 was good?

It was a remarkable document. This point about money-commodity relations had no practical significance at the time, but now it is the basis of what they write and how they educate our youth. Stalin edited the constitution; he headed the commission; everything was in his hands. It has played a colossal role.

[2-9-71, 6-13-74]

Is it true that after XIXth Congress Stalin said we had built a military-industrial dictatorship instead of socialism?

He said something else. In private conversation he confessed that we no longer had a dictatorship of the proletariat. He didn't state this firmly, but he said it. Only to me. Perhaps he was testing me, or perhaps he was trying to understand something himself.... If you read our constitution thoroughly you will see that it contains many points which contradict the dictatorship of the proletariat. Of course, it's all said in a very transparent form. There is something like this: our Soviet power was born in 1917 as the dictatorship of the proletariat and became the power of all the toilers. Notice, "all the toilers." That is why our country is administered by Soviets of Toilers' Deputies. Soviets have existed and remain, but they used to be Soviets of Workers', Soldiers', and Peasants' Deputies, fundamentally Soviets of Workers' and Peasants' Deputies. But this class division no longer exists. In my opinion this is a revision in diluted form: not the dictatorship of the proletariat but power of the toilers. There is a hint of this.

A theme runs throughout all of Lenin's *State and Revolution*. What about the peasants? They, the poor, they desire, but their worldview...

[6-30-76]

"The Economic Problems of Socialism in the USSR" was discussed at Stalin's dacha. "Any questions, comrades? Have you read it?" He gathered together the members of the Politburo, some seven or eight people. "What do you think about it? Any comments?" We said something or other.... I mentioned something not terribly important.

Now I confess, we underestimated the work. We should have gone into it more thoroughly. But no one as yet understood this. Unfortunately, people were bad at theory.

The more familiar I become with Stalin's "Economic Problems of Socialism," the more defects I find in it. I reread it today. How could he write: "It is obvious that after the disintegration of the world market, the spheres of exploitation of the world's resources by the major capitalist countries, the USA, Britain, and France, will contract, yet the cyclical character of the development of capitalism, the growth and contraction of production, will nevertheless be preserved." This is true. But further on—and this was written in 1952—"However, the growth of production in these countries will take place on a narrower base, because the volume of production in these countries will contract."

But nothing of the kind has occurred.

[3-10-77, 6-16-77, 11-7-85]

The fundamental law of capitalism is to secure maximum profit by one means or another. But how can a Marxist present the fundamental law of capitalism without including the downfall of capitalism? After all, in Marx everything moves in this direction. In his analysis of the development of capitalism, the system inevitably leads to its own downfall. That is the essence of Marx's work. All of *Capital* is built on the way capitalism develops. By dint of its internal laws, its fall and the transition to socialist society are inevitable. How can Stalin possibly speak about capitalism, about its fundamental law, without mentioning its eventual downfall? Impossible, of course! Herein lies the defect of Stalin's fundamental law of capitalism.

[1-14-73]

Give and give, that's what they taught you. Herein lies Stalin's error in his fundamental economic law. Just give, give! And Khrushchev included this in his party program [1961]. But there was also another, a valuable and indispensable element in Stalin. Khrushchev threw it overboard. He took the lesser, the secondary part of Stalin but forgot the main thing, and he tramples on both Stalin and Lenin. You see, all our woes stem from that. The Bolsheviks have never drawn up such rosy, such deceptive plans that promise that we shall live under communism by 1980. But Khrushchev promised it.

That was certainly a wild promise.

A gamble.

A gamble, and now you want more such gambles. . . . What can we give to the new generation? We ourselves understand very little, think very little, rarely and superficially look into what Stalin and Lenin taught. Stalin committed a gross mistake on this question in his unfortunate economic law. Khrushchev grabbed it and clung to it as if it were the sum total of or the main thing in Stalin.

They are pondering this in the German Democratic Republic. They have published a book on it. With them, first comes strengthening the socialist system—but only after the requisite growth and perfection of socialist production on a base of the most advanced technology.

Everything for technology, but how to strengthen the system—that's what Stalin overlooked. But the Germans have taken it up.

[3-11-76]

Stalin's last minister of finance was Zverev. I knew him very well. I valued him as a financier and often dealt with him. He was secretary of one of the Moscow district committees. At my suggestion he was moved to the People's Commissariat. Before this I asked for a list of those who had graduated from financial institutes—members of the party, reliable workers. I chose Zverev. He was called in to see Stalin. When he came he was very ill with flu, with a high temperature, bundled up with warm clothing. He looked a bit like Sobakevich, like a bear. Sholokhov called him "our iron minister of finance." He was derided for levying high taxes on everyone. But who to tax? Of course there were no bourgeoisie. He had to extract heavy taxes from our own, from peasants and workers. They say that orchards were destroyed—they were taxed only because fruit orchards near cities yielded supplementary incomes. You could get something out of them, so on went the tax. But just find another way. The state had to live somehow. No one would give us any money. What to do? In this matter, they say, Stalin acted badly—indeed, crudely, savagely, barbarically. But just put these "nonbarbarians" in those conditions, let them ensure the life of the state and prevent its breakdown. Just find the means. They were simpletons who did not understand the most elementary things! But Zverev was stalwart. I value him for this. He had competence, absolutely, and party-mindedness. He felt that it had to be done for the Revolution, for the party, that it was inescapable. He had a lofty consciousness plus a practical flair—he knew how to find monies to be snatched for taxes! Among the plain people he had a practical bent. . . . None better. To understand politics in the long term was not his suit. But he could think in terms of five-year plans. He would map

out a line. You knew it must be carried out come what may. Stalin
approved. Zverev would strive, in a more or less practical way, to find
the true path. He writes correctly that in the solution of financial
problems, Stalin knew how to identify the main task and inexorably
strive to accomplish it. Incidentally, not just in financial questions. . . .

Stalin wrote things out in his own hand or summoned Poskrebyshev
and dictated to him. He formulated things very tersely, very swiftly, very
concisely, not just as a rough draft. In most cases he produced a finished
document. Later, additions and corrections were introduced into the
final text.

■   **Everyday Life**   ■

At a large conference table in Stalin's office I had my usual place. But
it is difficult to say who sat where. It depended on the number of persons
present.

The way they show it in films is wrong. I'll have to draw it. I'm not a
good enough artist to draw Red Square.

Here is Stalin's office and the conference table. Here is Stalin's place.
A window, perhaps two or three. Here is the entrance. The security man
sat over there. Here was Poskrebyshev's place. A door here leading to the
sitting room. There maps, a big globe—we rarely used it.

The table accommodated about twenty persons. Portraits of Suvorov
and Kutuzov hung on the wall near a window. In the office was a death
mask of Lenin in a cabinet, on a pedestal, under a glass cover. A
separate table for telephones. A spacious office on the third floor. The
Eternal Flame can now be seen from a window.

Now about his apartment. Here on the first floor there were six or
seven rooms, a room for Svetlana, for a library, a bedroom, a room for
the servants. Servants were changed over time. There used to be an old
Georgian woman. After her, Valentina Istomina. . . . But she was at the
dacha. She served at table. If she also served as a wife, who was to know?

I read how Engels was straightforward in such matters. He did not
have a formal wife. He lived with his housekeeper, an Irish girl. He had
no time for marriage. When she died, Marx attached no importance to
this, which deeply offended Engels. Engels hired a second housekeeper,
the sister of his late mistress. . . .

Lenin had an affair with Inessa Armand—but he had no time for it.

Stalin's family life did not work out well. And the children . . . He had no time for the children. He was not up to the task—conditions were difficult.

Let's save paper. On a half-sheet I'll draw the dining room. It was a big longish dining table because often a large group of guests gathered around it. He had a set place at this table, too. A large room, probably with three windows. Here was a sofa. Frankly speaking, the apartment was not very comfortable. The cloakroom was near the kitchen. At the dacha there was a gramophone. It provided relaxation. After work it was here that we met most frequently. At night, after meetings, we would go to his place to dine. Naturally, conversation went on. . . .

Stalin forbade conversation in Georgian in the presence of Russians. Beria once violated this taboo and Stalin roundly upbraided him.

[8-16-77, 12-28-77]

Svetlana Allilueva writes that Stalin did not get along with his son Jakov.

I would say that Jakov was not party-minded. I met him at Stalin's, but quite rarely. Of course they were not on especially warm terms. Stalin received him stiffly. Was Jakov a Communist party member? Surely, but this side of him did not stand out. He had some kind of low-level job. He was handsome, a bit of a dandy. He served in the artillery. As a prisoner of war of the Germans, he bore up bravely and nobly. He perished, a hero. Stalin would not exchange a captured German general for Jakov. He said, "All of them are my sons."

Vasily [another of Stalin's sons], the militant communist, more or less, was a warrior in the Red Army, not as a communist but as a Soviet citizen with a taste for the military. He was a heavy drinker and, it seems, given to loose living. Considering the company he kept, it was impossible to expect anything good of him. He himself was wounded during the war—something exploded near him during a binge. He was good at carousing.

[12-21-79]

Vasily was not an important person. It cannot be said that he was all bad, but he did have many bad sides. People began to glorify him, and it pleased him. He had no observable talent. He certainly did not follow in his father's footsteps. He was weak-willed. On all sides he was showered with medals and regaled. But he was politically immature. As regards his cronies, they were unreliable and politically indifferent. He too was little interested in politics. Many of his cronies took advantage of him to feather their nests.

I had a talk with Artem Fedorovich Sergeev, the son of Artem, the legendary Bolshevik.

He was considered to be Stalin's son, but he was really his foster son. He was quite young when his father perished in an airplane accident.

He used to tell me about his life in Stalin's home before the war. It was in a two-story house in the Kremlin near the Troitskie Gates. In the hallway was a tub containing salted cucumbers.

I remember it.

"Stalin liked to wear his old military overcoat," Artem Fedorovich told me. "He had probably had it since the civil war. Some say he had it since his exile in Siberia. It hung in the hallway." Once someone tried to replace it with a new one. Stalin exploded with anger, "This one will last me ten years more!" He also had worn-out felt boots.

Tania, Tatiana Afanaseva, entered the conversation. "Back then, everyone dressed modestly. Viacheslav Mikhailovich had only one over-coat. All his life he had only one hat—you can see it in every photo-graph." Molotov treated new clothes as they do in working-class families. When he was given new clothing for his birthday, for example, a tie or a shirt, he was very happy and tried to hide his happiness. Then he would try it on. . . .

Stalin was very frugal. He had no clothes in which to be buried. He was buried in his old military suit which had been cleaned and repaired. . . .

Artem Fedorovich told me: "When Stalin returned home from his work, Poskrebyshev would follow him with a big bag of letters. Stalin sat down and read some aloud. He made notes on some of them and wrote brief resolutions. Mostly they were applications and complaints. . . . Miners wrote that they hadn't a bath house. . . .

" 'The director is an enemy of the people!' Stalin would say.

"Vasily and I were the same age. Stalin liked to read Zoshchenko aloud to us. Once he laughed to the point of tears and then said, 'Here, Com-rade Zoshchenko remembered about the GPU and changed the ending.'

" 'Ge-Pe-Oo!' Stalin said.

"Once he gathered his sons together: Jakov, Vasily, and me. 'Boys, war is coming. You will have to become soldiers.'

"Jakov and me," said Artem, "joined the artillery, and Vasily became a pilot. All of us went to the front—from the first day; Stalin telephoned to have us taken there immediately. It was the only privilege we got from him *as a father. There remain several letters from Vasily to his father. In one of them from the front, he asked his father to send him money. A snack bar had opened in his detachment and he wanted a new officer's uniform. His father replied: '1. As far as I know, the rations in the air force are quite sufficient. 2. A special uniform for Stalin's son is not on the agenda.' Vasily didn't get the money."*

[3-9-85, 10-4-85]

Viacheslav Mikhailovich drew the floor plan of Stalin's dacha in Kuntsevo (Blizhniya) and explained:

Here is the large hall, and another room to the right. Stalin spent time there when he was ill. Here was a large dining room where we gathered for dinner—if you could call it that at 10 or 11 at night—but not very often. Here is the big table, a record player, many records. He liked classical music. He often went to the Bolshoi Theatre, arriving in the middle of the performance. He liked Glinka, Rimsky-Korsakov, Mussorgsky—mostly Russian composers. He also liked the chorus by Piatnitsky. In the hall all the walls were covered with maps. Khrushchev said that Stalin used a globe in planning military operations. On the contrary, he liked wall maps, geographical ones. Here was Asia. Here was Europe. We spent a lot of time there. . . . He was interested in how to make use of the Arctic Ocean, the Siberian rivers, the treasures of Siberia, especially the mouth of the Ob. He planned to build a port at the mouth of the Ob River.

I have never been on the second floor, except once, after his death. In the office there was a desk. It was a good place for talks. But most talks were held in the dining room. While we waited for dinner we sat on the sofa and talked. Here is the bedroom. It's a little one. I have never been in it. He died in this big room. Near the wall there was a piano. Zhdanov used to play. He was something of a pianist, though an amateur. Stalin also had a billiard table, and I also played.

Stalin was not much of a sportsman. He didn't swim. He did like to shoot. He walked a little, not much. Voroshilov, Khrushchev, Andreev, and Malenkov liked to hunt. Stalin's arm was normal, but he held it in an unusual way, possibly as a consequence of an operation. In his childhood he was run over in an accident with a carriage. . . . He was very seldom on the second floor; only his daughter stayed there.

[7-28-76, 3-4-78, 4-10-79]

Bear in mind, I was not one to hang on Stalin's every word. I argued with him, told him the truth!

Only saints are infallible. The Lord God can be accused of unjustly creating the poor, the injured. . . .

Stalin was great in tactics. He did not delve deeply, but he knew how to get things done. . . . It took boldness, firmness.

[5-11-78]

In his last years Stalin was in failing health. He had been through so much! How he managed to bear up, I don't know!

[7-24-78]

Well, everyone grows senile to a degree in his later years. . . . It was then that Stalin was very jittery; he suspected everyone. His last years were the most dangerous. He swung to extremes. But in the editing and writing of essays he very scrupulously made certain changes in old formulations.

[4-29-82]

Once Stalin was at his dacha near Batumi, in Georgia, at a kind of resort. He decided to visit secretly another district. He invited his old prerevolutionary acquaintances—men and women—to meet him. They arrived and complained: bribery everywhere, thievery everywhere, and so forth. Stalin was indignant and dismissed Charkviany, the first secretary in Georgia, and appointed in his stead a new man, Mgeladze, who was transferred from Sukhumi.

But few problems are resolved by administrative remedies.

[10-21-82]

The Voice of America reported that Trotsky's assassin has died. He spent twenty years in jail, received the award of Hero of the Soviet Union, lived in the USSR for some time, and died in Cuba. Was he under our orders?

Of course. Trotsky said before he died, "Stalin found me even here."

[11-4-78]

I think Lenin was right in his evaluation of Stalin. I said it myself right after Lenin's death, at the Politburo. I think Stalin remembered it because after Lenin's death we got together at Zinoviev's in the Kremlin, about five of us, including Stalin and me, and talked about the "testament." I said I considered all of Lenin's evaluation of Stalin to have been right. Stalin, of course, didn't like this. Despite this we remained close for many years. I think he appreciated me because I spoke out about certain matters in a way others hypocritically avoided, and he saw that I addressed the matter of the "testament" forthrightly.

Although I had the best relations with Stalin, I would not oppose Lenin in this matter. I considered it necessary to support the "testament" in a way that would have an effect on Stalin. He never spoke to me about it. Lenin's "testament" is, of course, favorable for the most part to Stalin; compared with the assessments given the others, the one of Stalin was the most positive. But Stalin was then, it seems to me, dissatisfied with this characterization. Very dissatisfied. Lenin picked out two persons—Stalin and Trotsky. I can't recall just now how Lenin characterized Trotsky in the "testament." But Lenin had for the entire preceding period given many descriptions of Trotsky, and they were entirely negative. Lenin, of course, took this into account. He wanted to warn against this very dangerous enemy. That's why he juxtaposed the two—Stalin and Trotsky. So choose. His characterization of Stalin was shorter, but it was entirely positive; in closing, however, he did point out certain negative aspects.

Stalin was, of course, distinguished by rudeness. He was a very blunt person. But if not for his harshness I don't know how much good would have been accomplished. I think harshness was necessary, otherwise there would have been even greater vacillation and irresolution. But Stalin's willfulness, harshness, even brutishness, naturally repulsed people. He clearly, firmly, and unhesitatingly determined the main line, and this of course was very important for the party at that time. He was a complex man. He reckoned with Lenin's criticism. Yes he did, absolutely. In the early years he was very restrained; afterward, however, he became a bit conceited, as I see it. Conceited. I was always of this opinion. For people exercising such vast power this is most undesirable.

[11-1-77, 7-1-79]

A large number of the intelligentsia hold that Stalin distorted and deformed Lenin, and killed the best Leninist cadres, and that Stalin's misdeeds have left us in a mess ever since.

That's the rightist deviation. Its most recent manifestation takes less organized form but is quite widespread.

[8-26-79]

We would drive followed by security in a second car. Perhaps Stalin would also have a security man sitting in the front seat of his car. But only Stalin would have had a bodyguard sitting up there. Perhaps, but I did not know about it. Everyone knew about the second automobile. It went with him everywhere. . . .

In the early years, as I recall, there were no bodyguards. Back then we traveled by foot. Even Stalin. But fresh terrorist attempts resumed in 1928. Terrorists armed with bombs were apprehended at the border. Terrorists of the Socialist Revolutionary type. They were audacious. . . .

Back then it would have been enough to assassinate Stalin and another two or three leaders and everything might have come crashing down.

I recall a blizzard, snow was blowing. I was walking with Stalin along Manege Square. We did not yet have bodyguards. Stalin wore a fur-lined coat, felt boots, and a cap with ear flaps. No one recognized us. Suddenly a beggar beseeched us: "Give me alms, good people!" Stalin reached into his pocket, pulled out a ten-ruble note, gave it to him, and walked on. But the beggar followed us and cried out, "Damned bourgeoisie!" Stalin laughed afterward, "Who can understand our people! Give them a little, that's bad; give them a lot, that's bad, too!"

[3-11-76, 8-16-77]

They say Stalin had a double. He replaced Stalin on the mausoleum when Stalin got tired. I have heard this many times.

Nonsense! Someone is trying to make a joke.

[3-9-81]

In your opinion, did Stalin have negative features?

Negative? I never asked myself that question before. . . . He was by character an abrupt person, but at the same time fair.

All the same, he was liked, very much so. *Molotov did not seem to want to recall the negative features.*

Usually they cite Lenin's comment that "Stalin was too rude . . ."

You can see why. Of all the accusations leveled at Stalin, that is the strongest. But at various times different people regarded him quite favorably.

Stalin called the people "screws."

Screws are screws, but the important thing is the way they turn. They sincerely loved him. This is not mere puffery. People had a positive attitude toward him.

They puffed up Brezhnev's reputation, to no avail.

Why do you say that? It worked somewhat.

I met Brezhnev admirers in Canada, emigrés. They had hijacked an airplane of ours, and he had permitted them to go abroad. They had high praise for him but raged against Andropov, Lenin, and Stalin. . . .

[11-15-84]

In time Stalin will be rehabilitated in history. There will be a Stalin museum in Moscow. Without fail! By popular demand.

The role of Stalin was tremendous. I do not doubt that his name will rise again and duly win a glorious place in history.

[1-19-85, 3-9-85]

Stalin used to say, "Truth is protected by battalions of lies. . . ."

[8-17-71]

■ Kirov ■

At the XIVth Congress a majority of the delegates of the Leningrad organization were against the Central Committee line, but a small minority were for it. In fact the Leningrad organization was in Zinoviev's hands. The cadres were handpicked by Zinoviev.

Zinoviev was guided by Kamenev. He was the leader of the Leningraders. In matters of theory Kamenev was more profound than Zinoviev.

The Leningrad organization against the CC of the Bolsheviks? Well, then a special delegation of CC members was formed. In this affair I was the head and organizer of the shock group, the "savage division," as it was dubbed by the Zinovievites. Kalinin, Kirov, Bukharin, Tomsky, Voroshilov, Andreev, and Schmidt were members. Immediately after the congress we went to the Leningrad organization to remove Zinoviev. When we arrived Zinoviev courteously invited us to his office: "Just say what explanations you need, and I will tell you. When do you begin work?" "We shall begin tomorrow." "What do you plan to do, perhaps you can tell me?" "We shall go the factories, deliver reports, carry out elections."

Well, the group fanned out to individual factories. The next day I spoke at the renowned Lenin shipyards. I don't remember the others.

We removed Zinoviev. How? We went through all the factories, and everywhere they endorsed the resolution of the XIVth Congress that criticized the Leningrad group.

We could not afford to lose the major factories. To avoid this we first won over the smaller factories, as the Zinovievites still had powerful organizations in the big factories. They had a tight grip on the factory party committees. It was my responsibility that we not fail in this matter. Zinoviev asked, "Well, when will you go to the Putilov Works?"

I replied, "When the time comes. We are in no hurry."

The Putilov Works was their main base. All of Zinoviev's hopes rested on the Putilov Works. A delegation of Putilov workers came to me and asked, "Dear Comrade, why don't you visit us? We, the Putilovites, are workers too!" I said, "We will pay you a visit, a good visit to please you, all of us will pay you a visit. Just give us a chance to look into things at other factories."

It was important to encircle them. So we saved for last the two most important installations—the Triangle rubber works, a very large plant (it is no longer called Triangle, it is now called Red Triangle), we put off visiting this plant—and the Putilov Works, which were greatly under the influence of Zinoviev. But the moral pressure exerted by the workers of "Piter" [Petersburg] was turned on them. And we saved the Triangle plant for next to last. Almost our full group went there—Kalinin, and Tomsky. I do not recall whether Bukharin was there. Kirov was—he was precisely the one we would appoint to replace Zinoviev. We began the vote, for the moment on minor questions. Half for, half against. No way. They were continually confusing the rank and file. Those for the CC line on the left; those for the Zinoviev line on the right. It was so difficult to explain. They confused our rank and file; a majority was taking shape for us, but it was not yet a sure thing. Uncertainty, confusion reigned; the mass was split right down the middle. Deadlock. The opposition, too, marshaled its best forces. Only Zinoviev made no appearance, but his most persuasive speakers were there. Our speakers were top leaders, and the Zinovievites were their top speakers. For a long time it was not clear just which side would win the majority. The assemblage was so chaotic! There the mass of the party members were women. They arranged all kinds of discussions. I finally said to Kalinin, "Get up on the table and shout that you are the chairman and in charge!" He got up on the table and said, "Dear Comrades! Those who are for the CC stand on the right; those who are for the Leningrad group, the opposition, stand on the left!" He had clambered up onto the table; they had given him a hand; they respected an authoritative person, a worker. The hall quieted down.

The opposition was in the minority, but they sowed confusion in the ranks and blocked a decision either at meetings in the plant or in the cafeteria. Afterward the question of endorsing the CC resolutions was finally put to a vote. I don't remember precisely whether we had a majority or whether it was split fifty-fifty; certainly we won no less than half. There was a newspaper, the *Leningrad Pravda*, it is still published. I dismissed the editor and replaced him with Skvortsov-Stepanov.

He perished in 1937?

No, no. He was the translator of *Das Kapital*, a prominent theoretician, a fervent Leninist, and a backer of Stalin. He wrote a splendid booklet on electrification. Lenin had commissioned him to write it. Ivan Ivanovich Skvortsov-Stepanov was a highly educated man and a very staunch, old Bolshevik.

As soon as the day ended I discussed with him what was to be printed the next day so as to strike the hardest blow first of all in the factories we needed most. He went along with this. Thus every morning we fired off a barrage. Day after day for a whole week we skinned the Zinovievites alive, surely for a week and a half, no less. The last factory was the Putilov. Again we marshaled our most effective forces, and we won a thumping majority there.

In a word, we did not concede the opposition a single factory. We triumphed everywhere. Only at the Triangle was it a split decision. It was difficult to ascertain who had the majority; well, fifty-fifty, in my view, was the result. That's the way it was published.

We decided to convene a Leningrad City Party Conference. I attended it with Bukharin. It probably took place in 1926. It was a foregone conclusion. All the delegates were our people; the opposition had almost ceased to exist. After the factories, the district conferences supported us. Two or three weeks after this rout of the opposition in the factories, the Leningrad Conference was convened. Kirov and I stayed at the Hotel Europa, or later we stayed at some flat. Bukharin and I spent the night in the same room, and he informed me about the conference.

Bukharin was the political *rapporteur*. We triumphed at the conference. Kirov became secretary of the Leningrad party organization. Zinoviev did not speak, but neither did he capitulate. A vain man, he did not wish to experience public defeat. He dropped out of sight. For a time. He remained chairman of the Comintern. He was removed from Leningrad. Then he was excluded from the Comintern. They made Bukharin first secretary of the Comintern. The post of chairman was abolished, and a secretariat was created with Bukharin as a member. He supported Stalin's line.

[12-4-73, 4-19-77]

I have a question about the XVIIth Party Congress. Is it true that Stalin received fewer votes than Kirov at the elections to the Central Committee?

No. How can they say such things?

I don't remember exactly, but at one of the closed meetings the results of the elections to the Central Committee were announced. Only one candidate received no blackballs and was elected unanimously—Piatnitsky. Why? Because he worked as a secretary in the Comintern where he crossed no one. All the others received blackballs. In all probability even Stalin received two or three blackballs against, as did I.

Did you find out who voted against you?

What for? It was the party and not some kind of investigation bureau. What significance did it have? I am sure that at every election to the Central Committee, one or two votes went against Stalin. Enemies were always present. I admit there may not have been a single vote against Kirov. But the only such case I recall is that of Piatnitsky. But today no one knows or is interested in him.

There was a group at the XVIIth Congress led by a certain Oganesov, an old Bolshevik from prerevolutionary days, an Armenian. He hated Stalin, had been arrested and jailed. I once drove him out of my hospital room, saying, "If you talk that way, I want nothing to do with you!"

He recounted to me that during the XVIIth Congress [1934] they had elected Sheboldaev as party secretary of the North Caucasian Region. He once had worked with Mikoyan, had fled from the Whites in a boat. A good lad. He himself was not from the North Caucasus, a Russian, he worked in the CC under me as a deputy director of the Organization Department, a capable man. Well, he had gathered together eight to ten congress delegates, including this Oganesov.

"So that's why they jailed Oganesov, the scoundrel!" exclaimed Shota Ivanovich.

The group included quite prominent party workers of that time. According to Oganesov, during a recess the group met at a designated place in the hall. They called Kirov over to their meeting and informed him they would like to nominate him for the post of general secretary. But he derided and cursed them out: "You're talking rubbish! What kind of general secretary would I make?"

There were such people, unstable types. Their proposal was absurd. I was in the party back then, and of course I knew the leading cadres of that time quite well. Kirov was unsuitable as a leader of the highest rank. He was one of several secretaries, a tremendous speaker at mass meetings, but that's it. Kirov reported everything to Stalin, in detail. I believe that Kirov acted correctly.

They say that afterward Stalin made short shrift of these people.

No, afterward his repression cut a wide swath, including some of the people involved in the Kirov episode, but that is a minor matter.

And Kirov was not forgiven for enjoying greater popularity than Stalin.

Absurd! Just look up the stenographic records of the congresses. Who enjoyed greater authority, Kirov or Stalin? Just look at Kirov's speeches and collections of articles—what's there? "It is difficult to imagine a figure as gigantic as Stalin"—I quote from memory what Kirov said. But where are there political signs indicating in him the character of a top leader?

He had no such aspirations. He was not that kind of person.

Let's take 1917. Stalin was very close to Lenin, wasn't he?

Of course.

Recently I read that Stalin and Lenin overnight worked out the Brest pact together?

Perhaps. Kirov was far removed from it. It was extremely important. He had only worked on a provincial newspaper. It was absurd to nominate Kirov. This fact shows the mental horizons of such petty people. And Kirov derided them!

Some consider it to be a great misfortune for the party that Kirov didn't become general secretary in his time.

Let them say what they will, but what is valuable in Kirov from a political point of view? Just cite me his ideas that are distinguished by their value or utility—nowhere! Are they distinguished from what Stalin said by their originality, did they say something new?

"When we dealt with the Trotskyites, who did more than Stalin, who wrote Problems of Leninism?*" asked Shota Ivanovich.*

That's not the point, I said. They believe that Kirov was more humane. Second, if a palace revolution had been carried out in 1937 it would have placed at the head of the country intelligent people such as Tukhachevsky; they would have coped both with the country and with fascism.

That is absurd. Where is the evidence that Tukhachevsky could do something useful for the country apart from his specialty? Where is it? What kind of data? Whose? He was raised up by those who willy-nilly help betray bolshevist policy.

"I consider Zhukov a greater military man than Tukhachevsky. You knew them both?" asked Shota Ivanovich.

I knew them both, but they were different. Zhukov possessed firmness and of course a practical bent. Tukhachevsky was more highly educated, but of course less of a military man.

The point is, Tukhachevsky did not know where he was going. It seems to me that he would have veered to the right. He was closer to Khrushchev.

Well, all right, if you say that Kirov was better, what do you know about Kirov, what did he accomplish? We know about Stalin, he had his publications, articles, and we know where he worked. And Kirov? By and large he did not work in the Central Committee.

At the close of the XVIIth Congress I sat with him in the Presidium room where Stalin said to Kirov, "Now it is time to transfer you to work in Moscow."

I supported Stalin: "Yes, that's right." Kirov jumped on me: "What are you saying! I am not up to work here in Moscow. I can manage in Leningrad no worse than you, but what can I do here?"

He was in a rage. He was very much afraid he might be transferred.

His strong point was direct work with the masses. Such people are very necessary. In some instances he was more necessary than other people, in his place. But he did not measure up to anything above that.

He lacked training in theory. And he wasn't all that strong. After all, we had to remold the state and prepare for war, you know what that meant. . . .

How did you find out about Kirov's death? (I asked Molotov about this many times over the years.)

I was in Stalin's office when Medved, chief of the Leningrad OGPU, phoned to say that Comrade Kirov had just been murdered in his Smolny office. Stalin replied, "Boobs!"

The same evening we traveled to Leningrad—Stalin, Voroshilov, and I. We interrogated Nikolaev, Kirov's assassin.

Expelled from the party, he was an embittered man. He said he had premeditatedly committed the murder on ideological grounds. He was a Zinovievite. I think women had something to do with it. At Smolny Stalin interrogated Nikolaev's wife.

What kind of person was Nikolaev?

An ordinary person. An office worker. Short, stocky. . . . Apparently he was angered and affronted by his expulsion from the party. He was used by the Zinovievites. In all probability he was neither a genuine Zinovievite nor a Trotskyist.

They condemned not only Nikolaev but a whole list of people.

The point is that they were condemned not for the murder but for their participation in the Zinovievite organization. But as far as I recall, there was no direct documentary evidence that the murder had been instigated by a Zinovievite group.

Nikolaev, as it were, acted on his own, but, judging by his past, he was a Zinovievite.

[6-11-70, 7-28-71, 6-13-74, 4-28-76, 7-1-79, 3-6-81, 12-9-82]

A tenacious legend has been created that Kirov could have replaced Stalin. But where are his theoretical works?

But they were all practitioners then. You didn't necessarily need theoretical works to your credit!

Absolutely wrong. Kirov was a great agitator, though he lacked organizing talents. Frequently rightists gathered around him. In this sense he was not very perceptive. He had Chudov as second secretary, a right-winger. He later got burned, of course.

The general public knew nothing about Kirov before 1917. He was a communist, though not an active one. He needed a rostrum which was nowhere to be found then. Later he showed that he could speak to the masses, the workers, but in the years of reaction he was not very active. He would write short pieces for a local liberal bourgeois newspaper. He had no rostrum from 1906 to 1917.

But the legend persists that Kirov was supposed to have replaced Stalin as general secretary.

Was Kirov's personality wrong for the job?

Certainly not. He himself in no way aspired to it. He was capable of work but not in the leading roles. I can tell you bluntly that he would not have been acknowledged as number one, especially by the senior leaders. . . .

But they say: some type of Georgian ruled Russia. . . .

There were times when Stalin, as a Georgian, a "home alien," could allow himself actions in defense of the Russian people such as no Russian leader in his place could have contemplated.

[8-15-72, 11-7-79]

Kirov was a poor organizer, though he could work the masses rather well. We all treated him fondly. Stalin liked him. I would say he was Stalin's favorite. Khrushchev's casting aspersions on Stalin and insinuating that Stalin had Kirov assassinated—that was foul.

I used to be friends with Kirov. I can now recall that only Zhdanov received from Stalin the same kind of treatment that Kirov enjoyed.

After Kirov, Stalin liked Zhdanov best.

Stalin is said to have been afraid that Kirov would replace him.

That's absurd! Why should he have been afraid of Kirov? Oh, no no no. You must understand, eloquence came second. Eloquence alone isn't enough. We had to have either an especially outstanding person or a very fine group. Take Khrushchev, for example. He cobbled together a strong group for himself. Everyone then wanted a breathing spell, to live a bit easier. But Stalin's way demanded that the helm be held even more firmly.

■   **We Want to Live Well**   ■

With the war over, people certainly wanted to relax a little.

This included not only certain individuals but the bulk of our cadres and the masses generally. They were all exhausted. Not everyone in the leadership could stick to the new course, because it was extremely difficult. The change was never formally announced, but as a matter of fact the XXIVth Party Congress was concluded by Brezhnev, who spoke these words: "We can now enjoy breathing freely, working well, and living calmly." The "living calmly" part was particularly addressed to the Bolsheviks. The Bolsheviks could not accept that. With people enjoying a calm life, the Bolsheviks are no longer needed. They become totally unnecessary. The Bolsheviks are always in the thick of the fray, leading the people, overcoming obstacles. For what would they be needed if life was proceeding calmly? The Social Democrats would be much more appropriate. They would be perfectly suited. They would submit, so to speak, to this spontaneous movement of capitalism.

Under Khrushchev, bread and other foods were in good supply, and people liked that. He actually took advantage of that situation.

He was more adroitly manipulated than manipulator. Everyone wanted a breathing spell so that tensions would fade away.

"We want to live well," Shota Ivanovich said. "We live only once, and we want to have women and a good time."

Without women you can't get along. Women got Poskrebyshev and Vlasik into trouble. Having fallen out of favor then, I was rather on the margin. One day I heard that Poskrebyshev was no longer on the job. That was a surprise. Stalin had him removed but not imprisoned, since he could not be accused of embezzlement. But Vlasik did spend security funds for his personal pleasure. Neither damned Stalin for this. Later, when I was back in Moscow from... Mongolia? no, from Vienna, I happened to see Poskrebyshev on Tverskoy Boulevard. I didn't approach him, I just nodded and he nodded back. Poskrebyshev had intrigued against me industriously, and he was eager to recruit my interpreter Pavlov, who seemed agreeable to the secret assignment. Although he lacked the true character of a party member, Pavlov was an efficient worker, and I gave him the job. Pavlov knew English and German well. Of course, I was not enthusiastic about him lacking the qualities of a conscientious party member, but he could do a good job and he was not known to have any suspicious connections. . . .

When I was back at the foreign ministry after Stalin's death, I had Pavlov fired from his job there. Stalin had kicked me out of the ministry, and when I returned in 1953 Pavlov was an interpreter for Vyshinsky who had replaced me as foreign minister. So Pavlov started dropping in to inform on Vyshinsky.

I would tell him, "Look, Pavlov, why don't you just go to hell? I don't need you anymore. I know Vyshinsky inside and out. Why are you telling me all sorts of things about him? Consider yourself expelled from the ministry. I can't work with you any longer." I knew he had informed on me in the past.

Was Berezhkov any better?

I had him sacked from the foreign ministry earlier to be employed as a reporter. Security reported that his parents had stayed with the Germans in occupied territory somewhere in the Kiev area. Those could have been just rumors, but nevertheless I had the report and I was not in a position to have it verified.

So I promptly had him transferred to the *Novoe Vremia* [*New Times*] magazine. I just couldn't keep him on. I didn't even give him a reason for the transfer. Whatever the security people reported was strictly confidential.

But he was a young fellow then . . .

Poskrebyshev worked against me. . . . He was involved in intrigues in the higher echelons . . . mixing with the right people and spreading the word to middle-level officials . . .

He appeared to have remained loyal to Stalin. But he was involved in filthy affairs. Given the circumstances, women can serve as agents or weapons to have a man dragged into sordid business. One has to learn to reckon with that.

He was a capable man. He replaced Mekhlis. Before Mekhlis,

Tovstukha served as Stalin's secretary. A good man, he was. He died, his lungs.

The military didn't like Mekhlis.

Well, on the whole Simonov depicted him quite truthfully. Nonetheless, that man was loyal to the end.

[5-15-75, 7-17-75, 3-11-76, 1-9-81]

You said you too had been bugged?

I seem to have been bugged all my life. The security men told me about that, but I didn't check. You know, they treated me well. They would give me a straight warning to be careful when I talked. And they would do it without any ulterior motive, just so that I would be on the safe side. Whenever they were required to report they would add a good word. So we tried to be careful about what we said. . . . At times Stalin was extraordinarily suspicious of everyone around him. And he couldn't afford to be otherwise, no way. . . . Had I been compromised in any of the reports, you could easily imagine what . . . That was the difficult part . . . Most difficult.

As long as classes exist, that's life. Any loophole would be used against one, no stone would be left unturned. Whenever a direct approach failed, relatives and even the doormen of relatives would be approached. Anything that worked would be used. Favors could be granted for money. There are always some ready to engage in foul play. One couldn't fail to consider all this. But I had always been aware of it and always understood that I might find my future hanging by a thread at any time. One had to bear this in mind: there was no other way. Being cautious was the only sensible way of living. . . . One had to observe constantly a thousand constraints, though they did not guarantee one's safety. Nothing on earth is absolute, and that's how it is. Still, one could work for the good of the cause. We never forgot the *agent-provocateur* Malinovsky [the tsarist police-spy].

[8-15-75]

■   Voroshilov   ■

Stalin had been quite critical of Voroshilov in certain respects, especially after the war. Now and then Voroshilov would try to approach

Stalin, saying, "We became friends in Baku in 1907." And Stalin would respond, "I don't remember that."

Of course, I would say that Stalin never completely trusted him. Why? Well, all of us had our weaknesses and had acquired some ways of the gentry. We were seduced into that life-style, there is no denying that. Everything was provided for us, all our wishes were attended to. As a result, Voroshilov started to behave like gentry. He enjoyed mixing with artists and actors, he loved theatre and especially painters. He would often entertain them at his place.

In foreign publications Kalinin is described this way: "Kalinin's affection for Moscow ballet dancers is well known, and the fur coat that the all-Union elder gave to Tatiana Bakh was certainly provided by the funds of the state." Stalin allegedly told him, "If you aren't going to vote for me, then that fur coat . . ."

No, no, no. The problem was that Kalinin was then accompanied by a woman other than his wife, and everyone was well aware of it. . . . His wife came from Estonia. She was arrested. She had ties leading to Rykov.

Ballet dancers? Oh, no. That weakness should be attributed to Enukidze. He was friends with Karakhan, and both of them indulged in these kinds of affairs. Voroshilov clung more to the painters, and they were nonparty people for the most part.

Stalin regarded these affairs with great caution, and he was absolutely correct to do so. Had he been less careful, he might not have lived much longer. The situation was extremely tense. Voroshilov pursued his liberal ways. He took to drinking. When people drink their tongues become loose. Given the complexity of the conditions in which we lived, one had to be particularly careful about one's remarks. Voroshilov rather loved to pose as something of a patron of the arts. And the artists, for their part, tried to the utmost to reciprocate. Alexander Gerasimov, a very talented artist, painted Voroshilov riding on horseback, Voroshilov skiing. Their association appeared to be one of mutual back-scratching. Stalin was correct in his criticisms, for all artists are big-mouths. They are essentially harmless, of course, but they are constantly surrounded by ne'er-do-wells of every sort. And such connections were used to approach Voroshilov's aides and his domestics. It was out of the question to ignore this. Stalin himself could not have controlled the situation even if he had wanted to. The more critical issue was Voroshilov's personal life-style. This mattered in those years.

Voroshilov performed well at critical moments. He always supported the party's political line, as he came from a worker's family. He was approachable, and he could speak in public. His reputation was unblemished, and he was personally loyal to Stalin. Later his loyalty turned out to be not so strong. But in those years he very actively came out in support of Stalin, though as if he was not entirely convinced. This was also telling. This is a very complex question, and it has to be understood if you want to see why Stalin was somewhat critical of Voroshilov and did not invite him to attend all our conversations. At any rate, Voroshilov was not invited to confidential discussions. Sometimes he would just barge in, which invariably caused Stalin to frown.

Voroshilov showed himself in a particularly bad light under Khrushchev.

[3-4-72, 12-12-72, 3-8-74]

Shortly before his death Voroshilov is reported to have said, at a gathering, "I thank the Communist party and our dear Nikita Sergeevich for letting me live in this country house. I am faring very well, thanks to the solicitude extended by our beloved Nikita Sergeevich!"

I think his remarks were somewhat overstated, but that kind of boot-licking went on with respect to Khrushchev. Voroshilov did much to distinguish himself, and he achieved a great deal. But he went to pieces in the end. He didn't catch on to things.

He didn't have an easy time in the Ministry of Defense. Trotsky had installed so many of his own people there! Because of Voroshilov's connections and his circle of acquaintances, Stalin eventually ceased to regard him with the trust he had displayed earlier. Nevertheless, after the XIXth Party Congress, Stalin kept him on in both the Presidium and the Politburo, while I was kicked out of the Politburo.

[11-28-74]

Of course, much was expected of Voroshilov as commissar of defense. He wanted desperately to measure up, but he couldn't. It was necessary to adopt a new approach. Before the Finnish war he was opposed to providing submachine guns to the troops: "If we switch to submachine guns, where on earth will we find so many bullets? We'll never have enough!" Like it or not, we produced the necessary bullets. Given your enemy, you had to have no less than he. Of course, he lagged behind the times. "We will not have the capacity to do this," he would argue, and Stalin would respond, "How can you say that? Others have it, why not us?"

Stalin was a fast learner and was quick to grasp anything new.

[8-15-75]

During the Finnish war we found ourselves in a rather foolish situation. We had no machine pistols or submachine guns, but the Finns had such arms. They would ambush our troops amidst the trees. Our losses were heavy. We certainly did the right thing when we removed Voroshilov from the Ministry of Defense. Despite all the good qualities he had exhibited during the Revolution, he was now lagging behind the times. The Germans were then helping the Finns to procure arms. This made our situation very difficult. We had to take stock of all our deficiencies. Not everyone understood this.

[6-9-76]

"Voroshilov is a legendary hero of the civil war. Why did he allow himself to become a dishrag for three years under Khrushchev?" Shota Ivanovich asked.

That was a disgraceful page in his biography.

On a hunting trip near Tbilisi, Khrushchev once called, "Mo-lo-tov!" I think he cursed me as well.

No, he went on to say, "Molotov won't give up. Molotov alone remains true to himself." I admire those people who went to the gallows for their ideas. A man could be told, "Just one word—give up and you'll start a good life." But a Bolshevik chooses the gallows. He chooses the gallows!

"And did the Bolsheviks not go to the gallows?" asked Shota Ivanovich.

When Voroshilov died, Viacheslav Mikhailovich went to pay his last respects. Quietly and modestly he joined the line, but he was quickly recognized and approached by some generals who escorted him to his place in the guard of honor.

"You are making things up," remarked Molotov, and waved his hand in jest.

No, it happened. You did go to pay your last respects to our first marshal. . . .

Khrushchev was very eager to become a marshal of the Soviet Union. Marshal Golovanov once told me he had been approached with a questionnaire about whether he would approve Khrushchev's appointment to marshal. All of our marshals had to sign a sort of order to that effect. This idea, initiated by Eremenko, failed miserably. Zhukov, Rokosovsky, Golovanov, Kuznetsov, and other top-ranking military officers who had become marshals during the war refused to sign the order.

[1-16-73]

■   Kaganovich   ■

Kaganovich said his brother Mikhail had brought him into the party. Mikhail was commissar of aviation, and he later committed suicide. He was not a man of the highest caliber. Lazar, of course, was of high caliber, very energetic. He was a good organizer and agitator, though he floundered on questions of theory.

Generally speaking, we had few theoreticians. Genuine Bolshevik theoreticians were not easy to find.

Did the Mensheviks have more theoreticians?

The Mensheviks were nothing but theoreticians. . . .

Voroshilov was weak as a theoretician. Like Kalinin, he leaned a little to the right. But he was a tenacious supporter of Stalin, since Stalin's authority was high. . . . They were all afraid to break away from him. Twenty years have gone by since Stalin died. And who has remained loyal to Stalin throughout? Kaganovich and myself. I know of no one else.

Malenkov?

He's also held on well. No, he is not against Stalin.

Last summer I ran into Bulganin, and we walked together for about a kilometer and a half. Not once had he dared to drop in on me. Apparently Khrushchev had scared him to death! Nevertheless, he feels rather strange: peaceful coexistence is beyond his comprehension! And he shouldn't be this way! The theoretical level of a majority. . .

I met with Kaganovich at Luzhniki one day, for a walk. He lives in that neighborhood. . . .

Whatever I write, I mail to the Central Committee. I have concealed nothing concerning important issues. Naturally, I may be wrong, I may misunderstand things, or I may be behind the times. Nonetheless I keep working each day, and I don't think I am so terribly behind. . . . I do not merely exist, I work.

New elements certainly have emerged. I asked Kaganovich if he would have a look at a memorandum of mine, and he said, "Rather profound." Regrettably, he had no questions. I urged him to read carefully: "Go ahead and read it." He didn't criticize the Khrushchev program, and he didn't comment on my critical remarks either. And the new program was entirely unacceptable, because it was based on antirevolutionary groundwork.

[12-4-73, 12-30-73, 3-11-76]

Kaganovich visited me recently. His mind is active, but he is ailing. He has pains in his legs, in his arms, and so on.

How does he relate to you?

To me? Not badly. . . . He always used to be personally opposed to me. Everyone knew that. He would say to me, "For you it's easy, you are an intellectual, but I am from a worker's family." Even now he says things like this.

Poor fellow, he's not doing well. There is no one to look after him. He cooks for himself. "My only daughter helps to support me. I don't see anyone else. She has an apartment of her own," he would say. Another sad story. He is in a difficult situation. As a worker he had been very good.

[8-20-74]

Kaganovich was mainly an administrator but rather coarse, and not everyone could abide him. He not only knew how to apply pressure but also how to use something of a personal touch. A tough and straitlaced man. A great organizer and a fine public speaker. I clearly recall Sergo telling me about the two of them speaking at the same meeting. "Lazar made a great speech there! He captured the audience. He knew how to rouse the people." Sergo was ecstatic about Kaganovich's public speaking skills.

[1-14-75]

The Jews did not like Kaganovich. They would rather have had a more intellectual Jew in the Politburo. Even today Kaganovich is such an ardent supporter of Stalin that no one would dare to say anything derogatory about Stalin in his presence. Among all of us he was a 200 percent Stalinist.

He felt I didn't praise Stalin well enough. . . .

Now Kaganovich tells me, "We will be looking to you for leadership from now on." I take this with a grain of salt, of course. I know he loses no love on me, but he is honest."

[3-11-76, 10-21-82]

Last spring I invited Kaganovich to come and see me. . . . He declined my invitation. This is where his weakness shows, along with his one-sidedness and his inability to think independently. One shouldn't simply parrot another person. Stalin made mistakes, too. I always say that, and I wouldn't retract it. If I were to take back my words, I would cease to be the individual I am. I am poorly educated on many issues, but I learned and never forgot the main thing, and it is very difficult to lead me astray.

Stalin was an incarnation of his epoch, a different period from that of Lenin or Marx... an epoch that demanded profound scientific knowledge. And that science determined politics. This is where the difference lay. At a discrete stage Stalin achieved what had not—could not have—been achieved by anyone else.

Speaking of Lenin and Stalin, I would say this: the former was a genius, the latter was talented. Getting down to business, that's the way it turns out.

[4-28-76]

Kaganovich phoned. He feels badly about not being restored to the party.

He also phoned me before the congress and said, "I believe we'll be restored this time." I answered, "I don't think so. Who will do the restoring? The ones that did the expelling?"

[8-28-81]

Molotov observed the old relations of subordination in his communications with Malenkov and Kaganovich.
"Didn't you call Malenkov?" I asked.
Why should I make the call? It used to be them that called me!
Today is the fortieth anniversary of Victory Day. Kaganovich called. Molotov said this to him on the telephone:
"Lazar? Hello, hello there. My congratulations, too. What? I didn't quite hear you. I am becoming really deaf. I can't hear very well. Yes, I certainly realize that. Thank you. Accept my congratulations since that is our common cause—struggling for our army and our people, who are victorious. That is necessary, but difficult to accomplish. How are you getting on? How are you, I said. Poorly. And you got no reply? No answer whatsoever? That is too bad. I can't see why. I got the summons all of a sudden. It turned out all right in the end. I can't understand why they did not summon you? Someone must be getting in the way. As for Malenkov... I keep worrying about why you are angry with me about this? Is it really? No. Not like that. I have always felt and still feel that this problem would be resolved in your favor. Well, good luck. Thank you. All the best to you too. Goodbye."

Why Kaganovich has not been restored to the party, I can't understand. In those years we felt strongly about the struggle. We beat the right-wingers. . . .

[5-9-85]

■   **Comrades-in-Arms**   ■

Kosygin is an honest person, a genuine man of the party. Much better than the others.

Stalin would refer to Kosygin as "Kosyga." "Well, how are things, Kosyga?" he would usually greet him in a friendly manner, warmly and informally. And Kosygin rose very high.

[3-24-71]

A foggy day; the streets are slushy. Shota Ivanovich and I set off to visit Molotov. Tomorrow Molotov turns eighty-five. He looks hale and hearty. As we walk up the steps of his country house, he looks through the window and smiles at us. He promptly has both of us sitting at the table.

Sit down, or else nothing will be left for you. We are a serious people, keep that in mind. We are all Orthodox, and the Georgians are Orthodox, too.

Why do you say "too"? The Georgians were the first Orthodox people!

Stalin also took pride in this. Actually, we are denying historical facts.

Bulganin was buried recently. Did you attend the funeral?

I did. It was highly restricted, no regular visitors allowed. The cemetery was declared closed for sanitary inspection. I spent about an hour and a half there. Relatives, friends. They all arrived straight from the mortuary. No speeches were made.

But he was a military officer once, first a marshal and then a colonel-general. A company of troops should have been lined up, a gun salute should have been fired, and a military band should have played. These are military regulations.

The party regulations are different. They reign supreme.

[3-8-75]

Was Zhdanov a strong leader?

Not strong, though he had a few good works to his credit. I think his articles and his last public speeches were interesting.

Was he stronger than Kirov?

Than Kirov? Definitely so! Self-taught, as they say. Self-educated. Nevertheless, he certainly had some formal education. Stalin valued Zhdanov above everyone else. Stalin held him in exceptionally high esteem.

[1-14-75]

Despite my expulsion from the party, Budenny would always send me greetings on national holidays. His handwriting grew shaky, and yet he would keep mailing me his postcards.

Leafing through S. M. Budenny's memoirs in the magazine Don *I came across this passage:*

"Veterans of the Revolution went through some bitter experiences. They would often get into difficult situations and faced death more than once. But we never saw a greater danger than calling into question the revolutionary fervor and revolutionary deeds of the prominent leader of our party, the faithful comrade-in-arms of the Revolution's leader V. I. Lenin—J. V. Stalin.

"History belongs to posterity, and may it never serve as a distorting mirror."

Budenny's conduct was praiseworthy, but at the same time one could not demand too much of him. He was meritorious and popular with the people.

[3-4-78]

A friend of mine, an author, brought from Paris A. Avtorkhanov's Enigma of Stalin's Death *and gave it to me to read. I gave the book to Molotov, and after a few days I visited him to ask what he thought of it.*

It is so filthy. He depicts all of us as a gang of brigands! Nevertheless, the book contains a grain of truth. Beria was a man who, so to speak, was not so much a man of the past as a man of the future—in just one sense: he strained might and main to grab leading positions. Among the reactionary elements he was the activist. That's why he strove to clear the way for a return of private property. Anything else lay outside his field of vision. He did not avow socialism. He thought he was leading us forward, but in fact he was pulling us back, back to the worst.

On the book jacket are pictures of Beria, Khrushchev, Malenkov, and Bulganin. Molotov looked at them and went on to say:

Khrushchev was absolutely a reactionary sort of person. He merely hitched himself to the Communist party. He certainly didn't believe in any kind of communism. Bulganin didn't really represent anything. He never took a firm stand either for or against anything. He drifted along with the wind, wherever it blew. Beria, to my mind, was not one of us. He crept into the party with ulterior motives. Malenkov was a capable functionary.

You read this book and you become rather frightened. Bulganin played a minor role, while Malenkov, Beria, and Khrushchev constituted the nucleus of the new direction. I don't think Malenkov was very interested in issues of theory and problems of communism. Khrushchev was somewhat interested in these questions, though in a retrograde sense, in order to find out when and how things could be reversed.

Beria was unprincipled. On a number of occasions I heard that Beria, in his youth, had been recruited by some foreign intelligence service, and there had been some reports to this effect. But this has never been proven. But whether he actually was associated with the Baku commissars and served the cause in his youth should be verified.

In his younger years he worked with Mikoyan. They ended up hating each other.

They certainly hated each other. But then Armenians and Georgians are not, shall we say, well disposed to each other. Beria didn't trust any Armenian. He believed the Armenians wanted to seize the best land in Georgia.

Could these four have conspired against Stalin, as Avtorkhanov alleges?

The three, the threesome without Bulganin—yes, they could have had all sorts of plans. Beria's role is not entirely clear.

The book offers several accounts of Stalin's death, and each version features Beria.

This is true, and there is some basis for it. At times Stalin would change direction very suddenly. Khrushchev mentions Tito in this regard: "Stalin said that getting rid of Tito required no more than lifting his little finger." Stalin was certainly mistaken in this. To this day [1984] Tito is tsar and God in Yugoslavia, though not all communists share this view. But the fact is, he is securely ensconced among the Yugoslav communists.

You see, books like this are published abroad and then manage to make their way to us. I think you did the wrong thing last time when you mentioned this book with other people present. One shouldn't do this. People immediately besieged me, saying, "Give me the book to read!"

I thought we all were a close circle. . . .

A close circle we are, but all sorts of people were there. Most of them are not politically conscious with respect to communism. . . .

I have just finished reading a new book—Peter the First by Pavlenko. It's obviously a serious book and based on a great deal of material. Peter I acted very decisively and, as Marx said, used barbaric methods to drive out barbaric conditions. . . . But Marx highly valued Peter I as the reformer of the country. Peter I was, of course, a remarkable man. But his ways were far from modern and very drastic. Yet in order to accelerate the transition to a new society he had to act resolutely and often cruelly.

In my opinion, Stalin was not completely in control of himself during his last years. He didn't believe anyone around him. I'm judging from my own experience. But he promoted Khrushchev. In this Stalin was rather confused.

According to this book, he ceased to trust Beria.

I think so. He knew Beria would stop at nothing to save himself. This same Beria was responsible for clearing the security officers, and Stalin made selections from those whom Beria had chosen. Beria had tricked Stalin into believing that he himself had made the entire selection, but Beria was behind the whole thing.

Is it possible that they had poisoned Stalin when they were with him on the day before he became ill?

It's possible. Beria and Malenkov were close. Khrushchev communicated with them, but he had his own ambitions. He outwitted them all in the end! Khrushchev had a more solid social background, because philistinism was ubiquitous. He catered to the philistines. Khrushchev wasn't interested in ideas. He couldn't tell one from the other. He wasn't interested in ideas about the building of communism.

Did Stalin intend to retire after the XIXth Congress, as Avtorkhanov writes?

I don't think he was going to retire. He didn't seem to have any serious plans to that effect.

Could it be that he was just going to test the waters?

Yes, quite. I think it was this and nothing more. The circle around him was relatively close. Suggestions and ideas could be put forward rather informally at Politburo sessions. Stalin had nothing to fear in this respect, but there is reason to say that . . . It was just a probe or a test to take stock of sentiments and attitudes.

Avtorkhanov writes that after the XIXth Congress, at the Presidium of the Central Committee, Stalin asked to be relieved of the responsibilities of general secretary. . . .

Correct. That did occur.

After that he would become one of the Central Committee secretaries.

Not the general secretary. He was already that. Stalin suggested that the title "general secretary" be replaced simply by "secretary."

He also writes that Molotov assumed Stalin's place on the Central Committee.

This is not clear. At Stalin's suggestion, Malenkov delivered the report of the CC.

What role did Ignatiev play?

I didn't know him very well. He was not especially distinguished. A small man. He couldn't aspire to higher office, and he didn't. In the book his role is elevated beyond what it actually was. This is a fact.

The book cites Khrushchev at the XXth Congress, when he alleged that Stalin had said to Ignatiev, "If you don't get the doctors to confess, we'll have you shortened by a head."

I think that's improbable. I didn't know that. It seems to me unlikely.

Recently I went to see the Poskrebyshevs. I talked with Vlasik's daughter, and she told me that when her father was arrested shortly before Stalin's death, he exclaimed, "Stalin's days are numbered. He has only a short time left to live." He realized that Beria was bent on removing all the people who were loyal to Stalin.

That's right. At that time it was said that Vlasik had grown corrupt. More people from Stalin's intimate circle became corrupt as well. They were reported to have gotten involved with women from the outside. By that time, however, I was not exactly in the know.

Avtorkhanov writes that ". . . the only one who was candid in his relations with Stalin was Molotov."

Indeed, of the three who spoke at the funeral, I was the only one who spoke from the heart. . . . I would agree that it was so.

I don't believe Khrushchev grieved over Stalin's death.

No, he was extremely spiteful toward Stalin, and more so toward Beria. At times Stalin would express scorn for Beria. He wanted to have him removed. Whom did he trust? It's hard to say. No one, I would say. Khrushchev? There's no way he would have trusted that one. Bulganin was not the right sort. I don't think one can say that Malenkov was close to Stalin either. There was no one of prominence from the younger generation. He had cut off the Leningraders.

Avtorkhanov writes that Stalin had made up "the doctors' plot" in order to bring down Beria. [Nine Kremlin physicians, arrested and falsely charged with plotting the assassination of Stalin, were freed after his death.] Couldn't he have done it some other way?

These things are not that simple. It must be convincing to others. Otherwise people say nothing but are incredulous. . . .

The announcement about the doctors' plot contained a passage on the loss of vigilance in our state security agencies, a strong hint to Beria.

Correct. He saw that Beria was thorough but not completely sincere.

Avtorkhanov writes that Beria, Malenkov, and Khrushchev originally wanted to isolate Stalin, to ship him off to Solovky. . . .

Nonsense. That bears no resemblance to the truth.

Khrushchev told Harriman about his version of Stalin's death. Stalin invited "the four" to visit him at his dacha. On Saturday they had a dinner party, and on Sunday he didn't call. On Monday the chief of security reported Stalin's illness. "The four" arrived at the dacha but chose not to call the doctors. They refused to be seen with the sick man, and they all went home. The doctors were called only when it was clear that Stalin's condition was hopeless. The doctors were late allegedly because of slippery road conditions.

In a radio announcement on July 19, 1964, Khrushchev said: "Throughout human history there have been a number of cruel tyrants. All died by the very ax with which they had maintained their power." He also referred to the accounts of I. G. Ehrenburg and P. K. Ponomarenko, which are quite consistent. In late February Stalin had called a session of the Central Committee Presidium on the questions of "the doctors' case" and the deportation of Soviet Jews to a separate zone within the USSR. Stalin's resolutions were not passed, after which he fell to the floor in a faint. Beria was silent at the session, and then he too distanced himself from Stalin.

I concede that Beria was an accomplice in that affair. He openly played a very treacherous role.

[1-13-84]

Stalin spent most of his life at his dacha in Kuntsevo. That was where he died. During his last days I had in some sense fallen out of favor. . . . I had seen Stalin four or five weeks before he died. He was absolutely healthy. They called for me when he was taken ill. When I arrived at the dacha some Politburo members were there. Of non-Politburo members, only Mikoyan and myself, as I recall, had been called. Beria was clearly in command.

Stalin was lying on the sofa. His eyes were closed. Now and then he would make an effort to open them and say something, but he couldn't fully regain consciousness. Whenever Stalin tried to say something, Beria ran up to him and kissed his hand.

Was Stalin poisoned?

Possibly. But who is there to prove it now?

He was treated by good doctors. Lukomsky was good, as was Tareev. Kuperin was more of an administrator. Someone from the Politburo would always be on duty. I was on duty too.

But all hell broke loose the moment he died.

[4-22-70]

I repeatedly clarified with Molotov the details of Stalin's death. I recall that once, when we were walking in the woods, I felt I wasn't getting anything substantial from him. So I ventured to ask him a provocative question.

Beria himself was said to have killed him.

Why Beria? It could have been done by a security officer or a doctor. As he was dying, there were moments when he regained consciousness. At other times he was writhing in pain. There were various episodes. Sometimes he seemed about to come to. At those moments Beria would stay close to Stalin. Oh! He was always ready. . .

One cannot exclude the possibility that he had a hand in Stalin's death. Judging by what he said to me and I sensed. . . . While on the rostrum of the Mausoleum with him on May 1, 1953, he did drop hints. . . . Apparently he wanted to evoke my sympathy. He said, "I did him in!"—as if this had benefited me. Of course he wanted to ingratiate himself with me: "I saved all of you!" Khrushchev would scarcely have had a hand in it. He might have been suspicious of what had gone on. Or possibly. . . All of them had been close by. Malenkov knows more, much more, much more.

[8-24-71, 6-9-76]

My primary responsibility, as I see it, is not to write a truthful history, although that is a big, important task. A much more important, and more difficult, undertaking, which is more complicated to manage, is to help to restore and continue the work of Lenin and Stalin. This involves not only history but also the future.

To analyze the past as seen from the perspectives of the future and the present seems to me a most important undertaking. I cannot take on this task, of course. I don't have the strength for it. Nevertheless, I could offer some sort of assistance and impart a more correct way of thinking to such a study, which I consider to be essential nowadays.

[3-8-74]

Stalin was working on the second part of his *Economic Problems,* and he gave me some materials to read. Now no one knows what was done with these papers.

Could Beria have taken them?

No. Beria had no interest in that sort of thing. He was eager to know who was against whom and how to take advantage of one and bash the other. Most important to him were the conflicts between individuals and how he could make use of them. And, when necessary, to be able to produce some sort of document that declared, "Look what you reported about him!"

In short, he sought to provoke fights.

Mgeladze recounted how Malenkov and Beria formed a new government.

Malenkov made this announcement: "Comrade Stalin is in very critical condition. He is unlikely to pull out of it. Should he recover, he will need at least six months before he can resume his duties. Therefore the country cannot go on without leadership."

After that, Beria announced the members of a new government. He looked cheerful, as if he wanted to show that nothing terrible for the country had occurred.

That's possible. I can't remember those details. . . . Before he died, Stalin raised his arm. He raised it, but. . .

[6-30-76]

I am reading to Molotov excerpts from Avtorkhanov's book which describe the events of June 22, 1941: "We arrived at his dacha and suggested that he address the people. Stalin refused point-blank. Then Molotov was instructed to do it. . . ."

Yes, that's right. That is approximately what happened.

"It was proposed that Stalin head the high command of the Red Army. And he refused."

Why should he have assumed all these responsibilities? At any rate, he remained at the head, and he didn't immerse himself in trivial, secondary questions. Of course, he did the right thing in this respect.

"When the Politburo members started to remind Stalin of his personal responsibility in the event of catastrophe, Stalin switched to a counterattack and accused Molotov of treason. . . ."

Molotov?

Yes. ". . . For signing the pact with Ribbentrop."

Why, that's absurd! Stalin himself had been there. More to the point, he initiated the whole thing.

"He charged Voroshilov and Zhdanov with sabotaging agreement with the Anglo-French military missions..."

That is totally wrong.

"In response to protests that all had been done under Stalin's personal supervision, Stalin, with uncharacteristic fury, jumped up from his seat. He cursed everyone at the table and disappeared to one of his hideouts...."

Well, well.

Then Avtorkhanov cites Khrushchev: "I know what sort of hero he really was. I saw him paralyzed with fear before Hitler. He was like a rabbit hypnotized by a boa constrictor."

He certainly had a difficult time after the German attack, but he never appeared to be like a rabbit. He stayed at his dacha and didn't come out for two or three days. He took it all very hard, certainly. He was even a little depressed. But it was difficult for everyone, and he especially so.

Beria is alleged to have visited him and Stalin reportedly said, "All is lost. I give up."

Certainly not. It's hard to say now if that was June 22 or 23. One day just ran into the next. I never heard him say, "I give up." I never heard those words. I consider that to be improbable.

Avtorkhanov writes about Evgenya Allilueva, Svetlana's aunt, who came to see Stalin in August 1941 and was staggered by his mood of panic.

No. By that time he had already straightened himself out. When was he appointed war minister? June 30?

"The supreme commander-in-chief was formally Stalin, though in fact the responsibilities were fulfilled by his deputies: Zhukov in the army, Beria with the NKVD troops." Well, what do you think?

That's impossible to say.

"Politically the supreme command was handled by Beria and Malenkov."

Nor can one say this.

He writes about Zhdanov's intrigues against Malenkov and Zhukov and about how Zhukov was Malenkov's protégé....

Malenkov supported Zhukov to some extent. But to say he was Malenkov's protégé is going too far.

"Zhdanov enjoyed the support of Molotov, Kaganovich, Voroshilov, Andreev—all resentful Politburo members."

No. At that time we were not resentful at all.

Then he writes that after the war, Zhdanov was promoted, as were Voznesensky and Kuznetsov. Kuznetsov became a Central Committee secretary in charge of state security, and he proceeded to purge the security organs of those who were loyal to Beria. Beria then decided to bring Malenkov back from exile in Turkestan and to crush Zhdanov. "The Leningrad affair" was brewing.

Malenkov might have been in Turkestan, but I have no recollection of it. He might have stayed there a short while.

Then Zhdanov was taken to the hospital, where he died, and the others were arrested. . . . Dimitrov proposed that the Bulgarians and Yugoslavians form a Balkan federation. Did these things happen?

They did, though it remains unclear what part Dimitrov played in that affair.

In February 1948 Stalin said to Dimitrov, "You didn't consult me? You gab like women at a crossroads and say the first thing that crosses your mind!" But Dimitrov advised the Yugoslavs to remain firm in their disagreement with Moscow.

That's also unlikely.

Dimitrov never returned from his trip to Moscow.

It looks as if the Politburo had been filled with gangsters!

Avtorkhanov argues that Beria and Malenkov forced your break with Stalin.

I didn't believe so at the time.

They presented your cohort—Molotov, Voroshilov, Kaganovich, Mikoyan, Andreev—as a weapon in a Zionist plot. Furthermore, you might very well have been portrayed as a British-American spy.

Quite right, for a change.

"Stalin had gone as far as to suspect that his doggedly loyal Voroshilov was a British spy. He ordered that a listening device be planted in Voroshilov's apartment."

That could be. But he never accused Voroshilov.

Thoroughly amoral characters—that's the impression left by the book. Authors now seem willing to go to any extent in order to . . .

"Stalin never killed out of love for killing. He was no sadist, and even less was a paranoiac. . . . At the XIXth Congress Stalin turned out to be totally isolated from the other members of the Politburo. Stalin voted down six Politburo members. Nonetheless, they were all reinstated in the Politburo at the plenary session of the Central Committee. This was an historic, unprecedented defeat for Stalin." Did it happen that way?

That never happened.

And there is another detail. He writes that February 17, 1953, Stalin received the Indian ambassador Krishna-Menon. He kept making sketches of wolves in his notebook in the course of the meeting, and at some point he allegedly commented, "The peasants act wisely by killing mad wolves!" It appeared that he had certain members of the Politburo in mind.

He was just amusing himself.

[1-13-84]

■ Collectivization: We Extorted the Grain ■

On January 1, 1928, I had to go to Melitopol on the grain procurement drive. In the Ukraine. To extort grain.

From the kulaks?

From everyone who had grain. Industrial workers and the army were in a desperate situation. Grain was all in private hands, and the task was to seize it from them. Each farmstead clung to its stock of grain. We fanned out to the localities to get it. It was my first such mission—I remember it well.

I arrived in Kharkov. The capital of the Ukraine was still there, and the Central Committee of the Ukraine was still located there. The party activists were convened. They were told that the Ukraine must hand over its grain immediately, without delay. We criticized the slackers and traveled on to the countryside. January 1 I arrived at Melitopol. It was a holiday, everyone was celebrating the New Year, but I went straight to the regional party committee's building and ordered: "The party activists must meet here today." It was a large town, the administrative center of a large territory, a grain surplus region. That's why I was sent there to get all the grain.

The activists' meeting was held late in the afternoon, around five o'clock. I turned on the pressure: "Give us grain! It is high time to put the squeeze on the kulak!" and so forth in that vein. A resolution was adopted—to require, to fulfill the collection plan, to direct. . . . It was a peasant district, all the peasants lived on and worked their own farmstead. . . . We took away the grain. We paid them in cash, but of course at miserably low prices. They gained nothing. I told them that for the present the peasants had to give us grain on loan. Industry had to be restored and the army maintained.

Then I went out to the countryside, to the Greek and Ukrainian settlements. I applied utmost pressure to extort the grain. All kinds of rather harsh methods of persuasion had to be applied. We started with the kulak. If you don't put the squeeze on the kulak . . .

I traveled around the Poltava, Dnepropetrovsk, and Melitopol regions by special railroad car. I lived in it, protected by a security detail. By day I went out to the villages but did not stay there overnight. I returned to the railroad car to spend the night.

Soon I returned to Moscow. Stalin met with the most experienced grain collectors. I reported how I used pressure tactics and other ruses. I mention it because after that meeting Stalin wanted to go to Siberia on a grain-procurement campaign. That was his celebrated journey.

Did you stay to sit in for him?

Yes, I did.

Was there ever an instance when both of you were out of Moscow?

No, never, I believe. He said then, "I would cover you with kisses in gratitude for your action down there!" I committed these words to memory: ". . . for your action." He too wanted that experience, and soon afterward set off for Siberia. Stalin was interested in the grain areas. He wanted the peasants there to take better care of their crops. He visited the main centers—Novosibirsk, Altai. Before the trip he had carefully studied the reports I and others submitted, and he suggested that a special resolution be passed on the issue. From then on, the kulaks who failed to meet the quotas fixed for grain deliveries would face repressive measures. The kulaks were first of all held accountable if they failed to meet their procurement quotas. They were liable to violent measures: confiscation of their grain and execution. When the decree was published everyone began to sense that grain procurement had the force of law. It greatly increased the pressure, and grain flowed in. I went to the Ukraine, Stalin himself went to Siberia, and I believe Kaganovich and Mikoyan too traveled on grain-procurement missions. After that we went seeking grain every year. Stalin no longer made the trips. But we went out for grain five years in a row. We pumped out the grain.

In 1927 I delivered the report on collectivization. In 1928 we allowed a bit of a letup in the drive. In 1932, after I had already been appointed chairman of the Council of People's Commissars, I went to Siberia to procure grain.

There, apparently, an attempt on my life was made. In a road accident we rolled over into a ditch.

[6-21-72]

Were there any instances when the instructions issued by you, the Politburo, or Stavka [Supreme Command] went unheeded locally?

Such instances did occur. And they occurred not only during the war.

They were chronic, but especially during grain-procurement drives. We used to go to the villages for grain. "Hand over the grain!" "We've got nothing left!" "Nothing left? Go and get it! You surely have something cached away!" We never knew what they hid away, but often they did hold back stocks of grain. "Come on! Give it up! Quick!" Those drives were well warranted then. To survive, the state needed the grain. Otherwise it would crack up—it would be unable to maintain the army, the schools, construction, the elements most vital to the state. So we pumped away. Of course, we did not always succeed. We were sitting targets for criticism. They would say, Look, the center is demanding the impossible. Such talk was rife. Only the overwhelming authority of the center, with Stalin at the head, enabled us to fulfill the plans.

[7-31-72]

■ Famine, 1933 ■

Among writers, some say the famine of 1933 was deliberately organized by Stalin and the whole of your leadership.

Enemies of communism say that! They are enemies of communism! People who are not politically aware, who are politically blind.

No, in collectivization, you can be sure, hands must not tremble, you must not quake in your boots, and if anyone begins to shiver—beware! We get hurt! That's just the point. Now everyone demands everything ready-made! You are like children. The overwhelming majority of present-day communists come to us hands outstretched. They just demand that everything good we have be handed them on a silver platter. They act as if that is the meaning of life. But it is not.

People will be found who understand this. Such people will come along. The struggle against the petty bourgeois heritage must be merciless. If life does not improve, that's not socialism. But even if the life of the people improves year to year over a long period but the foundations of socialism are not strengthened, a crack-up will be inevitable.

But nearly twelve million perished of hunger in 1933. . . .

The figures have not been substantiated.

Not substantiated?

No, no, not at all. In those years I was out in the country on grain procurement trips. Those things couldn't have just escaped me. They simply couldn't. I twice traveled to the Ukraine. I visited Sychevo in the

Urals and some places in Siberia. Of course I saw nothing of the kind there. Those allegations are absurd! Absurd! True, I did not have occasion to visit the Volga region. It is possible that people were worse off there. Of course I was sent where it was possible to procure grain.

No, these figures are an exaggeration, though such deaths had been reported of course in some places. It was a year of terrible hardships.

[12-12-72, 8-15-75]

■   We Could Not Have Waited Longer   ■

At the XVth Party Congress you delivered a speech on the peasant question.

On collectivization.

Yes, on collectivization. You took a very interesting position. I would like to know, what did you mean by "cultured master of the land"?

I have forgotten what I said back then, but a "cultured master of the land" was a well-to-do middle peasant—well, even a kulak. We had not yet fully broken with the kulaks, as it were, because it was too soon. At this stage the relevant party decisions called for limiting kulak proclivities, not liquidating the kulaks. Not until two years later did we decide to liquidate the kulaks as a social class.

This was, perhaps, a preparatory period?

Yes, it was. The line back then was, don't alienate the middle peasants as a class, but put the pressure on the well-to-do middle peasants.

On December 11, 1927, at the XVth Congress, you stated: "He who now proposes that we adopt a policy of forced loans, of compulsory requisitioning of 150 to 200 million puds of grain [one pud = about 36 pounds] from about 10 percent of peasant households—that is, not only from the kulaks but even from part of the village middle stratum—however well intentioned, is an enemy of the workers and peasants, an enemy of the alliance of workers and peasants (Stalin, from his seat: 'Correct!'), who is pursuing a line leading to destruction of the Soviet state."

These are your words in 1927. But, look, I should like to clear up what ensued. Just a month later Stalin goes to Siberia to collect grain and says that we must liquidate...

Not a month later.

When was it? The Congress was held in December 1927, and he set out on his trip in January 1928.

He went later than that.

No, it was not more than a month later. Stalin went on a grain procurement trip to Siberia on January 15, 1928.

But we had not yet launched the slogan of liquidating the kulaks as a class.

And Stalin demanded that the grain be extorted without delay and that Article 107 of the criminal code be applied.

He went to Siberia after I had been to the Ukraine to get the grain deliveries completed.

Correct. But what happened right after the congress does not jibe with what was said at the congress....

Why not? Restricting the kulak is one thing, liquidation of the kulak is another. Back then our position was restriction of the kulak, not liquidation. Not until the autumn of 1929, in October or November, did Stalin launch the slogan of liquidation of the kulaks as a class. Two years had passed. Some delay was necessary for the conditions to be right for the collectivization campaign. Then we struck while the iron was hot. All the same, with our grain procurements we cleared the way for the next phase. You see, we would say to the peasant that the grain was needed, neither the working class nor the army could get along without it. But the kulak would not hand it over. What were we to do? So, a year passed, then another, by which time the liquidation of the kulaks as a class had been prepared. There was no other way.

[10-9-75]

Would Lenin have delayed the collectivization project a bit? Would he have launched the campaign later than Stalin?

No. I don't think so. No.

Wasn't collectivization started prematurely?

I don't think so.

Some argue that Lenin would have carried it through differently.

They are opportunists. They just don't understand. They are obtuse. They are unable to get to the heart of the matter.

Some writers now argue that Stalin and Molotov declared they would not rush ahead with collectivization, but as a matter of fact they...

We couldn't have delayed it any longer. Fascism was emerging. Soon it would have been too late. War was already looming on the horizon.

Some also argue that the muzhiks [peasants] should not have been so cruelly treated, and that Lenin had had different ideas on that score....

Lenin could also operate with resolve. Our situation, especially after Lenin was gone, became very dangerous.

The muzhiks were ruined, their will to work the land was destroyed. In general, the whole business was ill prepared. . . . That is what people say.

Of course, certain errors were made then. . . . It was a very complex undertaking. The Revolution occurred in a country where the petty bourgeoisie prevailed.

[2-3-72, 9-3-81]

At what point did the fate of the Revolution hang in the balance?

The transition to the New Economic Policy. Lenin said then, "We do not entirely enjoy confidence any longer. We are not trusted by the peasantry. If we do not find a way out of this situation, we'll be driven out." That was made public. He was most outspoken—"We'll be driven out." The peasant is a petty proprietor. As long as he is engaged in small-scale farming, he cannot do without trade. He is prepared to take to market the last of his produce to buy a length of cloth, shoes, and clothing. He has no alternative. We would have been ruined if we had not realized that. And that was the first critical moment.

Before this, of course, there was the crisis over the Brest peace treaty. Had we not concluded the Brest peace at that point, the Soviet government would have collapsed. Another critical moment arrived with collectivization. After that, industrialization. All this was evident. But as regards NEP, according to Lenin, it was our strategic retreat from socialism. He was condemned when NEP brought so much disappointment among the intelligentsia! Party membership cards were turned in. Well, those things happened. That was quite a turn, a drastic one, of course! During that period the NEP saved us from ruin.

Collectivization and routing the leftists and the rightists—particularly the rightists—were closely linked. The struggle against the right-wing deviation also raged around collectivization. But the struggle against the Trotskyite, the so-called left-wing, deviation had already been fought out.

By the time we passed through NEP to collectivization, we had already won reliable support. NEP was adopted at the Xth Congress. At the XIth Congress Lenin summed up the results of the new policy and said that if we had not abandoned our earlier policies and had not restored public confidence, Soviet power would not have survived. That was essentially his analysis of the NEP one year after it was launched. In 1922, at the XIth Congress, Lenin delivered the political report, and I delivered the report on organizational matters.

Our policy was flexible but forward-looking. Just at that point the workers' opposition started up. Among workers as well as among peasants, an entirely new party began in fact to take shape. They accused us of jettisoning our line, of renouncing socialism, of renouncing leadership of the working class, of drifting with the current toward capitalism. . . .

But otherwise Soviet power would have been lost.

[7-31-72]

■ That's Not the Long Term ■

Something is wrong with our agriculture. . . .

The writers need to be placed in the Ministry of Agriculture, then they will put things right there.

The Americans are jubilant. They have concluded another grain deal with us. They say they have never had such a profitable contract. The new one is for a number of years. It's unpleasant.

Unpleasant but a trifle. It's a trifle for the state. But we must have adequate supplies for the future. To achieve that goal we will have to work hard for another decade if we don't want to be affected by bad harvests. We want everything. We are like fairy-tale heroes who want everything right then and there. But we are not heroes, not entirely at least. I think the current situation indicates that we need to develop our agriculture along the path of socialism, while we . . .

The five-year plans now do us some harm. They pin us down, hold us back. In their time they were useful—not only useful, even necessary. But now the five-year span no longer affords full clarity. . . . If there were, so to speak, a long-term plan, which was broken down into five-year plans, we would have clarity. In practice now, many details are inscribed in the plan, but properly speaking there is no due clarity on where we are going. . . . We seem to lack the brains to think through the long-term prospect, while the five-year plan is not long-term any more. It used to be.

When we had nothing?

When we were drafting the first five-year plan—and this was typical—we stood for a five-year plan, but the rightists, Rykov and Bukharin, favored a two-year plan and fought hard for it.

Why?

We had to get out of a critical situation in agriculture. To prevent a collapse, what could we do in the next two years? And they actually wanted to mark time! We would not have been any closer to collectivization in two years. We would have issued some specialized directives, avoiding the main issue. And today we have all kinds of specific instructions crammed down our throats but no long-term outlook. After all, we need a political line. Improving the living conditions of the people is not a long-term outlook! We have been at work on that since the October Revolution. That is not a long-range goal for communism. We are building the material and technological basis for communism. But how are we building it? How are the current tasks related to the future? Take metallurgy—this, that, and the other are on the whole being accomplished to improve the situation of the people and thereby to undergird efficiency. This is correct, but this tells us nothing specific about a way of life. If the general line is set on peaceful coexistence, we don't need revolution.

[12-24-75]

. . . We did a pretty good job of carrying through collectivization. I believe our success in collectivization was more significant than victory in World War II. If we had not carried it through, we would not have won the war. By the start of the war we already had a mighty socialist state with its own economy, industry, and so forth.

I personally designated districts where kulaks were to be removed. . . . We exiled 400,000 kulaks. My commission did its job. . . .

[12-18-70, 5-9-72, 5-11-78]

■   **Frumkin's Letter**   ■

Vasily Belov, an author, wanted me to ask you about Frumkin's letter to the Politburo.

Right, I do recall a man by the name of M. I. Frumkin. It was the summer of 1928.

Exactly! You have a great memory. . . .

I can still remember the main events. He criticized me in that letter of his. He was a radical right-wing theorist, a Bolshevik. As we pressed on with collectivization, he wrote in opposition to it. In 1927 I was entrusted to deliver a special report on collectivization at the XVth Congress. As a matter of fact, I was then chairing the rural commission in the Central Committee, and the entire responsibility for... I myself come from a village, but I didn't know rural life well.

Frumkin contended that the struggle against the kulak would lead to the degeneration of agriculture and that we would be left without bread. So if we put the clamps on the kulak, we would face famine. He attacked me as I was, so to speak, among the instigators of collectivization. He said I was wrong. There was such a letter, and it was sharply condemned by the Central Committee. But behind Frumkin stood Rykov and Bukharin. He was in touch with them at all times.

Frumkin by and large had won a reputation for being quite independent in his judgments as far back as 1911, when he was the first to speak out on an important issue. In Petersburg a struggle was raging between Bolsheviks and Mensheviks. The Mensheviks had already become "liquidators." We roundly cursed them out because they wanted to liquidate the party. We, however, regarded the party as an illegal, strictly clandestine organization which at the same time had the ability to work within legal organizations wherever possible. The very flexible, well-balanced, and highly intelligent line pursued by the Bolsheviks set them off from the Mensheviks. The question then arose: What should be the main slogan of the workers of Petersburg? The Mensheviks proposed: In Piter let's build a workers' palace as a center for cultural work among the workers. But Frumkin proposed not a workers' palace but a workers' daily newspaper. He was supported by another well-known worker, a baker, who later became an anti-Stalinist. The former baker died in the 1960s, having deteriorated mentally. Back in 1911 he had supported Frumkin's idea.

The Bolsheviks stood for the workers' newspaper rather than for the workers' palace. That was how *Pravda* originated. The Mensheviks then launched a daily paper of their own.

Frumkin's role was a small one, but it has stuck in my memory, and from time to time I recall that he...

He wrote to the Central Committee: sown area is growing smaller, harvests are declining, grain marketings are falling, the country is without bread, but you persist in attacking the kulak. You are pushing the country toward the abyss.

Frumkin was a very straightforward man. I knew him well. A man of integrity who confronted the Central Committee openly and head-on. He explicitly wrote that he would not support collectivization and would criticize whomever wanted it, both the party congress and Stalin....

What became of him?

He too got mixed up with right-wingers, I think. The second wave.

Before the XVth Congress Bukharin and I worked on all the decisions pertaining to collectivization. We drafted the resolution on collectivization, and I delivered the report on it. Three of us had examined and reworked it: Stalin, Bukharin, and I. We worked out the fundamental decisions and line. . . . It is true that earlier, in 1925, Bukharin had told the peasants, "Enrich yourselves!" That statement, as it turned out, was no accident.

[2-3-72]

■   The Results Were Better. . .   ■

Bukharin and I drafted a resolution on my report at the XVth Congress. Later Stalin scoffed at Bukharin. To camouflage his opportunistic line Bukharin argued at one of our meetings, "You say I am defending the kulak, but in fact I favor a forced offensive against the kulak!" Stalin responded with a laugh, "Bukharin now favors a forced offensive! Even we didn't suggest that! But as long as he insists, all right, let us have it recorded that way—a forced offensive against the kulaks!" Bukharin was cornered.

But then Bukharin, of course, carried on as before. He subjected the party line to scathing criticism. The famous formula signed by Bukharin, Rykov, and Tomsky went like this: The Central Committee is pursuing a Trotskyist line on questions of the village and the peasantry. It is a policy of military-feudal exploitation of the peasantry.

First, we favor applying pressure—strong pressure—on the kulak. But not pressure that will be extended to the mass of the peasantry.

Trotsky did not believe we must count on the peasantry. He believed they were people who could not stand for socialism.

Flexibility of policy would help us in a very healthy way. Economic measures, Bukharin said, would suffice to finish off the kulak.

Trotsky betrayed the party by mounting military-feudal attacks on the peasantry which were merciless robbery.

[2-3-72, 4-13-72]

Stalin and Molotov pointed out in their speeches that the peasantry should be handled with caution, without illusions, that NEP would last a long time. . . . Had we proceeded with that kind of policy, we wouldn't have the problems we are trying to correct even now. Instead people started hiding grain in pits, and drunkenness increased. Although the kulaks amounted to only 3 to 4 percent of the peasantry, the numbers repressed were incomparably greater.

Molotov replied that, true, they had said such things, but then time told and circumstances demanded a much more rapid transition to collectivization.

The peasants were quick to respond to collectivization. The process advanced at a turbulent pace we hadn't expected. As far as de-kulakization goes, the Central Committee resolution of January 5, 1930, precisely designated the areas where collectivization was to be carried out. But of course there were more than a few excesses. Stalin pointed this out.

As to the NEP, it was never formally abandoned. Some of its elements are still practiced today.

I understood the feelings of those who wrote about rural life. They took pity on the muzhik. But what could you do? Sacrifices were unavoidable. Some argue that Lenin would have never pursued that kind of policy. But in matters like that Lenin was more severe than Stalin. Many suggest that Lenin would have reexamined his stand on the proletarian dictatorship, that he wasn't a dogmatist, and so on. But this is said by people who very much would have liked him to revise his views!

[5-11-78]

■ We Are Still Not Up to It ■

People now say, "Under Khrushchev it was bad, but now it is even worse."

It is not possible for everything to be good as long as imperialism exists. Imperialism must be destroyed. We have much building to complete.

Socialism is a cause of worldwide significance. There must be meat, there must be this and that. Well, what if we concentrate our main efforts on that? We may achieve a certain success, but we shall then be back where we started. Period.

Imperialism is still there.

But facing imperialism is socialism, the adversary. Why should they have plenty of everything, and we don't?

We are still not up to it.

Do you think collective farms could now be disbanded?

Not all at once. But we have to proceed in that direction. A big step in that direction was made with a recent decision of the Central Committee. The objective should be deeper specialization, wider cooperation, and a switch to industrial rails, to an agro-industrial way of development. The tasks that have been set are quite correct. I think my letter was of use in that regard. But there is no time to lose in this matter. It is a very important path along which the kolkhozes [collective farms] must evolve so as to heighten the very level of socialization, that is, to be transformed into sovkhozes [state farms]. There is no other way. That was stated by Marx, Engels, and Lenin.

Apart from the land we nationalized, our collective farms are not consistently socialist. Plants and factories are, which is most significant. Certain laws must be thoroughly reconceptualized and updated. The process should begin with specialization and increased amalgamation of kolkhozes, followed by the creation of agro-industrial complexes.

But the well-off kolkhozes will be against this. They find themselves in a favorable situation. At the expense of the state, they get land melioration and so forth; they deliver part of their output to the state and retain the rest—a very advantageous situation, indeed. This Marx and Engels feared.

In my opinion, the kolkhozes have already seen their day.

Things should not be rushed, but there is no reason to procrastinate either, because that would apply the brakes to an upsurge in the rural economy. Stalin's *Economic Problems* has a correct idea, a very correct idea on this question.

[6-3-76, 10-25-80]

The drought is not the problem. It is imperialism. This must never be forgotten. We are not likely to have it easy as long as we have to face imperialism. Of course we would like to live better. We deserve a better life. But improvement will be a slow process.

But people can't find meat for sale anywhere in the country.

To hell with the meat! Just let imperialism drop dead!

This bad drought . . . Everything we have is concentrated on it, and of course this is quite natural, correct, and necessary. But I would nevertheless approach it differently. It is probably because I've got all I need. No, not merely because of that.

And our assisting others is not an end in itself but has to do with the struggle against imperialism.

[11-4-76]

■ **Repression** ■

... Nowadays you don't get the real facts handed to you on a silver platter. They are mixed up and corrupted in every way, so to speak, and obscured by all kinds of other facts. It would now seem impossible to find a way out of this predicament. But for all that, there is a way out if one thinks and strives to sort things out. First, our country moved to the front line, so to speak, and has lived with two fundamental problems since the onset of the Revolution, which it could not surmount in a brief period and which are not yet fully surmounted. The first is our internal backwardness. To move to the most advanced positions for the destruction of capitalism and the building of socialism in a backward country—that, after all, is a Herculean task. The overwhelming majority hold that this task even contradicts Marxism, and they would depict Lenin as having departed from Marx. They try to do that in the West, though Lenin was a consistent champion, thinker, and revolutionary in the spirit of Marx and Engels. Marx constructed his theory objectively, but Lenin, they say, introduced a subjective, a new element to a degree not found in Marx. This is wrong, of course, but to a certain extent corresponds with the facts. He faced a new element in the backwardness of the country. The second problem is that the developed capitalist countries have remained capitalist. That is the external factor. It's undeniable.

These are the two problems, not to mention others, with which we must cope. They present colossal difficulties which might be overcome only under special conditions. In the early years, even after the victory of Soviet power, Lenin conceded that we had failed, so to speak. He frankly stated that if we proved unable to build a socialist society, we should nevertheless do everything we might toward that end. He would concede nothing as concerns the general line of advance. But have you seen what [Vasily] Grossman writes?—the problem is not Stalin but Lenin. Even here there is a grain of truth, because Lenin did not have the potentialities that became available to Stalin. Would Lenin have tolerated the opposition that surrounded him if he had been in a different position?

But what could he do? His genius lies in his ability to hold out under those conditions. That is real genius.

1937 was necessary. Bear in mind that after the Revolution we slashed right and left; we scored victories, but tattered enemies of various stripes survived, and as we were faced by the growing danger of fascist aggression, they might have united. Thanks to 1937 there was no fifth column in our country during the war. Even among Bolsheviks, you know, there were some—there still are some—who are loyal and dedicated as long as the nation and the party face no danger. But as soon as something dangerous appears, they first waver and then switch sides. I don't think we did the right thing to have rehabilitated many of the military who were repressed in 1937. The documents have not yet seen the light, but in time things will be cleared up. It's unlikely those people were spies, but they were definitely linked with foreign intelligence services. The main thing, however, is that at the decisive moment they could not be depended on.

Molotov was speaking in response to the persistent argument that if Tukhachevsky and Yakir had not been executed, the war's beginning would not have been so terrible for us. "Just the latest fashion in falsification," he said.

[12-18-70]

A friend of mine, a professor, comes to see me from time to time. "How shall I explain that period?" he asks. I say, "But what would have happened if the right-wingers had been in charge? Where would the course of history have turned then? If you look closely at the details, you will see the answer."

[2-19-71]

As long as the state exists, certain ills come with it; but neither survival nor progress can be achieved without the state. Unequal living standards, depending on what position you currently hold, a minister or... These things are all intertwined, and they should never be disregarded. As long as we have the state—and we will be living with it for many years to come—as long as we have money—and it is here to stay for some time—these are the fundamental factors that spawn all kinds of bad things, including bureaucracy, careerism, money-grubbing in every form, and, of course, cruelty.

The party purges are fully in keeping with the principle of democratic centralism, though apart from the Bolsheviks they have never been practiced by other parties. Only recently the Czechs have run a party purge, while we had several very thorough purges. Very sweeping and very harsh. Quite a few mistakes were made in the process, too.

So 1938 was too soon for rehabilitation? What do you think? Was it because of the imminence of war?

It was because of war and confusion about who was to verify whom. Distrust was pervasive. It was not only the flagrant rightists, not to mention the Trotskyists, who suffered but also many waverers who irresolutely implemented the line in which they had no confidence, those who at a critical moment might betray, might go back on their word.

Despite all that, people like Khrushchev and Mikoyan survived, and not only they. . . .

Yes, but it's a shame that many good people perished.

The struggle was so intense. . . . In such an intense, complicated struggle, fought by people often untested, sometimes they—perhaps maliciously—helped to destroy good people. There were undoubtedly such cases.

Testing for loyalty and reliability, you know, is very complicated. Herein lies the danger for a state, especially a dictatorship of the proletariat, any dictatorship—it requires harsh, unquestioning discipline. But who is to maintain it? People who do not always want it, down deep oppose it, and oppose it in practice as long as that is possible. But the moment they sense danger, they go too far to curry favor and to protect their careers. Many, many deeds have been committed by such people, because we do not have ready-made pure people, purged of all sins, people who would carry through a very complicated, difficult policy fraught with all kinds of unknowns. Verify or not, verification itself is not always appropriate. To stage a purge of the party is very dangerous. The best people are the first purged. Many people who are honest and speak frankly are expelled while those who keep everything in the dark and are eager to curry favor with the party chiefs retain their positions. This was to a certain extent inevitable as long as careerism and time-serving held people in their grip.

"1937 was the continuation of the Revolution," concluded Shota *Ivanovich.*

In a certain sense the Revolution has not been completed to this day. In a way, yes. Socialism has not yet been completely built.

To those people who arrive after the task is completed, it seems everything is easier. . . .

[2-3-72]

■   **"Had the Leadership Flinched Then..."**   ■

These things must be properly sorted out. Trotskyism and particularly the rightist deviation need to be recalled. You see, in 1937 there were many who wavered and vacillated. Many honest communists perished then. There is no smoke without fire. The security people overdid it. They were overzealous in fulfilling their tasks. But many wavered, and good people often perished as a result.

[2-18-71]

Some were offended, others were demoted. People had different motivations for their criticism. But there were critics who were unable to appreciate our accomplishments. They were prepared to do damage. . . .

A great many people cheered "Hurrah!" and were for the party and for Stalin in words but vacillated in deeds. Khrushchev, who was a Trotskyist in his time, presents a striking example. . . . In many cases it was difficult to sort things out. But back then one had to be very much on the alert.

Now we have all become wise after the fact, know-it-alls, and we lump together discrete time periods. We passed through dissimilar time periods. One must closely examine each period and each historical actor taken separately.

Socialism demands immense effort. And that includes sacrifices. Mistakes were made in the process. But we could have suffered greater losses in the war—perhaps even defeat—if the leadership had flinched and had allowed internal disagreements, like cracks in a rock. Had the leadership broken down in the 1930s we would have been in a most critical situation, many times more critical than actually turned out.

I bear responsibility for this policy of repression and consider it correct. Admittedly, I have always said grave mistakes and excesses were committed, but the policy on the whole was correct.

All the Politburo members, including myself, bear responsibility for those mistakes.

The allegation persists that the majority of the condemned were innocent and were wrongly punished. But in the main it was the guilty, those who needed to be repressed to one degree or another, who were punished.

[12-6-69, 7-29-71]

Policy is one thing, but its implementation is another. Had no brutal measures been used, there would surely have been a danger of splits within the party.

Office-seeking within party ranks also played a negative role. Each person clung to his position. You know, with us it has always been like that—once we launch a drive, we push it steadfastly to the limit. The opportunities for abuses in such circumstances are tremendous when everything is on so large a scale.

[4-27-73]

Marxist thought must be constantly replenished. We can't know whether or not there will be a "personality." May God grant there be not one "personality" but many good ones!

Citing these mistakes, some people have tried to impugn our entire system. They say: You were wrong! That's no way to build socialism! But who built it better? We were the first. . . .

[8-15-72]

I justify the repressions despite the grave mistakes committed in the process. Bear in mind it was not merely overdoing it—not with Yagoda heading state security. He explicitly told the court that the oppositionists had remained in high offices for so long only because he had assisted them. "Now I confess my mistakes and wrongdoings; I therefore ask you to spare me. Let me live, for I have rendered a good service to the court!"

I have the transcript of his trial. He said, "Indeed, the rightists and the Trotskyists sitting here in the dock were exposed so late because I was the one who prevented that. And now I am condemning them all! Can you guarantee life to me in exchange for that service?" What a skunk! A communist, a people's commissar. And that scoundrel sat next to Dzerzhinsky! As Dzerzhinsky's closest aide he was gradually, after Menzhinsky, moved up to take the job of people's commissar for state security. What kind of man was this? What filth!

I used to know him well in those years, and I regret he was such a close aide to Dzerzhinsky. Dzerzhinsky was a radiant, spotless personality. Yagoda was a filthy nobody who wormed his way into the party and was only caught in 1937. We had to work with reptiles like that, but there were no others. No one! Now you understand why so many mistakes were made. They deceived us, and innocent people were sometimes incriminated. Obviously one or two out of ten were wrongly sentenced, but the rest got their just desserts. It was extremely hard then to get at the truth! But any delay was out of the question. War preparations were under way. That's how it was.

[1-9-81]

And that was in 1937. It took twenty years. Not twenty exactly—they were thrown out of the Politburo earlier than that, but they were in it for quite some time. There were so many open and heated debates on a variety of issues! First it was Trotsky, then Bukharin in 1928–1929. Confrontation with Trotsky started even earlier, under Lenin; then, starting from 1925–1926, it was Zinoviev and Kamenev. The right-wing opposition—Bukharin, Tomsky, and Rykov—emerged in 1928–1929. It has received little coverage, but at the time it was the chief threat because essentially it reflected the interests of the kulaks and of many well-to-do peasants who followed them. That right-wing opposition was and is even today extremely hard to fight. But no one writes about this or tries to explain it.

Of course we committed a number of grave errors in the matter. But in fact those errors were many fewer in numbers than people think today.

[4-29-80]

Yes, even now I believe that the Central Committee acted correctly in 1937 and in the late 1930s. To have done all this smoothly and graciously would have been very bad. After all, it is interesting that we went on living with the oppositionists and oppositionist factions until the events of the late 1930s. After the war there were no oppositionist factions, a relief which enabled us to set a good, correct policy. But if most of these people had remained alive, I don't know whether we would have been able firmly to stand our ground. It was mainly Stalin who took upon himself this difficult task, but we helped correctly. I do mean correctly. Without a man like Stalin it would have been very, very difficult, especially during the war. There would no longer have been teamwork. We would have had splits in the party. It would have been nothing but one against another. Then what?

We overdid it and committed many errors. That's indisputable. . . .

You should never forget that if there hadn't been repression, the opposition wouldn't have been so fearful.

Yevtushenko writes in his novel that what was built on fear could not be regarded as victory.

If heroes like Yevtushenko had been placed on a pedestal, would we have won the war? We were a backward country of small-holding peasant farms, as Lenin said. The fact that we survived, that socialism endured and after the war moved forward, all of this, in my opinion, is our greatest accomplishment of this period. Yes, in this achievement the epidemic of repressions itself played a crucial role. In the spring of 1921 Lenin, at the Xth Party Congress, said that merciless struggle must be waged. In that case could we tolerate further discussion? No, no more discussion! But discussions went on and on interminably, though on a reduced scale. Under Lenin there was no alternative. But early in 1923, as soon as Lenin was incapacitated, we had to reckon with a new situation. Under Lenin it was one thing, without him, another. Under Lenin there were so many disagreements, so many opposition groups of every conceivable stripe. Lenin regarded this as very dangerous and demanded resolute struggle against it. But he could not take the lead in the struggle against the opposition or against disagreements. Someone had to remain untainted by all repression. So Stalin took the lead, assuming the burden of responsibility in surmounting the vast majority of these difficulties. In my opinion he generally coped with this responsibility correctly. All of us supported him in this. I was one of his chief supporters. I have no regrets over it.

[12-9-82]

Was Stalin correct about the class struggle becoming more intense under socialism?

It was correct in view of the periods analyzed then. It implied certain periods of intense confrontation rather than continuous struggle.

[1-1-83]

The service rendered by Stalin's leadership in strengthening the unity of the party—and of the world communist movement as well—is tremendous. Stalin was a man of integrity.

[1-1-83, 6-16-83]

I have heard that Stalin and you issued a directive to the NKVD to apply torture.

Torture?

Did you?

No, we never did that.

Vyshinsky is charged with abolishing legal procedures. A person's future was decided by one man.

Well, he shouldn't be charged with that. He was never the one to make those decisions. Of course there were such excesses. But there was no other way out.

An individual could be sentenced at the will of a district party secretary.

That was possible. The true Bolsheviks could not afford to hesitate on the eve of World War II. It's most important to realize that.

It is also said that Stalin and Molotov considered only themselves to be true Leninists.

There was no alternative. Had we not regarded ourselves as Leninists, and had we not attacked those who wavered, we could have been weakened.

[10-14-83]

Concerning 1937 someone has written: "So many families had a loved one arrested! Weren't Stalin and Molotov aware of that?"

Philistine talk. Such talk is inevitable.

[1-1-85]

Recently a chauffeur drove me here from Moscow. He was an elderly man whom I had never seen before. I accept any driver they send over to me. I normally listen to the Maiak [the news radio station] to get the latest news and enjoy some music. But this time my driver wanted to talk and asked if I would turn off the music. I wondered what he would say. I tried to ask him a question to enliven the conversation.

He remarked, "Isn't it great that in Russia there is a Siberia!"

I said, "Yes, Siberia is a vast land. We would be worse off without it, and we will benefit from having it in many ways."

"Yeah, France has no Siberia, Germany has no Siberia, but they are not faring well."

I thought, what was he up to?

"What exactly do you have in mind when you mention the benefits of Siberia?" I asked. "I know we possess boundless wealth there . . ."

"I think you know what's on my mind. There was the time when all that human scum and rubbish had to be crushed. Stalin was far-sighted; Josif Vissarionovich was a man of vision. Those who had to be put out of the way were done away with just in time. Just in time because it was necessary to act strongly, resolutely, and mercilessly. Comrade Stalin took the job firmly in hand."

"Right. I agree with you," I told him.

Then he remained silent till we were close to the house.

The people see everything. What is it they say—is there going to be a second revolution, or what?

[11-1-77]

"I recall as a child," said Shota Ivanovich, "that it was terrible, it was horrible when NKVD agents appeared. It was a fear, I imagine, analogous with that inspired by the Gestapo."

Of course.

"They would come to take someone away. They took my father. He perished because he was not fond of Beria, and my mother suffered terribly. It was horrible, I don't deny it and I well remember it, but admittedly without the state security agencies there would be no Soviet power today."

Certainly.

[8-16-77]

"You know why my mother was arrested?" asked Shota Ivanovich. "For being a member of the family of a traitor to the Motherland. Just a family member. And nothing else."

I understand. And why was your father arrested?

"It seems he was a right-winger. A party member since 1905. He had been to jail three times as a Bolshevik."

Even if he was a member since Napoleon's time, at some point he was a Bolshevik and then he apparently ceased to be one.

"He was always a Bolshevik. After the rehabilitation decree was issued, my mother received a special pension on his account as well as a free voucher for a stay at a spa. Mother was a housewife. She came from a poor peasant family."

From the kulaks, probably?

"Like my mother, father also came from a poor peasant family. Stalin and you looked on from the Lenin Mausoleum when the holiday marchers filed past bearing placards inscribed, 'Ezhovy rukavitsy' [Rule with an iron rod]. Did Stalin approve this?

No one voiced any objections then. . . . Ezhov was a prerevolutionary Bolshevik, a former industrial worker. He was never affiliated with an opposition faction. He was a secretary of the Central Committee for a few years. He worked in the Central Committee for quite some time. At one time he was secretary of the Kazakh regional party committee. He enjoyed a very good reputation, but I can't rule out the possibility that he became somewhat demoralized and corrupt. I still retain some impressions of him. . . .

In A. S. Yakovlev's book The Goal of my Lifetime, *Stalin says of Ezhov, "You call the ministry, he's left for the Central Committee; you call the Central Committee, he's left for the ministry; you send a messenger to his apartment and there he is, dead drunk. . . ." How then is Ezhov to be perceived? He had been honest but then committed all kinds of follies. Could that be so?*

You could say he overreached himself and committed all kinds of follies. When a man is afraid of losing his job and turns overzealous . . . that is called careerism. It is tremendously important because it keeps growing and is one of the main defects of our time.

By that time Ezhov had sunk to a point of degeneration. You are not the first to tell me that Stalin said this. I have read Yakovlev but don't remember everything. They started to accuse Ezhov when he began to set arrest quotas by regions, on down to districts. No fewer than two thousand must be liquidated in such and such region, no fewer than fifty in such and such district. . . . That's the reason why he was shot. His official conduct, of course, had not been subjected to oversight.

Didn't the Politburo err in placing excessive trust in the security agencies?

No. There were deficiencies. . . . You could say that Molotov is not bald. But that does not mean he has curly locks. If you say that a man is not tall, that does not mean he is short. I did not say that Ezhov had an unblemished record, but he was a good party worker. Closer oversight was needed. Oversight was inadequate.

Didn't the security agencies place themselves above the party?

No, that's not so. The acute danger of deviations should not be dismissed. There was not enough time. We lacked resources. I did not say that the Politburo was overly trusting, but I did say that insufficient oversight was exercised. I disagree that we were overly trusting. The oversight was inadequate.

[4-27-73]

There were things we have spoken about that broke people. And all of these oppositions? Friends today, enemies tomorrow, caught up in ferocious struggle. There were good people even among the rightists, of course. Of all the members of the Politburo who worked under Lenin, Stalin alone remained. All the others went into opposition at one time or another: Trotsky, Zinoviev, Kamenev, Rykov, Tomsky, Bukharin. . . . Of course, for Stalin it was an unbearable situation—how to suffer criticism from all quarters, not to mention dissatisfaction, grumbling, and distrust. He needed nerves of steel to withstand it. Stalin too valued Bukharin highly. Yes, he did! Bukharin was highly educated and cultured. But what can you do?!

[6-6-73]

■ The Trials ■

In the first place, as chairman of the Council of Ministers, I am accountable for all the repressions. I am responsible for...

I knew Ukhanov quite well. He was quite a good, likable fellow. Handsome too, by the way. A worker, a metal worker actually, from the Dynamo plant, and a revolutionary. He was chairman of the Moscow Soviet. He became associated with the rightists. I am responsible for everyone inasmuch as I signed most—in fact, almost all—the arrest lists. Of course we debated, then made a decision. In the end, however, the decision was based on trust in the GPU's word. Haste ruled. Could one go into all the details?

But you must remember that quite a few right-wingers were operating within the NKVD. Yagoda was a right-winger through and through. Ezhov was different. I knew Ezhov very well, much better than Yagoda. Yagoda was also a prerevolutionary Bolshevik, though not from the working class....

But their results were the same.

No, there was a difference, a political one. As concerns Yagoda, he was hostile to the party's policies. Ezhov had never been hostile, he just overdid it because Stalin demanded greater repression. That was somewhat different. Ezhov had no ulterior motives. The machinery rolled—stop it where? Sort everything out properly? But the sorting out was often done by rightists or even by Trotskyists. Through them we obtained a lot of incriminating materials.

But when a regimental commander gets arrested merely because he knows Yakir? Or because he saw him once from a distance?

One didn't necessarily have to see him to be in his group, or be a friend of his for that matter. Did each of Stalin's supporters know him personally? Each Stalinist just had confidence in his line and policies and fought for them.

Those public trials are surprising in that people like Bukharin, Rykov, Rozengolts, Krestinsky, Rakovsky, Yagoda confessed to things that seem ridiculous. Yagoda said, "I am no better than any spy operating against the Soviet Union." That was manifestly preposterous. Why did they do that? People who know Rykov and Bukharin, even Rozengolts, were deeply shocked—how was this possible? I think it was another stratagem of theirs to carry on their struggle against the party at the public trial—to so malign themselves as to make all the other charges seem unbelievable.

I would even say that their confessions contained only 10 percent absurdities, perhaps less. They confessed to certain things on purpose in order to show how preposterous the whole trial was. That was a struggle against the party.

You refuse to take into account the psychological and political dimensions of the matter because you wonder, could all those charges have been true?

The confessions seemed artificial and exaggerated. I consider it inconceivable that Rykov, Bukharin, and even Trotsky agreed to cede the Soviet far east, the Ukraine, and even the Caucasus to a foreign power. I rule that out. But some kind of talk revolved around this matter, and the prosecutor later oversimplified it. . . .

[12-4-73]

The time will come when everything will be sorted out. Solzhenitsyns could also be found in the party leadership. Then they had to be tolerated. Things are no different today. By 1937 they had lost a platform to stand on and the support of the people. They voted for Stalin but were double-dealers. It was shown in court that the right-wingers had Kuibishev and Gorky poisoned. Yagoda, the former chief of the secret police, was involved in arranging the poisoning of his own predecessor, Menzhinsky.

[1-8-74]

Did Stalin himself have any doubts about 1937? Did he speak of any extremes or excesses?

How could he not have had doubts? And not just doubts. Ezhov, chief of state security, was executed by firing squad.

Didn't Stalin merely make a scapegoat of Ezhov, thereby placing all the blame on him?

Too simplistic. That version is pushed by those who misunderstand the state of the country at the time. Of course the demands originated with Stalin, and of course there were excesses, but all that was permissible, to my mind, for the sake of the main objective—keeping state power!

Some fiction now includes episodes in which Stalin is tortured by doubts about the victims of 1937.

Poor things! Pity them? Don't forget, they worked to ruin the cause!

Stalin is said to have apologized to Rokossovsky.

Quite possible. Rokossovsky was a good man. Meretskov was also in jail before the war.

[2-29-80]

After the trial Trotsky called Zinoviev and Kamenev pathetic creatures.

Here's what Bukharin said at the trial. ". . . I admit that I am guilty of the dastardly plan of the dismemberment of the USSR, for Trotsky was negotiating about territorial concessions, and I was in a bloc with the Trotskyites. This is a fact, and I admit it. . . .

"I already said when giving my main testimony during the trial that it was not the naked logic of the struggle that drove us, the counter-revolutionary conspirators, into this stinking underground life, which has been exposed at this trial in all its starkness. This naked logic of the struggle was accompanied by a degeneration of ideas, a degeneration of psychology, a degeneration of ourselves, a degeneration of people. There are well-known historical examples of such degeneration. One need only mention Briand, Mussolini, and others. And we too degenerated, and this brought us into a camp which in its views and features was very much akin to a kulak praetorian fascism."

He was very articulate about that. Go on.

"For three months I refused to say anything. Then I began to testify. Why? Because while in prison I made a reevaluation of my entire past. For when you ask yourself: 'If you must die, what are you dying for?'—an absolutely black void suddenly rises before you with startling vividness. There was nothing to die for, if one wanted to die unrepented. And, on the contrary, everything positive that glistens in the Soviet Union acquires new dimensions in a man's mind. This in the end disarmed me completely and led me to bend my knees before the party and the country. . . .

"I feel it my duty to say here that in the parallelogram of forces which went to make up the counterrevolutionary tactics, Trotsky was the principal motive force. And the most acute methods—terrorism, espio-

nage, the dismemberment of the USSR, and wrecking—proceeded primarily from this source.

"*I may infer a priori that Trotsky and my other allies in crime, as well as the Second International, all the more since I discussed this with Nikolaevsky...*"

Who is Nicolaevsky?

A *Menshevik living abroad.*

"*... will endeavor to defend us, especially and particularly myself. I reject this defense, because I am kneeling before the country, before the party, before the whole people. The monstrousness of my crimes is immeasurable especially in the new stage of the struggle of the USSR. May this trial be the last severe lesson, and may the great might of the USSR become clear to all. Let it be clear to all that the counterrevolutionary thesis of the national limitedness of the USSR has remained suspended in the air like a wretched rag. Everybody perceives the wise leadership of the country that is ensured by Stalin.*

"*It is in the consciousness of this that I await the verdict. What matters is not the personal feelings of a repentant enemy, but the flourishing progress of the USSR and its international importance.*"

He is a little hypocritical at this point. . . .

"*I once more repeat that I admit that I am guilty of treason to the Socialist fatherland, the most heinous of possible crimes, of the organization of kulak uprisings, of preparations for terrorist acts and of belonging to an underground, anti-Soviet organization. I further admit that I am guilty of organizing a conspiracy for a 'palace coup.' ... These are profoundly practical matters. I said, and I now repeat, that I was a leader and not a cog in the counterrevolutionary affairs.*"

A good speaker. Very articulate. Pure diction. Now they have managed to trample these trials under foot. They don't appear in print any more. The entire proceedings, you know, were published for all to read. Attending the trials were foreign reporters, both left-wing bourgeois and Hitlerite press, diplomats, ambassadors. . . .

Past mistakes and losses of life had been great because we proved too trusting of individuals who could no longer be trusted. Their degeneration was already complete, and we got rid of them belatedly.

Personal ambitions could also be traced in that affair. The "palace coup" schemes. . . .

Personal . . . ? I can't agree with that. That conclusion would reduce the whole affair to mere trifles. Each of us, bad or good, has his own personal interests. But why should those individuals have initially proceeded in one direction and then made a U-turn to march in the opposite direction? Personal ambition would be something petty and narrow. The trouble was that they no longer believed; they had lost all faith in the cause and consequently had to seek a way out. But only implacable enemies of Soviet power could point to another way out. Either I defend the October Revolution or I am against it and look for allies among its enemies.

You see, it's never easy when you must grapple with difficulties. Not everyone has sufficient stamina for it. But the party keeps moving forward. It keeps advancing. The opposition desperately looked for a crack in which to hide. No way. You are known by the public. You are Trotsky, you are Bukharin. You feel you are supposed to say what you have always said. They repeated their past affirmations of faith, but down deep they no longer believed in the cause. Here you have what turned them into such spineless creatures in the end. . . .

[8-14-73]

At the trial, how did Bukharin put it? "What have I left? Should I hide anything? What for? Now I've got nothing. I face nonexistence, so I am prepared to tell everything. . . ." They sensed they could not squirm out. They were caught.

But now it is said that the accusations had no basis in fact whatever, apart from the confessions of the accused, which still cannot be taken as proof of guilt.

No other evidence was required. We were absolutely certain they were guilty. They were enemies! You just read Bukharin. What an opportunist! And what about the kulak revolts?

Their innocence was out of the question, then?

Absolutely. Look, they strained to reduce their testimony to the point of absurdity because they were so terribly embittered by defeat. Victory over them was complete. Of course Bukharin had a very high opinion of himself, and failure was not to his taste. Very embittered, indeed.

[11-9-73]

They now say the trial was conducted with actors in place of the accused. Then I pose this question: "The Germans just once arranged a show trial of a single individual. Goering presided over the trial, and the whole affair ended in a flop the very first day!"

Correct. But in our country everything was made public with the exception of two military tribunals. For reasons of military secrecy these were closed trials. The enemies of Soviet power have always been good at concocting ingenious stories. The open trial lasted for twelve days, with the world press attending and with twenty-one individuals, all well known to the public, sitting in the dock. . . . Our enemies also attended the trials.

[1-8-74, 3-8-75]

Nowadays it is said, "Yes, many lives were sacrificed in order to defend Soviet power. But who needs a system that caused so many millions to perish? Wouldn't a monarchy or a constitutional democracy have been better?"

Every well-off individual in bourgeois society will talk that way, but those not well off—the worker, the peasant, the poor man—can't agree with this. Lives were sacrificed under the old regime, and if not for Soviet power the number of lives lost would have been greater; there would have been ever more wars without end. That would have been inevitable.

Just try to prove it!

It does not require proof. Life will demonstrate it to those who still don't see it. But the masses of workers and peasants do.

[6-13-74]

Those who allege that the trials were badly scripted are, in their obtuseness, simply allied with the White Guards. No GPU or any other security service could have fabricated the trials that way. Three major trials were held: in 1936, 1937, and 1938, with much material released to the public. The defendants were totally demoralized, and they divulged a great deal about their operations. I think and assume that in their testimony they withheld information and tried to mislead on certain points.

To say that people like Krestinsky and Rozengolts, people like Yagoda, like Bukharin and Piatakov all followed some kind of script is absurd!

As long as there is imperialism all of this will be repeated time and again. There will be rightists and leftists. As long as imperialism exists, we shall not be delivered from this.

"Had you not prevailed in 1937, the Soviet government might no longer exist," said Shota Ivanovich.

No, that's an extreme supposition. There would have been more victims. We would have prevailed in any case. But it would have required millions more victims. We would have had to beat back the German invasion and fight the internal enemy at the same time.

[6-16-77]

You are reproached inasmuch as Stalin allegedly killed off the most talented people in the country.

The most talented being Trotsky, Zinoviev, that ilk? With such talented people we would have crept backward. There is talent and there is talent. . . .

[12-28-77]

A new version has developed with regard to the open trials of the 1930s. It is said that the defendants were promised life in exchange for exhaustive confessions—something on that order.

That's a White Guard version. It's their fabrication. Such notions appeared earlier, too. Are they complete fools, or what?

[4-28-76]

"Some people reproach you," said Shota Ivanovich, *"for not having done a thorough job in 1937. There should have been greater repression because many covert enemies remained untouched. You have shown in your memorandum that double-dealers were ensconced in the party!"*

Yes, both in the regional party organizations and in the people's commissariats. In the Politburo itself were people who did not believe in our cause. Rykov, for example. And Zinoviev, too. Rykov was convinced there would be an uprising in the Don area.

Now, how can we explain the bitter struggle within the party before the war? That's a very important question, an extremely significant idea which I couldn't entirely grasp at first.

The exploiting classes had not yet been finished off, and this was reflected in the party.

The exploiting classes are now said to have been eliminated by then. By 1937 there was not a single kulak around. . . .

The job was considered done the day after all the kulaks had been deported! Now, let me address what was not completed. The kulaks were defeated, yes. But that was not complete victory. The kulak mentality can still be seen today, and on a grand scale, too. Party members defend the kulaks! "They're hard workers..." some argue. Many writers say such things. Complete blockheads!

People say Lenin would never have treated his opponents the way

Stalin did. Stalin displayed a despotic character. Lenin spent so much time on a person like Trotsky!

That was a different era, and there were no other alternatives. That was it. "I will leave the party CC. I will leave the government," Lenin threatened [if the opposition to the Brest peace treaty did not come around to his position]. You see, that's how far things had gone!

Of course Lenin displayed more flexibility in certain cases. Stalin was less tolerant. But, on the other hand, Lenin demanded that Zinoviev and Kamenev be expelled from the party in the days of the October Revolution, and Stalin defended them. It could go either way depending on the case. But it cannot be said that Lenin was soft. He didn't spend his time wiping children's snotty noses. Lenin should not be portrayed like that.

[6-30-76]

We could not pause [in the 1930s] to go into a person's record thoroughly and get the objective facts about him. We did not have the time or the resources to defer action. In certain cases the fate of the cause hung by a thread. I believe we acted correctly, though it entailed certain inevitable, even grave, excesses in repression. But there was no other way during that period. If the opportunists had prevailed, of course they would not have followed our course of action. But later during the war there would have been much internal brawling, which would have impacted on all our work, on the very existence of Soviet power. We can and must be criticized, even charged with excesses. But I don't think we had an alternative then. It was the best of all possible alternatives.

Your opponents argue, "Had Bukharin prevailed, it would have been much better. Stalin and Molotov would have been removed, and there would have been less bloodshed."

A genuine communist cannot talk that way. It's not just that we overdid repression. Our mistakes, including the crude mistakes, were justified. Alternatively, the rightists would have dealt with all of us, and a rancorous struggle would have raged inside the country. We would not have submitted to Hitler, but he would have gained much by this. Of course, it would have inflicted a blow on the entire future movement of communism in Europe. (In China the movement was not yet on a firm footing.)

I believe we are being accused by people who are incapable of thinking and acting like Bolsheviks. Yes, we are to blame because we were the leadership, but that is a more complicated question. The role of the personality—Stalin, in particular, to say nothing of Lenin—was certainly tremendous.

Take the example of Chile. Allende laid a hand on no one, but what came of it? What bloody terror!

Of course, given the international situation, brawling within the Central Committee and the party would have played into Hitler's hands. Hitler would have gained assistance from the Bolsheviks. Back then we could not know how it would end. Nothing good could have been expected from internal discord. I, for one, understood that certain people bequeathed us by Lenin were nevertheless non-bolshevist types. People such as Zinoviev, Kamenev, and Bukharin had once played a great role in the party but now were against it. Consequently, on questions of overriding importance we had by and large worked out a correct position.

[10-14-83]

■ We Were Diverse Individuals ■

We had a variety of personalities. Many of them are still to be investigated. Take Vareikis, for example. He suffered in the repression, then he was rehabilitated though he had been an agent of the tsarist secret police. That's a fact. There are papers to substantiate it. But I assume that his worldview had changed. You know, there were no fools in the secret police then. I served time in jail, and I was in exile. I know. They were often smarter than the fellows we have today. . . . In 1919 I was sent by the Central Committee on an assignment to see Vareikis in Ulianovsk (Simbirsk). Vareikis was opposing Lenin's line, and I had to deliver a special report on that. He started to dodge my criticisms and make comments totally at odds with what he had said a short while before. I realized then what kind of man, what kind of Bolshevik I faced. And there were many like him.

[12-6-69]

People have good memories of Postyshev. . . , Kosarev. . .

Postyshev made a good impression. He had good qualities, too. But in his later years he made mistakes and drifted toward the right wing. Kosarev was from the younger generation; he came from a worker's family. As a Komsomol member he was very active, though definitely a rightist. He was a Bukharin-Slepkov type. There was such a youth faction which included Slepkov, editor of the magazine *Kommunist*. That faction included Maretsky, the actress's brother. Astrov... Astrov later began to write books on party history, thereby "completing his convalescence," as they say. A few more names can be mentioned—Eikhenbaum and others.... The youth group of the rightist faction was led by Slepkov. This Moscow organizer wasn't bad, but a kulak type, very troublesome.

Under the influence of the neo-Bukharinist "go-slow" lobby, a great deal of damage had been deliberately inflicted on the national economy.

What else could you expect in a country of peasants? Not only in a peasant country but even in Germany, and especially in Britain, where workers constitute the majority, the ruling class, fearful of losing its property, created a workers' aristocracy. This tendency cannot be checked by halfway measures.

Khrushchev? A person like him could have switched sides in a flash. The times were most difficult.

[2-19-71, 5-1-81]

Bourgeois democrats call you "inhuman." You have people shot because of the views they hold. In a bourgeois parliamentary system, senators are never placed before a firing squad.

That's because in bourgeois democracies they don't do what needs to be done. Initially we did not take everything into account, we did not understand everything that was going on. Of course we did not believe that everything would go smoothly, but certain developments escaped our attention. When wrecking began, however, we quickly began to understand. If the communist Rukhimovich, according to our information, participated in wrecking—I personally knew him well, he was a very nice fellow—but look, he was already a waverer.... At the Central Committee plenum of 1937 I named him as a wrecker. He admitted it. There was testimony. Yes, it's possible the testimony was concocted and fictitious, but not to the extent that innocent people pleaded guilty. Now Rudzutak—he never confessed to anything about himself. He was executed by firing squad. A Politburo member. I don't think he was a conscious member of any faction, but he was too easygoing about the opposition and considered it all nonsense, just about trifles. That was unforgivable. He didn't realize the danger of his attitude. Up to a certain point he was a good comrade. He was unquestionably a very intelligent man. Unlike many of the Latvians, he was flexible. The average Latvian is given to oversimplifying a bit, not to deliberation. The party never had an outstanding thinker from among the Latvians. But Rudzutak was distinguished by his well-known braininess. He excelled in this, and that's why he made it into the Politburo. An ex-convict, he did hard labor for four years. He was sentenced to hard labor as a Bolshevik, apparently in Latvia. A person of merit.

When he served his sentence at hard labor, Rudzutak acquitted himself well; he maintained his reputation so to speak. By the end of his life, however, I got the impression when he was my deputy that he was too interested in feathering his own nest. He was no longer waging genuine struggle as a true revolutionary. Back then this had vital significance. He was given to leisure. He did not especially distinguish himself in energetic, dedicated work. But as a highly capable man of vast political experience, he was useful in discussion. A highly intelligent, perceptive fellow. But there was that bit of a disposition toward leisure and leisure-time activities. . . . He did not take to drink, he was not a drinker. Kuibishev, another deputy of mine, hit the bottle rather heavily. He had a weak spot: falling into convivial company he would become the good sport. He would recite poetry and sing. He was easily influenced by the company he kept.

But he soon acquired new companions from a philistine crowd. It was hard to understand what he found in them. In general he kept his distance from us, favoring his own friends who also liked a life of leisure. He didn't put forward any new ideas to help the party along. We realized he had been at hard labor and now he wanted to relax a bit, so we didn't press him. All right, take it easy for now, if you like. But he indulged too much in partying with philistine friends. He was a boon companion. But that certainly could not have lasted indefinitely.

He was a rather versatile individual, good at maneuvering. At heart he was a Bolshevik, without any doubt. In 1920 Lenin referred to him by saying that we in the Politburo were to blame for disregarding his notes on the trade-union issue which were directed against Trotsky. Apparently Lenin needed a launching pad, so he referred to Rudzutak. But the notes had not been written by Rudzutak. In Petrograd there was a noted trade-union functionary named Tsyperovich. He too was an intelligent and competent individual. Both he and Rudzutak defended the notes, which I believe had been written by Tsyperovich. But Rudzutak had apparently picked them up instinctively. Trotsky pressed for administrative methods of work in the trade unions, while the notes inclined toward an emphasis on ideological, social, and organizational methods, which Lenin in fact believed to be fundamental for the trade unions. Lenin said, "You see, people working in the unions have already suggested these ideas, but you still persist with your tighten-the-screws policy, while here we have exactly what we need. Rudzutak is right!"

Rudzutak immediately rose in our estimation. But I still refrained from praising him. It is difficult to say at what point he got burned. But I think it was his getting mixed up with cronies who harbored God knows what kind of nonparty aims. The Chekists [secret political police] apparently had observed everything and had reported it. It's most unlikely his case was concocted. Most unlikely. He did hold up well facing the Chekists. He showed character. I recall we arrived at the NKVD building—Mikoyan, myself, some other Politburo members—to meet with him. I can't remember now if Beria was there; he must have been there as chief of security. There were two or three from security.

Rudzutak complained that the Chekists were using intolerable methods with him. He offered no evidence.

"I don't admit anything I'm being accused of," he said. That was at the NKVD building. Rudzutak said he had been badly beaten and tortured. Nevertheless he held firm. Indeed, he seemed to have been cruelly tortured.

Could Beria have been involved?

He must have been.

Couldn't you have protected him since you had known him for so long?

But one must not act just on personal impressions! After all, we had materials incriminating him.

If you were confident . . .

I was not 100 percent confident. How could one be 100 percent confident if they say that . . . I wasn't that close to him. He was my deputy, I met him at work. A fine, intelligent fellow. At the same time, however, I saw that he was entangled in personal affairs, mixed up with the devil knows what kind of people, with women. . . . A member of the Politburo and my deputy at the Council of People's Commissars, he had gone too far.

Your first deputy?

There were no first deputies then. Rudzutak was one of four.

What was he accused of?

I can't remember now. He said, "No! That's all wrong! I absolutely reject it. I have been tortured here. They are using force. I will sign nothing."

Was that reported to Stalin?

It was. He couldn't be acquitted. "Do as you have to with him," Stalin concluded. And Stalin had always had good relations with Rudzutak.

And then he had him shot?

Shot.

He might never have been guilty of anything?

Well, I couldn't vouch for his absolute integrity. He was friendly with Antipov, Chubar.

Pravda *now writes positively about him. . . .*

Tukhachevsky is also receiving a good press. He was rehabilitated and now is even being eulogized. . . .

Judging from the evidence produced at the trial, Rudzutak was an active accomplice of the right-wingers in their terrorist schemes and designs to overthrow the Central Committee and the leadership. So I consider him a guilty individual who doggedly put up a great deal of resistance. The very fact that he didn't want to talk with the security men . . . But who then did he want to talk with, in such a position?

At one time I even expressed certain doubts that he had been justly condemned. But when I read the fresh material . . . The trials fully exposed him as an active accomplice of the rightists. He actually had personal associations with Rykov and Tomsky.

Everything was strained to the breaking point. In that period it was necessary to act mercilessly. I believe our actions were fully justified.

Today such actions would be completely unjustified. By the time war broke out, when the purges had been completed, and after the war, when there was a general recovery, such a danger was gone. But if the Tukhachevskys and the Yakirs, with the Rykovs and the Zinovievs, had started an opposition during the war, there would have been cruel internal strife and colossal losses. Colossal. Neither side would have given up; the battle would have raged relentlessly until the end. Each side would have set out mercilessly to annihilate the other. Both sides would have been doomed. Someone would of course have triumphed in the end, but both sides would have suffered enormous losses.

The right wing already had a channel to Hitler even before this. Trotsky was definitely connected to him, that's beyond any doubt. Hitler was an adventurist. Trotsky was an adventurist, too. They had something in common. Linked to both of them were the rightists Bukharin and Rykov. They were all linked to one another. Many of the ranking military officers were also involved. That goes without saying. With the holders of high political office having ties to Hitler, the people in secondary positions followed suit. Tukhachevskys and the like. It could have started simply with their doubting that we could retain power, but it would have ended with their transforming our country into a colony for a period of time.

But Rudzutak should not have been handled so . . .

You say they shouldn't have, but here is another case for you. I was in Beria's office when Chubar was interrogated. He was also one of my deputies, and charges had been leveled against him. He was a former worker, a Ukrainian. For a long time he had been chairman of the Ukrainian Council of People's Commissars, then he was transferred to Moscow to become a Politburo member and deputy chairman of the USSR Council of People's Commissars. He was generally known to profess some rightist views. We all knew that. He also maintained a personal relationship with Rykov. A very cautious and smart person. Not very active though.

He was implicated by Antipov—who was already imprisoned—who had also been my deputy, a Central Committee member, and chairman of the Soviet Control Committee. We were listening to Antipov, with Chubar sitting next to me, still a free man. He had been summoned to the NKVD building: "Sit down, listen to what some people have to report about you."

Antipov was Chubar's personal friend. My dacha was not far from Chubar's and Antipov's, and I saw the Antipovs frequent the Chubars' dacha.

Although he might have been telling lies, Antipov said, "I tell you that you said this, that, and the other to me!"

Antipov too had been a worker—a Leningrad Bolshevik with underground experience. I knew them both very well, but here they were denouncing each other. Chubar said to him, "What a viper! I have clasped a viper to my bosom! A provocateur!"

But they didn't believe him?

They didn't.

Did they believe Antipov?

Not entirely. But I sensed he might be talking nonsense. . . . Stalin could no longer rely on Chubar. None of us could.

So Stalin treated people altogether mercilessly?

What do you mean, mercilessly? He got reports, they had to be checked out.

People would slander one another. . . .

We would have been complete idiots if we had taken the reports at their face value. We were not idiots. We could not entrust accused individuals with jobs of responsibility, because they could have reverted to type at any time.

Had we not resorted to the harshest methods, who knows what this unrest could have led to? The officials and people in leadership positions did not get down to the roots, to the peasants. But we stayed most vigilant regarding the performance of the high officeholders—were they unsteady, wavering, doubting? Too many complex questions had to be handled at the time to be entirely confident about anything. You might have felt confident about someone, but others did not, and they produced evidence. And now you talk. . . .

My first secretary got arrested, then my second secretary got arrested, too. I sensed danger gathering around me. . . .

Were there any reports on you?

And how! But I was never informed about them.

Stalin did not accept them?

How not accept them? My first assistant was arrested. A Ukrainian, from a worker's family. Not a well-educated man, but I relied on him as an upright man. So he was arrested. Evidently he was under great pressure. He didn't want to talk, and at the right moment he just threw himself down the elevator shaft at the NKVD building. That was all the staff I had. . . .

1937 was a very grave year. Had we not done what we did, our losses would have been greater. This I don't doubt. Had the opposition prevailed, we would undoubtedly have incurred even greater losses.

"You know what Khrushchev said about you?" asked Shota Ivanovich. "He recalled some woman from 1937. A list of convicts was reported to him: women sentenced to ten years in jail. Molotov crossed out the verdict printed on the paper and wrote, 'To be shot.'"

This excerpt is also in Suslov's report on the China question—of 1961, I believe. But you are not quoting it correctly. He said that in one instance I had written in my own hand next to the name of a woman on a list that the decision in her case must be handed down by a military tribunal. I should add there actually was such an instance. I was authorized to have access to this list and to amend it. And so I did.

What was the charge against her? Who was she?

It's of no importance.

Why were the repressions extended to wives and children?

What do you mean, why? They had to be isolated somehow. Otherwise they would have served as conduits of all kinds of complaints. And a certain amount of demoralization. That's a fact, definitely. That was evident at the time.

. . . In 1960 or 1965, as Polina Semenovna and myself came out of a metro station, we were stopped by Rykov's daughter. She recognized Polina Semenovna. She greeted me but preferred to talk with my wife. They talked a little in the crowd at the metro. She didn't say much of interest. That was how we met once.

[4-13-72, 6-13-74, 8-16-77, 1-26-86]

Without their resolve to take extreme measures, neither Lenin nor Stalin can be understood. No, without their resolve we might not be alive today, much less trying to understand.

The military now say that Stalin bequeathed us a splendid army.

The heart of the matter is this: I believe we had to pass through a period of terror, because we had already waged a struggle for more than ten years. The terror cost us dearly, but without it things would have been worse. Many people who should not have been touched suffered. But I believe that Beria on his own could not have done it. He carried out the orders, very harsh orders issued by Stalin.

It really never occurred to Stalin that we could not possibly have so many enemies of the people?

It is indeed sad and regrettable that so many innocent people perished. But I believe the terror of the late 1930s was necessary. Of course, had we operated with greater caution, there would have been fewer victims, but Stalin insisted on making doubly sure: spare no one, but guarantee absolute stability in the country for a long period of time—through the war and postwar years, which was certainly achieved. I don't deny that I supported that line. I simply could not study every individual case. But people like Bukharin, Rykov, Zinoviev, and Kamenev were closely linked with one another.

It was difficult to draw a precise line where to stop.

They say the whole thing was fabricated.

That's out of the question. They could by no means be fabricated. Piatakov kept Trotsky informed.

They were beaten up—not everyone could stand it. After someone is beaten, he is often ready to testify to whatever is required of him.

Stalin, in my opinion, pursued a correct line: let innocent heads roll, but there will be no wavering during and after the war. Yes, mistakes were made. But look, Rokossovsky and Meretskov were freed.

And how many others like them perished?

Not many. The terror was necessary, and it couldn't have been completed without mistakes. The alternative was to carry the internal political debates into the war years. . . . Had we been spineless then . . .

Vlasov [a captured Soviet general who voluntarily organized an army from among fellow PWs to fight the USSR] would have been as nothing compared to what might have happened. Many people were wavering politically.

Could they have gone over to Hitler's side?

I don't think so, but their wavering would have been very dangerous.

[4-29-82]

The 1920s and 1930s. I consider that period absolutely remarkable.

It is referred to as the bloody period.

I don't consider it the bloody period.

There was bloodshed.

There was. But only philistines see nothing but the repressions. You can find many people like that among the communists, too.

[1-15-75]

At the Lenin Library I asked for whatever they had by Tukhachevsky. Everything. My order arrived the next day. Before that visit I had heard of only one book by him, *Questions of Modern Strategy*, published in 1926. So I said, "I would like to have that book and everything published after that."

First I went through the books at the library, then I secured permission to take the materials home. I still keep some materials with me. They contain nothing revealing. I just wondered how he proceeded since he could not come out publicly against the prevailing policies. Most of the materials were Tukhachevsky's speeches at large gatherings. All of his works, as a matter of fact, amount to nine thin booklets, twenty-five to thirty pages each. That was his legacy. I got everything the Lenin Library had. Each booklet is protected by a hard-cover binding. The works of a genius are always exciting to look through. I have read all of the booklets. There was not much to read actually: a lot of italicized quotations from Stalin, Molotov, Voroshilov. He mostly quoted from them when he appeared before the sessions of the Supreme Soviet. . . . In all of his speeches up to 1936 he invariably eulogized our leaders and our people and emphasized that the Germans would be smashed should war break out. That's all, there is nothing to find fault with. Nevertheless, he organized an anti-Soviet group in the army.

He was accused of being a German agent.

Borders don't count in this matter, because he calculated politically. It turns out that before 1935 he was somewhat afraid and he procrastinated, but beginning in late 1936 or the end of the year he hurried with plans for a coup. Both Krestinsky and Rozengolts testified to that. It makes sense. He feared he was at the point of being arrested, and he could no longer put things off. And there was no one else he could rely on except the Germans. This sequence of events is plausible.

I consider Tukhachevsky a most dangerous conspirator in the military who was caught only at the last minute. Had he not been apprehended, the consequences could have been catastrophic. He was most popular in the army.

Did everyone who was charged or executed take part in the conspiracy hatched by Tukhachevsky? Some were certainly involved. Others might have been implicated by mistake. There could have been sympathizers among them. It was different with each individual. But two categories were easily distinguishable: the dangerous officers who enjoyed popularity among the military for some time, and the officers who were misled and who could have returned to the right track. Rokossovsky could have been one of those implicated without sufficient evidence. He had been in jail for some time. Surely there are other cases that need to be reviewed.

But as to whether Tukhachevsky and his group in the military were connected with Trotskyists and rightists and were preparing a coup, there is no doubt.

Recently I was approached by the author of a book on Tukhachevsky. I asked, "Have you read the transcripts of the trial?" "No," he responded. There's an author for you. "But he has been rehabilitated," he said.

"Yes," I replied, "but have you read the transcripts? Those are documents. And where are the documents on his rehabilitation?"

He opened his eyes wide in amazement.

If the Trotskyists are referred to in this fashion, Trotsky himself will be rehabilitated.

[3-8-75, 6-16-77]

How have we come to our present condition, Viacheslav Mikhailovich?

This is how. As I talk with different people, I come to see that people are too easy to please. They lose all their enthusiasm whenever they don't get what they expect. It's good that a struggle is going on. How good it is that a new crisis is beginning!

"Here is another thing I don't understand," said Shota Ivanovich. *"People engaged in anti-Soviet propaganda, like Yakir's son, are being freed. Why is that?"*

It's a pity to feed him at the expense of the state.

Siniavsky has left for France.

He shouldn't have been allowed to leave. The Jews can be let go. To hell with them, since they don't want to stay here any more. But letting a Russian leave is a sign of weakness. But they—they have a homeland of their own. Leave, by all means!

But what kind of homeland? Israel is a bourgeois state.

Let them go, let's wash our hands of them. If they do not accept life with us, they are just members of the bourgeoisie. But don't let them return—what is our country, some kind of hotel? Trotsky was let out, and he hatched all kinds of anti-Soviet plots. Nevertheless, I believe we did the right thing in letting him out. He would have stirred up more trouble here. . . .

Couldn't he have been killed in 1928 or 1929?

Impossible. That would have been a blotch on our reputation. So we keep living with enemies. . . . People now seem to dote on technical gadgets. Politics decide everything, but politics come second. Solzhenitsyn, for example, could be easily killed today [1970]. But I believe sending him to jail would be a better solution. I think so, yes. But even if that swarm of insects is squashed, our troubles won't be over. We just have to keep fighting them. Anatoly Kuznetsov is another so-called author. What's his real worth? Nothing! Not worth a rap! He also left. Good riddance! But Sakharov, of course, has to be reckoned with. He cannot simply be ignored. I don't think he or his friends and colleagues would cooperate. In a certain sense the people now must be dealt with by creating the right kind of environment.

[12-18-70, 1-14-75, 5-24-75]

Viacheslav Mikhailovich, the dissidents held a demonstration on Red Square and handed out anti-Soviet leaflets.

Ah, there you are! One steeple has fallen, they have shaken the world.

[8-18-76]

Bukharin and Rykov were not in Petrograd in October 1917. They were Muscovites, Moscow bourgeoisie. The Moscow uprising proceeded at a very slow pace. Extremely slow. It was protracted. One leader of the uprising then was Arosev, a very close friend of mine. Later he became an author. I kept some of his books with his autograph. Some time ago at a jubilee party in his honor, I was foolish enough to give all these books to his eldest daughter.... Several of his daughters are still alive. One is an actress at the Satire theatre, another is an author....

A very nice man. We had been together since school in Kazan. His mother was executed by Kolchakites. After the October Revolution he was our ambassador in Czechoslovakia. I keep his letters from Prague.

Later he worked as deputy chairman of the All-Union Society for Cultural Ties. He perished in 1937. A most dedicated man. Perhaps he wasn't particular about making friends. He could not have been involved in anti-Soviet matters. However, his connections... Hardships of the Revolution.

Didn't you know about it?

How not know? I did know!

Couldn't he have been saved?

Out of the question.

Why?

The evidence. How could I have said, "Hand him over. I'll question him"? Impossible.

And who produced the evidence?

Who the hell knows?!

Could it all have been fabricated? Enemies were also at work.

Definitely. They were active. Very active. They wanted to undermine us.

You knew Arosev quite well. A dedicated man. It all defies one's understanding.

It may defy one's understanding because those cases were very, very complicated. Even my wife was arrested when I was a Politburo member.

Then Stalin is to blame for all that?

No. You can't say Stalin is...

Who then?

It couldn't have been done without his consent, of course. He was in desperate straits. There were so many people around him who changed....

You knew a person, Stalin knew him, and this person enjoyed a positive evaluation, yet he was done for....

In that sense the line was exceedingly harsh.

What was Arosev's crime?

He might have committed just one blunder: dropping a wrong word at the wrong place.

Almost anything could be the wrong word!

He could have taken up with some woman who... The struggle raged. The right-wingers had a potent nucleus: Bukharin, Rykov, Tomsky —a powerful trio. They were very assertive. They would send formal letters to the Politburo, signed: Members of the Politburo Bukharin, Rykov, Tomsky.

Stalin was never overtolerant. In those matters Kalinin wasn't overtolerant either. He always lent his support, though the initiative was never his.

[4-13-72, 12-30-73]

Tomsky shot himself, at his dacha. He had been expelled from the Central Committee though he retained his party membership. By then he had grown into a real bureaucrat. Until 1905 he was a Bolshevik. Then he vacillated. ... In the summer of 1917 we advanced the idea of launching a newspaper to be published by the Petrograd party committee. Heated debates were held on the question at meetings of the Petrograd committee and the Central Committee. It was late May–early June 1917. He disappeared when the going was toughest. But later—it was already after the October Revolution—he turned up in Moscow. Here is a prominent leader for you! What steadfastness! Nevertheless, he was a good organizer of the masses. ...

"Suppose we here are all Politburo members," said Shota Ivanovich, "and one of us suddenly vanishes. His seat is empty. Were these situations addressed by the Politburo?"

No. There was always the leading team in the Politburo. Under Stalin that team never included Kalinin, Rudzutak, Kosior, or Andreev. The materials pertaining to a matter would be forwarded to all the Politburo members in advance. Before the war we received intelligence reports. But all the issues of cardinal importance were first addressed by the Politburo's leading group. That tradition started under Lenin.

"Did Stalin interrogate Tukhachevsky?"

No, he didn't need to.

"How could you let people that you knew well be sent to meet their death, to say nothing of the thousands who perished in the provinces?"

I would like to see you in our positions then. I wonder how you would have coped.

[3-9-73]

■   **"I Send Them Letters After Each Congress..."**   ■

Let me tell you my news. Last Tuesday [1971] I received a call inviting
me to visit the party commission. I had a conversation with the chief of
section about my application to be reinstalled in the party. He asked
whether I wished to add anything to my letter. I said no.

"Your evaluation of the policies in the 1930s?"

"I hold myself responsible for those policies," I said, "and consider
them to be correct. I admit that grave errors were committed and things
were stretched too far at times, but on the whole the policies were
correct."

The first accusation against me was the abuse of power in the 1930s,
the second, my involvement in an antiparty group.

"Yes," I said, "we opted for factional fighting because we wanted
Khrushchev removed, which the party later did. We believed that should
have been done several years earlier."

The chief of section asked no further questions and made no more
comments.

[8-17-71]

I send letters to the Central Committee after each congress asking
them to consider my application for reinstatement in the party. Once,
after the XXIVth Party Congress [1971], I was summoned to the Central
Committee for a hearing. I write after congresses so that the new
members of the Central Committee will look into my case with fresh
eyes. Last time they merely heard me out and, inasmuch as I continued
to consider the policies of the 1930s to be correct despite certain errors
that might have been made, they concluded: "Original decision confirmed." That was it. I was actually rebuffed, the message in effect being,
"Molotov doesn't know he has lost touch." I was no longer accused of
being a dogmatist, which Khrushchev liked to call me. I have never
been a member of the opposition. I have been an active party member
all my life; all my activities have been aboveboard. Of course I made
mistakes. I can't deny that.

Lenin also made mistakes and admitted to them. At the XVIIIth
Congress Stalin declared communism could be built in one country.
That conclusion certainly runs counter to Marxism-Leninism. At that
time I didn't agree, but I didn't speak up. How could I? I would have
been kicked out like some rag that was in the way. Everyone cheered,

everyone wanted communism. Stalin wanted to show he was moving forward. The current party program is no different.

[4-29-80]

. . . We are out for a walk. Molotov is recounting a recent experience.

A friend of mine told me, "They would like to reinstate you in the party, but you keep sending critical letters to the Central Committee." He is an economics professor. I think only a few people would like to have me back in the party. Too many negative reports about me have reached the top, and now they simply can't do it.

I am portrayed as a Stalinist before the Western communist parties. If they reinstate me, would Stalin follow?

No, I don't think they could do that.

I wrote them another letter before the congress. I handed the letter to the right person. This is also a critical letter. Alas, I got no response or acknowledgment from them. I understand no one enjoys being reproved.

[5-1-81]

I've been to the party control commission today. On the question of being reinstated in the party. This was my second visit. The previous decision was once again left standing. On July 15 I was summoned to the commission in connection with the application I addressed to the congress. Handling my application was a member of that commission, who later filed a concluding report on my case. The original decision was confirmed. I asked for the last report to be given to me to read. They acquiesced, and I went over today to have a look at that report.

The charge against me is the same: abuse of power. The report written by that commission member (I don't remember his name—it was Russian but strange-sounding) says that 1,370,000 arrests were made in the 1930s. That's too many. I responded that the figures should be thoroughly reviewed and that unwarranted arrests did occur, but that we couldn't have survived without resorting to stern measures. Take Tukhachevsky, for example. On what grounds was he rehabilitated? Did you read the records of the trial of the right-wing and Trotskyist bloc in 1938? Bukharin, Krestinsky, Rozengolts, and others were on trial then. They stated flat out that in June 1937 Tukhachevsky pressed for a coup. People who have not read the record go on to say that the testimony was given under duress from the Chekists.

But I say, had we not made those sweeping arrests in the 1930s, we would have suffered even greater losses in the war. So today I looked through the party report and wrote, "I have read the report. I shall submit a written reply."

I wanted to send them a written response to the report. It matters to me that I am not reinstated in the party, and I want them to have a record of my views on the past repressions. I stopped short of asking them why they hadn't posthumously expelled Stalin from the party.

Now only Kalinin is in good standing. Even Dzerzhinsky committed gross mistakes, regarding the Brest peace and in the trade-union discussion. But surely Kalinin was not so active?

Right. A worker once told me that before World War I Kalinin had intended to open a beer stand.

But they write that he led an underground political study group.

That's possible. I too led such a group, and Kalinin used to attend my classes.

Did Kalinin really enjoy a solid reputation, or was his image only propped up for public consumption?

Mostly for the public. . . . He was loyal to Stalin. He was particularly close to the peasants, who didn't know any other Bolsheviks. He was certainly a nice person. At one time he wavered toward the right, but he did his best not to become separated from us. Voroshilov also leaned toward the right. . . . We had an army made up of peasants, after all.

You have not been reinstated in the party. Why then are you reported by all encyclopedias to have been a party member since 1906? Not a word about "the antiparty group."

That's the question. I've seen that in four or five encyclopedias. Apparently, having me recorded in the books as a former party member, now expelled, would make them feel uncomfortable. Generally speaking, I now receive neutral coverage in most of the publications, with the exception of a recently published book on the party's history edited by that candidate for the Politburo in charge of international relations, what's his name . . .

[7-22-81]

At the XXIInd Congress Khrushchev alleged that Molotov, Voroshilov, and Kaganovich recognized the court's ruling on Tukhachevsky and others to be incorrect and welcomed the rehabilitation of Tukhachevsky and others. . . .

Emphatically no.

Khrushchev said, "At a session of the Presidium of the Central Committee, we were told that neither Tukhachevsky nor Yakir nor Uborevich committed any crimes against the party and the nation. Then we asked Molotov, Kaganovich, and Voroshilov, 'Are you for their rehabilitation?' 'Yes, we are in favor,' they responded. 'But you were the ones to have those men executed,' we added with indignation, 'so, when did you act truthfully, then or now?'" Those were Khrushchev's words.

I understand. I assume that Tukhachevsky engaged in some misconduct and then found himself an enemy not only of Stalin but of the party as well. But I did not have the relevant documents, though I do recall something of this period.

Khrushchev asked if you were prepared to support their rehabilitation.

No.

"'Are you for their rehabilitation?' 'Yes, we are in favor,' they responded."

No. Moreover, I had not agreed to it.

Then Khrushchev distorted your words?

Definitely. He was never dependable. He was a man without scruples. Slapdash. Very primitive. The issue was never addressed in my presence.

Kaganovich told me nearly the same story. "Khrushchev never asked those questions. Nothing of the kind occurred at that meeting."

[12-9-82, 5-9-85]

■ **How Is 1937 to Be Viewed?** ■

I believe there were deficiencies and mistakes. It couldn't have been otherwise with our enemies operating within the security agencies in charge of investigations. . . . The major deficiencies were that the security agencies had been left without due oversight by the party during certain periods. The negligence was not purposeful. The resources for adequate oversight were insufficient.

That policy of repression was the only salvation for the people, for the Revolution. It was the only alternative in keeping with Leninism and its basic principles. Today that policy would be out of the question, of course.

. . . Almost every time I saw Molotov we talked about the repressions under Stalin. Molotov touched on the subject in his book, Facing the New Tasks *(on completing the construction of socialism), which was never published. He presented me with an autographed copy of his manuscript in February 1977. The book repeats much of our conversations, but it was entirely written by him. Here is a brief excerpt from his book:*

In the 1920s and particularly in the 1930s the extremely hostile anti-Leninist faction of the Trotskyists threw aside all restraint and grew aggressive and insolent, though they continued to pose as fighters for communism. Trotsky was deported from the USSR in 1929. In his writings published abroad he implied—and in his letters to partisans in the USSR explicitly ordered—that now the struggle against the party (against "the Stalinist leadership") should resort to all means up to and including terror and wrecking within the country, and dirty, traitorous political deals with governments of bourgeois states, including Hitlerite Germany. Trotsky and others maintained ties with the intelligence services of bourgeois countries with a view to speeding up an armed attack on the USSR by the aggressive imperialist nations. Then they could utilize this attack to carry out an antisocialist coup within our country. Following in the footsteps of the Trotskyists was the Zinoviev-Kamenev faction—suffice it to recall that they confessed [at the public trial in 1936] to their complicity in Kirov's assassination. In the 1930s and even earlier Trotsky's and Zinoviev's bloc included the right-wing clique (the Bukharinists) that reflected the aspirations of the petty bourgeois elements seeking a quieter life and coexistence with the kulaks—doomed to extinction—and the other exploiter classes under socialism.

As time passed, the leaders of those factions (and other smaller groups) turned into miserable bourgeois degenerates, who were intimidated by imperialism and had lost faith in socialism. In fighting the party and its leadership they had gone so far as to become, in fact, rabid enemies of the party and socialism, gangs of conspirators who aimed to overthrow Soviet power. They drifted closer and closer together to plot their infamous conspiracy and military coup in order to turn the country back to capitalism and to restore bourgeois government. Obviously they counted on being better off under that kind of government. In the forced, urgent implementation of resolute measures to root out and rout these counterrevolutionary groups and the criminal bands organized by them who were preparing a coup d'état—and this was confessed by the accused themselves in public trials—there occurred, of course, grave errors and injustices, which cannot but evoke profound regret. These errors were largely caused by the fact that at certain stages the investigations fell into the hands of people who were later exposed as traitors guilty of heinous, hostile, antiparty acts. These belatedly exposed degenerates—traitors within the security agencies and party organizations—obviously at times, with malice aforethought, pushed certain incorrect measures against honest party members and nonparty people. The party and the Soviet state could not permit delay or postponements in carrying out the punitive measures which had become absolutely necessary. At the same time the abuses of power and other injustices committed in the course of numerous investigations, which were laid bare, were eliminated. Party organizations were informed about this in detail in a special letter from the Central Committee. For crude abuses of power People's Commissar for Internal Affairs Ezhov, guilty of certain crude distortions of party policy, was unmasked and then condemned to the "highest measure of punishment" [the death penalty].

[2-1-77]

■ A Conversation with Marshal Golovanov ■

. . . Today we decided to go to see Molotov at Ilinskoye. There were three of us: Shota Ivanovich Kvantaliani, Chief Marshal of Aviation Alexander Evgenevich Golovanov, and myself. . . .

"Guests are always welcome in this house," said Molotov, *"though I can't boast of too many coming to see me."*

"It's good when the guests are not too many," remarked Golovanov.

No, that's also bad. You can't do without people.

People keep writing to me. Some letters are good. And it's always exciting to read spiteful letters.

They come from the heart. I keep getting letters from a man who puts his messages in verse: "Your wife is down there, and why should you still be here?" His letters are always signed, "Sincerely yours, Well-wisher." Quite an educated man. And he knows my address, too.

You can't do without fighting in politics. There were a little over 200,000 communists in the October Revolution. The more exact figure would be 240,000.

The country's population was 150 million, more than half illiterate; socialism had to be built with hostile forces encircling the country and within. We somehow had to find a way to drag the country onto the high road of progress. Nothing could have been achieved had we not utilized the services of temporary allies, even if they were only one-quarter allies. Unaided, we would have been incapable of building socialism.

1937—we could not have done without it. The very saints could not have accomplished anything with their sweet talk in those critical periods. They would have failed miserably. You can't do without harsh measures against ferocious enemies. Admittedly, innocent people suffered too.

"Indeed," agreed Golovanov, "1937 witnessed the bitter struggle against the fifth column—a struggle that went too far."

The threat would have been worse otherwise. No one knew which way Tukhachevsky might turn. . . .

Golovanov said, "Tukhachevsky was arrested, then a thousand, ten thousand, a hundred thousand were arrested. The process was totally out of the control of the leadership. People began informing on each other to the security agencies. Some scoundrels emerged and began to profit from the lawlessness. . . ."

Many errors were committed. Many.

"Stalin himself had to admit in 1938 that something had gone wrong and that things had to be sorted out," said Golovanov. "I am lucky to have had a very close escape then. Later I was expelled from the party, I was nearly arrested, I was out of work. My family starved, with one loaf of brown bread for a week. My sister's husband, a noted security officer, was shot. I wrote about those years in my book. I believed then that Stalin had gone on a rampage to destroy everything. But after I met him and worked for him for a few years, I came to realize he was different. In fact, he was the man I have portrayed in my book of reminiscences. The fact that I or Konstantin Konstantinovich Rokossovsky, who also suffered in 1937—to say the least!—hold such a high opinion of Stalin and won't allow his name to be trampled into the dust, is especially unpleasant for many people.

"When Khrushchev asked Rokossovsky to write some filth about Stalin, Rokossovsky responded, 'Comrade Stalin is a saint to me.' The next day Konstantin Konstantinovich comes to his office and finds Moskalenko sitting at his desk, who hands him the orders on his retirement. That was how it was arranged. Rokossovsky says, 'I get up in the morning, stretch a little, and realize I have no job to go to. No one needs us these days. We are merely stumbling blocks for those who wish to portray the past in their own way.'

"At one government reception someone toasted Nikita Sergeevich and everyone came up to him with his glass, the lame Meretskov being no exception. At that point Rokossovsky and myself were somewhere in the center of the crowd, and we didn't budge. We just went on with our conversation, which evidently could not have gone unnoticed, since we *seemed to be the two tallest men in the crowd. We have never been invited to those receptions since. . . .*

"*If you want to know what I think of '37, I will tell you—it was a national calamity. Millions suffered. But it would be wrong to conclude that Stalin was 100 percent responsible. Who did he have as his principal assistants? Mekhlis supervised the army, Nikita Sergeevich Khrushchev supervised nonmilitary matters, the Moscow party organization. Fifty-four thousand people in the Ukraine were sent off by Khrushchev when he chaired the notorious troika. It was he who signed the verdicts! Certainly Stalin is politically responsible for all of that in the first place as head of state. But you can't say all of the individual verdicts were sanctioned by him. It would be impermissible to look at 1937 and fail to see the five-year-plan periods, political struggle within the party, acts of terrorism reported all over the country, not to mention how the Great Patriotic War turned out.*

"*Let me tell you this,*" *said Golovanov.* "*I went over to the Central Committee building one day. As we got down to business, I said, '1937 is all clear to me. It all went on before my own eyes. I remember how it all was arranged. But about the Leningrad affair [postwar purge of Leningrad leadership], I was not close to Stalin then and couldn't understand much.' I got this response: 'The Leningrad affair was framed behind Stalin's back.' Well, it occurred to me then that if it all had been done behind Stalin's back, it surely had to be done by the inseparable three—Beria, Malenkov, and Khrushchev. But now we hear that Stalin regarded Voznesensky as his possible successor both in the party and in the government.*"

I haven't heard about it. I don't know everything about that affair, but I have my conjectures. Stalin could not have remained unaware of it when it all occurred while he was in power. There was a touch of Russian nationalism about the Leningrad affair. I can't see the whole picture, but I do know that an issue of that sort was discussed in high offices, which infuriated Stalin.

Without the consent of the Central Committee, an all-Russia fair was planned for Leningrad. As deputy chairman of the Council of Ministers and chairman of the state planning committee, Voznesensky encouraged this plan. Apparently there was a hint of or an attempt to put together a separate group on economic or, so to speak, business or practical grounds. Officials from Leningrad and Gorky began covert negotiations to arrange a deal. Voznesensky was the moving force. Stalin was left out of the picture. No formal reports reached him. I have no idea what kinds of reports might have reached state security. Apparently they saw it as an attempt to set up a legal group promoting economic and business affairs. I didn't perceive them as a separatist group. But evidently some compromising materials and documents were made available to the top leadership. Remember, Beria was fearful of Voznesensky and very much against him. Voznesensky was unquestionably a highly educated, experienced, broad-gauge worker. But in no way could he lay a claim to leadership of the party. Stalin made him first deputy chairman of the Council of Ministers, which displeased Beria no end.

Beria telephoned me and said they had been to see Stalin, to persuade him that Voznesensky's promotion was wrong. Stalin agreed and had Voznesensky removed from the first deputy's job. It seems that the security people had completed a report on him at the time. I don't know what was in it. Malenkov received instructions from Stalin to look into the matter. Stalin didn't operate single-handedly in cases like that. Malenkov was thorough and dedicated in his work. In such affairs none of us could make decisions on his own then. In the end, Malenkov was made a scapegoat.

"*You know, Viacheslav Mikhailovich,*" *Golovanov continued,* "*I have listened to you very attentively. Of course I don't know all the details, but given the system that existed then, this could not have happened without Stalin's knowledge. When I was told at the CC offices that this was done behind Stalin's back—this frightful affair—I was taken aback. Moreover, while Stalin is accused of every crime under the sun, the 'Leningrad affair' is never mentioned. This matter is not clear to me even though I have worked ten years with the Cheka on questions of intelligence and counterintelligence in the most critical positions and times. That is where I was tempered. I believe the fair alone could not have served as the cause underlying the 'Leningrad affair.'*"

Some group was set up, and that's all I can recall. Beria stopped keeping me informed during Stalin's last years. I was on the sidelines then. Under Khrushchev I was entirely in the dark about some events. Voznesensky was not discussed in my presence. I do know that Beria was extremely jealous of him. They were both the same age—the younger, ambitious generation moving up. Some selfish or careerist considerations could have been involved.

Voznesensky wrote a book on the Soviet economy during World War II. He did it well—but he could write, of course. He had his weak spots, but I would say he was more outstanding than the others. Young and energetic, he was definitely moving up. Beria, fearing a rival, was capable of anything.

One of my readers sent me a letter saying, "Stalin never shot anyone without reason."

What does he mean, without reason? That's stretching the facts. I think Voznesensky was executed without reason. The same surely applies to Kuznetsov as well.

Kuznetsov, yes. He was a Leningrader, and in my opinion a good lad, good indeed. I liked him. I supported him in every way. He was among the best of the people I knew. Stalin had a good opinion of him, but here you have that Voznesensky group. . . . Whether he dirtied himself with that group, I don't know, and perhaps they were too hasty in his case. I was told very little, and I myself may have barely survived. But on whom could Stalin rely? And I was not without error. He himself used to say, "Only he who accomplishes nothing is error-free."

Yes, of course, I too am to blame, though at that time I had already been removed from things by Stalin. But I stayed on longer than most of the others in the top leadership of the party.

But to bestow leadership of the party on Kuznetsov would have meant letting things slip out of control. He was ill-prepared for this. I repeat: he was a good man, devoted to the party, deeply devoted, but he did not go carefully into everything. Many things about the "Leningrad affair" have remained unclear. Yes, party affairs are not simple.

I think Voznesensky and Kuznetsov were incorrectly charged. It was surely a mistake. Kuznetsov was a fine chap. He wasn't particularly active or ambitious, but he was a straightforward and dedicated man. During the enemy encirclement of Leningrad, he acquitted himself well. He showed no desire to rest on his laurels.

"Could Stalin have been fooled?" asked Shota Ivanovich.

Not in matters like that.

"I have never heard anything of the kind," said Golovanov. "I think Beria feared Stalin more than anyone else. To my mind, Beria was the greatest intriguer ever born. True, he could not be compared with Talleyrand, but he could have arranged quite a few frame-ups. All the Politburo members in their very being feared Beria. During the war years Khrushchev, Malenkov, and Beria were close friends . . ."

That was not a fast friendship though.

"Beria thought that if Khrushchev was to be first secretary in the party and Malenkov chairman of the Council of Ministers, he would follow them. . . . But Khrushchev outsmarted him."

Outsmarted, yes.

If Stalin knew everything and did not rely on bad advice, he bears direct responsibility for the executions of the innocent.

That conclusion is not entirely correct. Understanding the idea is one thing, applying it is something else. The rightists had to be beaten, the Trotskyists had to be beaten, so the order came down: punish them vigorously. Ezhov was executed for that. If tough measures are rejected, the great risk is always that at the critical moment the nation may be torn apart and the devil knows how it may end—leading only to greater losses. Millions may die, and that may mean total collapse or at least a very deep crisis.

That's true. Ezhov was executed, but the innocent were not released.

But, when all is said, many of the verdicts were justified. The cases were reviewed and some people were released.

"People were released in 1938," added Golovanov.

But most of them stayed in the camps!

A commission on Tevosian was set up after he was arrested. Mikoyan, Beria, myself, and someone else worked on that commission. Tevosian was a Central Committee member, a most upright man, an excellent specialist in metallurgy. An extremely competent man. A report came in that he was a saboteur and that he was working to damage our steel industry. He had intensive training in Germany with the Krupp works, and upon returning home he most perseveringly and effectively worked in our steel industry. But soon a lot of evidence given by specialists and managers was received. At Stalin's initiative, a special commission was set up to review his case thoroughly. We went to the NKVD building to examine the evidence. We heard out one engineer, two, three. Each one insisted Tevosian was a wrecker because he had issued such and such instructions. Tevosian was in the same room and listened to all those accusations. He easily exposed and rejected all the charges. We compared the evidence with the facts and concluded that the charges were absurd. Sheer slander. Tevosian was acquitted. He remained a member of the Central Committee, and then he continued to do his job. We reported to Stalin, and he agreed with our conclusion.

Regrettably, my assistant, who, at my instructions, had collected the materials to substantiate Tevosian's acquittal, perished just after that. Who did him in?

"Solzhenitsyn writes," said Shota Ivanovich, "that Stalin himself placed Ezhov in that job and made him slaughter the party's key workers."

That's not so. Ezhov was a rather prominent worker who had been promoted accordingly. Short in stature, slightly built, he was nevertheless a highly energetic, outstanding worker. But when he was placed in a position of enormous power and given sweeping directives, it put a strain on him, and he began to carry out repressions according to a production plan. Before him, Yagoda had paid for this. But overnight a man does not show himself in everything. The trees were felled, the chips began to fly, so to speak. To say that Stalin did not know about this is absurd, but to say that he is accountable for all these cases is of course also incorrect.

"I hold this point of view," said Golovanov. "Peter I was head of state. True, he built Leningrad on human bones. True, they don't talk much about this, they talk about his opening a window onto Europe. If Stalin had been a sadist, had killed people, devoured them to satisfy his sadism, that would have been one thing. . . ."

Some people believe he was a sadist.

"But I knew him well. He was no bloodthirsty tyrant," said Golovanov. "A struggle was raging. There were various political currents and deviations. The building of socialism required firmness. Stalin had more of this firmness than anyone else. Was there a fifth column? There was, no question about that. And they were prominent leaders, not underlings. I can't imagine myself being arrested like Tukhachevsky and testifying before the court the next day that I am a German spy or station chief of the Polish intelligence service. Beatings? Devil take it! Let them beat me up. Let them cripple me. Some people were suspended on meat hooks and they would just spit in the executioner's face. Had Tukhachevsky been different he would have spoken up, and all would have been revealed. Had he possessed sufficient willpower, everything would have ended much earlier. But as he admitted to everything at the trial and implicated so many people on the first day, even the forged document coming from Benes . . . After that, it all proceeded as before.

"Look at Rokossovsky. He was tortured, nonetheless he denied all the charges. He implicated no one. And no one else was arrested. He was incarcerated in the Shlisselburg prison. Then he was released. Konstantin Konstantinovich is still respected for this by the army. Stalin held Rokossovsky in very high esteem. By the way, after the Stalingrad battle he became the second military officer after Shaposhnikov whom Stalin began to address by given name and patronymic. He considered Rokossovsky a great military captain. It was no accident that Rokossovsky commanded the victory parade on Red Square. It was to honor service he rendered! Stalin asked, 'Konstantin Konstantinovich, did they beat you up there?'

'They did, Comrade Stalin.' 'We still have a lot of yes-men in our country,' Stalin concluded.

"Stalin also tried to find out from me who had me expelled from the party. I realized that if I indicated that person to him, the next day the man would be out of the Politburo. I never divulged the name to him. A lot of people kept informing on their colleagues and neighbors. People were forced to send in reports on Tevosian, for example. I met people like that in the past, and I know some of them now. They look at me and say, 'Alexander Evgenevich, I sent reports on this person, that one, and the other.' 'Why?' 'I was just scared.'"

That's true.

"There were others who informed of their own free will. We are looking into the issue as a whole. But we must also examine the details. Why did Khrushchev act the way he did? Did he expose enemies of the people? A friend of mine, a division commander, told me about Khrushchev visiting a garrison in the Ukraine. He arrived, assembled the troops, and declared, 'Comrades! Enemies of the people are all around us!' Then he turned to the commanding officer and asked, 'How many enemies of the people have you exposed?' They arrest, they jail. These are the kinds of politicians they were."

Khrushchev brought his lists of enemies of the people to Stalin. Stalin doubted the numbers reported—"They can't be so many!" "They are—in fact, many more, Comrade Stalin. You can't imagine how many they are!"

"I have a friend who used to work with me as flight engineer when I was a pilot in civil aviation. He studied at the political academy, switched to research work, and taught at the general staff academy. As the campaign of exposures and denunciations was launched, he was transferred to the Institute of Marxism-Leninism to pore over documents in search of execution orders and so forth signed by Stalin. He did not find a single paper of that kind bearing Stalin's signature."

Such documents certainly can be found. Both of us signed those papers. The lists were reported to us. We discussed them in great detail; all the Politburo members were present. Signing the lists was Stalin for the party and myself for the government. Those lists made a lot of people suffer.

I was told by the military that Khrushchev also signed.

He certainly did. I would sign whatever was signed by Stalin, and then I would have the paper forwarded to Beria. I signed lists containing the names of people who could have been straightforward and dedicated citizens. The Central Committee was also to blame for running careless checks on some of the accused. But no one can prove to me that all those actions should never have been undertaken. That claim could only come from someone who had never been a Bolshevik with prerevolutionary experience.

"Did Kalinin also sign?" asked Shota Ivanovich.

Yes. Kalinin and the others. Not all the lists were signed by the Politburo members. In many cases the verdicts arrived at by the security agencies were taken on trust.

"On trust, of course," confirmed Golovanov.

Not all the cases could be checked out. . . .

■ **The Benes Letter** ■

"I was particularly interested in Benes's letter to Stalin," said Shota Ivanovich. "Here is what Churchill writes on this score: 'Soviet Russia, surrounded by a cordon sanitaire of anti-Bolshevist states, sulked in its isolation. No progress in the East was achieved, though we continued our effort. I was never against attempts to give Germany greater satisfaction on its eastern borders. However, over these few years hopes in this were left unrealized.

'. . . Laval now went on a three days' visit to Moscow, where he was welcomed by Stalin. . . . Stalin and Molotov were, of course, anxious to know above all else what was to be the strength of the French Army on the Western Front: how many divisions? what period of service? After this field had been explored, Laval said: "Can't you do something to encourage religion and the Catholics in Russia? It would help me so much with the Pope." "Oho!" said Stalin. "The Pope! How many divisions has he got?"

'. . . In the autumn of 1936, a message from a high military source in Germany was conveyed to President Benes to the effect that if he wanted to take advantage of the Fuehrer's offer, he had better be quick, because events would shortly take place in Russia rendering any help he could give to Germany insignificant.

'While Benes was pondering over this disturbing hint, he became aware that communications were passing through the Soviet Embassy in Prague between important personages in Russia and the German Government. This was a part of the so-called military and Old-Guard Communist conspiracy to overthrow Stalin and introduce a new regime based on a

pro-German policy. President Benes lost no time in communicating all he could find out to Stalin. [There are reports, however, that the information Benes received had been made known to the Czech police by OGPU, which wanted Stalin to be advised of the information by a friendly foreign source. That news by no means diminishes the services rendered by Benes to Stalin, and should not be viewed as significant.] Thereafter there followed the merciless, but perhaps not needless, military and political purge in Soviet Russia, and the series of trials in January, 1937, in which Vyshinsky, the Public Prosecutor, played so masterful a part.

'Although it is highly improbable that the Old-Guard Communists had made common cause with the military leaders, or vice versa, they were certainly filled with jealousy of Stalin, who had ousted them. It may, therefore, have been convenient to get rid of them at the same time, according to the standards maintained in a totalitarian state. Zinoviev, Bukharin, and others of the original leaders of the Revolution, Marshal Tukhachevsky, who had been invited to represent the Soviet Union at the Coronation of King George VI, and many other high officers of the Army, were shot. In all not less than five thousand officers and officials above the rank of captain were "liquidated." The Russian Army was purged of its pro-German elements at a heavy cost to its military efficiency. The bias of the Soviet Government was turned in a marked manner against Germany.'"

I'm not quite certain the question is recounted correctly. Benes was interested in maintaining good relations with us. Stalin could not trust a letter coming from a bourgeois leader since he scarcely trusted most people. The point is that even without Benes we knew about the plot. We even knew the date the coup was to be staged.

■ **Wages and Prices** ■

Is it true that real wage levels will rise but that prices will be kept stable whenever possible? Price reductions are not even mentioned.

"Price reductions would have been better," commented Shota Ivanovich.

You know, price reductions look good, but it's easier for the state to raise wage levels.

"Why then did you reduce prices right after the war? Almost every year?"

We appear to have differences on that score—not for the first time. We gained tremendously in terms of morale. That was a powerful plus.

Things have to be seen as they are. Of course, the temptation is there to whitewash the prewar scene because I myself was deeply involved in those events. In the 1930s we also kept raising prices.

"Times are different. Today the Komsomol officials have Chaika limos waiting at the door, but then you were dressed in work clothes and toiling at the construction site. Times are different, indeed."

They are different, nevertheless one must be objective and not oversimplify, Shota Ivanovich, for people now live quite a bit better than they did before the war. It could not be otherwise. To live better is what we fought for. Of course, this is a plus. But there is another danger: growing inequality. That's the trouble, that's the seat of the ulcer, not a decline in living standards. Despite the fact that on average the worker and even more the peasant now have a higher living standard, there is also a highly negative trend: inequality is growing. Here is the ulcer.

In our country the differential between the lowest wage and the highest is 1 to 30.

In remarks printed in *Pravda*, Gus Hall, chairman of the Communist party of the U.S.A., correctly judged the measures we initiated in Czechoslovakia during the events there. He said the Soviet Union, with other countries, acted correctly by intervening in Czechoslovak affairs, notwithstanding the fact that the Communist party of Italy was opposed, the French party was opposed, the British party and others were opposed. Although he lived in America, he was nevertheless faithful to the truth when he said the action was absolutely necessary. As concerns Czechoslovakia, he said it would have been better if in the preceding years the wage level had risen more slowly and the socialist system had been more firmly consolidated. That's the heart of the matter. In our country this is imperfectly understood. That's what I am trying to say. Wage levels had to be raised—without a surge in living standards there can be no socialism. That is the very meaning of socialism. I too favored allowing living standards to rise more slowly, but to make up for it, strengthen the system of socialism. Then we should have had nothing to fear. That's the main thing. That's why we prevailed in the 1930s despite all our shortcomings.

Did Stalin boldly pursue this policy?

Absolutely, unreservedly, more than anyone else. Of course there were many shortcomings despite our good intentions, especially with Stalin, who most tenaciously carried out the policy. Of course it would have been preferable to raise living standards and reduce prices, providing we had stability. But stability was the very thing we lacked. Today it would be even better if we reduced prices, but for all that I would shift the focus from this question to another one—inequality.

Price stability strengthens commodity-money relations rather than undermining them as is necessary for socialism.

Not necessarily. Commodity-money relations consist not only of prices. It's a more complex question. Price stability alone speaks neither for nor against commodity-money relations. I favor aiming at the gradual reduction of commodity-money relations. But price stability as such is no barrier to this.

But how are we going to reduce the role of commodity-money relations unless we go ahead with price cuts?

After the war we had no choice but to reduce prices, and that bold policy certainly is to Stalin's credit. But that kind of policy is now insufficient because of growing social inequality.

So price stability remains on paper.

In fact, prices keep rising, and that's bad.

"*Comparing the wage increase with the price increase, everything is topsy-turvy,*" argued Golovanov. "*Wages rise, but prices rise even faster.*"

We are increasingly influenced by consumerist thinking. These arguments will scarcely persuade the authorities that it is time to make changes.

According to directives of the XXIVth Congress, a 36 percent increase in labor productivity will secure an 87 percent increase in production. In other words, if we raise labor productivity 100 percent, output will triple annually!

That's wrong. You take the figures but play "If." Your supposition is totally groundless.

"*Why?*" *asked Golovanov.*

Because labor productivity can only be raised by 37 to 38 percent, and every percentage point up to 40 is extremely difficult. How can one talk about raising productivity by 100 percent?

"*Viacheslav Mikhailovich, I will cite your own report from the XVIIIth Party Congress to refute you,*" *said Golovanov.*

What do you mean? I can remember what I said then on this issue.

"*Your report focused attention on questions of labor productivity—what Lenin said about it, what everyone was saying about it. The problem, however, is this: to talk about it is one thing, but to do something about it is another. Elements of Kosygin's report have something in common with yours. Productivity is given pride of place. To fight absenteeism and lax labor discipline, in your day those who showed up twenty minutes late for work were haled into court. This got real results. But now, of five million construction workers in our state, a half-million do not show up for work each day. Incidentally, that's not the way it used to be."*

Well, to a lesser extent.

Living out here, you can't see it all.

Probably.

"The difference between what appears in print and what really happens is like the difference between heaven and earth. The people complain; it is impossible to meet production targets. Economics determines politics. Loafers abound, absenteeism abounds. A new smelter goes into production in a ceremony dedicated to the convocation of a party congress and is then shut down. The Moscow Circus gave only one performance, after which the building was closed down. I recently visited Ust-Ilimsk. They report the fulfillment of plans. But there is no raw material. It goes to cooperatives. It's a vicious circle. . . . Stalin said that no propaganda, no agitation would be enough to unite the world proletariat around us. Instead we need to show that the people in our state live better than people live in America or in any other capitalist country. This would be the best kind of agitation, the best kind of propaganda."

Don't repeat the talk that's going around. I stick to my opinion.

"But can one really consider it right that living standards in the capitalist countries are twice as high as in our country? Are we always to be tightening our belts? I am younger than you, and I have never been on the Politburo," said Golovanov.

What does that have to do with it?

"I am saying this not because you have held a top position, but because you have a broader view than others."

And the point is?

"I consider Stalin's policy to be absolutely correct when he says that the nation should be based primarily on the material well-being of its people. Irrespective of our efforts in propaganda and agitation . . ."

I can't fully agree with you. You are oversimplifying things. Stalin never reasoned the way you ascribe to him. He never laid out his views in such a simplistic fashion. That kind of thinking could not be ascribed to Lenin either. No person sharing the Marxist position could support that viewpoint. You should emulate good communists rather than bad ones!

"I can swear I heard it from Stalin."

You did not get him right. You can't reason like that. Your figures are not right. I agree with you that the standard of living in the socialist countries is higher than ours, but by one and a half times, not twice ours. If we draw inaccurate comparisons, inevitably we pass over to rumor. I believe the standard of living is higher in the socialist countries; they consume more meat, have more footwear per capita. As to how much, I assume one and a half times more. But I also believe this serves our interests. Take another example. Our Baltic peoples live at a higher level than Muscovites. We need this. It is a policy that is in keeping with the interests of Moscow.

"I need to talk with your son-in-law Alexei Dmitrievich. He's a smart fellow and knows all the figures. I agree with your interpretation. People from the Foreign Ministry, experienced men all of them, tell me, 'If not for Vietnam, we would be much better off today.'"

The Vietnamese shed their blood for us! That has to be realized. No true communist would advance that argument.

After the Teheran conference, Stalin once told me he was sickened by the way they were deifying him, and that there were no saints. He said there was no such man as Stalin was depicted, but if the people created such a Stalin, if they believed in him, it meant this was necessary in the interests of the proletariat and should therefore be supported.

"If Stalin were alive today, the Soviet people would live much better, there would be five times greater aid to Vietnam, and we would have excellent relations with China and India," said Golovanov.

It's good to hear you say that, but we have lived through greater hardships and penury. In 1919 Lenin said we had made a workers' revolution but that the greater gains had accrued to the peasants. But complete victory was possible only if everything was in order in our villages. The politically conscious worker leads, the politically illiterate worker must be convinced, and the worker will gain only when he wins leadership over the peasantry.

The economic base is of primary importance. I'm no idealist, but if Stalin were alive today the British would surely have more than merely 29,000 communists, and our working class would be twice as well off as the workers in Britain.

. . . Molotov picks up the party program booklet and reads Khrushchev's conclusion that other nations will follow us once they see we live better than they.

You parrot Khrushchev's rubbish. That's nothing short of consumerism and even nationalism. Had the Bolsheviks waited for everyone to become literate, we would never have had a revolution. The workers in the Western countries enjoy better living conditions than we because their bourgeoisie robbed other countries as well as their own. Each Englishman used to have ten slaves. Then there was a workers' aristocracy. If we wait until we first raise our standard of living, expecting that others will then imitate us, we shall be nationalists who devote themselves solely to their own affairs, not communists. This is worse than Khrushchevism, this is utopianism.

"I heard from Stalin many times," said Golovanov, "and I say categorically that the way people live is the basis of everything. After all, neither Marx nor Engels ever said that when the people take power, thievery, absenteeism, drunkenness, and bribery would persist. It was assumed that the new society would be free of those vestiges. Last year twenty million tons of grain rotted in the fields. Now we buy grain from abroad and pay in gold. Unless we have another Stalinist hand firmly on the helm, we won't build communism. I hold that Stalin took the correct road and that we must continue this line. We must lay bare the ulcers. But what is going on instead? I recall how I first visited Stalin, long ago. I recall how during the war he offered me a dacha: 'We shall live side by side. While everyone talks about the great man, the genius, in the evening I have no one to drink a glass of tea with.' I declined the offer, and he said, 'Take it, or we will hand it over to Vasilevsky.'"

Vasilevsky had a very interesting encounter with Stalin. Alexander Mikhailovich told me about it. Stalin asked him to come over to his dacha and started questioning him about his parents. His father was a village priest, and Vasilevsky had been out of touch with him for a long time. "One shouldn't forget one's parents," said Stalin. "And it will be a long time before you pay off your debt to me!" He then walked over to his safe and took out a stack of money order receipts. It turns out that Stalin mailed money orders to Vasilevsky's father regularly. The old man believed the money came from his own son. "I couldn't find any words. I was just stunned," said Vasilevsky.

How much patience Stalin had for such matters! He called me one night, "Aren't you in bed yet? You have no security of your own, but we have posted some security men at your dacha."... I spent hours and hours arguing with him! I was like a kid then. Regrettably, I must admit that a man starts thinking sensibly only when he is in his advanced years.... Some people can't boast that even at an advanced age.

■   Dirty Politics?   ■

"I twice called Suslov about China," said Golovanov. "The country that Lenin spoke about in his day should not be treated the way we see today. The situation must be remedied. The chief culprit in this matter, second only to Khrushchev, I believe, is Mikoyan. After Khrushchev was removed, Brezhnev hoped that Mikoyan would succeed in patching things up with China. He was authorized to conduct negotiations with China. But in reply to Chou En-lai's question, Mikoyan responded that the position of the Central Committee toward China remained unchanged.

"Suslov said that Mao Tse-tung had written that we should remove Khrushchev from the CC. 'But Nikita Sergeevich is, after all, our CC!' said Suslov. The figure of Suslov is the greyest eminence operating in the background of our party's activity. Such a chameleon."

Suslov was a Stalinist.

He also made a statement upon Khrushchev's removal from office.

He was the first to propose that Brezhnev be awarded the gold medal of Hero of the Soviet Union.

"Politics is said to be dirty business," said Golovanov, "but still, some decency should be observed."

Philistines regard politics as a dirty business. Was Lenin a dirty operator? He was a politician, and we don't think he engaged in dirty work.

"'Stalin once said to Svetlana that politics is a filthy business," remarked Yevgeny Djugashvili.

That must be kitchen gossip. Stalin could not have said that. He spent his whole life in politics, that so-called filthy business.

"I was close to Stalin for four years," said Golovanov, "but Viacheslav Mikhailovich worked with him almost his entire life, for forty years. Stalin did not falter or blink an eye in repressing all kinds of scoundrels and crooks, and all this without a sign of indignation. That's what is interesting. But I believe he was very good to people."

Yes.

"There was a period when I didn't see Viacheslav Mikhailovich for some years. Then Stalin died. I wondered what stand Molotov would take on major political issues. After all, of all the Politburo members he held the most responsible jobs under Stalin. I must tell you quite frankly, I don't know what would have happened to Viacheslav Mikhailovich had Stalin lived on."

Exactly.

"Despite all his hard feelings and bitter experiences, it must be said that Viacheslav Mikhailovich regards Stalin truthfully and without bias. A lot of rumors used to be spread by Beria."

After all, it is not by chance that I am a party member.

"I did not experience 1 percent of what you had to go through. Stalin died. Only three days later I was summoned. They worked on me and offered me all kinds of offices. I am an honest man, but to slander a man with whom I had worked . . ."

"People say you have not returned your party membership card and you continue to pay your party dues," says Djugashvili.

No, that's not true. The matter has nothing to do with the party membership card. Before the Revolution none of us had a party card. Then Lenin received party membership card No. 1, Stalin No. 2. My card was No. 5. . . .

"I was a delegate to the VIIth Moscow party conference where Egorychev told us about how Molotov was expelled from the party," said Golovanov. "If you had sent in a letter of repentance confessing all your crimes, you would have been reinstated in the party! I say in my reminiscences that the younger generation would certainly profit from the memoirs of people like yourself who worked selflessly. Maybe I'm idealizing those years a bit. You are more careful in your remarks than I am. You had tremendous experience as chairman of the Council of Ministers, first deputy chairman, Minister of Foreign Affairs. I don't know if you ever took a break and relaxed. You always had the pallor of a man who obviously worked day and night. Everywhere I go I am asked, 'How's he doing?' Let me tell you, these days you look better than ever."

I sleep well. I usually go to bed at 11 p.m. I read off and on during the night. I get up at 6:30 in the morning. During the day I take a nap for thirty or forty minutes. It's not long, but it's fine. My brain is refreshed. . . . My blood circulation is improved. Twice a day I go for a walk in the woods. I always have lunch at the same time, 1 p.m. . . . The rest of the time I work a little, read something.

Everyone is looking forward to reading your memoirs.

That doesn't interest me. Lenin left no memoirs. Stalin left none of his own.

"Many believe your memoirs have already appeared in print," said Djugashvili. "Some say they have even seen the book and that it is titled Thirty Years with Stalin."

The postman congratulated me on my book being published. Some people even mention the number of copies printed. It's all nonsense! Everyone seems to have seen the book but me. . . . *Thirty Years with Stalin?* But I actually spent forty-one years working with him. . . . Of course, I can't remember all the details.

Do you remember your younger years and the Revolution best?

That's usual for an old man.

"I realized you have forgotten some details when I started to tell you about one particular event," said Golovanov. "We were about to fly to Teheran. I arrived at Stalin's dacha and heard him giving Beria a good dressing-down. I opened the door and saw Beria sitting in a chair with his ears all red. Stalin said, 'Look at him, Comrade Golovanov! He has the eyes of a snake! Our Viacheslav Mikhailovich can't see very well, and Beria keeps forwarding his messages in delicate handwriting, and he insists on wearing his pince-nez with blank glasses!' You were sitting on the windowsill at the time. I mentioned this to you, and you said you didn't remember. I thought it was a joke on your part."

You can't remember everything.

"Let me reconstruct for you a sitting of the Defense Committee. Sitting here was Viacheslav Mikhailovich. Over there, Stalin, though he would normally be pacing the floor. Apart from your job you were also responsible for a segment of industry as a Politburo member. I noticed you never got involved in the discussion because there were too many people at the meeting. But I could sense that Stalin and you were the two who made the decisions. I also recall the episode when Stalin received a letter from Churchill, apparently not the first time. As you handed the letter to Stalin, he started reading it and said, 'Hm . . . Churchill appears to believe he has saddled the horse and now he can enjoy a free ride. . . . Am I right, Viacheslav?' You calmly responded, 'I don't think so.' Stalin abruptly fell silent. I was so struck by what I had witnessed that I have remembered it to this day."

Disagreement is necessary. Nodding in agreement all the time . . . Shortly before his death, Stalin kicked me out of the bureau of the Presidium of the Central Committee, but I am not angry with him. I can stand on my own two feet; I hold my own opinions. Perhaps it did not always please him, nevertheless I used to tell him my frank opinion, even about his booklet "The Economic Problems of Socialism in the USSR." Back then I was not up on economics, but I can now judge economic problems far more knowledgeably. Back then I felt there were weak spots in his work and told him so. One must focus with great concentration in economics, and that was just what his work lacked. How can an economy be regarded as an independent variable? An economy may perhaps operate as the motor force, ideological or psychological. This may be regarded as an objective law, but right from the outset he indicates that an objective law is one that operates independently of the will of man. . . .

Well, what kind of economic law is that? What kind of law can set itself the task of directing society along a socialist path rather than along a capitalist path? Such laws do not exist. Initially his reasoning was correct, but he ended up in contradiction.

How did you address Stalin?

I used his party code-names: Stalin, or Koba. He would call me Molotov or Viacheslav. He often called me "Molotoshvili."

Malenkov is barred from coming into Moscow. He is the youngest of all of us. His mother lived at Udelnaya on the Riazan highway. He stayed there for some time, then he moved elsewhere. I don't know if Shepilov was expelled from the party or not. I think he was. A nice man. Very well educated. Good speaker and editor. He is competent on many issues, but he doesn't seem to have had sufficient experience in party work. A desk worker.

Let me tell you this: if Khrushchev could have seen farther than his own nose, he would have realized that it was necessary to build on Stalin's reputation, and he would have been forgiven everything by the people.

[12-2-71]

■   **"Be Grateful for Being Punished So Lightly"**   ■

. . . The three of us were out for a walk—Viacheslav Mikhailovich, Shota, and myself—along the path running between the railroad tracks and the fenced-off dacha compounds. Walking toward us was Alexei Ivanovich Shakhurin, minister of the aviation industry during the war years. The old men cordially greeted each other and stopped to exchange a few words about their health and problems at home. Molotov introduced us to Shakhurin, and then I ventured a question:

Alexei Ivanovich, why were you sent to prison?

"You'd better ask him," answered Shakhurin, and looked at Molotov. "He sent me there."

"You should be grateful for being punished so lightly," responded Molotov, tapping his cane on an icy patch on the path.

Shakhurin became pensive for a moment, then he looked at me and said, "He is actually right. It might have been much worse in those days. Nowadays people become Heroes of Socialist Labor for things that in those days could have caused their execution before a firing squad."

. . . We started talking about economics.

"Postwar taxation covered nearly everything, even privately owned cows," said Shakhurin.

"So what?" asked Molotov as he tapped on the ice with his cane. "Someone had to be taxed. It would never have occurred to me to have you taxed then."

"But what were the returns? We got scanty kopeks for our subsistence."

"Kopeks?"

"Exactly. When I was back in Moscow in 1953," recalled Shakhurin, "I saw lots of she-goats kept by individual owners all around the Moscow suburbs, which had never been the case before. 'Stalin's cows,' people used to say. . ."

"We had no other way out, dear comrade. It's time you realized that. Yes, yes, yes. It's time you realized that," said Molotov. . . .

"I am in a position to know that Stalin had very many positive qualities, because I met with him frequently—almost every day—for six years," Shakhurin said. "I know personally of his many rare, positive qualities and how much he accomplished. He had unique attributes, the mind of the greatest of statesmen. But at the same time he cannot be forgiven for having slaughtered our cadres—party, economic, and military."

"Could you explain that?" asked Shota.

"Better ask Molotov."

"He argues there was no other alternative," I said.

"He's a liar! How could he say that? No, not a liar. Molotov is a man of principles and integrity. He is firm in his beliefs. He does not try to justify himself; no, he is utterly convinced of his rectitude. I too have raised this same question with him. Molotov replies, 'Well, of course, not all of them may have been actual enemies, but the potential was there. . . .' I: 'What potential?' Molotov: "Take Khrushchev, for example.' In this case, he is of course right. I can agree with Molotov because Khrushchev in his ten years in power managed to do more damage than an enemy might have done. He is worse than an enemy. To have ruined what had already been built! Now they say that Stalin is responsible for our lagging behind. No, forgive me, under Stalin we so forged ahead that we must thank God!"

. . . I turned to Molotov with the question that Shakhurin refused to answer.

Of course. What did you expect? He wouldn't talk about himself. That's quite understandable. How could he be grateful to Stalin for sending him to prison for seven years of his life?

And Molotov proceeded to tell us about the reason for Shakhurin's arrest in 1946. Briefly:

After the war, the commander-in-chief of the air force, the chief marshal of aviation, A. A. Novikov, and the minister of the aviation industry, Shakhurin, arrived at the conclusion that one type of aircraft could do very well without a wingspar. The decision was not whimsical but was primarily motivated by the need to economize on metal and make the aircraft lighter. The move was made in violation of the Politburo's decision to prohibit any unauthorized alterations in the design of aircraft already operational in the air force. Some air crashes involving that type of aircraft were soon reported to Stalin. A special commission was set up to look into the matter, and, as a result, Novikov and Shakhurin were each tried and sentenced to eight years in prison.

Shakhurin was not a profound man, though he was a good minister, especially during the war. Everyone wants to be looked upon as kind. Well, if the Bolsheviks had been kind there would never have been any Bolsheviks. They had to go through terrible suffering and hardship. Look, pilots perished in airplane crashes, their families were bereft. . . . Is he not to blame?

[12-4-73]

■   The Tupolevs . . .   ■

Why did Tupolev, Stechkin, and Korolev serve time in prison?

Indeed, all of them were jailed. . . . They talked too much. And they were surrounded by dubious characters, so it was to be expected. After all, they never supported us. . . .

For the most part, our Russian intellectuals were closely linked with the well-to-do peasants who had a pro-kulak mentality. Ours was a country of peasants.

That very same Tupolev [an aircraft designer] might have even become a dangerous enemy. He had extensive connections with intellectuals hostile to us. And if he had helped the enemy, other people would, thanks to his prestige, naively have followed his lead in the mistaken belief that this would be beneficial to the Russian people. . . . And people were being compromised. In their time the Tupolevs were a very serious problem for us. Initially they were hostile to us, and it took some time to reconcile them to Soviet power.

Ivan Petrovich Pavlov [the famous Russian physiologist] used to say to his students, "Those are the ones who have ruined our lives!" pointing to portraits of Lenin and Stalin. Such undisguised enemies were easy to understand, but the ones like Tupolev were much harder to deal with. Tupolev was the sort of intellectual whom the Soviet state very much needed. But deep down these types opposed us and through their personal connections carried out dangerous and demoralizing activities. And even if they had not, they nevertheless breathed hostility. They could not have been otherwise!

What about Tupolev? Among Lenin's closest friends, in the end not one of those around him remained sufficiently loyal to Lenin and the party except Stalin. And Lenin had criticized Stalin.

Now when Tupolev won glory, that's one thing. But back then the intelligentsia took a negative attitude toward Soviet power. Look, we had to find a way to overcome this. The Tupolevs were put behind bars, and the Chekists were ordered to provide them with the best conditions, feed them as well as possible—indeed, better than anyone—but don't let them out! Let them work designing the military equipment needed by the country. These are indispensable people. It is their personal influence, not open propaganda, that makes them dangerous. We cannot overlook the possibility that at a critical juncture they could become especially dangerous. In politics such problems are unavoidable. Communists will not be able to build communism solely with their own hands.

I didn't see Tupolev very often, but I knew him well. I knew Ilyushin quite well. My daughter Svetlana was married to his son. Ilyushin is a communist, but Tupolev is a totally different type. Totally different. At one time he was certainly involved in anti-Soviet activities. We had to think hard and make quite an effort to straighten him out.

Ilyushin is a fine fellow, I think. He is good. A good communist, besides. He is a specialist. He didn't meddle in other business, but he knew aviation. He did a lot of good things. He used to come and see me from time to time. We would have quite good discussions on all kinds of questions. . . .

Yes, Ilyushin and Tupolev are different. One is a communist, the other is a bourgeois type. But Tupolev was, of course, pretty much Sovietized. Tupolev is the greater man. The difference is marginal, nevertheless.... Tupolev suffered great hardships while Ilyushin fell on to fertile soil and accomplished much. In depth of schooling, in this instance technical, it seems to me that Tupolev was superior to Ilyushin. Culturally, too, I think Tupolev was superior. There was competition between them. Ilyushin aspired to produce airplanes under the leadership of a Communist party member who would equal and perhaps better those produced by the nonparty member Tupolev. And we wanted and strove for this. On the whole he accomplished this task well. Ilyushin, in my opinion, is easier to understand. But to write about him will be difficult. He is not extroverted, and to get down deep inside him will not be easy. Tupolev takes some understanding. It's just not enough to depict him as a Soviet man. He is a far more complex figure than that.

We had other such cases, like that of Peter Kapitsa, the atomic physicist. I had to have him detained in the Soviet Union. He wanted to return to England to attend an international conference, but we proposed that he remain in the Soviet Union. He acquiesced but without enthusiasm. But he never spoke out, or at least he did not express his dissatisfaction publicly.

I heard that Ivan Petrovich Pavlov also spoke out against Kapitsa's going abroad.

Yes, I think so.

Pavlov reminded him against whom he would be working in England— against Russia! And this though Pavlov lost no love on communists.

No love at all.

But he was a Russian patriot.

Of course. But not just that. I read some of Pavlov's letters on the question of having people cleared to travel abroad. Then I met him at the International Congress of Physiologists in Moscow. We happened to meet there, since Pavlov was chairing the congress, and as chairman of the Council of Ministers I appeared before the congress with a welcoming speech. We were sitting next to each other, and I now recall Pavlov said, "I know rural life quite well, and I am watching closely to see what comes of your experiment." He referred to collectivization as an experiment. "I know the peasant well. I know he can complain in silence, then suddenly want to return to his old way of life from your collective farms. What will you do then?"

I said he did not fully understand real peasants. You say they want individual farming. But they have their own approach to this matter.

One must distinguish among the peasants: the poor, the middle, and the kulak. Now, you say that all of a sudden they will want to return to individual farming? This cannot be said about the peasantry as a whole. The kulaks are one thing—they really have something to be upset about. But what will the poor peasants, who constitute the majority, have to regret? And the middle peasants as well? As individual peasants they have a hard life and their income is small. They suffer all kinds of hardships.

Pavlov mulled this over a bit. I got the impression he did not brush off this response, but it did not suit him because he held the Social Revolutionary's abstract view of peasant society: well, there are individual kulaks, that's one thing, but the peasants as a whole are individual tillers, proprietors, which for them is the decisive question. In fact this is not so. It seemed to me that he mulled over this argument. That was toward the end of his life. The congress took place in 1934 or early in 1935. . . .

Let's return to Ilyushin.

A good communist and a good man. And his attitudes are generally commendable. He comes from Vologda. He is not merely a dedicated expert, he is also a dedicated citizen of the Soviet Union. He is loyal, too. He used his own mind and worked independently to reach the position he now holds.

But Tupolev was reported to have had close ties with the Paris-based anti-Soviet committee set up by emigrés and the wealthy living in Paris and other French and German cities. Later he moved closer to the Soviet people and conducted himself quite decently.

Of course, the White Guards wanted to keep him under their sway. They saw he was about to accomplish great things. He had hobnobbed with them for quite a long time. But afterward, in my opinion, he worked honestly. Although initially he had a negative attitude, in the end, during his mature years he came to Soviet power. He turned out well, quite well.

I know all of the best aircraft designers. They are all diverse in character. Some are friendly and have the right attitude, but there are also skeptics.

Did you ever have dealings with Polikarpov?

At conferences. In an official capacity, at conferences.

He used to be regarded as "the king of the fighter planes."

Yes, of course, he pioneered in this matter. In the early stages he held a top position in aircraft technology. But in my opinion he was a religious man, cast in the old mold. . . .

Tupolev possessed a good deal of entrepreneurial spirit. Sergei Vladimirovich was of course a more high-minded person.

Did Stalin ever meet with him?

Many times. On aviation matters. Stalin had a great instinct for technical things. Ilyushin designed a very good "flying tank." Stalin also put him in charge of the project that later became known as "IL-10."

Did Stalin pay much attention to aviation matters?

A lot. Quite a lot. In fact, aviation was one of his principal preoccupations before the war. Meetings then would quite often be held to address different questions, and Ilyushin would always be asked to attend.

[4-29-83, 10-14-83, 8-1-84, 4-30-86]

■   **"Why Was I Removed?"**   ■

. . . We are chatting about the repressed delegates to the XVIIth Party Congress.

Let us assume that the Central Committee consists of eighty members, of which thirty hold correct positions while fifty not only hold incorrect positions but are even active enemies of party policy. Why should the majority submit to the minority?

The question is incorrectly formulated.

But the point is, this is the way many people raise it.

Khrushchev did everything to have the question formulated in this manner. Everything, but everything. First, concerning democratic centralism. Is dialectical materialism to be applied to democratic centralism? Listen, there has never been a case where the minority excluded the majority. This was a gradual process. Seventy excluded ten to fifteen members, then sixty excluded another fifteen. Here you have the proper relationship between the majority and the minority.

That was evidence of brilliant tactics rather than evidence of correctness.

Let me say, this corresponded with the actual course of events and was not merely a matter of tactics. Everything emerged gradually in sharp struggle fought out in various sectors. In some places it was possible to be patient; we withheld action, though we mistrusted them. In other places it was impossible to be patient. Gradually everything followed the procedure of democratic centralism, without any formal violations. In point of fact this left a Central Committee consisting of a minority of the former majority, but without formal violations. This did not formally violate the principles of democratic centralism; it was a step-by-step process, though it proved a rather rapid process of clearing the way.

Over the course of two or three years.

But this is an achievement of colossal significance! The February Revolution is one thing; it was fought out under one set of conditions. But the October Revolution was another thing; it was already a socialist revolution. In only eight months what a colossal shift, and it involved a completely new set of people. . . . A radically new situation had taken shape. Then it took two or three years to show who stood where; rot persisted imperceptibly; one man had already begun to degenerate and deserved no trust as a leader. That is why one must reckon with the historical side; the materialist dialectic has great significance here. And if you look into the details of these events, you find no overturn of a majority by a minority but a historical sequence of events and clearing of the way. This is very essential. It is necessary to form judgments more concretely by taking into account the specifics of the given historical period and the political alignments that took shape within it. Likewise, one must take into account the past which left its imprint on these people. The struggle against Trotskyism did not remove everything Trotskyist either from the ranks of the party or from its central bodies. In this period the struggle shifted to a struggle against the rightists; they adhered most flexibly to the party. Back then they were regarded as the main danger. Even after the rout of the kulak class, after total collectivization, the rightists turned out, as was revealed, to be more numerous than was assumed. That was the main danger.

The XVIIth Party Congress went down in the history of our party as the "Congress of Victors."

Look, these labels were unimportant. It was just a slogan for use by agitators.

Were there no oppositionist questions raised at the XVIIth Congress?

The Politburo knew about what was out in the open. But it was impossible to know everything as long as no opportunity arose to find out. In order to throw some light on this question, let me ask you: what do you consider Khrushchev to have been back then, a rightist, a leftist, or a Leninist, or what? Khrushchev sat on the Politburo under Stalin throughout the 1940s and the early 1950s. And Mikoyan, too. We purged and we purged, yet it turns out that rightists still sat in the Politburo! Look how complicated all this is! It is impossible to understand this if you judge only by facts and figures and formal criteria. Impossible. There were such profound changes in the country and in the party too, that even given all the vigilance of Stalin to liberate ourselves of Trotskyists and rightists . . . Even in Stalin's time they served continuously in the Politburo, especially the rightists most adaptable and skilled in time-serving. Our rightists, so flexible, so closely and strongly connected with our own dear peasantry, resembled the muzhik in his ability to adapt himself ideologically to every twist and turn. Determining where Trotskyism begins and especially where rightism begins is a most complex subject, most complex.

In many cases the rightists comport themselves no worse than genuine Leninists—but up to a point. Like Khrushchev. At the XIXth Congress, when Stalin was still alive, Khrushchev delivered the report on the question of organization. I opened the XIXth Congress.

But they advised me—my speech of about twenty pages at the XIXth Congress lies before me even now—the entire Politburo said, "Don't give a speech! Stalin will be displeased. Don't, you must not speak." I had nothing special in mind, and of course everything I said was favorable to Stalin. In the end no one knew what I was going to say, yet they said, don't go out on a limb, you must not speak!

Why?

And why was I removed from the Politburo the very first day after the congress? Not formally but in fact. Yes, yes, you don't know this.

But according to all the newspapers you were on the Presidium of the Central Committee . . .

The Presidium of the CC consisted of twenty-five members. That was stipulated in the party statutes. But a plenum was convened, a Politburo had to be elected. They elected a Politburo that did not include Molotov and Mikoyan. I was included in the Presidium membership of twenty-five, but it almost never met. But there was a bureau of ten members, a fact which was not publicized at the time. It included Beria and Khrushchev.

In 1953 Stalin no longer invited me to attend official or informal comradely gatherings, to spend an evening together or to see a film. I was cut off. Bear in mind that Stalin in his last years took a negative attitude toward me. I believe this was incorrect. This matter should be thoroughly investigated. As for me, I had not changed my opinion of Stalin, but apparently someone was turning him against me.

Surely that group of three friends—Beria, Khrushchev, and Malenkov— were working on him?

Apparently, yes. Most likely, yes. All the same, of course, that's not the main thing. My wife was distrusted. That was an effect of Stalin's distrust of Zionist circles. But this was not, so to speak, fully reasonable.

[10-9-75]

The Soviet Encyclopedia *writes: "In November 1946, the General Assembly of the Academy of Sciences of the USSR elected V. M. Molotov an Honorary Academician."*

1946. I was abroad then. I was in New York when I received a telegram from Stalin. He wrote: "Some Academicians came to see me. They want to elect you an Honorary Academician. I request consent." I gave my consent and did a foolish thing. I signed off with a superfluous phrase on the order of "Your Molotov." Later Stalin said to me, "I am surprised. How could you sign like that?"

Yes, I said a real foolish thing. Well, I was overdoing it. That Academy, the devil knows what kind of motley crew composed it, so why "Your?" I wanted a simple sign-off. Inasmuch as they had nominated me, it was impossible not to accept. It was foolishness, of course.

Further on the Encyclopedia *reads: "In March 1949, V. M. Molotov was released from his duties as Minister of Foreign Affairs to concentrate his activity in the Council of Ministers of the USSR in his capacity as Deputy Chairman of the Council of Ministers of the USSR."*

There are no comments. Apparently Stalin had already started to crush you.

No comments? No, all this started earlier.

[4-19-77]

In January 1953 a certain Polish entertainer Dombrowskaya-Turskaya gave a concert here while on tour. The following day the newspapers reported that the concert was attended by Stalin, Molotov, and others. Period. I was listed in second place after him, following usual procedure. I myself read this in the newspapers. But in fact I was no longer being invited anywhere! He had already openly said that I was a rightist.

Wasn't it because of Polina Semenovna?

She suffered because of me.

Not the other way around?

They sought a way to get to me, they grilled her. So as to compromise me they had to humiliate her, accusing her of being party to some kind of conspiracy. They summoned her time and again and grilled her, saying that I was not a genuine proponent of the party's general line. That was the real situation.

Viacheslav Mikhailovich Molotov, the man, she said, who together with Josif Vissarionovich had become leading figures in the state long before you . . .

Since 1912.

Since 1912! Both of you were on the Central Committee in the most critical and complex moments of struggle. Both of you passed through the ultimate trial, the Great Patriotic War, when the question was, to be or not to be . . .

I did nothing special. My contributions to victory were few, so to speak. . . .

Didn't you fly to London?

We did, yes.

During the war probably no political leader risked the kinds of dangerous journeys you logged.

Well, it had to be done.

Viacheslav Mikhailovich Molotov was in actuality the second highest person in the state over so many years. Then suddenly . . . How do you explain this? Stalin by and large trusted no one? Or was his mind affected? How was this possible?

He succumbed to sickly suspiciousness. Stalin had undergone so many years of ordeal and had taken so much on his own shoulders that in his last years he suffered from impaired judgment. Impaired in the sense that a simple mistake might seem to him evidence of some dastardly plot.

But, look, by the early 1950s there were not and there could not be any people in the party who would try to pursue an anti-Stalinist line.

Just a minute. Stalin died in March, but as early as June or July Khrushchev headed this self-same Central Committee. How did it turn out that way? Khrushchev, Mikoyan, rightists, they sat on the Politburo where they pretended to be Stalin's greatest champions. Look at what Mikoyan said on the occasion of Stalin's seventieth birthday: "Stalin is the Lenin of today." You would not repeat that nor would I, yet in his article marking Stalin's seventieth birthday he wrote, Behold, we had Lenin, now we have Stalin. But several months after the death of Stalin he reversed himself! And Khrushchev? After all, he had put together a faction!—So much for our fortress, Nikita Sergeevich! Behold, how thoroughly the purges had been carried out! Behold, how we had put all that rightism behind us! As a matter of fact, we had still left nothing of that behind us!

I wrote an article in 1960 to mark the ninetieth anniversary of the birth of Lenin (I was ambassador to Mongolia back then), and sent it to the journal *Kommunist*. It was not accepted. Konstantinov, then editor-in-chief, one of the few editors who would even respond to my article, explained why it could not be published. First, he wrote, you do not refer even once to your errors; second, you discuss the February Revolution and say that it was a blow against imperialism, as if there had been no October Revolution; and third, you talk as if Lenin in conversation with you had criticized communists, said that our country was so weak, and so forth, which we cannot print.

Just what did Lenin say to me in 1921? The conversation was so concentratedly political that for me it was very important. Lenin said, "I want to talk with you concerning our economic affairs." Preobrazhensky, an oppositionist, was then deputy people's commissar of finance. Although he no longer completely adhered to the party's positions, he had not yet fully shown his true colors.

Lenin said: "Preobrazhensky is proposing financial reform, to change the parity of the ruble, so to speak, to carry out currency reform: instead of a thousand-ruble note, a one-ruble note. Reform in that spirit. Is it necessary? After all, the condition of our state is so parlous that the touch of a finger would be enough to cause the whole edifice to come crashing down!"

That's what I wrote. They replied to me: After all, to write such things would be misunderstood abroad, where it would engender fear of revolution.

Almost forty years have passed since Lenin told me this, so it is utterly absurd to say one cannot talk about it now. This shows how things were. It was under such conditions that, thanks only to Lenin's authority, the state survived. Thanks only to this! And afterward, thanks to Stalin. Much has been achieved and has turned out better than we deserved— after all, many of us lacked education. Stalin's authority was so great that plenary sessions of the Politburo or of the Central Committee did not have to be held to take up each complex question. Sometimes a certain matter had to be decided something less than democratically, but later the party as a rule endorsed the decision. Had we convened to make a democratic decision on each question that came up, we should have inflicted harm on the state and on the party, because this would have dragged out a solution to the question. In some cases a more extensive discussion of a question might have led to a better decision, but in certain other cases the very protraction of the decision-making process would have inflicted vast harm. Under such complex conditions formal democracy does not always resolve an issue.

Well, at the same time Stalin, bearing such a heavy burden, at times bent under the weight, yielded to bad advice, and swallowed incorrect information. He knew me like a book. He was familiar with my entire biography and had known me personally since 1912. We had worked together four decades and implemented the toughest decisions. On the whole I was an active participant in everything, never a passive observer. Nevertheless, he began to have his doubts about me, the devil knows why! He may have had a reason. Perhaps I vacillated on a question in 1940.

I was not afraid that I might sound like a rightist when I personally suggested: "Let us raise the procurement prices we pay for grain. The peasants of Central Russia are living in great hardship."

He replied, "What's this? How can you make such a proposal? What if there is a war?" I responded, "If war comes, we shall say openly to the people: Because of the war, we are returning to the old procurement prices." "Do you know what this reeks of?"

I said, "If war comes, we shall return to the old prices. The peasants will understand that we can no longer pay the higher prices." I believe I made a mistake. Patience was called for, so I did not start to argue with him. I had simply made a suggestion in a tête-a-tête conversation, with only the two of us present, at his flat. I changed the subject and did not raise the question again. In 1952 he reminded me of this incident. In the presence of others, he declared, "Just look at what Molotov proposed—to raise grain procurement prices, and he demanded that we convene a Central Committee plenum to address the issue!"

I couldn't have possibly demanded a Central Committee plenary meeting; I merely mentioned that to him privately. He appeared to have remembered that as my deviation to the right. He didn't accuse me directly of a right-wing deviation, he just said, "You are Rykovists!" Meaning Mikoyan, too. But as a matter of fact, Mikoyan is a Rykovist, a rightist, and a Khrushchevite. I see no great difference between Khrushchev and Rykov. And I have never supported Khrushchev.

The first to speak was Mikoyan. He claimed he had nothing to do with . . . Of course, the records of that meeting have never been made public.

Unaware of what lay in store for me, I also responded. "I do admit my mistakes. But that suggestion was just part of my private conversation with Comrade Stalin, nothing more." Even now I fail to see why Stalin got it mixed up. It was impossible even to tell him that his doubts were baseless.

But in my opinion this was a very important matter, because in Central Russia tension was running high.

At that plenary meeting, Stalin promoted Khrushchev. As far as I was concerned, I was not elected to the Politburo for being a right-winger. And that was no minor issue, either; my suggestion was not merely used as a pretext. It shows that I had made some deviations.

I'm not convinced Stalin was right on that question.

I think he was right.

Anything can be justified then.

Well, you shouldn't exaggerate. Being wealthier today, we practice policies detrimental to our main goal. Grain procurement prices should not have been inflated; there was no need for it. It was harmful to the peasantry, not to mention harmful to the country as a whole. The huge sums of money we squandered on procurement prices should have gone to increase the number of tractors, combines, and other farm machines, to enable the peasantry more quickly to increase agricultural production. . . .

In his later years Stalin's memory began to fail him. Someone was slipping him reports at just the right moment. He became obsessed with the idea that a Central Committee plenum was needed to expose Mikoyan, the rightist, and me. . . . Perhaps something more—I don't recall all the details. I spoke, I repented, I confessed my mistake.

This occurred after the XIXth Congress, in 1952, in October or November. I believe I had erred. But I did not persist in this error. . . . After all, twelve years had passed since this controversial question had come up. . . . Polina Semenovna had already been deported from Moscow.

[2-3-72, 10-4-72, 5-12-76]

I spoke, of course, in our very small leadership circle—I did not agree with them on a number of issues. When they discussed a new five-year plan—I always favored restraint in capital construction. Construction of capital projects was dragged out, dragged out, nothing was completed. But when we set planned targets that we cannot fulfill, breakdowns develop, we start plugging the gaps, yet we increase investments in other places. The plan had to be reworked anew. "Who is to blame?" Stalin asked. This is with six or seven of us at his dacha. He was chairman of the Council of Ministers and I was first deputy, around 1950. He said, "We cannot keep supplementing appropriations endlessly, taking from here, then from there. . . . Who is to blame?" "You are to blame!" I said to him.

He flew into a rage. "You are always stepping up the planned investments!" I said to him in the heat of the moment, in the presence of all our company, "They come to you with the plan, and you keep adding on more and more!"

I got into fights with many of them.

I believe Beria did me less harm than the others, Malenkov hardly any at all. I think some of the lower-ranking CC apparatchiks did me harm, but that was after he had already ordered an investigation.

To this day I am unable to understand. Why was I eliminated from the Politburo? Beria? No. I think he had even defended me in this matter. And later, when he saw that even Molotov had been eliminated, he became apprehensive. Beria! If Stalin no longer trusted Molotov, he could eliminate me, Beria, in an instant!

Khrushchev? Hardly. Some of us knew Stalin's weaknesses. In any case, I never gave him reason to mete out such treatment to me. True, I was never a yes-man to him. He appreciated me for this quality. In dealing with him my principle was to speak my mind straight out, right or wrong. One must not overlook that side of the affair. But then suddenly. . .

Throughout the war years we used to follow the same routine we had started before the war. We would work at the Central Committee late into the night. Sometimes we would spend long hours at Stalin's place, having supper and then—let's watch a movie! At 11 or 12 p.m. we would walk over to the movie theatre at the Kremlin, a small room to which foreigners were occasionally invited. Churchill visited it once. It was sort of a private theatre, comfortable: no outsiders were allowed in, though movie officials were invited for some shows. Bolshakov, chairman of the state movie committee, and some script writers could be found in the audience. Conversations would then focus on certain special problems, of course.

To this day there are some things I just can't understand. Stalin regarded Khrushchev very critically. True, he valued Khrushchev as a practical man, one who sniffed out things everywhere and strove to master details. Stalin needed such a person, one he could rely on more or less.

In Stalin's last years there was an economist on the staff of the journal *Problems of Peace and Socialism*, L. D. Yaroshenko, who was taken to task by Stalin in his last work. When Khrushchev was not around, Stalin used to remark about this, "The Khrushchev Affair!"

Stalin raked Yaroshenko over the coals, correctly in my opinion.

Doubts arose as to whether this matter had been looked into carefully, because it involved rather complex questions of political economy. But Stalin said Yaroshenko's discussion of economic theory had been engineered by Khrushchev, then head of the Moscow party organization, of which Yaroshenko was a member. I don't think this is possible. Khrushchev could hardly have thought it up; he was not at home in questions of theory. Stalin might have been duped. Intriguers always abound. Just drop a hint, pass on some insinuating document at the psychological moment, and finally, when the prey takes the bait, he gets more and more drawn into the web.

But Stalin, especially in his last years, did not fully trust anyone.

[10-4-72, 1-9-81]

■ "Polina Is Alive!" ■

. . . *On a hot August afternoon I arrived at the Novodevichy Cemetery to attend the dedication of Polina Semenovna Zhemchuzhina's tombstone. People had begun gathering in the corner of the old part of the cemetery by 4 p.m.—news travels fast, the news being that Molotov was to arrive shortly, the very Molotov whose formal portraits had disappeared from public view in 1957.*

"I recently rode with him on a trolley bus," a voice could be heard in the gathering crowd.

"Nonsense! He wouldn't ride on a trolley bus. He surely has a chauffeured Chaika limo of his own!" said another.

In fact, Khrushchev had deprived Molotov and other members of "the antiparty faction" of all the usual perquisites. Molotov lived with his relatives on Chkalovskaya Street on a pension of 120 rubles a month. To have laid away savings or valuables for his old age would have been out of character for him. He lived entirely on his meager state pension.

. . . Plainly attired in his navy blue suit and tie, Molotov was wearing his pince-nez. He was accompanied by his daughter Svetlana and son-in-law Alexei Dmitrievich Nikonov, a Ph.D. and professor.

The tombstone was hewn by Vuchetich who accepted no fee for the job. He took quite a long time to complete the order, saying the tombstone had to be "worthy of the name Vuchetich." The tombstone is a sculptured head in white bas-relief set against an upright slab of black marble. That is all. Very austere, nothing superfluous.

After spending half an hour at the cemetery, we went to the apartment building on Granovsky Street, apartment 61, and shared a funeral repast in memory of Polina Semenovna.

To me befell the happiness to have had her as my wife. Beautiful, intelligent, and, the main thing, a genuine Bolshevik, a genuine Soviet person. Because she was my wife, her life didn't go at all smoothly. Although she suffered through difficult times, she understood everything. She never cursed Stalin, and she wouldn't allow anyone to do that in her presence, for she realized that anyone who denigrated Stalin would in time be jettisoned as an element alien to our party and to our people.

"It seems to me," I told him afterward, "that it was you who suffered because of her, and not the other way around, when Stalin came out against you at that plenary meeting after the XIXth Congress and did not include you in the bureau of the Central Committee Presidium."

Why did he go after me the way he did? Perhaps she had something to do with it.

At the session of the Politburo when he read out the material on Polina Semenovna supplied by the security people, my knees began to knock. This was not a question of some intrigue. Security had done a thorough job on her. They had outdone themselves. What did they accuse her of? Of connections with a Zionist organization and with Golda Meir, the Israeli ambassador. Security charged that they sought to make the Crimea a Jewish autonomous region.... They had good relations with the great Jewish actor Mikhoels.... Security found he was an alien element.

Of course, she should have been more fastidious in choosing her acquaintances. She was removed from office but for some time was not arrested. Then she was taken into custody and summoned to the Central Committee. A black cat had, as they say, crossed our path. Relations between me and Stalin cooled.

She was in prison for a year and in exile more than three years. At the Politburo meetings Beria would walk past me and whisper into my ear, "Polina is alive!" She served time in the Lubianka prison in Moscow, and I didn't even know she was there.

And yet you continued to be the second most powerful man in the state?

Yes, formally. For the press and for public consumption. She was freed from exile the day after Stalin's funeral. She didn't even know that Stalin had died, so her first question was, "How's Stalin?" The news of his illness had reached her. Taking advantage of Beria's invitation, I arrived at his office to pick her up. Hardly had I walked up to her when Beria ran ahead of me to Polina and exclaimed, "A heroine!"

She certainly endured great hardship, but I repeat, she never changed her attitude toward Stalin. She always thought highly of him.

Shota Ivanovich added, "Once a relation of hers started to assail Stalin at a dinner, and she abruptly put him in his place. 'Young man, you understand absolutely nothing about either Stalin or his times. If only you knew the burden he bore in office!'"

[8-18-73]

In his last years Stalin suffered from a persecution mania. He was so overwrought, self-seekers had so irritated and worn him down, had incited him against this person and that—he had broken down. That's a fact. No man could have withstood it. In my opinion he was no exception. So he went too far. Consequently, able leaders such as Voznesensky and Kuznetsov perished.

Yes, he was definitely afflicted in his final years with a persecution mania. How could it be otherwise? Such is the lot that befalls all leaders who hold office too long.

[10-21-82]

I don't know on whom he relied! He promoted Khrushchev and mixed me up with Mikoyan as two of a kind. Well, there was no basis whatever for that. It was not only because of Polina Semenovna, though I assume this had some influence on him.

People say Stalin demanded that you get a divorce but that you refused. He demanded that you dissociate yourself from her.

In the first place, *they* had separated me from her. You see, back in 1940 when they voted to exclude her from the Central Committee, I abstained, that's true. Later he said, "People are talking as if you voted against." She had been a candidate member of the CC when she was excluded. They accused her... What didn't they think up! Everything was very confused. Zhdanov, it seems, laid out the case against her. Wreckers had been exposed in the fisheries industry where she worked. According to the charge, it all started in Uzbekistan. Later she worked in the cosmetics industry, in perfumery, and had allegedly employed some shady characters. (Naturally, there were no other kind.) German spies were uncovered there. They availed themselves of the presence of wives of our most prominent leaders, who went to her for the latest in cosmetics.

But when she was arrested in 1949 they accused her of plotting an attempt on Stalin's life. Vyshinsky then put in his oar. Before I was removed from the Ministry of Foreign Affairs, Stalin came up to me at the CC and said, "You have to divorce your wife!" She then said to me, "If the party needs this, then we shall get a divorce!" At the end of 1948 we were divorced. But in 1949, in February, she was arrested.

No accusations were leveled at me, but I received no sensible explanation. Putting two and two together, however, I grasped—and this was later confirmed—that the trouble stemmed from my stay in America, probably in 1950. When I traveled from New York to Washington I was given a special railroad car. I paid too little attention to this courtesy at the time, but obviously I had been assigned a car equipped with listening devices so as to eavesdrop on every word I uttered. I was accompanied by some kind of delegation of physicians from the Soviet Union who traveled to Washington with me without passenger tickets. What kind of secrets could they let slip out?

Stalin said nothing, but his secretary Poskrebyshev started to hint, "Why did they assign you a special car?" Later Vyshinsky told me that Poskrebyshev had said that our security men had checked out the car. Needless to say, not everyone is granted a special car. It had no precedent, so why did they offer it to me?

Should you have declined the offer? What could they suspect you of?

Perhaps the security men suspected that I had been gotten to when I headed the Soviet delegation to the UN. But the atmosphere was already palpably heavy with suspicion. After all, Stalin back in the 1930s had appointed Polina Semenovna people's commissar of the fisheries industry—and I had opposed this! She was the only woman people's commissar of an economic commissariat. A woman headed public health. Krupskaya had been deputy commissar of public education, but Polina Semenovna was then the first and only woman to head an economic commissariat.

On the one hand Stalin, as it were, promoted and valued Polina Semenovna. But, on the other hand, at the end of his life . . . He might have been influenced by anti-Semitic sentiments. Another of his extremes skillfully exploited by schemers.

[12-4-72, 3-10-77, 9-29-82]

Stalin took a very critical view of me. To this day I do not know precisely why. I sensed that he held me in great distrust, but the grounds for this remain unclear to me. My wife was arrested not without his knowledge; indeed, he personally ordered it. That's a fact.

Didn't Stalin tell you the reason why?

No, he didn't. Bad company, apparently. In this respect Polina Semenovna was too free and easy. That's the truth. She met with all kinds of people. Perhaps I'm a bit to blame inasmuch as I did not categorically oppose this. On the whole the friends and acquaintances in her circle were good, but there were also some acquaintanceships that were not fully defensible and even some that were indefensible.

Your personal enemies could have schemed against you.

Absolutely. There's no doubt about that. I had no open opposition on the Politburo, but concealed opposition was certainly there.

Then she was deported to Kazakhstan. Do you remember where exactly?

I certainly do. It was a city in the breadbasket of Kazakhstan . . . Kustanai!

That was all very odd, you being the second most powerful official in the state, and your wife under arrest. . . .

Kalinin's wife was also arrested. . . . She wasn't much, but she was probably mixed up with a motley crew of people. Such pathological suspiciousness—sickly suspiciousness. But who was left he could rely on? Khrushchev, whom he did not trust even earlier, was scrambling upward. And Stalin had good reason to distrust him.

Some people believe that Beria killed Stalin. I believe this possibility cannot be excluded. If Stalin did not trust me, whom could he rely on? Was anyone safe?

Western radio stations went into detail about the "doctors' plot," pointing out that it was to go to trial on March 5, exactly the day Stalin died. That sounds like a veiled hint that he was murdered.

That's possible. Of course this possibility cannot be ruled out. Beria was treacherous and unreliable. He could have done the deed just to save his own skin. The skein was badly tangled. I too am of the opinion that Stalin did not die a natural death. He wasn't seriously ill. He was working steadily. . . . And he remained very spry.

[3-11-83]

■   **From the Revolutionary Point of View**   ■

Stalin shouldered a burden so heavy that it naturally left him burned out. It was very difficult for him in his last years as he aged, but the main thing is that he was utterly drained in every way. Also he was afraid of taking medicine. He had good reason. Stalin had enemies enough who might put one over on him. His fear that someone might slip some poison either into his food or into his medicine, however, went beyond all limits. . . . To a certain extent this is understandable, because really it was very difficult to bear the entire burden on his own two shoulders. Apparently he had all kinds of doubts whether anyone induced to take up this burden would have the patience, the will, and the strength to bear it. That was his predicament.

Although these events did not leave me untouched, and although I might not have remained in one piece had he lived on, I have regarded him and still regard him as a great man who fulfilled such immense and arduous tasks as none of us, none of those in the party back then, could have fulfilled.

To speak of Kirov as some kind of deputy or successor to Stalin is entirely absurd to any literate and knowledgeable communist. That choice would have been totally at odds with the nature of the relationship between Stalin and Kirov, and above all with Kirov's own perception of his potential. It so contradicts the realities of that period that only a criminal type such as Nikita could go so far as to allege that Stalin had special reason to finish off Kirov.

True, Kirov had told Stalin at the XVIIth Party Congress that a group of delegates had proposed to nominate him for top office in the party. But Kirov as general secretary? Utterly, simply absurd! Kirov was a highly effective agitator and good communist. He was not and did not claim to be a theoretician. Never. It goes without saying that he was incapable of ideologically crushing Trotsky, Zinoviev, and Kamenev. Others were more capable, feasible, or likely as a potential leader than Kirov! Indeed, far more!

The 1920s and '30s witnessed an open struggle on the ideological plane—in the press a struggle of pens—but could we permit it to go on endlessly at the expense of the state, at the expense of the working class? If you want to spare the working class—the people were toiling, they wanted to live better, while we at the top and in the press were constantly clashing and at each other's throats. A most dangerous thing, assuredly!

In this connection I should like to ask a purely psychological question, which of course is most closely related to politics but is nevertheless psychological. You said that it might have happened, that repression might have even reached you, if . . .

Yes, it could have.

Could have?

Could have.

Especially as Polina Semenovna . . .

They were intriguing might and main against us.

Just imagine your plight. A man who gave many years to the party, sacrificed his health, life, everything for the cause of the party and the building of socialism, might suddenly find himself behind barbed wire!

Well, what of it? Oh, Lord! I look at this from the revolutionary point of view. At any time during those long years—both before the Revolution and after—I might have more than once perished.

But after all, you had done nothing so wrong . . .

And I tell you that I had made one definite mistake, and probably note was taken of more than one. . . .

A person who never sympathized with either Stalin or Molotov persistently asked me to arrange a meeting with Molotov. I made a strenuous effort to arrange it and finally succeeded. The conversation lasted about four hours, during which the most burning questions were raised and not a single one left unanswered. As we walked to the railroad station after the meeting, Molotov's interlocutor remarked, "Visiting with Molotov is like traveling abroad for the first time. If one were anti-Soviet he would grow more anti-Soviet after meeting with him; if one were pro-Soviet he would grow firmer in his convictions. I haven't started liking him, but I've definitely been struck by his reasoning powers and responsiveness. Those men are not to be trifled with! I wonder what kind of person Stalin was if he had a man like Molotov working for him?"

[2-3-72]

Four

SINCE
STALIN

As Molotov viewed the world in the last third of his long life, he did not like what he saw. Perhaps most old men and women take a jaundiced view of the world compared with the idealized memory of an earlier time. But Molotov had special reason to be dissatisfied. No one still alive in the Soviet Union had done more than he to create and shape that world, but the product bore little resemblance to Molotov's vision of socialism, however perverse. It bore even less resemblance to the classical socialist vision of a world without violence, domestic or foreign, a classless society living in equality, freedom, justice, and democracy.

To what did he object most? The triumph of his nemesis, "the right wing," which falsely proclaimed that full socialism, "real socialism," had been built in the USSR, even as inequality and venality grew. True, Molotov argued that the foundations of socialism had been laid. The means of production had been socialized; that is, productive wealth was owned either by the state or by cooperatives such as kolkhozes. But the USSR could not be regarded as socialist, first, because proletarian revolution had not triumphed in the major capitalist countries and ended "imperialist" encirclement of the USSR. Molotov claimed that Khrushchev and Brezhnev, intimidated by U.S. atomic weapons, had cravenly abandoned the goal of international communism for that of "peaceful coexistence" with imperialism.

Second, social equality had not been achieved in the Soviet Union. A socialist society must not only eliminate the "exploiting classes" (landlords, bourgeoisie, and kulaks), as had already been done. It must also eliminate the distinction between the two surviving social classes: the working class and the kolkhoz peasantry. Meanwhile, the kolkhoz system was failing so badly that the USSR had to import grain from the United States. Chuev suggested dissolution of the kolkhozes. Molotov recommended their transformation into sovkhozes. These would convert the kolkhoz peasant into a wage worker, like the factory worker employed by the state, making the country a truly classless society. Thus only state property, the "highest" form of socialist property, would remain.

Finally, a socialist society must reduce income inequality to a minimum by capping remuneration, abolishing money, and eliminating material incentives. This conception of socialism marked a throwback to the period of War Communism, 1918–1921, when it proved ruinous.

Most alarming in Molotov's valedictory is his vehement opposition to the policy of "peaceful coexistence" initiated by Khrushchev and continued by his successors. Molotov adhered to two of Lenin's cardinal tenets, unmodified. First, socialism could be initiated in Russia but achieved only on an international scale. And second, war is inevitable as long as imperialism exists. Molotov believed that both tenets fully applied, even in the nuclear age. The USSR must therefore not slacken its efforts to spread the Soviet system, even if doing so increased the danger of nuclear war. Any relaxation would embolden the imperialists to blackmail the USSR into abandoning socialism at home and abroad.

From Khrushchev on, however, Soviet leaders contended that the enormous growth of Soviet economic and military power, exemplified by atom-tipped ICBMs, kept the imperialists at bay; consequently, war was no longer "fatalistically inevitable." The prime aim of Soviet foreign relations must be "peaceful coexistence" with adversaries, détente marked by a search for means to reduce the danger and prevent the outbreak of a new war. Molotov opposed all such efforts while applauding Soviet occupation of Czechoslovakia in 1968 and the war in Afghanistan. In that connection, Molotov, as if reciting George Orwell, bluntly declared that "there can be no peace without war!"

In sum, Molotov's mind had frozen in the prenuclear age. The West as well as the Russians can be thankful that Molotov failed to unseat Khrushchev in 1957. Reason prevailed. One year before Molotov's death, President Gorbachev and President Reagan echoed and surpassed their predecessors, Khrushchev and Eisenhower, by agreeing at Geneva that "A nuclear war cannot be won and must never be fought."

■ "The Trinity" ■

In his recollections Molotov often referred to "the Trinity"—Beria, Malenkov, and Khrushchev. Asked why Khrushchev headed the Central Committee after Stalin, he replied that Khrushchev was friendly with Beria and Malenkov.

At that point Beria miscalculated. He started to do things behind Malenkov's back, and he refused to assume the position of chairman of the Council of Ministers because he didn't command sufficient authority.

Khrushchev was no fool. He succeeded in rebuilding the Central Committee after his own fashion.

[4-22-70]

What united those three—Malenkov, Beria, and Khrushchev?

Well, they certainly followed in Stalin's footsteps, and that united them. The Trinity. In my opinion they were not really united by any genuine or fast ties. There was perhaps a modicum of friendship, of fellowship. . . .

[4-19-83]

Molotov recounted that in 1953, after Stalin's death, he was returned to the Ministry of Foreign Affairs. The German question had to be discussed and a policy set. As a Politburo member Molotov was accountable for the German Democratic Republic.

After Stalin's death there were attempts to scrap our German policy. Beria took an active stand on the German question. But he didn't come across very well. We had never had easy times in Germany. In 1953 we began receiving reports that the situation in the German Democratic Republic was not particularly stable. I promptly went to the Ministry of Foreign Affairs and requested that Gromyko report to me on a Sunday. At the time I had two deputies—Gromyko and Vasily Kuznetsov, who is currently in the Presidium of the Supreme Soviet. I summoned Gromyko, who was more experienced in these matters. We discussed the problem and worked out some proposals in writing. The gist was what we should do about the GDR. At the head in Germany then was Ulbricht, a dedicated communist, a politically conscious comrade, who was somewhat blunt and lacked flexibility. It turned out that the German comrades began talking at the top of their voices about building socialism without having laid the proper groundwork for it.

We forwarded a draft proposal from the Ministry of Foreign Affairs to the effect that the leadership of the German Socialist Unity Party—we did not explicitly name Ulbricht—had mounted an all-out offensive against capitalist elements which was incorrect. An all-out anticapitalist policy must not be pursued; a more cautious approach must be employed.

In his time Bukharin had said, "Start an all-out offensive against the kulaks!" Stalin responded, "So, you want to use force!" "Yes, force is necessary," he answered. "Well, let's record it that way: use force," Stalin concluded. We were more cautious, and we never used the word "force." But Bukharin pushed himself forward and went off on his own. So it was recorded that way. He favored "force" because to "ease up" would be a contradictory policy. . . .

So we and our Foreign Ministry workers proposed the following: "Do not implement a policy of forced socialism in the GDR." But Beria suggested that the word "forced" be dropped altogether. We had proposed that the process not be forced, but he insisted that the word "forced" be taken out. Thus the proposal would have read: "Do not implement a policy of building socialism in the GDR." We asked, "Why?" And he replied, "Because all we want is a peaceful Germany, and it makes no difference whether or not it is socialist."

The point of our draft proposal was to instruct the Communist party of the GDR to hold to a course on socialism, but not to rush the process or divorce themselves from the realities of the situation, because too few preparations had been made. We forwarded our proposal to the Politburo, where they proceeded to examine the issue in more detail. Divergences of opinion arose. Beria, who was then becoming particularly active, advanced the following argument: "Why should socialism be built in the GDR? Let it just be a peaceful country. That is sufficient for our purposes. . . . The sort of country it will become is unimportant."

I took the floor to offer a new proposal. In my opinion the course pursued within the GDR mattered a great deal. It lay within the heart of Europe and was a highly developed capitalist country. Consequently, though it was only part of Germany, much depended on it. That is why it was imperative to set a firm line on building socialism but without rushing the process. When it became possible to take this or that step with confidence, then accelerate the process.

Beria kept insisting it made no difference whether Germany was socialist or otherwise, that the most important concern was that Germany be peaceful. The Politburo vote was nearly split on the issue. Khrushchev supported my position. I didn't expect that. But Malenkov was the centerpiece. Malenkov and Beria were supposedly great friends, but I never believed this. Beria on the whole took little interest in fundamental questions of politics; he attached no great significance to the question of whether Germany was socialist or capitalist. A stable Germany was good enough for him.

The arguments went on. Malenkov chaired the session because the chairman of the Council of Ministers always chaired the Politburo sessions. Malenkov remained silent, and I knew he would follow Beria. Since we failed to reach agreement, a special committee was created—Malenkov, Beria, and myself. I was in favor of not forcing a socialist policy, while Beria favored not supporting socialism at all. Malenkov vacillated. Beria, of course, had counted on Malenkov's support. Khrushchev was also his friend.

I was alerted to any eventuality. Malenkov wouldn't voice an opinion. I felt I could easily be isolated in that committee. When the session ended and everyone left, I looked out the window. Immediately I spotted the three together. Yes, it was in the Kremlin. Beria, Malenkov, and Khrushchev were out for a walk. Later, toward evening, I phoned Khrushchev and said, "Well, have the three of you agreed on anything? You know, you supported me on the German question, but then I saw you all walking together, probably reaching an agreement against me." "Oh no, I will support you. I think your position is correct. I will firmly support your proposal," he responded. And I valued him for that.

I was pleased. I thought Khrushchev would sway all those who were as yet uncommitted. That same night I received a telephone call from Beria, who said, "Look, why should we meet again? Let's just reach agreement on the telephone and consider the resolution passed. Why don't you drop your stand?!"

How did you address him? Lavrenti?

Yes, Lavrenti. He persisted: "Socialism isn't necessary in Germany!" "No, I will stand firm. This is a matter of principle, and it also relates to what might happen should war break out," I said. "To hell with you! Let's not go to another meeting. I agree with your stand," he concluded. He tried to understand the philosophy behind it, but he failed. Indeed, he didn't take special interest in fundamental questions of policy. His philosophy was that if you were powerful, no one would touch you. Or something close to that. At any event, he did not delve into this matter. I said, "Well, we have reached agreement, and you suggest we not meet again. And what about Malenkov?" "I will work it out with Malenkov," he said.

Malenkov didn't play a decisive role. I didn't speak with him. So we reached an agreement, everyone voted in favor of the resolution, and we all signed it. That was it.

In the end, Beria yielded to me. Khrushchev apparently talked him into it.

What was Stalin's thinking on it? Did he ever speak with you about it?

What Beria proposed would never have come up for discussion in Stalin's time. Stalin made a public statement when the GDR was created, that this was a new stage in the development of Germany, and that there could be no doubts about this. Stalin was the sort of man to sacrifice everything for the sake of socialism. He would never have abandoned the conquests of socialism.

We believed that the building of socialism in the GDR must unfold gradually in order not to alienate the population. Otherwise revolts might flare up, and then we would have to forcibly repress the very Germany we had only just started to rebuild. The work had not really begun yet, and we had to be patient and proceed slowly so as not to have to use force. Yet Beria said, "Don't follow this policy! The policy of building socialism should not be pursued in the GDR."

I objected that there could not be a peaceful Germany unless it took the road to socialism. Therefore all talk about a "peaceful Germany" implied a bourgeois Germany, period. Yet if it was only a bourgeois Germany it could never be peaceful. If it pursued a path toward socialism, not forcibly but cautiously, and maneuvering skillfully until our position was stronger, until then we would have to be extremely careful. We had addressed this question in May 1953 and already in July that same year revolts broke out. Had we gone too far then, we would once again have had to struggle against internal enemies in Germany, which would have roused most of the Germans against us. That was a danger and it had to be avoided. And Beria was saying then, "No, socialism is completely unnecessary. All we need is a peaceful country. . . ."

I consider Khrushchev a rightist, and Beria was even further right. We had the evidence. Both of them were rightists. Mikoyan, too. Still, they are all different personalities. Being a rightist, Khrushchev was rotten through and through. Beria was even more of a rightist and even more rotten. He showed this when the German question was addressed. Khrushchev had a streak of Russian patriotism about him, which Beria lacked. Hence Khrushchev supported me on the German question.

I believe that Khrushchev's measures of Russian nationalism helped him to understand the interests of our state. Russia certainly plays a significant role in the state, but had we been nothing more than Russian nationalists we would have strayed from Leninist thought. In any event, Khrushchev did not back Beria on that issue. Did our people shed their blood in vain? If the GDR does not proceed along the path of socialism, it will remain the old Germany.

[7-31-72, 6-6-73, 4-29-82]

Malenkov is an excellent executive, a "manager by telephone," as we used to call him. He was always on the telephone. He knew where to find things out and how to get things done.

Administrative and organizational matters, personnel assignment— that was Malenkov's department; to relay instructions to the localities, to have all things arranged. He pushed ahead, was effective. He was very active, lively, and courteous. But he was silent on critical issues. He had never led a single party organization, in contrast to Khrushchev, who had done this both in Moscow and in the Ukraine. Khrushchev was made a Politburo member in 1938 or '39, around the same time as Beria and Malenkov. I hear that Malenkov was recently allowed to return to Moscow. His mother had died here. . . .

We talked on the centennial of V. I. Lenin's birth, and Molotov remarked:

Each of our leaders would like to create Lenin in his own image. Lenin is now being falsified and exploited. Even Fotieva thinks she can speak in Lenin's name. But who was she back then? A technical secretary.

I remarked that old Mensheviks have now become the old Bolsheviks.

Not just Mensheviks but Constitutional Democrats and the Black Hundreds as well.

[4-22-70, 4-13-72]

I haven't heard from Malenkov for quite some time. He visited me once about two years ago. Could he feel offended? Probably he does not regard me quite objectively.

After Stalin died I spoke at the Central Committee plenary meeting and supported Khrushchev's proposal that Malenkov be removed from the position of chairman of the Council of Ministers. I criticized him for his line after Stalin died. His first failing was that he immediately fell into the grip of the rightists on political questions, and, second, his conduct in the office of chairman of the Council of Ministers was not worthy of a true Central Committee member.

[4-29-82]

Malenkov is certainly a decent fellow. Unfortunately, however, given existing conditions he is woefully unprepared in matters of theory. Apparently he cannot genuinely orient himself, and that is very telling.

He is very pedantic and can keep things orderly, but in my opinion he cannot perceptively and critically cope with economic and political questions. But without that ability it is impossible to master affairs. He sent me his best regards the other day. . . .

[4-27-73, 10-21-82]

Malenkov came over to see me twice. I told you. The second time was at least three years ago. I haven't heard from him since then. No telephone calls. Nothing. He is said to be living in Moscow now. I'm afraid he doesn't want to be seen with me. For a long time he was not allowed in Moscow. I have to say that, if I were him, I would have found a way out. I asked him last time, "Are you working on anything? Studying anything? Do you plan to dig into some issue?" He replied, "Yes, I am studying . . ." "What?" "Imperialism."

So I came to understand at that moment that he was studying international relations and the struggle against imperialism, otherwise how would he take advantage of imperialism? The key question is, when will it collapse? He doesn't know any languages. Imperialism? Imperialism is a tough topic if you don't have a command of languages. But knowing the languages is not the primary objective. He came over to see us, gave everyone a hug and a kiss, and then left. We didn't have time to have a good talk. So I really didn't arrive at any sort of understanding. . . .

[1-14-85]

At the plenum, when Khrushchev suggested that Malenkov be removed from the position of chairman of the Council of Ministers, I also criticized Malenkov for his failure to address critical policy issues. . . .

He is not an independent thinker. Take the German question, for example. . . . A chairman of the Council of Ministers who has no opinion on a series of cardinal issues . . . that was why I criticized him. Apparently he never forgot this. Later we met. Like most of the Politburo members, we found ourselves in the same group. This was not, frankly speaking, to our advantage.

Afterward Beria didn't express much of an opinion about the position I had taken. I considered then, and still consider, Beria to be an unprincipled man. He was a careerist engaged only in what was to his advantage. He was not even a careerist, or, so to speak, *merely* a careerist since he did not address most issues from a Bolshevik perspective.

He killed a lot of people.

I don't think Beria was the principal culprit.

He destroyed people for personal rather than party-related motives.

That's possible. He was unprincipled. He was not even a communist. I consider him a parasite on the party.

With respect to what you said, Beria is not to blame. It's not easy now to sort things out without documents, and I can't recall everything, but I'm under the impression that Beria was only a functionary at that time. He worked only to secure his own interests.

In my opinion there were excesses, but these excesses were brought about by Stalin. Beria himself was very much afraid of Stalin. He would not have gone that far, but Stalin, in my opinion, carried things a bit too far. I have defended and continue to defend Stalin in this regard and also with respect to matters of terror. I think that had we not used terror, we could hardly have survived before the war, and we could have failed to secure a relatively stable situation in the country after the war. I think this had, to a significant extent, been secured in the late 1930s.

[10-21-82]

No, I have never considered Beria to be primarily responsible for the terror. I have always maintained that the principal responsibility rested with Stalin and those of us who approved it and were active in it. And I had always been active and stood for adopting these measures.

I never regretted and will never regret that we acted very harshly.

But mistakes did occur, of course.

[11-1-77]

To this day, people still argue whether Beria had been an agent of some foreign intelligence service.

I don't think he was. But I think he was unprincipled. He was very afraid for his own life. He was afraid of Stalin. He had always been eager to curry favor. . . . He was a man of few ideas—probably of no ideas at all. But he was a capable person.

[10-14-83]

Whatever he did was a boon to imperialism. He played the role of an agent of imperialism, that's the point. There could have been no greater service to imperialism than if he had succeeded in renouncing socialism in the GDR. One does not have to be an official agent; but to act as he did means that you are playing the role of an agent of imperialism. Many people do not understand this, but you must.

I regard Beria as an agent of imperialism. Agent does not mean spy. He had to have some support—either in the working class or in imperialism. He had no support among the people, and he enjoyed no prestige. Even had he succeeded in seizing power, he would not have lasted long.

[7-28-71, 7-31-72, 4-29-82]

Stalin's wife was very antipathetic toward Beria. Had he not performed his duties effectively, he would have been replaced. He did a job that was difficult and unavoidable.

He had files on everyone, even on Stalin. Of course, he had a file on me, too. Not exactly a complete file but rather. . .

Shota Ivanovich recounted, "When the funicular was under construction in Tbilisi, Beria had a habit of visiting the construction site at night and having a look. He was a good organizer."

Though a big scum.

But wasn't this because of his position?

Dzerzhinsky also held that position. So it absolutely didn't go with the job. Before he took that position, Ezhov had been a rather fine fellow, too. But power intoxicated him and swept him off his feet. He tried to show off and curry favor. That's when careerism begins. False evidence, previously set quotas of enemies: "The numbers of repressed persons are not high enough!" So everyone tries harder. And what kind of work is that?

Perhaps they demanded too much, that all those who were not totally reliable be purged?

As a matter of fact, yes. But that should never have been done. That's wrecking. Even today that sort of person is everywhere. Beria overdid it.

Should it be repeated today, we would be the first to go to jail.

I may be there before you.

"Is it true that Beria wasn't articulate enough to speak without notes?" asked Shota Ivanovich.

I think so, yes.

He wasn't a bibliophile?

Oh, no, no, he was not. The Beria trial in 1953 was broadcast on the radio, and I would sit in my office and listen. Merkulov said he wasn't sure whether Beria had ever read a book. This is rather indicative of a man's character. He spoke Russian correctly. He was a good organizer, a good administrator—and a born security operative, of course. But quite without principles. He served his current master.

Was that why Stalin kept him?

Yes, indeed. In this sense he certainly was very useful in getting certain jobs done. Regarding the atomic bomb, that was his responsibility. The air defense ring around Moscow—that was entrusted to him.

He was reported to have briefed his intelligence officers this way: "A true knight can't be bought with anything. He can only be tempted by a beautiful woman. And a beautiful woman can always be showered with diamonds. Off you go and get down to business!"

He could have said that. Oh yes, he could.

[6-9-76]

I went to the cemetery last summer. As I stopped to look, I spotted [Soviet diplomat] Maisky's grave.

It turns out he was arrested two weeks before Stalin died.

Possibly.

On Stalin's orders?

Of course.

He was still in jail when Khrushchev came to power. Reportedly he was somehow mixed up in Beria's affairs.

Maisky said Beria wanted to recruit him after Stalin's death. He summoned Maisky to his office and proposed he turn informer. Maisky was rumored not to have declined the offer.

There were reports in the West that Beria had planned to appoint Maisky as minister of foreign affairs in place of Molotov in his new cabinet after a successful coup.

I don't rule that out. I told you I had a sharp clash with Beria the first week after Stalin's death. It is quite possible that I was not the one to meet either his or Khrushchev's requirements. Their policies would not have differed greatly. I think Maisky had probably given his consent to

Beria. When Beria was apprehended, Maisky was checked out too. Beria definitely intended to appoint him."

[3-10-77]

Kruglov was Beria's deputy.

He was. They appeared to perceive each other differently. In fact, Kruglov used to be critical of him. At times this was not merely implicit. Beria did not retain Kruglov by his own choice. Before he was transferred to the NKVD [People's Commissariat for Internal Affairs], Kruglov had been on an assignment in Georgia. He used to send critical reports about the situation in Georgia at the time when Beria was party secretary there. I remember that. Some of the reports seemed to have come out in print, though I can't quite remember now. But after his Georgian assignment Kruglov came to see me. I know he told me that Stalin had been informed of the situation there. Kruglov had been rather brave in his criticism.

"*Mgeladze told me,*" *said Shota Ivanovich,* "*how Beria once toasted Stalin: 'I first saw Comrade Stalin in 1926, with Ordzhonikidze. I showed them around Vladikavkaz.' At that point Stalin remarked sharply, 'I don't remember such a meeting with Beria.' Beria immediately changed the topic of the toast. Then Stalin concluded, 'I liked Beria because he kept me truthfully informed on the situation in the Transcaucasus.'*"

Why did Beria do that? First, when you have a boss, you do what you are told. But as the situation changes and you have some sort of choice, you start to speak your mind.

[3-17-84]

In Lenin's office I once saw the young Beria. He was reporting on the situation in the Caucasus. His information was apparently trustworthy, otherwise Lenin would have had nothing to do with him.

[11-28-74]

Did Beria ever argue with Stalin?

No. It's not that he would never speak up. He just didn't volunteer. He wasn't pushy. On certain issues, of course, he would argue, but not often. Whenever he had facts or reports, he would try to prove that he knew more about specific issues.

[1-14-75]

Shota Ivanovich said, "*Mgeladze was taken aback when I said that Beria had been obsequious to Stalin, that he did all the filthy work and otherwise wouldn't have been kept on."* "He was a servant, indeed!" added *Akaki Ivanovich.* "He could just as successfully have served Hitler or Mussolini."

He would have been completely suitable for the job. He didn't go that far, but he was, in any event, a dangerous character.

[6-6-73, 8-20-74]

There was a book published on the history of the creation of Bolshevik organizations in the Transcaucasus. One or two Georgians wrote the book. I can't remember their names now, but one author was—Beria. It later turned out he hadn't even read the book.

[10-14-83]

Beria is called a diehard enemy of Soviet power.
I don't know whether he was a diehard or some other kind of enemy, but I do know he was an enemy.

[3-8-85]

After Stalin's death a question was raised about the need to remove Beria. Nikita called me and said, "You have nothing against the Central Committee building? Come over, if you can!" My office was at the Foreign Ministry building on Smolenskaya Street.

[3-4-78]

If you are interested in this episode, the final Politburo session on Beria, you must bear in mind that some preliminary work had been done before that. In this Khrushchev showed he was an exceptionally energetic and effective organizer. The initiative was in his hands as he was the party secretary. He was definitely a good organizer.

He summoned me to the Central Committee building, and I came over. "I'd like to talk with you about Beria. He can't be trusted."

I said, "I fully support this idea. He must be removed and expelled from the Politburo."

Then he turned to Mikoyan and suggested that Beria would have to go, that he was dangerous, and so on. "But no, why?" said Mikoyan. In short, he didn't consent. He took a wait-and-see position and offered his own objections. Malenkov had talked to Mikoyan before that, I believe. And Malenkov supported him. Khrushchev then appealed to Voroshilov, who at that time happened to be in his office of chairman of the

Presidium of the Supreme Soviet. He immediately agreed and started to cover the telephones to prevent being overheard. He immediately rushed to cover the telephones. He began to whisper and quickly gave his agreement.

Khrushchev apparently had talked with Voroshilov right before the session. He talked with me two days before that, and he contacted Mikoyan still earlier. . . . Immediately before the session we agreed that expelling Beria from the Politburo would not be enough. He had to be placed under arrest.

Evidently Khrushchev warned Kaganovich and others. I can't remember it all now, but apparently he notified most of the Politburo members. Two days later we all gathered in session. Beria was still in the Politburo, and there Khrushchev declared that Beria could not be trusted. . . .

As party secretary Khrushchev then performed the duties of first secretary, though he was not yet elected first secretary. He was the organizer of the entire affair. Why? He worked at the Central Committee. Apparently he had been informed that Beria was up to something. And Beria had troops under his command. Aside from his personnel, he also had a Ministry of Internal Affairs division at his command.

In short, he was preparing a coup. Is that right?

Yes, yes. . . . He was arrested during the Politburo session. Discussion ensued. Malenkov chaired. I don't remember who first took the floor. I was among the first to speak, possibly even the first or second speaker. The session began in the usual manner. We were all friends. Since we had agreed beforehand to have Beria arrested during the session, it was initially made to look like a normal session, but later it changed. . . .

Other questions were also addressed at that session. I don't remember them exactly. Probably we started with that question, moving it to the top of the agenda. Someone apparently suggested that Beria's conduct had to be discussed, and I was one of the first to speak. I said that Beria was a degenerate, that he could not be taken seriously, and that he was no communist. Perhaps he was a communist at some time in the past, but he was a degenerate now, and alien to the party. That was the essence of my remarks. I did not know Beria's past well. I had just heard some rumors and all kinds of talk. I believed he had been a communist when in the lower ranks, but in the end he had just lost all these qualities as he moved up.

Shortly after my remarks Khrushchev took the floor, going into polemics. "Molotov says Beria is a degenerate. That is incorrect. A degenerate is one who used to be a communist but has ceased to stay one. But Beria has never been a communist! What kind of degenerate can he be?"

Khrushchev careened to the left with his remarks. I offered no objections. I didn't argue with his observations. Surely they were true.

Then Beria took the floor to defend himself. No one was prevented from speaking. He said, "Of course I have made mistakes. But I ask you not to expel me from the party. I have always carried out the party's decisions and Stalin's directives. Stalin entrusted me with the most critical and secret matters. And I have always duly completed them. So it would be wrong to expel me. . . ." No, he was no fool. Malenkov pressed the button.

Beria and Malenkov were friends. Khrushchev would often join them. He was eager to befriend them.

Beria had arrived at the session totally unaware of what lay in store for him. . . .

Mikoyan spoke against Beria's removal, characterizing Beria as a good worker, and so on. Apparently he was afraid of Beria's gaining the upper hand in the end.

The room was securely guarded, but sitting in Poskrebyshev's room, which adjoined the meeting room, was a group of military officers headed by Zhukov. The group was waiting to be called in to arrest Beria. Malenkov pressed the button. That was the signal. Malenkov chaired the session, so he controlled the button. The group of officers led by Zhukov entered the room.

Malenkov says, "Arrest Beria!"

"What rotten friendship!" exclaimed Shota Ivanovich.

Their verbal exchanges were even more bogus than their friendship! How can you talk about a rotten friendship? Malenkov's performance precisely showed the good side of his character. In spite of everything, he came to himself. What kind of friendship? . . . The Trinity. I always said they would stay together up to a point. I never changed my view about them. Indeed, the three of them used to stay together. . . . Malenkov held a subordinate position. No strong will, a weakling. Khrushchev appeared to have started his plan with me. And I said that I consented. I have no regrets about it now. On the contrary, I believed, and I continue to believe, that this was to Khrushchev's great credit. That's my opinion.

Was that a complete surprise for Beria?

Exactly. First he felt somewhat at ease. Then he started to bang his head against the wall.

"I fell into a trap!" he cried. He didn't expect that from Khrushchev.

Moskalenko also was involved. Khrushchev had him promoted to marshal.

The connection was there. I can't recall whether he was among the group of officers that arrested Beria, but Moskalenko was put in charge of the jail where Beria was kept. That seems to be the reason for the promotion, which was definitely initiated by Khrushchev.

Shortly before that Beria had been dispatched to Berlin to suppress the unfolding revolt there. He was excellent in cases like that. We had passed a decision to use tanks. We had approved the use of drastic measures to put down the revolt, the most ruthless measures. Let the Germans rise up against us?! Everything would have turned shaky, the imperialists would have taken action. There would have been a total collapse.

As soon as reports of the events in the GDR started to come in, Beria was among the first to say, "We must act! Unhesitatingly! Ruthlessly! Most urgently!"

[7-2-71, 6-6-73, 11-1-77, 3-17-84]

■   **Conflict with Khrushchev**   ■

The development of the virgin lands began prematurely. It was unquestionably an absurd undertaking. On such a large scale it was adventurism. I never opposed cultivating the virgin lands, although Khrushchev charged me with being the principal opponent of the virgin lands project. From the very start I supported cultivation on a limited, rather than on a grand, scale. To do it in a big way demanded tremendous resources, huge investments and expenditures, which could have yielded faster returns had they been used in the areas already settled and cultivated. That was the only sensible approach. Look, you have a million rubles and no more. Should the money be allocated to the virgin lands or to settled regions with unused potential? I proposed investing the funds in the non-black-earth regions and opening up the virgin lands gradually. Alas, the resources were scattered over a vast area, and as a result each locality got very little. Moreover, storage facilities and good roads were lacking. The harvest could neither be stored nor shipped out. It rotted.

At a session of the Politburo I said: Listen, we have just received crop data from the TsSU [Central Statistical Board] on the harvest in those areas we call the virgin lands. The yield is two or three centners [one centner = 100 kilograms] per hectare [one hectare = 2.471 acres]. The average yield over a period of five to ten years in the arid lands is five or six centners. A small yield, but the infrastructure is already there. If we till ten million hectares in areas where crop prospects are better and the area more manageable than the twenty million hectares of virgin lands, then we shall get a harvest. . . .

Khrushchev exploded: "So, you are against the Virgin Lands Program!" "What do you mean, against the Virgin Lands Program? We must make the necessary calculations. Otherwise how can we conduct affairs of state?"

Khrushchev was so carried away with his idea that he was like a runaway roan! An idea alone solves nothing conclusively; it may be helpful, but only to a limited extent. You have to make the right calculations, weigh alternatives, consult experts, sound out the people. You can't just shout, get going! get a move on! He bit off more than he could chew—about 40 to 45 million hectares of virgin lands to be opened up. This was unmanageable, absurd, and unnecessary. Fifteen to 17 million hectares would probably have produced better results and would have made more sense.

Khrushchev reminded me of a livestock dealer. A small-time livestock dealer. A man of little culture, certainly. A regular livestock trader, a man who deals in cattle.

Stalin's mistake was that he had not trained anyone to fill his position. Khrushchev took over, not by chance. Of course he was not the right man for the top office. But we had no unity in our group, and we had no program. We merely agreed to have him removed, but at the same time we were totally unprepared to assume power.

I certainly opposed opening up the virgin lands on such a vast scale. Even today I think it was a bad idea. I suggested the project be done at half the size. There weren't enough people nor enough machinery. The counterargument: "We'll take the necessary resources from the other regions."

I opposed economic decentralization in the form of Sovnarkhozy [regional Councils of the National Economy] and wrote a letter to the Politburo arguing that the project lacked preparation.

I opposed division of the party into rural and urban branches as contravening both the constitution and the party statutes. All that was sheer idiocy.

[1-1-79, 12-9-82]

Khrushchev gathered writers together one day at Stalin's remote dacha, two hundred kilometers from Moscow. There he announced for all to hear that he had differences of opinion with me. His move particularly displeased me because he announced it at a nonparty gathering. It all started with an article in the journal *Kommunist* in 1955, where I argued that we had constructed only the foundations of socialism in our country. Shortly before that I had gathered reporters and distributed the article to them. There were some queries on the article. But I said I believed that socialism in our country was not yet complete. . . .

Under Khrushchev, Molotov was reproached for saying that in our country, only the "basis of socialism" had been constructed and not "socialism basically," and he confessed his mistake in the journal of the Central Committee, Kommunist.

No, I had to. They forced me to. At a session of the Supreme Soviet I delivered a report on the international situation. By the way, I still believe that both conclusions were correct. Then, a letter signed by Pospelov and Rumiantsev was published. They contended that "socialism basically" and its "basis" had been built long ago. I then said at the Politburo: "I don't see any contradiction in terms there. One can say that both "socialism basically" and "basis" have been built. "Basis" is a narrower concept, which places greater emphasis on the economic side of things. "Basis" or "basically"—just so much talmudic hairsplitting. I wrote that both formulations were correct, consequently there could be no objections to my position as being incorrect, because "basis" is the same as "basically." To see a difference between the two one would have to be a pedant.

At that time Khrushchev started undermining you.

Why started? He had always been doing that.

They seem to have been eager to incriminate you somehow. They launched a campaign against you.

Not just over some issue or another. Not just any issue. This question was absolutely crucial. To say that socialism had triumphed completely and definitely was to oversimplify our achievements, and this contradicted Marxism-Leninism. No one wants to dig into this now, but exasperation with this situation is sure to mount. Younger people will take up the issue and agree that the wrong conclusion had been drawn.

Was Khrushchev adept in matters of theory?

No. He was extremely weak in that regard. We were all "practicals," all practitioners. Before the Revolution we read all the books and newspapers, now we read nothing. Had I not spent so long in prison and exile, I wouldn't know many things either! I read publications written by our opponents too, and we had to participate in heated discussions. . . .

[2-19-71, 12-12-72]

"You were attacked after Stalin's death," said Shota Ivanovich. "But you were right."

Of course I was right. Khrushchev made Pospelov and another one, Satiukov, I believe, write a letter to the effect that Molotov was in error on this issue. The letter was distributed to all Politburo members and discussed at the next Politburo session. I responded in writing, confirming my viewpoint. I wrote: My point is, "basically" the victory of socialism and the "basis" of the victory of socialism have both been achieved. I said that in our country the basis of socialism had been built, and in another place I said that in our country socialism had basically triumphed. Is there a difference or not? Basically or basis? In essence, no, but of course . . . So I wrote in reply that I see no difference in the two wordings.

Khrushchev said, "How's that!? It only shows Molotov belittles the accomplishments of socialism." And so on, and so forth. . . . Everyone would nod in agreement. I thought, why the hell should I harp on these differences. "To hell with you," I said. But the written document is and has remained in my possession.

Now you can find the nuances in books written by our scholars. It is all right to say "basically." Indeed, "the basis" had been achieved first, but later socialism was built "basically." But this is utter talmudism . . . real nonsense. The trouble, I say, is that in the present situation it is impossible to offer a definition of socialism. There is no complete clarity on this question. One can only depict distinct stages, fundamental phases.

[3-8-75]

■   **Khrushchev and the XXth Congress**   ■

Everyone knew that Khrushchev was going to deliver that [anti-Stalin] report at the XXth Party Congress. The report had not been discussed in the Central Committee, but we knew the essence of it. I had tried to speak on the Yugoslav question in 1955 in criticism of Khrushchev's policy, but the comrades didn't support me. Nevertheless, I enjoyed some prestige in the party. True, later they said I was right. Take Lenin, for example, who enjoyed tremendous prestige. A good many people understood that they must follow him. Ten years passed and Stalin gained tremendous prestige, and people began to follow him. Take Yaroslavsky. You can't imagine how many factions he had been associated with. But one day he said, "That's it! From now on I shall not be dragged into factions. I will just follow Stalin. That's for certain." After Stalin's death, many were confused: where are we to go?

                                                                        [4-22-70]

When Khrushchev delivered his speech at the XXth Congress I was already sidelined. And not only at the ministry. . . . People made it a point to keep their distance from me. I got the news only at formal sessions. . . .

People often ask why you didn't speak against Khrushchev at the XXth Congress. Meaning, you and your group.

I think the time has come for me to answer that question of our party. At that time I analyzed my predicament at length and from various perspectives. The party was not ready for such an analysis. We would simply have been kicked out. I still hoped that if we remained in the party we would be able to correct the situation gradually. To speak out would have been unexpected at that time, and no one would have supported us. No one. We had to make a few preparations.

I did have a different opinion. I will merely say that some of my amendments on the question of socialism were passed, but I refused to initiate a substantive discussion. The danger was that our group comprised a great diversity of aims, a whole mix, and a split could have ensued. This would not have done any good at all, as the party as a whole was completely unprepared for the event.

Was Khrushchev's report discussed in the Politburo?

It was. The majority supported it without reservation.

The people weren't prepared for a critique of Stalin, but at the top, it seems, everything was ready.

It was not supported openly, but in fact people were drawn to it. Yes, they were. There was instability in these questions.

To this day there are many people who approve this report. At worst a split in the party might have occurred. I was afraid of this too, an open split. To heal it would have been very difficult.

The initiation of this affair was perfectly attuned to the prevailing mood in the party. Given the atmosphere in the party at the time, if we, or even I, had presented our views, we would have been easily expelled. This would have provoked a split at several levels in the party. That split might have run very deep. Tevosian, then minister of ferrous metallurgy, shouted at me, "How come!? How come!?" He was a Stalinist, yes. Yudin, too, our ambassador in China. Both of them came up to me at the congress.

It's best to admit it! Some people holding pretty much the same view blame me: "Why did you keep silent at the XXth Congress?" It was not that simple. But was it correct to say nothing? These things cannot be easily explained. To keep silent, they say, is tantamount to consent. That's how it turned out: I kept silent and thus consented. No one, not even my adversaries, could charge that I had agreed with Khrushchev, only that I remained silent, and that is a fact.

People keep asking, "How did you allow Khrushchev to deliver that report?"

The majority vote. Everyone was supposed to vote. . . . I can't remember if the speech was presented for us to read. But it was read out.

That speech of his turned politics upside down. It all started with that.

It didn't exactly turn politics upside down, but it helped. The change didn't start there. If you think about it, you'll recall that it certainly started earlier, of course. The Yugoslav question came up in 1955, a year before the XXth Congress. I think the turning point was already completed with the Yugoslav question. Of course I made an attempt to speak out, but everyone opposed me, everyone, including those who supported me for another year or year and a half.

So the turning point came before that, and insofar as it was completed, Khrushchev had selected to the XXth Congress those delegates who would keep cheering "Hurrah!" to him. I openly came out against him.

Why did he come out against Stalin so drastically?

Because he pursued a different policy. He is a rightist. . . . The rightist and the Trotskyist extremes come together. The main threat in the 1930s came from the rightists rather than from the Trotskyists. They had close ties with the village. Their social base was the kulak class. That's where Khrushchev had his roots.

Pospelov is said to have written the report?

It would seem so. Either that or he helped to prepare it. He had no firm theoretical grounding either, but still. . . . He had once been a staunch Stalinist. . . .

[1-8-74, 3-11-83]

Deep down Khrushchev was an enemy of Stalin. On the surface
Stalin was the be-all and end-all, but deep down it was another matter.
Personal bitterness animated his every step. His bitterness toward Stalin
stemmed from the fact that Khrushchev's eldest son got himself shot.
Driven by such bitterness, Khrushchev would balk at nothing to be-
smirch the name of Stalin.
   Nikita disowned his son, didn't he?
   Yes.

                                              [8-15-72, 1-8-74]

His son was something of a traitor, which also reflects on Khrushchev.
A good political leader with a son like that?
   Khrushchev's wife did not distinguish herself in any way, but she lived
more or less honestly. She has a house in this neighborhood. She is very
isolated here; no one comes to see her, no one stands in a shopping line
next to her. . . . She is a very demanding person, however. . . . When
Khrushchev had just come to power, she told Polina Semenovna once
that Nikita Sergeevich was uneasy because he had to handle very
complex questions; not everything was turning out the way he wanted,
and he was uncertain about the Yugoslav question. She was afraid he
was overdoing it and might go off the deep end. . . .
   He not only overdid it, but she could do nothing—she wasn't up to it.
I still have things to say about Khrushchev.

                                              [6-30-76, 10-30-80]

Stalin didn't want to pardon Khrushchev's son. And Khrushchev
personally hated Stalin. Of course, that added to his animosity, but that
was not the main thing about him. He was not a revolutionary. He
didn't join the party until 1918—some militant! Ordinary workers had
joined the party earlier. Some leader of our party he turned out to be! It
was absurd, absurd.
   Khrushchev was four years my junior, but he was no child. Our first
revolution took place in February 1917. He was active in Yuzovka, but
this was a center of Menshevism. . . .

                                              [6-16-77, 12-9-82]

Khrushchev opposed Stalin and Leninist policy. He wanted changes
in the Leninist policy pursued by Stalin and ultimately by all of us who
supported Stalin. You know what the rightists were after? In the party?
The rightists wanted to block us from pressing for the liquidation of the

kulaks; they were champions of a pro-kulak policy. Even after the kulaks had been destroyed they continued to hold right-wing political views. So they maintained afterward that Stalin had pushed things too far, and that this had been a mistake. We saw this in Khrushchev, and spoke about it, and this was even openly acknowledged by the Central Committee under Stalin. Everyone makes mistakes. Lenin made mistakes, and Stalin made mistakes. Khrushchev was no exception. I had my own mistakes. Who is infallible? If, however, one has good intentions but is in error, he must be corrected. . . .

[1-8-74]

Khrushchev hinted that Stalin had Kirov killed. There are some who still believe that story. The seeds of suspicion were planted. A commission was set up in 1956. Some twelve persons, from various backgrounds, looked through a welter of documents but found nothing incriminating Stalin. But these results have never been published.

Who else was on that commission?

As far as I can recall, Shvernik was on it, I think, Suslov, Kaganovich, Furtseva, Procurator-General Rudenko, also someone who used to work in the Cheka . . . what's his name? In all, there were ten or twelve people. I don't remember exactly. I think Mikoyan was there, too. But I can't be absolutely sure. Voroshilov, I think, wasn't included in that commission. Or he might have been there after all. I can't recall all of them.

The KGB [Committee for State Security] made a special report. Rudenko's group authenticated and examined the material—and there was a great deal of material. We used all the materials sent to us as well as those we managed to obtain ourselves.

The commission concluded that Stalin was not implicated in Kirov's assassination. Khrushchev refused to have the findings published since they didn't serve his purpose.

[7-1-79]

Khrushchev got by because we had many Khrushchevites. Stalin was firm, a firm hand—that was Stalin—and under that strong hand everyone sang the same tune. But as soon as that hand grew weak, everyone began to sing his own tune.

In 1957 Khrushchev was relieved of his duties for three days. This happened at one of the Politburo sessions. This, of course, had to be announced. He was chairing Politburo sessions; he was merely relieved

of the chairmanship. Nothing more occurred then. He wasn't removed
from his job, and he couldn't be removed. The Central Committee
plenum would decide this. How else could he have been removed?

[1-8-74]

At the XXth Party Congress a Presidium [the name adopted in 1952
for the old Politburo] consisting of eleven members had been elected.
Later, in 1957, we decided to remove Khrushchev. At the Politburo he
chaired its sessions; we decided to replace him with Bulganin [chairman
of the USSR Council of Ministers, 1955–1958]. The point was that
starting with Lenin—and it was always so—the chairman of the Council
of People's Commissars [from 1946, Council of Ministers] always chaired
sessions of the Politburo. This was a Leninist tradition. From the
beginning, Lenin chaired—when he was ill, Kamenev sat in for him—
then Rykov chaired, then I, then Stalin. Khrushchev was the first to
break with this Leninist tradition. He began to act like a regional party
secretary. . . . He was not chairman of the Council of Ministers, nevertheless he chaired Politburo sessions. . . . Now we had Bulganin chair.

Did Khrushchev remain silent?

No way! He screamed, he was furious. . . . But we had already reached
an agreement. We were seven out of eleven, and his supporters were but
three, including Mikoyan. We had no program to advance. Our only
goal was to remove Khrushchev and have him appointed minister of
agriculture. Commotion could be heard behind the door. Furtseva,
Serov, Ignatev were there. They convened the members of the Central
Committee.

The Central Committee plenary meeting was held the following day.
Furtseva and Suslov were Central Committee secretaries who played
roles. Serov played a major role. He employed the staff to best advantage. He had all the Central Committee members promptly summoned
to Moscow. They all gathered in Suslov's office. Serov helped out,
though his role was purely technical. Inasmuch as Khrushchev remained
the first secretary of the Central Committee, the entire staff was in his
hands.

Suslov is such a small-minded politician! And he is a big bore, too.

He and Khrushchev are birds of a feather. Zhukov is a great military
man but a poor politician. He played a decisive role in elevating
Khrushchev to a pedestal in 1957. But Zhukov himself cursed him soon
afterward. . . .

We failed to have him removed as first secretary; we just didn't manage it. They convened a plenary session of the Central Committee, and the plenum sided with them—the game was over!

And they did not allow you to speak at the plenum?

No, they did, though I had to insist on it. Just let them show the stenographic record of my remarks to someone!

They still won't do that. But how did the plenum respond?

They yelled, they bellowed. I didn't talk about Khrushchev personally, I talked specifically about his leadership. No, I can't recall all that was said, but I indicated in particular that a commission on Stalin's archives was set up in 1953, with Khrushchev as chairman and myself as a member. Since 1957 the commission has not had a single meeting. Mikoyan was a member of the commission, along with some others. . . . The Stalin archive was entrusted to the commission. Do you see how Khrushchev was behaving?

Khrushchev apparently had been listening in on our telephone conversation. And he had his own spies. I spoke at the plenum and the audience wouldn't listen. They shouted. Later they doctored my remarks and published them. Initially the three of us were labeled "the antiparty group"—Malenkov, Kaganovich, Molotov—then they also added Shepilov who had joined us. After a while they included Bulganin and Voroshilov. Initially Voroshilov had been one of us, but then he repented. You can judge for yourself, from reading the published material, how he conducted himself. He behaved badly. He lost his head. He didn't know whom to look to. And Khrushchev was very sly. Voroshilov's becoming president didn't add to his prestige, which he had enjoyed since the civil war. . . .

Each year following I sent one or two letters to the Central Committee with a critical analysis of their policies. My last letter contained a critical review of the new party program which I considered deceptive and anti-Leninist. Khrushchev raised the question, and I was expelled from the party. Malenkov and others were absolutely unaware of my letters. They just minded their own business. But it was awkward to have me alone kicked out of the party. The "antiparty" group had to be removed, and four of us were expelled.

[4-22-70, 1-8-74, 5-9-85]

I don't think I precipitated this expulsion. Kaganovich, Malenkov, and myself were expelled. Shepilov too, though he was not part of the group. I don't know how well Shepilov knew economics, but he was a good speaker. He was a man of integrity. He sensed that the anti-Stalin campaign had gone far beyond objective truth, and he stuck with us and supported us.

He refused to be Khrushchev's servant, even though Khrushchev had very much counted on him. Apparently I tripped up Khrushchev in that case, though Shepilov was hardly aware of it.

[12-4-73, 12-30-73]

I don't consider Khrushchev an especially dedicated communist. He was capable, unquestionably. But he only fluttered about. . . . He had no serious interest in ideology. There is more than meets the eye in the fact that he succeeded in making short work of Malenkov, Kaganovich, and me. The reason is that there was no genuine bolshevist stability during that period. I ought to have been punished, true, but expulsion from the party? Punishment, of course, because sometimes the ax must be used without sorting things out. I believe we had to pass through a phase of terror. I am not afraid of that word, because back then we had neither the time nor the opportunity to sort things out, for not only Soviet power in Russia but the international communist movement as well were at risk.

[10-14-83]

I sent a letter to the Central Committee from Geneva, where I was on the International Atomic Energy Commission, and wrote that Khrushchev was continuing to repeat the same error Stalin had made when he argued that communism could be achieved under conditions of capitalist encirclement. I was recalled to Moscow and expelled from the party at the meeting of the Council of Ministers party nucleus. Lesechko and some women, whom Khrushchev had brought to the meeting, raged more than anyone else. I was expelled, but I appealed. The party bureau confirmed the expulsion. I appealed again. The Sverdlovsk District Party Committee and then the Moscow City Party Committee approved my expulsion. I appealed again. Demichev was particularly adamant against me. He took my party card. . . . The only person who conducted himself decently was Shvernik. He did not vote against me and refused to involve himself in that campaign. Four times I applied to be reinstated in the party. I wrote to Brezhnev. Not once did I get an answer. Asked about my party membership status at a party conference, Shaposhnikova explained to the communists that "he didn't apply to be reinstated in the party." I am going to send another application to the XXIVth Congress.

When I was expelled from the party, people like Serdiuk screamed about the repressions. But after all, I was not expelled from the party because of the repressions but rather because we spoke out against Khrushchev and wanted to have him relieved of his duties. When the repressions were condemned at the XXth Congress, I was not only not expelled from the party but was even elected to its Politburo!"

[2-19-71]

Were you charged with the repressions when they expelled you from the party?

I was. They claimed the antiparty group was fearful of being exposed. But as a matter of fact, Khrushchev was the one who should have been fearful of exposure. The game was played out rather well. . . .

As soon as you relieved Khrushchev of his chair functions, why didn't you appeal to party organizations, to the people?

The party organizations were not in our hands.

Anyway, you failed to take advantage of that moment.

Indeed, I wasn't able to take advantage of it. We had another disadvantage—we were not prepared to put forward a counterprogram of our own. But Khrushchev did exactly that: "Life under Stalin was hard; from now on it is going to be better." People bought it. The overwhelming majority voted against me. A good many people bore me a grudge.

But they were all high officials.

Not only high officials but the rank and file as well.

But the working class was for you.

The workers also bought the line: "You will have it easier now, and there will be no more rushing ahead."

Viacheslav Mikhailovich, you said that when Demichev took your party membership card from you at the Moscow Party Committee, you made his task easier for him.

I don't think I made it easier for him. He simply said, "You must hand in your party card." Quite a crowd was gathered. A few people were selected to speak. I was the first to take the floor to offer my explanations. But as I was rabidly attacked, I was brief in my remarks. Criticisms mostly referred to the events of 1937. The chairman of the Moscow Soviet also spoke. When I worked in the Central Committee and then in the Council of Ministers, he was in charge of construction projects, and I often had to deal with him. A capable worker. I had no disputes or run-ins with him. He began cursing me out. Well, in such cases he was obliged to act so. He was chairman of the Moscow City Executive

Committee, but the party secretary, of course, shows the way, so to speak. How could he remain silent? I looked at him with utter astonishment.

Didn't they feel awkward about it?

Who knows? I am not going to speculate about that.

"Children were shot to death in Georgia in 1956," said Shota Ivanovich. "They removed Mikoyan's portrait and hung it in an outhouse, where his home was supposed to be. They hitched Khrushchev's portrait to a streetcar, but they carried your portrait at the head of a marching column of protesters that demanded, 'We want the Central Committee headed by Viacheslav Mikhailovich Molotov!' Did it really happen like this?"

Children died then, and you know which children? Those whose parents were in jail in 1937. The children that were shot to death were not allowed a decent burial. People wailed, they couldn't understand. "Your parents perished at the hands of Stalin, but you are for him?"

[1-16-73]

In theoretical matters, wasn't Malenkov also weak?

He too. I know it for a fact.

"And what a grand name—Malenkov!" said Shota Ivanovich.

For peasants mostly. In that regard he was also involved in a lot of demagoguery. A special decision had been taken. Khrushchev was furious then, because he was supposed to announce the new policy. Everyone was preoccupied with office-seeking and gossiping, who said what. But in fact it was all sheer demagoguery. They couldn't do without it. Of course, there were cases when we overdid it. After all, back then we were wringing the last ounce of energy out of the workers; we had them on the rack. The same with peasants who owned any property.

I can't say I am not to blame, that I could not have been arrested for this, that, or something else. . . . Khrushchev thought it was right to defame me for potato deliveries to Moscow. That might have appealed to the layman. As chairman of the Council of Ministers, I thought it best to break the established procedure. Food shortages were our constant headache. So we used all the means at our disposal to wring potato supplies out of Belorussia, the northwestern regions, Novgorod, and the Chernigov regions. We took their last supplies. My task was to put pressure on the Moscow region where the possibilities were far from being maximized. The Muscovites were obliged to produce more potatoes in their region, and we reduced shipments from Belorussia where local food shortages were reported. We squeezed to the maximum just to provide food supplies in the capital. Khrushchev rose to his feet: "Just imagine, when we didn't even have enough potatoes to eat, Molotov reduced our food rations. . . ." It was all published. In his reports on agricultural issues he would now and then take potshots at me. I would like to know what he would have done had he then been in my shoes? Alternatives were nowhere to be found. In the end, when the Muscovites were hard up, we urged them to provide at least part of the food themselves.

Food deliveries had been on the rise anyway. Had we not brought in food from the provinces, we wouldn't have known where else to turn in order to satisfy the demand. In the Kremlin too we went without. In any case, Moscow enjoyed a privileged position. But we never resorted to purchasing food from abroad. We didn't want to do that because we needed equipment and metals in the event of war. . . . That consideration came first, and no one could deny it.

[12-4-73]

Khrushchev often traveled to the provinces, to the collective farms and state farms. He would often serve as a kind of walking delegate, and in this he was above reproach. This was precisely his positive quality. He was everywhere—stables, boiler works—he was interested in everything. . . . Of course, he mixed with peasants and workers more than Lenin or Stalin; in casual environments, too. There is no denying that. People would treat him like one of their own, and they would be absolutely at ease with him.

[4-27-73]

Khrushchev asked former KGB chairman Semichastny to find all the documents related to his work in the Ukraine. That was done, by the way, in the heat of the anti-Stalin campaign.

Surely, measures were taken to destroy all the documents on repressions in the Ukraine that he had ever signed.

How did Khrushchev happen to be moved up to the top? From the grassroots? How did he get on the Central Committee? He found a good many allies there. Many would have preferred a more dependable leader, but Khrushchev promised a quieter, more relaxed life at the top. Many went for this instantly. And he made promises to the common folk. People welcomed the change. But it was all deception, though many used the change to take it easy and enjoy themselves. A very dangerous thing. Stalin was quite apprehensive in that regard. So Khrushchev promised better living conditions, and a good many people took the bait, though it was a deception. They were deceived.

All the same, I think he was not so much pulled up from the top as pushed from below. From party cell secretary at the Moscow-based Industrial Academy he moved on to the job of secretary of the Krasnopresnensky and then the Baumansky District party committees in Moscow. This showed he had support in those places. Stalin's supporters would hew to the party line, but Khrushchev was always clever enough to adapt to that line. He was quite a capable man. You can't say he had been merely a lucky fellow. He could very well have become a Bukharinite, but he moved in the opposite direction. He sensed it would be more secure that way. Khrushchev in essence was a Bukharinite, but under Stalin he was not a Bukharinite.

You say that the Germans supported Hitler. But wait a minute—in nationalism our Black Hundreds, though they were not great in number, even outdid the Germans.

Not all Germans to a man followed Hitler; it would be wrong to say that. I'll prove it to you. To all appearances, under Stalin everyone in our country was for Stalin. But when it became possible to express one's true feelings, the majority turned out to be against him. The reason is that the leading role is so demanding, and that the individual under those circumstances plays such a powerful role, that the multitudes bite their tongue, follow the leader, and groan. . . . Even Khrushchev used to address Stalin ingratiatingly, "Father Stalin! Dear father Stalin!" You just can't imagine how it all was. He remained a small-minded man, indeed. You just read his speeches. And he slandered others.

Nonetheless, Stalin did enjoy popular support, however hypocritical it was.

The same applies to Hitler. Do you think the industrial workers were eager to support Hitler? They were constrained to do it when they were told that if they did not the German people would perish. How and why perish? They had no idea. They were simply told, Support Hitler or you will die miserably. We know the names of prominent individuals who opposed Hitler, but in the working class there were many such people, not just Ernst Thaelmann [leader of the Communist party of Germany].

But what good did they do if they kept their anti-Hitler thoughts to themselves and did not undertake a single organized action against fascism?

If the people keep their thoughts to themselves, what good does it do a leadership, however powerful, to think: "Thank God! No one is speaking out"?

Surely Hitler thought that too: Thank God! No one is speaking out.

His cause is lost, but ours won and is winning.

He certainly did not think his cause was lost.

But there is an objective side to the question. In spite of Hitler thinking that, the upshot was the opposite. Inasmuch as there is a GDR, part of Germany stands as the diametrical opposite of Hitlerite Germany. Something of the same is true in our country. Despite many of our people still having doubts and in fact being pulled away from communism, a timely change in course was effected, which constrains them to help build socialism, even if against their will.

[6-6-73]

Hitler wasn't a fool. On the contrary, he was a capable man. Khrushchev was a capable man, too. But as he was pushed up, promoted, and placed in the highest office, it occurred to him that he could singlehandedly manage all the affairs in a state like ours, and in a party like ours. And backing him with his preconceived ideas were those who would also like to live easier. They hoped that the cause initiated by Lenin and Stalin could be promoted without difficulty. That was a deception. Lenin and Stalin never said that while imperialism existed we would easily advance along the path we had chosen. There are inevitable hardships along the way. If you don't agree with this, then go to hell or wherever you please, but if deep down you understand this, if you have reasoned it all out, then you are very useful to the cause. Khrushchev was a sleight-of-hand artist, a good practical worker and energetic leader.

[6-6-73]

"Stalin was absolutely right in his judgment on the kulak sentiments," said Shota Ivanovich. *"Czechoslovakia has shown . . ."*

And we haven't? We had Khrushchev promoted to the top office! That too proves something.

Josif Vissarionovich was to blame for that.

He seems to be blamed for everything. For whatever. It all happened because we are a bit on the Social Revolutionary side. It was not bad that Khrushchev, a rightist, was made to toe the line. He had his reservations, but he toed the line, which was good. He performed well for some time, but then . . .

In any case, he realized full well he would be better off following orders and making appearances. He was a conscientious worker.

You remember the editorial in *Pravda* on agri-towns, where he was corrected like a youngster?

Right after the war he pushed the idea of merging cities and villages into so-called agri-towns. Agri-towns. Stalin scoffed at this and set up a commission. I was placed on that commission, and Stalin instructed us to give Khrushchev a good lesson.

Stalin is reported to have let slip once, "My little Marx!"

I remember that. . . . Stalin said, "To have Khrushchev taken down properly, we need to put Molotov on the commission, too!" Chairing that commission was Malenkov, and I was actively involved in all its functions. When we reported our draft conclusions, Stalin started slowly to shake his head. Electrification as perceived by Lenin is one thing, but rural electrification is another. The two could not be equated. They are different things. A power plant is no doubt a useful facility, but it is not tantamount to electrification. To build socialism is to create an integrated system of electrical generating stations covering the entire country rather than to merely build small power stations. . . . So he went over our draft and remarked, "Soften it up a little bit."

Kaganovich suggested that the new teaching should be called "Leninism-Stalinism." Khrushchev supported this, of course, but Kaganovich pushed it most vigorously.

[2-3-72, 6-6-73]

The part played by Khrushchev was very bad. He unleashed those same sentiments he lived by. . . . He himself could not have done this without popular support. Unlike Trotsky, he created no special theory, but he made it possible for the beast to tear itself free, the beast which is now, of course, inflicting terrible harm on society. But it's not just Khrushchev's doing.

But this beast's name is democracy.

No, it's called humanism, but in reality it is petty bourgeois philistinism.

[7-9-71]

Khrushchev was for Soviet power but against the Revolution. This is his distinguishing feature: he was against everything revolutionary. Here you have what is interesting or typical about him: to him, of course, collectivization—which in our country was carried out by Stalinist methods—was impermissible. Yes, impermissible. But no alternative was proposed.

He is against collectivization. He is without doubt a Bukharinite. His view did not rise above Bukharin's but was on a par with it. He found a cozy niche for himself.

"He was promoted by Allilueva," said Shota Ivanovich.

Look, we had been watching his performance for fifteen or twenty years after that.

He was your servant.

Exactly. He was a capable man. He got things done.

"He considered Stalin to be an uneducated man," said Shota Ivanovich.

He might have said that, of course. That could have been expected of him, especially when he threw a tantrum. But I don't believe Khrushchev truly considered Stalin to be uneducated. Arrogance and conceit would apply rather than educational level. Actually he never considered Stalin stupid since he was so fearful of him!

I meant, after Stalin was gone.

After, of course.... He was never seriously interested in or thought about the meaning of Leninism or of Marxism. But just look at how tricky he was.... He wanted to rehabilitate Bukharin, Rykov, and Zinoviev. Zinoviev had gone over to another group, the Trotskyite, while Bukharin was a rightist. Khrushchev wanted to rehabilitate everyone, but everyone.

[4-25-75]

Khrushchev and Mikoyan posed as arch-Stalinists, but deep down they were not. Confronting us were so many complex, unresolved, and very difficult problems, many of which persist even now. Certain people were still not conscious of who they were really, but to them everything seemed clear. The entire top leadership united around Khrushchev. Yes, the entire top leadership. Under our conditions, how much deeper, more energetic work we needed; the surmounting of how many obvious problems the Revolution required! But none of this came to pass. Even people who, as it were, had been tested, did not measure up. There are no accessible documents, articles, or speeches on it, but Stalin reckoned with all of this, and, of course, not without violations of formal democracy pursued this policy in the 1930s and 1940s, right up until the 1950s. There of course was that strong hand without which we would not have been able to hold out. So great was Stalin's prestige that it was unreservedly acknowledged both in the party and among the people. Of course, not all the necessary formalities were observed or always carried out. Nevertheless it was impossible to adopt a really better, more democratic way; any other way would have left us in an even worse plight. Thanks to the prestige of Stalin in this period, even where there were many very weak, many unreliable, people, we stayed the course only because he was feared. Fear played its part. And perhaps this wasn't so under Lenin?

[2-3-72]

"By the way," argued Shota Ivanovich, "documents can still be obtained to prove that many thousands of communists, were destroyed on Khrushchev's initiative. The lists are kept at the Moscow Party Committee and in the Ukraine, and he reported them to Stalin."

Definitely, of course. He couldn't have been promoted otherwise. But such were the times. . . . That's clear to any reasonable person. He was a half-educated man, alien to the party. Alien, absolutely alien. He couldn't stay at the top for long. You see, his former supporters finally got rid of him and had him quietly buried at Novodevichy cemetery. Now they all behave as if they had had nothing to do with him.

Didn't you pass by there to have a look?

No. I avoid his grave.

"You'd better not go there. Somebody might inadvertently spot you there, and immediately tales would be spread: 'Molotov has been there to see the grave!' All sorts of tales abound these days," cautioned Shota Ivanovich. "Don't go there even once."

To hell with him. . . . But I attended Bulganin's funeral.

[4-25-75]

Stalin and Khrushchev. As for Khrushchev, he is not worth one of Stalin's fingernails. Stalin's achievements, despite everything, are enormous. He was the great transformer. He did not complete certain projects, which has slowed our progress, and this speaks against him. Now his errors are being repeated, his very shortcomings on the peasant question are being repeated. While they strive to efface his colossal achievements.

[4-28-76]

Speaking of Khrushchev, Stalin is to blame, as I and all of us are to blame, for failing to see that it was not merely a matter of Khrushchev, a typical anti-Leninist, but of a trend, that of playing up to public opinion.

Khrushchev was a good worker under good leadership. But there are many such people even now, and there will be many in the future. Isn't that so? He worked in the Ukraine, then in Moscow. He rose from below, from district committee to Moscow Committee. But one should not exaggerate; he played a secondary role. Stalin discerned in him certain qualities and he wanted to utilize them. He did.

In his book Khrushchev spoke about me in a rather restrained way, though in one passage he poured on the scorn; about Stalin, however, he vented bestial malice. *[In his memoirs Khrushchev said in one place, "Molotov impressed me as a strong-willed, independent, thinking man."]*

Do you believe Khrushchev was unintelligent?

That's not the question. You can't say he was unintelligent; he was very shrewd. The labels, the kinds of accusations he pinned on people!

In his own words he denied that Stalin was a communist.

One can't say that, but hatred is a terrible force. Since Khrushchev himself was not a communist, how could he judge whether Stalin was a communist?

He writes at length about Beria—most negatively, too. He also mentions Malenkov rather scornfully. He was his close friend! "He was a functionary, unable to operate independently. Good only to act under orders." He recalls Bulganin derisively too.

Whom does he speak well of? Mikoyan, surely?

Yes, Mikoyan.

[4-25-75]

In the summer of 1920 I was replaced by Mikoyan in Nizhny Novgorod. A capable man, quite capable. . . . A man of very few principles, unrestrained and easily influenced by others. . . . He began to be closely associated with Khrushchev after Stalin's death. That relationship had not existed before. It only developed in Khrushchev's later years. Khrushchev's best friends had been Malenkov and Beria.

"I do not doubt," said Shota Ivanovich, "there will be a party resolution on Khrushchev sooner or later. What do you think?"

Of course there will be a resolution on him! I don't doubt it either, but everything takes time. We have been thrown from one side to the other. And it will take time to restore stability.

[4-19-77]

They say that Mikoyan suggested to Khrushchev that Stalin be toppled.

I don't rule that out. Khrushchev's champions could only be proud of him. The true communists wouldn't be among that crowd.

It was absolutely stupid to divide the party into rural and industrial units.

At the time it was considered progressive, a fresh approach.

Fresh? It was rotten! That Anastas himself was rotten through and through.

Mikoyan was most closely linked with Khrushchev. I think it was he who induced Khrushchev to take drastic measures. . . .

At one time Khrushchev and Mikoyan went as far as to try to prove that Stalin had been employed as an agent by the tsar's secret police. But they failed to fabricate documents to that effect. They may even have tried to implicate me in something like that.

One author told me that Molotov had never been in prison, and that this story was made up after the Revolution.

Made up? But my entire life story has been covered in different publications. Such detractors abound. What can you expect if some of the people among the formerly repressed have tried to prove that Stalin was an agent of international imperialism? Here is hatred that will go to any lengths. . . .

[7-16-77]

Mikoyan played a vile role. He was a chameleon. He kept adapting himself to the point of embarrassment. Stalin was not overly fond of him either. At times Stalin put him under great pressure. But he was, of course, very competent in practical matters: the economy, trade, and the food industry. It was precisely there that he learned how to be so adaptable. He negotiated good deals, worked perseveringly—he was a very industrious person. That's a good quality that Armenians generally have.

[8-28-81]

Khrushchev knew as much about matters of theory as a shoemaker. He was a real foe of Marxism-Leninism, a real enemy of communist revolution, a covert, cunning, skillfully camouflaged enemy. . . . No, he was no fool. Why would people follow a fool? They too would have to be fools! The thing is that he reflected the spirit of the overwhelming majority. He keenly sensed the disparity [between policy and the state of opinion]. That's why he went no further.

[6-21-72]

We are out for a walk. Molotov has been greeted by Spiridonov, who proposed at the XXIInd Congress that Stalin's body be removed from the Mausoleum.

Sometimes I would join him for a walk. I know he is a Stalinist; he was just a disciplined party member then. But Mzhavanadze refused to come out with such a proposal. Khrushchev asked him to make the proposal at the congress, but he ate so much ice cream that he lost his voice. Khrushchev cursed him out. The chairman of the Georgian Council of Ministers, Dzhavakhishvili, spoke then.

I recall Dora Lazurkina making her comments.

A sheer witch! She appeared to have dreamed that Lenin was swearing at Stalin.

[4-10-79]

Was Khrushchev correct in alleging that the policy of gradual retail price reductions conducted under Stalin after the war was adventurist in character?

Incorrect. Price cuts after the war were good policy. People well recall how they welcomed the news.

[1-1-83]

Two years after the war, food rationing was abolished. A staggering event! I recall how happy everyone was on December 15, 1947. I was starving and I was taken to the dystrophy station for children. I was six then. I used to lick the cupboard shelf where we had always kept bread. . . . Those who went through all that will never forget that day.

I can't say I have ever experienced what you have. But there were periods in exile when I had to go hungry, too. My friend Arosev, a writer, who was there with me, would tell me, "Well, we have nothing left. Let's eat up the sugar! What's left of it. . . ."

That decision was quite a serious event.

After the war, from 1947 to 1954, we had seven price cuts. Over the seven-year period the price index went down two to three times. That was a significant achievement. It was just great! At the time, food rationing was still in effect in England.

[4-28-76, 8-18-76]

Cutting prices and stabilizing the ruble was a good and sensible policy conducted by the Central Committee and Stalin in particular. You must not forget that throughout the 1930s prices had been rising. The price rise was particularly high during the war. But even before the war we had no alternative. Now and then, for one reason or another, prices would climb. We had to reverse the process. Gradually the price cuts grew smaller and smaller until all possibilities of further cuts had been exhausted. But after the war, when tensions slacked off a bit, this was a very astute measure. Tremendous increases in prices have been occurring in all countries over the past several years. In our country too on trifles.

A ruble is a ruble all right, but preparations for a new war must be tremendously expensive. On that score don't stint on anything so long as the Americans don't. We have taken upon ourselves a great task—to help achieve the overthrow of imperialism. This is a very costly undertaking. It is everyone's concern, and may God grant that all of us measure up to the task.

[12-4-73]

After Stalin gave me a "bashing" at the Central Committee plenary meeting in 1952, my prestige was undermined. Khrushchev's promotion could in no way depend on me. I can't see why Stalin got so mad at me. No idea. Because of my wife? It did matter, but that was not the main thing. I never refused to work with Khrushchev. He approached me a couple of times: "Let's work together! Let's be friends!" "Let's. But on what grounds? Let's first reach some understanding."

Nothing came of it because we had different outlooks. He desperately wanted to build his reputation, primarily by means of releasing inmates from the camps. I particularly disagreed with him, of course, when he began to rehabilitate avowed enemies.

When I asked him, "On what grounds?" I intended to restrain him a little. He wouldn't listen. We couldn't have worked together. But Mikoyan built a good relationship with him.

[10-16-80]

Khrushchev must not be condemned for leading the country as if it were a military unit: "Column right, march! Column left, march!" Under conditions of dictatorship this defect persists. Only under a very great mind is this defect minimized. Lenin, of course, was the exception in this regard. Stalin was a very firm man, but of course he too had his defects. No one is perfect.

It's not just that Khrushchev lacked the capacity to address large-scale problems of state. It goes without saying, he didn't have it. But he was a skilled tactician, nobody's fool, and worldly wise. The main drawback is that he was not a revolutionary, that was the core of the problem. From my point of view, his attempts to besmirch everything connected with the name of Stalin shows that he was not a revolutionary, though I would not go so far as to say he was a counterrevolutionary. While Stalin was a revolutionary, Khrushchev proceeded from an alien ideology.

I am sure you know I had been out of favor with Stalin in his last years, which culminated in my expulsion from the Politburo. That was most adroitly arranged by Stalin. Of course, I could not agree with this. I still don't think I did anything to deserve that punishment. I did criticize some of Stalin's views in the past, and I would offer my opinions to him personally. I think a communist and a Politburo member of thirty years' standing without his own viewpoint would have been no more than a chatterbox. That was why Stalin valued me. He saw I had my own views and my own thinking on the issues. Of course, I can't say he would always agree with me, but I must say he did frequently agree with me. Otherwise we wouldn't have worked closely together for thirty years.

[6-16-77]

■ **Self-financing** ■

I've just read the article by Rudnev, minister of instruments manufacturing and communication equipment. This is the only ministry since 1970 that has switched to a self-financing basis. He believes it expedient for other ministries to make the switch. But I deem it a harmful undertaking. Self-financing in the ministries? Entire ministries? The approach is totally syndicalist. But the author, while a minister himself, is absolutely ignorant. He does not concern himself with the ideological and political aspects of such an enterprise. He merely describes possible benefits, with not a word about the losses, not a single critical remark.

In his report to the XXIVth Party Congress [1971] Kosygin mentioned in passing that self-financing is necessary, which means it is to be extended ever further. In my opinion this is very dangerous.

But where's the danger?

The danger? Throughout the existence of the Soviet government we have had only one ministry shift to self-financing. Self-financing grew from the grassroots—from factories and plants up to the so-called industrial trust. Now as in the past, we have some ardent champions of self-financing at the workshop level, but not once has an entire ministry been allowed to shift to self-financing. Why? Because there is no monitoring of those who are out by any and all means for profits. If there is a check at the top, it can to some extent brake this drive. But what if everyone from top to bottom is profit-driven? Everyone will be drawn into the race for profits. Who, then, will bring them back into line? If they are all after profits at any price, and through profits bonuses, and everyone from top to bottom is so driven, there is no lever that might moderate this drive, place it within limits, and halt various kinds of excesses. And there is not a word about the drawbacks of self-financing. I believe it will not only incur losses, it will also strengthen elements of corruption. Without monitoring, everyone goes after the same thing.

The author is simply obtuse. He is ignorant of theory and lacks political perception. Proponents of self-financing regard everything from a utilitarian point of view. But this is a question of principle. If all ministries are now permitted to move to self-financing—and the author does, after all, want to see other ministries make the switch—what will happen then? Everyone will be out for his own good, above all for profits. The ministries very likely will be transformed into monopolies—a construction monopoly, a coal-mining monopoly, and so forth. That's what he leads to.

[8-15-72]

The self-financing policy is just wrong. We must finish it off, but still they tout it. At some period it is necessary, even inevitable, but our MAs and PhDs melodramatically sing its praises to the skies. . . .

[7-28-76]

Self-financing in Rudnev's ministry has drawn extravagant praise from advocates of the NEP mentality. Not being a seasoned communist, he is pleased by this. Ironically, it has turned out that on certain questions he is at the cutting edge. On the whole this is positive when it does not exceed certain bounds, but where are these bounds? I am opposed to switching all ministries to self-financing, though many people have long dreamed about it. This is a throwback, in my view, to NEP, but in our country NEP is past history. But while we impose ever narrower limits on NEP, we have yet to fully renounce it. Otherwise progress toward the elimination of social classes would be impossible. But if we roll up the boundaries delineating ministries and individual economic entities, we will head in a direction different from the one we have mapped out for ourselves.

[3-11-83]

According to Khrushchev, we should by now [1983] have free transportation, free meals, free medicines, and the like. . . . He showed he did not understand the meaning of socialism. It is not merely the handing out of goods and services. It is a lengthy period during which everything is regulated, calculated, and consumed in keeping with a definite plan. It is an entire period devoted to preparing the country for the transition from socialism to communism.

In principle the idea of self-financing would not be bad, but we are not ready for it. The process has not gone beyond one ministry. A ministry is an administrative apparatus, but in fact it is administered with difficulty. That is why we have not succeeded in switching all ministries to a self-financing system.

[3-11-83]

What you refer to as "material incentives" Lenin called a capitalist method. I can look it up and read it to you—I keep that volume close at hand. You are underestimating this dimension. . . .

"Now we see mixed companies emerging. . . ." He refers here to the joining of socialist with capitalist elements. Such companies were practically nonexistent back then. They were only just emerging. "Mixed companies in the present case, like the whole of our state trade and all of our New Economic Policy, represent the application by us, by communists, of commercial methods, of capitalist methods." See, he calls all of this "capitalist methods." But these were necessary, as they say.

But we have never moved away from them.

That's just the point. This requires understanding. It's just what Khrushchev and his ilk don't understand. They think in a bourgeois way. Unfortunately our literature on this question remains scanty. No one recalls it, but Lenin spoke about it several times. "In this field we are setting up practical competition between capitalist methods and socialist methods. . . ."

[8-20-74]

■   **"The Bukharinists, Most Likely. . ."**   ■

How does the saying go? "Our land is vast and abundant, but there is no order in it. Come to rule and reign over us." In school I learned this in our history class. We spit in our own face!

[10-14-83]

I have just read that the star of Hero of Socialist Labor has been conferred on Chernenko. Brezhnev said Chernenko was awarded this decoration for loyalty to the Politburo. This is tantamount to saying, "for loyalty to me."

[4-28-76]

New portraits of Brezhnev have appeared. He is ruining his own prestige, in my opinion, with all this pomp. So many gold stars! Ridiculous! There is no room left on his chest. . . .

[12-7-76]

[Brezhnev's funeral, 1982, shows] that he had lost all sense of modesty and proportion.

In past funeral ceremonies one decoration would be displayed on an individual cushion, but at his funeral there were seven decorations on each cushion!

He didn't spare himself when it came to medals. This is disgraceful.

[12-9-82]

A friend of mine, a former KGB man, mailed me a good deal of negative information about Kunaev [the party boss of Kazakhstan].

That's to be expected. Over there the local bosses were the true masters, and they protected one another. But the choice of possible leaders there was of course very limited. Aliev [party boss in Azerbaijan] made an unpleasant impression when he met Brezhnev. So much glorification, praise, and boasting! The Azerbaijanis even outdid the Georgians! Shevardnadze is kicking himself!

[10-29-82]

We are long on avarice and short on thoughtfulness. We need a different culture, a different ideology. . . . We have so many drawbacks, so many excesses, so many extremes—the rich and the poor. All of this should be quite different. It seems to me that the repeated attacks on leveling are not at all correct—to a degree leveling ought to be obligatory. But that is not the leveling which has been criticized of late.

[12-9-82]

I am confident Stalingrad will one day be Stalingrad again. It is unlikely to happen this time around, but the city is sure to be renamed Stalingrad. I have no doubts about that.

All over the world you can find city streets and squares named after Stalingrad.

Khrushchev clearly indicated he was no communist. He would never get to the heart of a matter, to the cardinal issues. We used to have a lot of open enemies, and they still abound. In the past, when Stalin was praised, Khrushchev didn't dare criticize him; but as Stalin began to be criticized and damned, Khrushchev readily got involved....

[10-30-84]

Bukharin and Dubcek are now counterposed to Stalin.

They are both right-wingers, kulaks who escaped. Bukharin and Dubcek have a lot in common, by the way.

[7-24-78, 11-4-79]

A struggle still lies ahead for the party. Khrushchev was no accident. We are primarily a peasant country, and the right wing is powerful. Where's the guarantee to prevent them from gaining the upper hand? The anti-Stalinists in all probability will come to power in the near future, and they are most likely to be Bukharinists.

[8-14-73, 3-8-74]

■ Dissolve the Party Organization ■

I do not favor jailing all crooks at once. Time should be taken to troll, to play them on the line a bit as we did with Trotsky, as we did with Bukharin. Now, more than ever, rationality rather than haste is called for.

We were talking about Fedoseev, deputy minister of aviation, who had defected to the West.

Unstable? A crook. A man who did not accept our system and believed it did not have long to live, therefore grab, take, thieve! How did Soviet power endure it? All of this had to be endured. There was so much rot and filth of all kinds gathered around it!

We were talking about Shchelokov, about Colonel General Pakilev, about crooks who had been brought to trial.

They are subject to execution by firing squad. Where was the party organization they were registered in? Why isn't this discussed?

The leadership is not to be criticized. Do you know how they are elected now [1983–1985]?

I know something about it.

You are accused of, among other things, having introduced this system in which it is forbidden to criticize the leadership.

These accusers are people who are prepared even now to defend those who should be judged and punished. They have found an out.

Now things have gone so far that they are even condemning Lenin.
And the Lord God?

They now say that we made the Revolution too early and that it should not have been carried out.

Not only now; they started to talk that way even before the Revolution.

It may have started before the Revolution, but later you forced people to forget about this.

You can't force people to forget.

Just the same, you applied great pressure.

To a certain extent, yes. But why aren't these leaders being discussed in the party organizations? How could this have happened? But what came to pass is not as important as why it came to pass. That's what requires explanation.

There is a lot that needs digging into.

Not a lot. You don't have to dig down into Lenin or dig down into Stalin.

But after all, when you were in power the top echelons were not discussed either.

Okay. But it is certainly necessary now, because so many misdeeds have been committed. They have to be stopped. Otherwise we have a misunderstanding of democratism, an unwillingness to take an independent stand in these questions.... But look, these questions are not being discussed. That's intolerable. They must be discussed.

In cases of thievery and bribe-taking, the entire primary party organization must be dissolved and its members expelled from the party.

[11-10-83, 1-1-85]

■   What Is Socialism?   ■

Our newspapers no longer print even mere half-truths. Just take the reports on the XXVth Party Congress—do they say much about our shortcomings? And there are heaps of them. I am not certain what can be said publicly. But what shall we do then, and what will come of it all?

It won't right itself, yet we simply hold our tongues. But life marches on. People are saying, you meet communists—I don't see that many people, nevertheless I see people from here and there—and people ask, don't you see, things are going wrong? You see it, but why don't they see it at the top? Evidently they do see it, but in the first place they lack resolve, and in the second place one must not only speak the truth but draw the correct conclusions for action. But they are not up to it. Lenin—he was. Lenin and Stalin spoke the harsh truth. People believed in them.

[4-28-76]

Lenin said, "Uneven economic and political development is the absolute law of capitalism. Hence it follows that the victory of socialism is possible initially. . . ." Initially, do you see the word "initially"? What does this "initially" mean? "The victorious proletariat of this country, having expropriated capitalism and itself organizing socialist production . . ."

How precisely everything is stated! But five years after the victory of the October Revolution, in 1922, he writes: "An elementary truth of Marxism holds: the victory of socialism requires the joint efforts of workers of several advanced countries." That is, it is possible to seize power, it is even possible to organize socialist production, but only initially in one country. In order to triumph, joint efforts are needed. So far the advanced countries have not arrived at this juncture.

At first, simple victory rather than complete victory is required. It is possible to triumph initially in one separate country, to liquidate the exploiters, to organize socialist production. Victory is possible in this sense. But to triumph fully, according to Lenin, is for the present impossible. Continued existence of the socialist state alongside capitalist countries for a long period is inconceivable. Either one or the other will triumph. But Trotsky did not believe in the possibility. . .

Can't this be expressed in the language of mathematics: Trotsky thought in the fixed categories of arithmetic, but Lenin thought in the differential categories of higher mathematics?

Correct. It's a rough analogy, but it may be drawn. Trotsky did not believe the peasantry could follow our lead. That was his most flagrant error.

"We are attending 'Molotov's Academy,'" said Shota Ivanovich.

Everything is stated quite clearly in Lenin, but nowhere is it explained today. Lenin has been so badly distorted that Academician Pospelov, in his published biography of Lenin, quotes the first part of the statement on the possibility of victory in one country but omits the second part, about the joint efforts required. Even in a specially published collection of quotations from Marx, Engels, and Lenin, the first part of the quotation is given but not the second.

Yet Lenin explicitly stated that the victorious proletariat, if required, raises up armed insurrection in other countries, and if necessary wages war. Some defensist, that Lenin!

Lenin stated it explicitly, but now this is inconvenient because of the policy of peaceful coexistence. But even peaceful coexistence is class struggle. Capitalism does not intend to yield peacefully, and once we set about this revolutionary affair only two outcomes are possible: either we have to grow so strong, not only internally but also externally in other countries, by overthrowing capitalism in several leading capitalist coun- tries—that is, France, Italy, Spain, and Portugal—so that imperialism will not be in a position to declare war on us; or we must gird ourselves for the contingency that an early outbreak of revolution might prompt the imperialists to undertake counterrevolutionary armed intervention, in which case there will be an atomic war. This contingency cannot be ruled out. Consequently, another very intense exacerbation of tensions is possible. It follows logically that victory as such in one country does not close the question.

Look, Germany invaded us yesterday. And America could strike us tomorrow. After all, that is what the whole issue boils down to. So to say that class struggle is coming to an end is of course untrue.

[7-29-71, 12-12-72, 6-30-76]

At the XXIst Party Congress, which is mentioned nowhere, Khru- shchev had said that in our country socialism had triumphed fully and finally. But if fully and finally, what are we building? As an excuse the current leaders say: now we are building communism. What is the purpose of this argument? To provide a beautiful façade behind which they can avoid drawing revolutionary conclusions about unfinished work. The task of doing away with social classes is arduous and revolutionary. But "we are building communism" is only a lame excuse for avoiding this question and concealing an effort to escape revolution- ary tasks. Communism, they say at the top, comes automatically as classes are abolished. This is a typical rightist position. They say, don't destroy the kulak, he will do it himself. . . .

Here you have the morality of the rightists: they say, let us find an explanation for needless cruelty; we must be humanists, and laws must be obeyed. But this morality is not revolutionary, it does not advance the cause. It glosses over difficulties, evades questions. And the pretext for this?—we are building communism.

Lenin said that classes must be abolished. The current leadership says, "We shall achieve this under communism. Of course we are steadily eliminating classes; for the present we are allowing it to happen of itself." Without hardships. This is a quicker way—peaceful coexistence. . . . With this thesis Khrushchev won out or gained an ideological majority. But you just take Lenin. He says that our ideology has no room for or against divine consolation, for one religion or another. Our ideology is: overthrow capitalism by socialist revolution! That is our ideology.

If we adhere to Lenin's ideology, our morality will be revolutionary, aimed toward fulfillment of these tasks. Our humanism is Marxist, it cannot resemble bourgeois humanism. Their humanism is such that it offends no one, that's their humanism. Christian or anti-Christian, it is bourgeois humanism. People are taught not to lay a hand on the bourgeois system. So Trotsky preached. Because he was a landowner, he could not understand that without changing the system you could not change man.

If we direct morality toward instilling good qualities in man but leave the system as it is—with bribery, with embezzlement—if we leave this intact, this morality will remain corrupt. But if we set the revolutionary task of smashing the system, of revamping it, then we must adapt morality to this goal, to the struggle for victory. This is a different morality. But today everyone wants to avoid all this. Therefore all talk about morality, about humanism, is false through and through. If there is no primary objective, what is there to struggle for? If there are no goals, what are we struggling for, and where are we going? If toward peaceful coexistence, then this calls for another morality.

In our country we do not yet have socialism. We have bribery, we have embezzlement, we have every kind of scandal imaginable. . . .

Trotsky was a crook, a 100 percent crook, and he pointed out to Stalin that it was the bourgeois philosophers who discovered the law of capitalism's uneven development. Indeed, the bourgeois philosophers produced a great many different definitions which were not too far from the truth, and they stood for revolutionary ways as long as they remained confident of their powers. In short, they lived to see King Charles of Great Britain beheaded and Louis XVI of France executed, and they showed no remorse. But the revolutions didn't stop at that point. A great revolutionary feat was achieved with the expulsion of the landlords. That was the point beyond which the bourgeois thinkers refused to travel. Initially the working class was not a powerful force. But can we stop at that? No, we cannot. Today's revolutionary tasks need to be properly understood. They rest not on verbiage about communism or the blessings of peaceful coexistence but on the struggle to eliminate social classes. I see no other decisive revolutionary tasks for today. If you know of any, you are welcome to come up with them. . . .

They are not discussed nowadays because they are revolutionary tasks. Classes cannot be eliminated overnight, so let's discuss how it is to be done. But no. No one wishes to tackle the issue. But does any other way exist?

Work habits are deteriorating. People need to be educated for good job performance. Wage increases play a role, of course, but educational work is also important. Regrettably it is nowhere to be seen. Everyone seems to believe that things can be achieved with money alone. But our morality can only be revolutionary. Our revolutionary tasks have not yet been achieved. We must make every effort to prevent world war, but still more we must not surrender our positions but consolidate them. How can that be achieved? By struggle. But struggle is dangerous. So choose!

[12-7-76]

Now let me quote from Trotsky: "Is it conceivable that European socialism would start to decay within the next forty or fifty years and that the proletariat would be incapable of achieving the revolution?" Fifty years have already elapsed. There lies one of his major blunders.

"In what sense does my theoretical or political responsibility as a communist oblige me to adopt the premise that the European proletariat may fail to seize power within the next forty or fifty years . . . ?"

And they did fail to seize it!

"I maintain that I have no theoretical or political grounds to think it will be easier for us with the peasantry to build socialism than it will be for the European proletariat to seize power."

Here is my marginal note. "The thesis has no theoretical grounding."

Back to Trotsky: "Even Stalin in 1924 wrote that the efforts of one country, a peasant country, are insufficient for the building of socialism. . . ."

In February 1924 it was stated that it was possible to begin socialist production, but impossible fully to construct socialism in one country.

On this point Trotsky seemed to hold Marxist views of a sort.

He very skillfully pits Marxism against Marxism; that's it in a nutshell.

Some kind of line of demarcation must be drawn between socialism and communism.

That goes without saying. The line is already sharply drawn. Under communism there is no state, while Stalin allowed for the existence of the state under communism. That is absurd from the point of view of Leninism. Stalin said, under communism there should be no state, but if capitalist encirclement remains...

There will be an army and state apparatus.

What kind of communism is that? Good housing, good living conditions, everything provided for—this is enough from the philistine's point of view. If all the poor live more or less well, they say, that means we already have socialism, not capitalism. But this in itself is not complete socialism. . . .

Marx holds that in a society based on collectivist principles, producers will not engage in exchange of their commodities. There will be no trade. Will they then dump their goods into a garbage pit? No, they will get along without trade, without commodity-money relations. Here you have socialism.

In that case, what distinguishes communism from socialism?

A lot. The point, you see, is this. When classes do not exist, when there are no money-commodity relations, and the level of production is still not high enough so that each receives according to his needs...

To fully satisfy his needs?

No, not fully, but for the most part. Generally speaking, maximum satisfaction of human needs will never be achieved. Stalin's assertion that it would be is empty, a banality so to speak. What does maximum satisfaction of needs mean? Everyone gets himself a piano? everyone gets himself an automobile? That's absurd. Socialism means satisfaction of all basic needs, not maximum satisfaction. Everyone will have the right to use publicly owned facilities. Along with the other former ministers— and not only ministers—I will have my meals at a public dining facility. I pay sixty rubles per month and take my meals. Having completed one hundred work days, you would be entitled to a certain remuneration. Marx says that everyone will be paid according to the number of days worked. If you have produced a hundred pairs of shoes, for example, within a hundred days, you are allowed to take home a pair of shoes and other products you need equivalent to the remaining ninety-nine pairs of shoes.

What kind of accounting would be practiced? Socialism is accounting.

The most rigorous, rigorous accounting. Communism is a higher stage than socialism, because there will be such abundance that it will be possible to eliminate the distinction between physical and intellectual labor as well as to eliminate social classes. It will also be possible to eliminate the distinction between town and country, but differences in standards of living will remain.

If class distinctions are eliminated, then how is it that a distinction between town and country remains?

Engels said there will be no peasantry—mountain folk will live under different conditions, yet they might not want to live in the valley. They will have their choice. To level everything and everyone is neither possible nor necessary, and no one will stand in the way of your preference in this regard. If you want to live in a village, fine. But you will have fewer cultural amenities at your disposal. You will have fewer theatres to attend. But it's possible you will have a television set and access to a cinema.

And human relations will be different.

Yes, different. This may please some and displease others, as it were. To eliminate the differences in social relations will of course take some time. They cannot be completely eliminated at a stroke, which is all the more true of the difference between intellectual and physical labor.

Material abundance will not be achieved overnight. Probably rationing would still be practiced. But then, under socialism, Lenin said, no official will be paid a higher wage than the average worker's. None of the officials, including the general secretary of the party and the chairman of the Council of Ministers, should receive compensation higher than that of the average worker. This principle was practiced by the Paris Commune. But do we?

No, we cover up unfinished business. But the chief thing is that it is impossible to overcome bureaucratism so long as some get a hundred rubles per month while others get a thousand rubles per month. . . .

Organization can be achieved only by the working class, but infusion of the ideology of socialism is the mission of scientifically educated people, that is, the intelligentsia.

Was calling the intelligentsia a social stratum correct?

Correct. If not, then what is it?

Well, this term sounds demeaning.

Well, social layer, stratum. You gain nothing by calling it a class. Lenin demanded the abolition of classes.

The West asks, haven't the Bolsheviks renounced world communism?

Oh, Lord! When we were a weak power such talk did not scare us. What do we have to be scared of now? Let them talk. We have renounced nothing, we are just a bit confused.

. . . Now we have a powerful country and a commonwealth of socialist states. We have nothing and no one to fear but our own laxity, indolence, and indiscipline, which must be combated in order to strengthen the cause of socialism.

Life has grown more complex. But in the past life was more difficult, much more difficult.

It's up to you to look into things thoroughly. You are young, and I'm too old for that. Seeing and understanding things is of vital importance. Unless you do that, you will proceed blindfolded and will be pulled from one side to another.

What can serve to replace material incentives under socialism? I disagree with Zlobin's work crew being glorified. He's merely a good subcontractor, and there were lots of them under the tsar! In my essay I put forward six substitutes for material incentives under socialism.

Competent and scientific planning of production.

Socialist competition.

Selection of personnel.

Social orientation—all organizations should work toward a single common goal.

International socialist economic integration.

The party's ideological education—covering all internal and external policies.

[7-17-75]

■ The Program Impedes Progress ■

I hold to the opinion that for the education of youth—and not just youth but even for senile elders and indifferent middle-aged citizens—there is nothing to rely on except Lenin. But Lenin is considered passé, and it is believed that something new is required. But the essence of the matter is that the struggle must be raised to a new stage at which the entire picture will appear in a new way. We shall have to look at a great deal in a new way.

I advise you to read Lenin's *Politics and Economics in the Epoch of the Dictatorship of the Proletariat*. It was published at the end of 1919. I can give you the gist in my own words, after which you can read it to examine its profundity. In any event, I convey his thought precisely.

What is socialism? Lenin says, socialism is the abolition of social classes. The abolition of classes is possible only under the dictatorship of the proletariat. Without the dictatorship of the proletariat, it is impossible to abolish classes.

In our country we need to abolish exploiting classes. But look, the peasant, the kolkhoznik, is coddled. If you really want him to be happy, you must not coddle him. He must be freed from the kolkhozes by turning him into a toiler in the new socialist village. The self-styled champions of the peasant, of democracy, are the real reactionaries; they want to preserve the peasant in his present form, they want to freeze things as they are. They have sunk into the torpor of their petty bourgeois philistinism.

[7-29-71, 12-12-72, 6-30-76]

Everyone keeps referring to Lenin. The historian Gleizerman refers to Lenin's "great initiative" in concluding that communism is a classless society, and that eliminating the classes is a lengthy process to be completed only under communism. And this idea is being pushed. But the point is that the whole of Marxism, the whole of the Marxist dialectic, unconditionally postulates a process of historical development. Everything is considered in terms of development, and nowhere does the process ever cease. Therefore Lenin is right in saying that socialism is the abolition of classes. This means that the differences will not be permanent but will of course eventually be obliterated. After all, a person develops from a child into a scientist or scholar. There is infancy. Youth. Then a young man in his student years is already a young scholar, then a mature scholar. As you see, it is impossible to draw a fine line between these stages of development.

All the same, Lenin did presume the abolition of classes under socialism.

He did not presume it, though it is fully in keeping with his teachings. But this is far from saying that everything will be put off until the end; it will be an ongoing process. He doesn't put off the abolition of classes until communism. That's the heart of the matter. But there are those who do put it off and count on this. They lack revolutionary spirit. One must not put it off. Sometimes it is necessary to defer action, to clear the way, but say so when this is the case. Yet they have postponed the abolition of classes until communism comes. The whole point is that you cannot arrive at communism without having resolved this question. That's the main thing. They are trying to skip over a difficult question.

Petty bourgeois democrats, said Lenin, have an aversion toward the class struggle of the proletariat. They dream of getting along without it, they strive to smooth out and reconcile contradictions, to round off sharp corners. But Marx said, in the transitional period between capitalism and communism there can be nothing other than the dictatorship of the proletariat. Yet everywhere in our country they now contend that this applies only to the period between capitalism and socialism! Our entire literature is being revised accordingly. Even the new program of the party adopted in 1961.

[4-28-76]

"We have brought an end to class struggle," said Shota Ivanovich.
We have not yet brought an end to anything.
Within the country.
Even within the country we have brought nothing to an end. We have only laid the foundations.
Khrushchev said we have completed the edifice.
It was not completed under Khrushchev, and it is still not completed. Quite the contrary, the ideology contained in the party program only hampers progress.
Good heavens! The program is incorrect!
Not just incorrect, it impedes the building of socialism. The workers toil and move the cause forward; the peasants, kolkhozniki, work slowly but are advancing. They lack genuine leadership. In reality the people are preoccupied with problems of daily life. A socialism in which money dominates is not the socialism of Marx, Engels, and Lenin. There is no such socialism. Just try to find it. Yet in our country such "socialism" exists. There is no genuine socialism in which two kinds of property exist, neither in Marx, Engels, and Lenin nor in a developed, completely built socialism. Instead of overcoming these vestiges of the transitional period, we have preserved them and applied the brakes to further progress. And we claim we are already building communism. It's absurd. That's what this ideology leads to.
In "Economic Problems of Socialism," didn't Stalin address this problem correctly?
Correctly. He started off cautiously, but in the end he took a firm position. He alone addressed the question correctly. We didn't understand all of it back then. He made some mistakes, and I called them to his attention. He let me read the manuscript of a part which was then published, and the second part on which he was still working. But I

repeat: there is nothing in Marx, Engels, and Lenin to suggest that you can have socialism while money, the purse, holds sway.

The kolkhoz is a transitional, and only a transitional, form. No socialism, no complete socialism, exists while there are two forms of property, state and cooperative. Yet we say that we have a developed socialist society, delude ourselves in this manner when in fact we are slamming on the brakes. We must liquidate this delusion and unleash the full energy of the people. This step will turn things white-hot but will work itself out. Nevertheless, our present leadership [under Brezhnev and Kosygin] doesn't understand this, while those who slip them ineffectual memoranda are simply mindless, petty bourgeois ideologists. We have only built the foundations; true, this is irreversible. But lo and behold, they proclaim: "This is developed socialism! Let us pass on to communism!" and so forth. We are passing on to nothing. Look, Brezhnev, in spite of himself, is one of those leaders who doesn't understand this, one of those who live according to a vulgar, petty bourgeois ideology. We have a lot of that around in our country, and it cannot but impede progress. Most interesting is the fact that you won't find any serious people pondering this problem. Have you heard of anyone who says that we must somehow change so as to build the socialism of Marx, Engels, and Lenin? You won't find such a person.

But how to change, begin with what, with the kolkhozes or what?

Yes, with the kolkhozes.

Liquidate the kolkhozes, turn them into state property?

Yes, exactly. To do this, however, vast preparatory work must be done, but we are not yet doing it because presumably socialism has been fully built, a claim that hinders preparation for the liquidation both of the kolkhozes and of money. I must say that apart from Stalin no one has embarked on this work or even grasped its necessity. I read and discussed this matter with Stalin. In his booklet Stalin at first writes hesitatingly but in the last letter very categorically. Twenty years ago he wrote that the kolkhozes were already beginning to block progress. Today the kolkhozes can rely on their own funds. But what if the state should invest in this matter? The rate of growth would rise phenomenally. The party program states that the sovkhozes [state farms] should serve as a model for the kolkhozes. If we have already built socialism and if we are building communism, why not transform them into the model? Mere endless babbling about this must stop. Undermechanization is the major reason for our agricultural problems. In America there is no shortage of grain, cotton, or sugar beets. Why? Because of complete mechanization and integration, down to the smallest detail. If we were able to do this we would outperform them. Nevertheless, instead of concentrating everything on this and moving forward, we are now making colossal investments in the rural economy as it stands. . . . But if we pass over to the sovkhoz model of structuring agriculture, in which the state does everything to ensure mechanization and agricultural-industrial integration, the results would be remarkable, simply remarkable. I hold that the rural economy presents no problem for us. We shall not, however, solve it quickly until we have enough machines adapted to the conditions of various regions of the country and each farm unit, crop, and variety is integrated with the others. If we mechanize realistically, in a scientific and efficient way, we shall easily cope with these tasks. We must not lag behind in military technology. It is here that we have concentrated all our strength. . . .

Priority for industry is our first concern.

Of course. More than anything. We now find ourselves at a very advantageous position as the only country in the whole world not dependent on foreign oil or gas. America is dependent in this regard, as are France, England, all. . . . We are fully self-sufficient in energy. We lack only machines and educated people. But the main thing is mechanization. If we clearly understand this and firmly carry out mechanization, we shall speedily move forward.

But we need to understand, really understand, what socialism means.

Generally speaking, no one even discusses this today.

What do you mean, no one? They are discussing it. Indeed, too much so. Philosophers and economists are discussing it. We have two books recently published on the foundations of scientific communism, edited by the director of the Institute of Marxism-Leninism, Academician Fedoseev. Just look at the nonsense he read into Marx, Engels, and Lenin.

He is confused?

Totally. The contributors just sow confusion: peace, peace, peace! Nixon will never hand it to you on a silver platter. A bitter struggle for peace lies ahead; it is not yet avoidable. Our ideologists disingenuously shout peace, peace! Better the hand wither than write this nonsense! Peace, peace! It must be fought for and won!

We have scored gains in some places. We now have a foothold in the Near East. But it will be harmful if we go too far. I believe it was utterly foolhardy to propose in the UN that for the sake of peace in the Near

East we should send a contingent of our troops there if our partners agree to it.

And the Americans would send a contingent of theirs.

Why go out on a limb? Look, the proposal is unwarranted. We have used Sadat in order to supply arms to the Arabs to stiffen their resistance to the imperialists who are now forced to a certain extent to bow down to the Arabs. The Arabs have grasped the idea that they must unite. They are starting to raise their oil prices and to reduce oil exports to the world market, which can only benefit us. Let Sadat keep busy with this; what's so bad about that? Given our assistance, he will be active in this direction. But if we stand aside we shall perform a service for the imperialists. . . .

"Would Vladimir Ilyich Lenin and Josef Stalin have acquiesced in Sadat's destruction of the Communist party of Egypt?" asked Shota Ivanovich.

But why do you ask? Look, Lenin accepted the Brest peace, and Stalin signed a peace with Hitler. Our leaders were intelligent men, not stupid. Your approach to the problem is very primitive.

Back then we had no alternative.

You must understand, when it came time to make full use of the obscene Brest peace treaty, Lenin signed while Trotsky was opposed. How intelligent, that Trotsky! We concluded a peace agreement with Hitler, but the Germans invaded us. How stupid we were! But in fact we gained almost two years to prepare!

We have signed a nuclear test-ban treaty with the imperialists of America and England, a treaty directed against socialist China. Why bar China from having nuclear weapons? China just shrugged off the ban and developed its own bomb. France disregarded the ban. We proved to be helpless as a newborn babe, and we gave Mao Tse-tung his main reason to break with the Soviet Union. The imperialists signed this treaty to foster the split between China and the Soviet Union. It is now almost impossible to rectify that blunder. The Chinese further deepened the rift because they are semi-Marxists rather than true Marxists.

Khrushchev apparently instigated it.

Instigated it? He literally dragged us into it. So, we signed the treaty: peace, peace! But there can be no peace without war.

We are handing out billions in Soviet money to foreign states, but the recipients have collapsed.

Can you name just one?

Chile, for example. You yourself once told us several years ago that Chile could not hold out for long.

All right, that was Chile. There will still be many Chiles—victories and defeats.

Assistance to Sadat.

That's philistine talk of the kind heard in bazaars.

What if he takes Egypt back to the American camp?

What if? He will without fail!

Okay, I'll shut up. There are some wise words: we shall see what we shall see. History proves... As Churchill said in his Second World War...

You are going about the study of history badly if you study it only in Churchill; you will fall into many gross errors if you rely only on him.

But we are not relying on him exclusively.

You are, you are.

But no one can deny that Soviet billions have gone to foreign aid.

Oh, you philistine, you! Just a philistine! No one can deny... Come on...

Khrushchev just whiled away the time and departed.

Well, where were you in the meantime? Where did you while away the time? Just putting the blame on others. No, that won't do.... At times I let fly at you. For instance, in your opinion it will take two hundred years before we have socialism in our country. It would be better if we went into that question.

... This is that wonderful American fruit, grapefruit. I think the Georgians ought to grow it.

"We do, but very little," said Shota Ivanovich.

But you must, it's a very good fruit, I recommend it....

If before the war we had not unswervingly put every kopek into the economy and instead had disbursed our funds on all kinds of projects, we would not have won the war.

For everything there is a season. Now is the time for us to sort things out.

It's up to our propaganda to explain matters.

But we should not repeat the errors of our propaganda and its shortcomings.

On television they show a sports complex that we have given to a foreign country, but it is dedicated without mentioning that it is a gift from the Soviet Union.

Take grapefruit, American or Cuban...

Cuba is a burden on us. Let it be?
It's not at all.
And Chile would have been a burden, too.
No, don't go on that way. I am very sensitive on this topic. . . . You are a great philistine in matters of politics, Shota Ivanovich.
Viacheslav Mikhailovich, I clearly recall your words of last year. I said I would not grudge my monthly pay for Chile, and you replied, 'Your monthly wage? So what. One must be ready to sacrifice one's life for the revolution!' Those are your words."
We are still far from the point where it's a question of sacrificing one's life.

[11-9-73]

■   **Peaceful Coexistence**   ■

Am I right, the slogan "peaceful coexistence" was not used under Lenin?
It was never used, and Lenin never used it. And I think the reason is quite understandable. In those days it would have been naive, utterly naive, to talk about peaceful coexistence. As if we would have begged, "Please give us peace!" The imperialists would have given us no kind of peace whatever. They went their way, we ours. Along the revolutionary way, our policy was affirmed and gathered strength. In my view it is a correct slogan today, but we must bear in mind that some people, pacifistically minded people, incorrectly interpret this slogan. The very idea draws people toward a pacifist way of thinking. Under Lenin the old program condemned such views. Pacifist ideas are pernicious. Lenin was very punctilious, most precise in this regard. But today it's another matter.
Khrushchev even included it in the party program. . . .
I personally tried to avoid this expression and still do, while Khrushchev, in contrast, tried to make it the touchstone of party and state policy. Elaborating on it leads to no improvement. Another aspect of it needs to be stressed.
In 1921 we made no use of the slogan. We stood for peace, we were for the development of relations with the bourgeois countries. We intended to attack no one. But we were opposed to pacifism. This was stated very sharply, even scathingly, in the party program, that is, the

Lenin program. I took the trouble to reexamine the program to check on this. It does not contain this slogan. Even during the struggle over the Brest peace treaty, when Lenin defended the necessity of peace, even then this expression was not employed, at least not by Lenin and his closest associates. Today it is widely and eclectically bandied about. The general line on this has already been fixed. We are, as it were, begging for peace. But to beg for peace means exposing one's weakness. And to show one's weakness to the strong is politically disadvantageous and inexpedient. For Bolsheviks it is unseemly. The expression was widely used by Khrushchev, who did not always speak correctly to questions of theory and questions of a profoundly political, principled character. One finds in him all kinds of similar crude formulations. . . .

Stalin's published works contain no slippery expressions such as peaceful coexistence. I don't recall any. Absolutely none at all in Lenin. But in Lenin there are many apt expressions such as "We stand for peace," "We stand for normal relations with other states." Of course we struggled for peace back then.

Stalin said, peace will be preserved and strengthened if the peoples take the cause of peace into their own hands and uphold it to the end.

Yes, into their own hands. This expression is much stronger; it does not beg for peace. Just as in Lenin.

[4-29-82]

The impression is being given that we have consolidated the peace, when we have done nothing of the kind. We have consolidated nothing. In dealing with imperialism is it possible to say, live and let live? If so, permit me to ask: what are we living for? If it is for the overthrow of imperialism, can we possibly coexist peacefully without overthrowing imperialism? Are we renouncing the overthrow of imperialism? No, we are not. How then is it possible to combine peaceful coexistence with the overthrow of imperialism? According to the *Communist Manifesto*, "The communists do not conceal their views. They stand for the violent overthrow of the entire existing social order." This is basic to Marx and to Lenin. Everything is reasoned out so as not to contradict this teaching, but now we preach peaceful coexistence. How does one fit in with the other? If they do jibe, then explain how. The real purpose of this expression is to set people's minds at ease.

More than a hundred years ago we were not afraid to speak out openly, and we rallied people into insurrection. But today we who have grown strong talk about peaceful coexistence. There can be only one long-range goal if we are to move forward: only international revolution. There is nothing, no alternative, more reliable than this.

It is our duty to preserve peace. But if we believe that without international revolution we can fight for peace and delay war, if we still believe that it's possible to arrive at communism in this way, that is deception from a Marxist viewpoint, both self-deception and deception of the people.

Revolution is on the march, it is growing stronger, everything is moving forward, but not without sacrifices. He who thinks it is possible to advance to communism without sacrifices and without mistakes is naive. The fewer the mistakes the better, but there are bound to be some. Big mistakes that create illusions and spread complacency do not prepare us for decisive battles which are absolutely unavoidable. Thus nothing will be gained, and we shan't move forward. This means that very big battles lie ahead. We are not preparing for them. This is the main danger as I see it.

We must maintain peace in every way and delay the onset of a new war, especially war against the socialist countries. But we must not get too deeply engaged in favor of the Arabs and others when they put their national interests first. We ought to help them, but within limits. We are going too far.

We stand for peaceful coexistence in the sense that we stand for peace. We must in every way stand for peace—we are the most peace-loving country—insofar as this does not impede the strengthening of socialism and the growth of the national liberation movement. As to world communism, that goes without saying. If we do not struggle for communism, for world communism, we won't have socialism either. Insofar as this peace does not impair the gradual deepening of the pit under capitalism—we don't speak of this openly—we preserve peace for the purpose of overthrowing imperialism.

In fact, when Khrushchev launched "peaceful coexistence," he did so for the most self-serving of reasons. After all, by playing up fear of atomic war, we help bring it on. Much lies ahead to be done. We proceed from the premise that our positions must be strengthened.

[1-4-75, 7-17-75]

"What struggle? Capitalism has collapsed," said Shota Ivanovich.

Well, well. A formidable struggle lies ahead. And the further we go, the more formidable the struggle. There is no book whatever that will provide a solution to this question. Marx's *Capital* is the most all-encompassing book, but it does not provide an answer to all problems.

How about State and Revolution?

It is based on Marx. Marx said, here is my book. It is a bomb of a kind more powerful than any bomb that bourgeois society ever had or will have. Indeed, this bomb will blow up bourgeois society. No atomic bomb has this power. Nor will any bomb help bourgeois society. Marx's teaching has proved to be a teaching, which, if adhered to—and Lenin undeviatingly adhered to it and very ingeniously applied it to our country's conditions—was capable of blowing up our society. But it has not yet proved capable of this in other countries.

[1-8-74]

Is the bourgeois system better than the socialist system? Better? In what respects? Better because it is infected through and through with Khrushchevism? But Khrushchevism is the bourgeois spirit.

I told Khrushchev this straight to his face, and I who had always been considered a man of the party was later considered superfluous to the party. I say to you, we must not follow in Khrushchev's footsteps! Khrushchev is not alone. We have very many "Khrushchevs" in our country; indeed, they are the overwhelming majority. We who believe that we must take fundamental positions different from Khrushchevism should have looked into things a bit more deeply.... Why do we have such a situation in our country? What is its cause? Is Khrushchev alone to blame? It would have been so easy to kick him out. But we are surrounded by little "Khrushchevs," and they keep mum—but now they have come to understand.... Everyone wants to live, it's a legitimate demand. But if we who consider ourselves dedicated communists devote all our attention to this, we will begin to move through bourgeois floodwaters to the aid of Khrushchev. We will cling to him so as not to fall behind.

We just talk about socialism in generalities and refer only in passing to the difficult questions. We deliberately avoid these questions.

[6-21-72]

■   To Consolidate the System   ■

... A hot July day like the one colorfully described by Boris Zaitsev in his stories, when our summer can be a genuine summer with daytime

temperatures reaching 86 degrees. Shota Ivanovich and myself arrived at
Ilyinskoye by train at noon. Molotov was outside his dacha waiting for us
at the door.

"I suggest we take a half-hour's walk if you don't mind." Molotov took
his cane and put on his pince-nez. "Others can do without a cane, but I
always take mine along." He's wearing his usual grey slacks, a blue shirt,
and a pair of light summer shoes. We started for the woods nearby.
Shortly we took up the issue of so-called "consumer socialism."

Khrushchev took advantage of the widespread philistine mentality:
"We just need more goods! Never mind they are low quality, all that
matters is that they be cheap!" Buildings with low ceilings have been
constructed, the builders copying from foreign capitalists who are interested only in cramming in more and more workers! In our country we
have only laid the foundations of socialism, and even that has not been
completed. The building of socialism is not an overnight affair but
requires an entire epoch. That's just the approach economists in the
GDR [German Democratic Republic] take, though their work contains
ambiguous formulations.

. . . Molotov believes that imperialism should be finished off in the
twentieth century.

In January 1917 Lenin did not know that in ten months he would
become the head of government of the first socialist state in the world.

It's possible to achieve optimum satisfaction of material and cultural
needs just in the course of a decade while this prepares the way for total
collapse in the next decade. If you set a course on satisfaction of material
and cultural needs, this requires that priority be assigned to development
of light and food industries, right? To meet the needs of the people.
Gradually heavy industry is neglected. If you take this byway you forget
the need to take heavy industry in hand, and material consumer
satisfaction itself will be undermined. This is the heart of the matter and
what I want to emphasize. As the socialist system is consolidated,
emphasis on consumer satisfaction will become correct, but if one
branch of the economy is separated from the other. . . What kind of
satisfaction then? None. If we neglect heavy industry, if we forget about
abolition of classes. . . I tried to persuade Stalin to bring this up in his
"Economic Problems," but everyone else was cheering, "Hurrah! Hurrah!"

In my opinion there will be improvement in living conditions, but let
it proceed somewhat more slowly; and to make up for it, let us
strengthen the system and steer a course on abolition of classes.

To wrest the working class from the clutches of capitalism is possible only with sacrifice. Anyone who wants to overthrow capitalism without sacrifice would do better to enroll in another party, the party of pacifists, idlers, babblers, and incorrigible bourgeois ideologues. Period. In short, the working class can tear itself away from capitalism only through the greatest of sacrifices. If this is not to one's taste, then just go on living in slavery. There is no alternative. Why spin fantasies? Life has demonstrated this long ago. Thanks only to our Soviet people, the Russian people, thanks to our Communist party and above all to Lenin, we have cleared the way forward and in fact won a place of honor among all peoples.

[7-28-71]

For communists the party program is scandalous. Communism in 1980! Well, here it is 1981. Where is communism? It can't be built today, and it could not have been built yesterday. It was impossible under 1980 conditions, because first socialism must be built.

This is not at all a misfortune or a crime; it is more in the nature of things.

This formulation of communism by 1980 was apparently dictated by Khrushchev on his own, recklessly, on a day when he must have got out of the wrong side of the bed. He was like a runaway horse. Absolutely unbridled. And many small unbridled horses ran after him. Communism is impossible to realize without the requisite internal and external conditions, as science shows. Communism will unconditionally require both the former and the latter—to complete the building of socialism and at the same time to move things forward. But in our country, even now, socialism has yet to reach completion. That is why I insist that completing the building of socialism remains the political task of our time. May God grant this take no more than a five-year plan or even one decade.

[3-6-81]

I am beginning to see why the party inscribed in its program that we should have communism by 1980. It happened in November 1961. Why did it happen? Shouldn't there be some explanation? Why was such a mistake committed?

It is not by chance that I target two Academicians, Fedoseev and Pospelov, one a philosopher and the other a historian of the party. In the book edited by Fedoseev, *The Foundations of Scientific Communism*, he treats the building of communism just as the program does: socialism exists when the exploiting classes have been abolished, while classes on the whole will be abolished under communism. He wrote this, and no one objected! Why, it is even inscribed in the program.

The party proclaimed from the lofty tribune of the party congress, "The present generation of Soviet people will live under communism." This proposition is so remote from reality that the people have ceased believing anything. As never before, the slogan "The people and the party are one" rang true. The party deceived the people, and the people, having lost faith and working slapdash, began to deceive the party.

I have often thought about this and have come to the conclusion that this happened because there was no correct conception of what constitutes socialism.

[4-28-76]

At about the same time, in the 1960s, Mao Tse-tung spoke out about communism and about socialism. I do not recall just where, but Mao, who was proclaiming the building of communes in China, had already stated that two hundred to three hundred years were needed to build socialism, the first stage of communism, in China. But he did not at all renounce the building of communes. This is difficult to imagine, and there is no need to try. . . .

Nevertheless, all this showed how superficial was our conception of socialism. Our current leaders speak of "developed," "mature" socialism! Such idle chatter! It seems to me that long ago we had already entered the stage of developed socialism—but only just entered it. We are in its very initial period. But in order to do what is necessary to achieve socialism in a separate country, the whole economy must be turned into the property of all the people. This is the main thing. In this connection Lenin simply, clearly, and succinctly said, "Socialism is the abolition of classes." Nowadays people don't like to talk about this. The same applies to our most senior spokesmen. On the elimination of classes there is not a word in the party program. But this is the knottiest question of socialism. It is the main issue.

Labor productivity is currently on the rise. But when we have all the production links smoothly coordinated and integrated, labor productivity will rise significantly. Labor discipline is important in this regard, but not discipline alone. It is important to be thorough in ensuring the smooth flow of supplies, on time and according to plan, to every link in the production process. At present this is not the case. Many workers waste time waiting in vain for what they need to do their job. What does this mean? It's not a genuine planned economy. We have a lot of boasting about exceeding output quotas, but in all these years we have never even met them. Accurate, timely, and precise coordination and integration of all links in the chain of production are the crucial elements. Of course this is difficult in so vast an economy, but this too is socialism; herein lies its main problem. We just go along in the old peasant spirit of "perchance"! This "perchance" has survived into the Soviet period. For a long time I have wanted to write about this but haven't managed. I am unable even to get started, though the main point is clear to me.

Cautious praise is due Andropov. He has introduced a fresh stream of thought and a good direction. For the present, however, it is not quite clear whether this will really prove itself and how long it will last. But the first steps, in my view, have a positive character.

[3-11-83]

Andropov, judging by the way he looks, is not a healthy man. All the same, considering the times, he is a godsend. I do not know or see anyone else of his caliber in this circle. He does not indulge in verbiage. His thought is not obscured by his language.

Andropov says, "We are addressing the question of perfecting the relations of production. The foundation is social ownership of the means of production. In our country, as is known, it takes two forms: state-owned property and kolkhoz-cooperative-owned property. In the long term, we see the fusion of these two forms into a single form of property, that of all the people. . . ." This is in keeping with your views.

Yes, yes.

"We, Communists, see in the long-term the growing-over of Soviet statehood into public self-administration."

Absolutely correct, yes.

"And this will take place, as we see it, by means of the furthermost development of the state of all the people."

The state of all the people, from my point of view, is incorrect. On this point I part company with the Central Committee. Poland and certain other states show that the concept of the "state of all the people" is not a particularly sound one. At least for the present, that is, as long as imperialism exists.

[6-16-83]

I shall write my commentary on the new constitution and send it on. If they don't evict me from the dacha after this . . . But whether they evict me or not, I shall send it on.

In our country it is forbidden to persecute a person just for opinion.

"With the exception of cases in which . . . ," and so forth [Molotov laughed]. The chief flaw in the constitution is an even greater departure from the class struggle against imperialism. Shall I be more specific? The dictatorship of the proletariat has supposedly already fulfilled its role and is to be replaced by the state of all the people; as in the party program, there is nothing new in this. This flagrant departure from the class line was begun as far back as the program and is simply continued here in the constitution.

This has a bearing on the entire international movement, because this is a fundamental question, a question of state power. It was imperative in the constitution to speak intelligibly about what constitutes a developed socialist society, but it contains only rumination on this matter; nothing is explained. Neither its authors nor the body of our political literature show any understanding of this. I stand ready to call both into question. No one understands a thing about this.

Similar confusion was injected into this question by the 1961 party program—indeed, total confusion—when it stated that we were to have communism by 1980, that is, three years from now. Does anyone really believe this? Absurd, utterly absurd.

They say that instead of communism in 1980 we shall have the Olympic Games.

Something like that, yes. Everything is topsy-turvy. From my point of view, the only thing that would justify a new constitution would be to explain what constitutes a developed socialist society. In that case we should radically have to amend both the party program and the constitution.

[6-16-77]

I consider the draft constitution unfounded in principle, though it contains many good points. But its premises are baseless. That poor fellow Brezhnev parrots what they write for him, but the upshot is no improvement. Inasmuch as we are marking time in economic policy, under conditions that still preserve part of NEP—we are in an analogous transitional period—we must overcome these vestiges of a transitional period in production and distribution. Substantial vestiges of a transitional period persist: two forms of property and commodity-money relations. No one objects, no one dares object, and these questions are evaded in underhanded fashion. The leadership consists of able, practical men, but they lack experience in politics at the All-Union level, and they are not seasoned. Moreover, they have not been properly trained in scientific socialism. But that is their misfortune, not their fault.

If these basic mistakes are allowed to go uncorrected, damage will ensue along three avenues. First, renunciation of the dictatorship of the proletariat. Marx and Lenin believed that pending communism, the dictatorship of the proletariat is needed, without which it is impossible to do what is necessary to prepare the way to communism. Renunciation of this, from my point of view, is baseless, though of course the dictatorship may assume other forms, another character. Everyone must recognize this. As long as the state is necessary, it can only be the dictatorship of the proletariat.

In all capitalist countries the dictatorship of the bourgeoisie holds everything economic and political in its hands. Is the dictatorship of the proletariat to be different in this regard? Must the proletariat march bare-handed against an armed enemy? This is absurd, this is the most harmful rubbish!

Our leaders now apparently proceed from the premise that the working class has already won out, so who would the dictatorship be directed against? This notion arises from the fact that the petty bourgeoisie and peasant masses have crept into our party and hatched all those theoreticians who have no revolutionary tempering, who have not genuinely participated in class struggle, all of those Fedoseevs en masse. Read them and see: they are afraid of revolutionary measures! I believe that the task of liquidating two forms of property, of transition to one form of property, that is, the task of abolishing classes, is a revolutionary task, but they are afraid of shouldering it. And it can be fulfilled only by the dictatorship of the proletariat and none other. A peasant, even the best, is and remains a peasant. The peasants cannot pass to positions of abolishing classes; this is beyond their ken as long as they are peasants. For a long time they will hang on to their old ideology, their old psychology, and be peasants, not revolutionary proletarians. They serve splendidly as allies of the proletariat, as is the case now, but they have no will to see things through to the end, and they lack full understanding of the cause. Only the working class has what it takes!

Second, I criticize the notion of a "state of all the people." Despite everything that's said, I believe that in our country the dictatorship of the proletariat obtains. A state that represents the interests of the working class *and* of the kolkhoz peasantry *and* of the intelligentsia is not possible. The intelligentsia is not a social class; in our country there are only two social classes: the workers and the peasants. But the intelligentsia expresses the will and the interests of either workers or peasants. The draft documents generally refer incorrectly to the intelligentsia, and it is mentioned just in passing. Moreover, the intelligentsia includes many former class enemies; they cannot struggle for the dictatorship of the working class. . . . Not only Narodniki, even bourgeois leaders when enfranchised say, "We are representatives of the people!" To a certain extent this is true. They are representatives of the people who are under their thumb, in their power, and who do not rise up against them.

Thus we, Marxists, must not falsify reality—as if we express the will of both the working class and the peasantry! Marx and Lenin said that in order to establish socialism, the cause must be taken in hand by the working class. When we renounce the dictatorship of the proletariat, we renounce the working class. To whom then do we pass it on? Well, let us assume both to the workers and the peasants. But this is impossible. The working class is more revolutionary, more advanced. The working class is in alliance with the peasantry, but the working class alone leads. Consequently, all this talk about the "state of all the people" is only a change of names. The harsh word "dictatorship" is not pleasant. Nevertheless, in the West they are getting used to it. But it is being falsified there; they [presumably the Euro-Communist movement] don't comprehend that without the dictatorship of the proletariat, they will never be able to move forward. However much they babble, the truth remains: either remain slaves of capitalism or, if you want to wrench yourself free, it is possible only with the aid of the dictatorship.

When the working class in our country made up probably no more than 15 percent of the total population, we proclaimed the dictatorship; no matter, the peasants assented to it because the dictatorship gave them land, gave them the struggle for peace, gave them farm machinery; so how could they be against it? No force can suppress the bourgeoisie and the landlords more effectively than the working class. It offered the peasantry the most hope. It is not by chance that in the theory of the state there is no room for "state of all the people." Nowhere has it ever existed in reality. What kinds of tasks are assigned the "state of all the people" that have not been fulfilled by our dictatorship of the proletariat? What kinds? Name them! There are none!

Third. I revert to the issue which was a mistake both in the Stalin constitution of 1936 and in the current one: "from each according to his ability, to each according to his work." Ninety-nine percent of the readers won't even notice this, and will then go on parroting it. I call your attention to a phrase in the new constitution, which compared with the preceding constitution is even worse: "from each according to his ability, to each according to the quantity and quality of his work." This has been deftly crafted by our bureaucrats to line their own pockets. The gist is this—I am a conscientious worker and I am unusually qualified, so my remuneration should be five times the norm; as for you, remuneration one-fifth of mine would be enough. I am a minister, which means remunerate me at six times the norm; but you have lesser qualifications, so just keep quiet with what you get, if you please.

I don't deny that for the present we must reckon with qualitative factors. Lenin declared in 1918 that we could pay the top bourgeois specialists more than others. However bad, we could find a way to pay two thousand especially distinguished experts a total of 50 million rubles or even 100 million rubles. This would be a bourgeois principle, a deviation from the principles of the Paris Commune, a deviation from communism, but we could tolerate it as a temporary expedient.

Instead we now sanctify such disparities in pay. Naturally this is very harmful. There is no such thing now as a party maximum remuneration, nothing of the kind. I have higher qualifications than others, therefore pay me ten times as much as you pay them.

That's the kind of constitution you are about to have!

They boast that this is a kind of Communist Manifesto! They are utter idiots!

This disparity won't last long, I believe, because the question "How come?" is already being raised.

But now they will have the cheek to say to the workers: "How come? The constitution stipulates remuneration 'according to quantity and quality...'"

A woman who happened to be in the neighborhood of the dacha approached me and asked, "Where does Molotov live?" "I am Molotov." "You are Molotov? Very good." And she shared her news and views with me. She was not at all a simple person. I met with her on three occasions at her initiative. Either she lay in wait for me or something of the kind. Apparently she had a high opinion of me. She told me she had been working for ten years at a chemical plant in Riazan. "Look," she said, "although I am young, I am already an old woman. On the job, working conditions are intolerable, very injurious to the workers' health. I have appealed everywhere, but in vain." And she started to tell me very frankly that she had gone as far as to turn to foreign correspondents and even to the American and Japanese embassies. Foreign radio stations, she said, were already beginning to publicize her case. Through foreign correspondents she had succeeded in calling attention to her plight.

I told her, write to me about your working conditions. Write to the Committee of People's Control, and send me a copy detailing how things are going and why you are such a dissatisfied person.

Some two weeks passed. She met me not far from home and handed me some papers. I read: "I have not written to the Committee of People's Control because I believe it futile, but I transmit what I have written to you." I got a copy of her memorandum and sent it to Arvid Pel'she, with a brief note saying, "I request your attention to this matter."

About another two weeks passed. I was taking a walk outside the dacha area and encountered her. She said, "It's you? Hello!"

I said, Look, I have read your memorandum. I see that you are a person who has no desire to help Soviet power but one who works against it. I'll no longer speak with you. Either you cease appealing to foreign embassies—she had appealed also to the Turkish embassy—or I'll have no more to do with you. I walked away from her. She did not show up again.

The point of my story is that she had lost faith. The people are losing faith. They appeal every which way but find no understanding. She had appealed also to local officials. According to her memorandum, a conference of representatives of the ministries was convened in Riazan which included representatives of the executive committee of the regional party organization. Apparently something was done about her complaint, but nothing substantial.

She represents just one example of how people are losing faith. Similar examples are brought to my attention informally by various individuals, showing that there are many such cases. Her case is not an isolated one. Naturally this is very sad. Yet the constitution is being praised to the skies! It's just so much verbiage! True, the constitution also records real gains. The right to housing, for example. Nowhere, in no other country could that be inscribed in the constitution. But it is little enough to write. What's needed is an understanding of where we are headed. Instead we have this hullabaloo—it goes beyond all bounds.

Here you have the commentary I have drawn up.

[11-1-77]

■   **I Am Against the Tranquil Life**   ■

Viacheslav Mikhailovich recounts that he had read in the journal
Kommunist *a pronouncement attributed to Lenin regarding developed
socialism. Molotov had written a letter to the editors challenging the
authenticity of this alleged pronouncement. The journal's editor-in-chief,
Kosolapov, phoned Molotov, saying, "We have to have a talk." "My
pleasure." They sent an automobile to take him to the editorial offices. I
rode with him to the office and back.*

Actually, Lenin said nothing of the kind. Kosolapov said I was right;
he had no rebuttal to my refutation. But you and I are communists
[Molotov, smiling, emphasized this phrase—after all, he had been
expelled from the party!] and understand party policy.

"You understand," said the editor, "unfortunately I cannot print your
letter."

"I do not insist," I said, "but the people must not be deceived."

[12-28-77]

*We touched on events in Czechoslovakia, their causes, and the grave
economic situation.*

I sometimes muse, what if we had something like that in our country?
Because we are now in a deep economic slump. Raising prices is not the
way out. I think we have to change social relations. To start with, let's
impose a party maximum, a cap on remuneration of party members.
This would have a tremendous material effect on the country and its
morale. The trouble is that Khrushchevites still dominate, even in the
Central Committee. Since Stalin's death we have lived on the reserves
built up in Stalin's time.

I propose a toast—to Stalin! No one else could have borne, no one
else could have endured the burden he carried on his shoulders. None
but he had the iron nerve and strength it took!

[12-18-70]

I sent a request to the Institute of Marxism-Leninism. I wrote,
inasmuch as I am researching certain questions of party history, to
request permission to look into the materials held by the institute on the
party maximum. About a month later I received a reply. They sent me a
packet of information concerning the resolutions and decisions adopted
by the party on this question—but only the titles and dates of these

actions, not the texts. Nevertheless I was grateful for this. The document abolishing the party maximum was dated 1932. Actually abolition started earlier, but the formal abolition took place in 1932.

According to institute rules, by decision of the Central Committee, as someone explained to me later, only party members are permitted access to the holdings of the institute. I take this to be perfectly correct. So, regarding me as a nonparty member, they sent me this information.

[3-11-86]

"Go your own way!"—if that's the policy we are going to follow regarding Poland, then we are in for trouble at home.

We are all interconnected. Our planned economy should be strong. Otherwise some will live at the expense of others. But this requires a firm hand. No one is to be aggrieved, but neither is anyone to be pampered. That's the only way to maintain order. And a general line, a common goal, is needed. Not empty words but strict, consistent regulation and setting of norms beginning with production. And in distribution, no one is to get anything extra at the expense of another, of an honest worker. That's the only way. You receive what you earn. Under communism it will be different, but for the present we don't have communism. Lenin said, socialism is the strictest control over production and distribution. But how is this to be assured? By setting norms. This is a very complex matter, but there is no alternative. If we don't come to our senses, things will only get worse.

[10-16-80]

Everyone wants to live well, but imperialism won't allow it.
I know it won't.
You understand nothing of the kind. You pay only lip service to this truth. In fact, an ever more ferocious and perilous struggle is unfolding. Only we don't want to recognize this, because we want both to live well and to struggle. But we can't have it both ways.

The events taking place in Poland could, in my opinion, be repeated in our country. If we pursue the smug policy in which each day is taken up merely with writing greetings. . . . This is just chatter, self-advertisement. We need struggle, however arduous it may be. Meanwhile we are sowing illusions. . . .

I laugh when I receive New Year's greetings: I wish you a tranquil life, and so forth. They want a tranquil life, but I know it is impossible. I am against the tranquil life! If I craved a tranquil life, it would mean I have been "philistinized."

Take Stalin. I believe that toward the end he suffered a monumental failing: he turned complacent. True, for decades, like no one else, he had overstrained himself. All the same it was a failing, because he was not Lenin.

[11-9-81]

Should or should not money exist under socialism? It ought to be eliminated.

Reduction of prices, a fixed wage, bread laid out free for the taking at public dining facilities . . . People have gotten used to easy living.

Free distribution of bread was far from correct; it came too soon. This too is dangerous, this was at the expense of the state. If it were to be done at the expense of the state, then it should have been done competently and carefully. We must think also about bureaucratism in the state, because if the state is bureaucratized it will gradually rot. There is an atmosphere of rot in our country because thievery is rampant. They play this down, saying it exists only in isolated cases, no more! This, they say, is a disease inherited from capitalism, elements of which we cannot do without. Nevertheless, we have in our country developed socialism! Not just developed socialism but even mature socialism! What kind of socialism is it that abides money and social classes!

They are incapable of comprehending what constitutes socialism. I am of the opinion that our country is in the initial stage of developed socialism.

And what about mature socialism? This is improbable, because we are surrounded by capitalism. If we are in mature socialism, then how come capitalism continues to prosper? Capitalism does and can exist because our socialism is still young and is only beginning to mature, to gather strength. Everything conspires against it. Both capitalism and internal enemies of various stripes are very much alive; all are striving to break down the socialist foundations of our society. . . .

They curse our socialism, but for the present nothing better is possible. As for socialism in Hungary, Poland, and Czechoslovakia, it is possible only because of us, because in our country the economic foundation belongs to the state. Apart from the kolkhozes, everything is state-owned.

In our country only one party holds state power. When it speaks, you must submit. It has set our direction.

But what if the direction is wrong?

Even if the direction is wrong, one must not go against the party. The party is a great force, but it must be used correctly.

How then are mistakes to be corrected if you can't speak out?

That's not an easy question. One must learn. . . . All the same, there is nothing better than the party. Ours has its flaws. Most party members are politically illiterate. They live with ideas of socialism that date back to the 1920s and '30s, which are no longer adequate. We have passed through difficult periods, but in my opinion even more difficult ones lie ahead. For one must reckon with ever newer circumstances without forgetting lessons of the past. But they are difficult to retain. Much is being forgotten. A stage is passed—it has left its mark on some, not on others—and for some time they recall its lessons, but then they begin to think increasingly about how to get along in the new stage, and ideology is adapted in like fashion.

[6-16-83]

Molotov is working on a new report and has invited four of us over to discuss it. November. We are gathered around a table at his dacha. The time is 3:30 p.m., and it is already dusk. We turn on the light. Molotov has placed on the table several sheets of paper containing draft theses in shaky script. His hands have started to tremble more and more, and in the stillness is heard the rustling of paper. He places his watch on the table and begins.

My report is entitled, "The USSR and the Struggle for the Construction of Communism."

In his report he, as it were, summarized many of our previous conversations. I cite certain of his theses.

Where does communism begin? At which stage of socialism? Lenin emphasized that the state under which the building of socialism is to be completed is to be a state of the dictatorship of the proletariat. But the 1961 party program proceeds from the premise that the dictatorship of the proletariat is no longer necessary and that we shall have a state of all the people. But Lenin in his *State and Revolution* said that a state of all the people is senseless and a deviation from socialism. A state of all the people does not and cannot exist. That kind of state can only be bourgeois or petty bourgeois. To speak of the present state as being a state of all the people is absurd and a step backward.

They say now that Lenin could not foresee everything.

People who say that are blockheads. In his article "On Cooperation,"

Lenin wrote that power should belong to the state, that is, to the working class. But the working class alone cannot make socialism a reality. What is needed?

In politics, not a state of all the people; in economics, not the continuation of the oppression of money but its overthrow; in ideology, the scientific communism of Marx and Engels. And a party of all the people in our country? Utterly absurd. Lenin held that viewing social questions without a class approach yields nothing. If the party is one of all the people, then it expresses the interests of the petty bourgeoisie and small landholders. I will not renounce my view whether the party restores my membership or not. We can only be a party of the vanguard, of the working class. We must go through this difficult phase of renouncing the petty bourgeois ways taught by the program. We have started to abandon the position of the working class for that of "all the people."

They may say that Lenin would speak differently if he were alive today. This speaks not against Lenin's old pronouncements but against those philistines in the party, of whom there are many.

In 1920 Lenin signed a decree on the liquidation of money...

But without money it is impossible to build socialism.

But we need to abolish money. Money is part of bourgeois society. Planning is decisive in the abolition of money. Units of labor time will replace money. This will cost so many hours of labor, that will cost so many hours. Because the majority believe that we cannot get along without money, you are smoothing over the harmfulness of money!

[11-7-83]

Soon seventy years will have passed since the Revolution, but social classes remain and money is acquiring a large role. Neither Marx nor Lenin foresaw this.

Although it gives me great difficulty, I am trying to write about this, for the need is great.

An opinion now has it that it would be good for labor discipline if we had a small percentage of unemployment. Some people believe this.

Such people can be found. This is philistinism of the worst kind.

Well, there are lots of idlers.

Measures ought to be taken.

So, under socialism how will everyone be compelled to work?

In my opinion that's no problem. But since we do not recognize the need to abolish classes, we do not make haste in this regard. This has a demoralizing effect.

Thievery, speculation, and swindling are rampant. It's just capitalism in another form. No real struggle is being waged against it; it's being combated merely in words. Under capitalism such evils are customary, but under socialism they should be impossible. This radical distinction between the two systems is not acknowledged, and the question is evaded.

Revolutionary spirit has greatly diminished.

Revolutionary spirit never existed. It was a bourgeois democratic spirit and never went beyond that. So now our theoreticians have quite renounced the aim of abolishing classes.

They say that kolkhozes and sovkhozes are now one and the same; all institutions are subordinate to the plan, to the regional committee of the party; consequently, a great difference between the two is no longer visible.

There is no big difference, but the difference that exists has a corrupting influence. Somehow this matter must get special attention. It requires special discussion. For the present this is a very confused question. But if we don't hit on something we shall unquestionably revert to capitalism.

There is also the opinion that Stalin had overhastily abolished the New Economic Program.

Unfortunately Stalin gave too little thought to this. We did not abolish NEP, we simply moved beyond it.

Many people believe we would have been better off staying with NEP.

Now there's a classical example of philistine thought.

But there are many such people.

Many! Indeed a majority, I would say a majority. They don't sort things out. This is not taught or written about anywhere.

If NEP had continued, would we have won the war?

Unlikely. Would NEPmen have marched off to fight? For reassurance they will say this denial is just dogmatist talk. Early in the century, Lenin too was accused of being a dogmatist by Mensheviks, "Economists," and opportunists. One of the main tendencies had been the so-called Economists. In their view the task of the working class was the struggle to improve the economic situation, not the political. . . .

[1-13-84]

■ Two Surprises ■

Now that Andropov has come to power, perhaps you will resubmit your application for readmission into the party?

Application? No, that would be out of place, and I won't do it. The political situation has changed, so why climb back into the party now? That would be unseemly.

On the other hand, reinstating you to the party would disconcert those who excluded you. . . .

You may look at it that way, but that's sheer speculation. I believe that reapplying would be unseemly on my part. I expect I will get in through some loophole.

[1-1-83]

Of course I will submit an application to be reinstated without waiting for some special occasion. I would be quite justified in doing this so as to avoid the appearance of counting on some special occasion to request amnesty.

[10-1-83]

It's the sixty-sixth anniversary of the October Revolution. Several guests and relatives have already gathered at Molotov's around the table set for the holiday. Viacheslav Mikhailovich rises, glass in hand, and extends holiday greetings to us all. Then he asks all of us to think of what good deed we should do by the sixty-seventh anniversary. Molotov delivers the final toast, which comes as a surprise to me. He says:

To our party and its Central Committee, to Comrade Andropov and to his health of which he is apparently in need!

I have never before heard Molotov propose a personal toast to any of our leaders.

I believe the appearance of two men has marked a great achievement for us communists in the past few years. First, Andropov. His accession to office came as a complete surprise to me, though I had been thoroughly familiar with Bolshevik cadres over the years. Gromyko, whom I had promoted, measured up. Andropov was the first surprise but a pleasant one. It turns out that he is firm in politics, a man with broad horizons. A reliable person. Apparently he has been seasoned by years of responsibility. He has proved to be quite trustworthy. He measured up when he worked with me.

And the second surprise is Jaruzelski. I had not even heard of that name before his appearance as first secretary of the party in Poland. Bolsheviks among Poles were precious few. But there were some. Dzerzhinsky, for example. He was a man of the highest caliber. Back then the Poles were worse than they are now.

Jaruzelski, in my opinion, has come to our rescue. . . . Until Jaruzelski the only pleasant surprise of that kind I had previously was Fidel Castro.

[11-7-83]

We see in the New Year, 1984. Molotov asks:

How do our experts on international affairs see things? In this past year did the danger of war increase or decrease?

Increased, says one of our guests. "Increased," muses Molotov.

So many events have occurred since we saw you last. Andropov has died.

It's a pity. He was just beginning to find himself politically, in foreign affairs . . .

People have a high opinion of him. This is palpable.

Yes, yes, you're right. This must be looked into to find the reason.

As soon as Andropov was elected general secretary, Sofronov, editor of Ogenek, *said he phoned Andropov's assistant seeking advice concerning a portrait of the new general secretary to be placed in the magazine. The assistant put him through to Andropov who said, "No need for a portrait." "But we customarily run a portrait of a newly elected general secretary. That has always been done." "Well, it's going to be different now," replied Yuri Vladimirovich. Even* Pravda *ran a story about his meeting with the workers of the ZIL automobile plant, but without a photograph.*

But Chernenko on the whole is the type of person foisted on the people. We seem unable to nominate a real president. Few people will look ahead; for that reason we will get the unexpected. It's not really such a difficult matter, but we can't seem to manage it.

If something happens to Chernenko, they say Gorbachev will be next. He is the youngest of the lot.

How old is he?

Fifty-three, I believe.

Good. To the surprise of all, he too might somehow be promoted to head the party.

Andropov obviously was not on the side of Khrushchev nor on the side of Brezhnev for that matter.

The Americans are already openly declaring that the days of Soviet power are numbered, that only the façade of the edifice is left, and that the interior is rotted through and through.

Questions arise. I think the dreams of counterrevolution will not come true. Our state, like the entire socialist camp, is still the strongest in the world. Meanwhile it is precisely the condition of the bourgeois system that is unstable. Who is in charge of ideology now?

There is no chief ideologist. It used to be Suslov, but now we don't even have a Suslov.

Thank God we don't have one! There are so few who understand.

[8-1-84]

■ Reinstatement in the Party ■

It's about 8 a.m. Sarra Mikhailovna [daughter of Molotov's niece] phones me: We have wonderful news! The party has reinstated Viacheslav Mikhailovich! I take the train to Zhukovka. Molotov is in a white shirt and is seated on the sofa watching television. I congratulate him and ask him for the details.

Yesterday what's-his-name received me . . . Chernenko. He gave me a decision to read, which contained a line: to restore to Molotov his rights as a member of the Communist party of the Soviet Union . . .

A decision of the secretariat?

I can't exactly say. Apparently it was a decision adopted by the Politburo. It was the Central Committee that had excluded me and it must therefore reinstate me. The current minister of culture, Demichev . . . As concerns the party card, it will be made out in a few days.

This took place in the Kremlin?

No, at the Central Committee building on Old Square. It was all very simple. But I have some questions. Thanks, so to speak, to the activity of Ponomarev, the latest edition of *The History of the CPSU* describes me as a "conciliator." If I am a "conciliator," can you name anyone who is less a "conciliator"?

Have you noticed that you are no longer referred to as being a member of an "antiparty group"?

Long ago. The charge was just a product of Khrushchev's malice.

Did they phone you yesterday?

Yesterday, in the evening.

That means after a session of the Politburo. Yesterday, Thursday, they held a session.

The Politburo customarily meets on Thursday, just as in Lenin's time.

Today's Pravda *reports a session of the Politburo. At the very end the report reads: "The Politburo session examined and adopted decisions on a number of other questions of economic and social policy of our Party. . . ." That means you. Apparently, after the Politburo session Chernenko received you. Did they send an automobile to pick you up?*

Two cars, Volgas.

They phoned, says Sarra Mikhailovna, and asked for Viacheslav Mikhailovich. "Who is calling?" "It's from the CC." "I'll call him to the phone." He came to the phone, they said they would come for him.

Did they say he was being reinstated?

No, they didn't, but I guessed. I had already sent the Politburo a letter, May 14.

But they could have refused you, as they had before.

Of course.

So, you entered the office . . .

What's special about that? He was alone in that big office.

Stalin's office, no?

No. He received me in his office which is near the large room where the Politburo meets. He sat behind a conference table. When I entered he got up from behind the table to greet me, shook my hand, and then we sat down opposite each other at the conference table. He said something but I did not quite hear what, and he made some small talk. Then he showed me the decision. I said to him, "I have been a party member since 1906 . . ." He said, "That is stated in the decision."

To indicate continuous length of service?

Yes, yes.

Well, you now hold the record for longest continuous membership— eighty years in the party!

Yep.

Longer than anyone.

Well, there is Father Christmas.

What did Chernenko say to you?

Nothing special. There was hardly any conversation at all. He said I was hereby reinstated in the party and handed me a copy. . . . He congratulated me, nothing more.

Did he allow you to take a copy with you?

No, he did not. It all took two minutes, no more. I did not catch what he told me; I said I did not know the reason for my being expelled and the reason for my reinstatement. . . .

Molotov stuck to his guns. He reached his goal without groveling in repentance and without writing a self-abasing recantation, which had frequently been urged on him.

We were sitting at the table. Molotov was speaking about economic questions, of how he had proposed increasing investment in soil-improvement of Russian farmland, for which Khrushchev called him a dogmatist.

He called me a dogmatist simply because I read books. The struggle still goes on in other forms, but a hard-fought struggle is raging. What do our brothers the writers say about this?

I attended a meeting at the House of Writers that featured Valentin Berezhkov [who had been in the Soviet diplomatic service during the war]. I struck up a conversation with him, and he told me that the complications for our diplomacy created by Stalin and you had closed off all our loopholes or escape hatches, so to speak. Because you and Stalin had pursued such a hard-line policy, it was now difficult to have any dealings with the capitalists.

That, in my opinion, is very superficial reasoning. To assert that Stalin did not understand the ABCs of diplomacy is sheer nonsense.

They are trampling on Stalin in order to get at Lenin. And some people are even starting after Lenin. They say Stalin is his continuator. In what sense? In the worst. . . Lenin started the concentration camps, established the Cheka. Stalin just continued them . . . No less!

So what else are they talking about?

About Gorbachev, about the struggle with alcoholism.

Yesterday I heard him speak on television. I think it was quite a good speech. I don't think I ever met him.

He is young, born in 1931. You were already head of the government the year he was born.

Well, I too was pretty young then—indeed, the youngest chairman of the Council of People's Commissars. The Japanese ambassador remarked what a young prime minister I was. And an American, too—I forget his name, one of their big capitalists.

Concerning alcoholism, that's a matter we greatly neglected, a difficult problem that must be solved. It's a peasant country, the right-wing deviation is preponderant. Many people do not like socialism. . . .

Why do people drink? History and geography have a lot to do with it. We are a northern country. A lot of people drink, but never so many as now. We have become richer, that's the first thing. We have become edgier, that's the second. Sedatives are needed. There used to be less drinking.

[11-15-84, 2-16-85, 10-4-85]

Recently I brought Molotov a long memorandum written by E. F. Grundin, a member of the Kranopresnensk District Committee of the party. Molotov read it with great interest.

Grundin wrote that under Lenin the Sovnarkom [Council of People's Commissars] was vested with plenary executive, economic, and administrative power while the party served as an assistant.

Under Lenin that was true.

In a letter addressed to Molotov in March 1922, Lenin wrote: "Finally, it is necessary to delimit far more precisely the functions of the party and the CC on the one hand and of Soviet power, on the other. . . ." According to Grundin, too much is now left to the party.

Just try to lead the country in another way. In most cases Grundin's criticism is correct, but he can't draw conclusions. This is very difficult.

He proposes to leave to the party overall leadership of the work of the state, but without petty intervention.

That's difficult to put into practice, given our conditions. A very difficult question.

He wants to investigate why people work so badly.

The reason is that we are bad communists, bad communists in our majority. Thank God we are nevertheless finding some leaders who, despite all shortcomings and little understanding of the entire complex of questions, have held together a certain core of the party and have not let go. . . .

Yes, the role of the soviets must be strengthened, but this won't come about at once. We need everything; we are still accumulating crumbs. We need to strengthen the party line to prevent philistines from getting the upper hand. Yes, more than a few who desire a restful life will be found out there.

At our next meeting Molotov continued the conversation on Grundin's memorandum.

[1-26-86]

I have reread this memorandum. It's not quite clear. He almost holds that we have accomplished nothing, that we have no socialism whatever. He swings from one extreme to another. But we have retained state power; industry is in the hands of the state; the peasant has broken with the old way of life and has taken the path of collectivization. We have thrown on the scrap heap what had been very difficult to scrap. We are moving forward over contradictions, but they will last more than one more five-year plan, since it is necessary to gather experience and understanding of what is taking place. The contradictions riddling our socialist society are still substantial. While they are not dominant, they do affect things. All the same, the guideline, the dictatorship of the proletariat, will triumph. But in Grundin it turns out that bureaucrats possess everything. In practice, bureaucrats have seized a lot, but this is a social category which has been virtually decapitated. Nevertheless, difficulties remain.

That is why I reread the memorandum. It reflects an almost despairing view of our situation. But we are moving forward despite the fact that much of the old still slows us down, like leg irons, making it difficult just to walk. But there is no power in the world that could force us to turn back. We are undeviatingly moving forward, but more slowly than is desirable. That's my opinion. I don't know, what's yours?

What would you advise Grundin?

First, to continue the line we are pursuing. It is Leninist, it is socialist, but not enough. The socialist elements in the economy, in the culture, and in the party itself must be strengthened. It is difficult, but we have set about attaining a difficult goal toward which we are victoriously advancing. Much of the old still blocks and befouls our path. No soothing phrase will clear it away. Do I make myself clear?

Not entirely. Grundin sees our shortcomings and is thinking of ways to correct them.

That's what I am saying. We are moving forward, but many difficulties remain, including those it would seem we had already easily overcome. But nothing will come easy to us because we live in a petty bourgeois country. We are building socialism and moving toward communism because state power and the vanguard of the people rest solidly on the policy pursued by the party. That's the main thing.

In our country the vanguard is preserved, it is growing in strength, it is socialist, communist—this is the main thing. To sink into pessimism is wrong. Our work in the Soviet Union affects all mankind and is making progress, though slowly. It could not be otherwise. There are still the Trotskyists and Bukharinists—they emphasize our difficulties and short-comings, they are voices of despair and unbelief, as if we were moving backward rather than forward. They are wrong. In five to ten years everything will have become clearer, but even then we will still have to face many vicissitudes. Beyond what is being done, I cannot recommend something specific, but I believe it is being done well. And our work has penetrated the life of the people so deeply that it is no longer possible to go back. As for leaders who, as it were, might be able to propose something new, they are all too few. These new elements have not yet crystallized. No one new has been pushed to the top, have you noticed? Who is being talked about, what kinds of articles are being written? Yes, many new men have been pushed up, but their caliber has not been tested. That's the way things stand.

What do you think about the proposal to grant the soviets greater power?

It is correct. Imperative. But it will take time because political literacy here is still all too rare. Today it is not enough just to read about and understand a situation; one must still decide what course of action to adopt. The party is doing this and, in my opinion, is doing it correctly. Overhastiness must be avoided.

What are you reading now?

Churchill's memoirs. He excoriates you, alleging that you helped Hitler in 1940 during the battle for France. You congratulated Hitler on his victory over France. Also, Stalin and Molotov should have known that in one year they would have to fight Hitler!

We knew, we knew it very well. But Churchill took a great fall. He did not see things in the long term. He did not see—more precisely, he did not want to see. He was a man of great character and perseverance. But character is not enough; one must have understanding.

Viacheslav Mikhailovich, the people of Irkutsk have asked me to have you write a few words on your photograph for the museum in Manzurk village. Kirov, Frunze, Ordzhonikidze, and you had been in exile there.

Molotov took up a pen and began to fidget with it pensively. I tried to dictate a greeting for him: To the Museum of Manzurk . . . But he wrote, after thinking a bit in his own way, in trembling hand with effort, but without glasses:

"To my Siberian comrades in Manzurk and in other distant places: I wish you every success. From the former exile, V. Molotov. February 1986."

I hold the photograph he inscribed.

"I can't make it out," Molotov said, and put on his glasses to read what he had written. *Only recently he had in a firm hand inscribed on his photograph presented to the Museum-House of J. V. Stalin in Gori:*

"I am proud to have worked many years with J. V. Stalin. V. Molotov."

[2-7-86]

On Sunday, March 9, 1986, Molotov celebrated his ninety-sixth birthday. I congratulated him, and he replied: "Let's stick with this policy right into the future." He smiled.

How did the XXVIIth Party Congress strike you? [Molotov had seen twenty-seven congresses in his lifetime.]

It lacked specifics. Acceleration, acceleration. Haste should be avoided because the problems to be solved are so complex that no one has ever found a solution. Most people don't even think about such problems. Many words but so far few deeds. We adopt a five-year plan but don't fulfill it. That's awful and doesn't look good—but inevitable in the early stages. Everyone is required to fulfill and exceed the plan, but it is just impossible. Every new and momentous step must be carefully prepared. The desire to struggle for socialism is there, that's the main thing. That desire is not always a conscious one, but people sense this is the only way out of our plight. We still live in straitened circumstances. Life for many is still not especially good, but long-term prospects bode improvement. Or so it seems to me. . . .

The party has a sound core, but gathered around it are many rotten elements. . . .

If we had not supported Stalin those years, I don't know what might have happened. But Brezhnev pinned medals on everyone, and persons who cannot be trusted on any account have wormed their way into leading positions.

Guests began to arrive. V. P. Mzhavandze arrived with three people. He delivered a brief but eulogistic opening toast. Molotov rapped his fork against a glass and demanded, "Finish up." . . .

[3-9-86]

On April 30, 1986, my 139th and last meeting with Molotov took place.

I fully expected the congress to tick off the causes of our country's falling behind.

Russia was a backward country at the start of the Revolution, then came a big war and hardship so terrible that in the West they did not believe the Soviet state would survive. Indeed, the majority in the West were of this opinion.

Forty years have passed since World War II. I believe the Brezhnev period slowed us down terribly.

He did slow us down, no question about that. Khrushchevism was repeated in the Brezhnev period. This is so. This speaks to the fact that we have many rotten apples within the party itself and much backwardness, ignorance, and undereducation in the country. Nevertheless we are, on the whole, beginning to emerge from this sorry plight with some success. . . . Of course complacency must be avoided, much work remains to be done. . . . The danger now lies in the sugar-coating of criticism.

This year marks your eightieth year of membership in the party.

Yes, I have seen too much. I had not intended to live so long. All of my contemporaries have long been in the grave. What are you working on?

On a biography of Ilyushin [the aircraft designer]. People have finally noticed a serious problem in our country: the loss of mastery in many fields. I am surprised our planes manage to fly. They are so badly made. It is unconscionable.

That's just a result of the fact that a peasant stratum has risen to the surface. A vast layer has lifted itself from illiteracy and semiliteracy. They have not yet digested new things. How it will turn out. . . But it rises, then falls back. . . . We have girded ourselves technologically, but we need to double or triple our effort. . . .

We speak about writers, about Bondarev, Rasputin, and Isaev. I say I intend to go to Afghanistan.

You must drop in and tell me all about it!

These were the last words I heard from his lips.

[4-30-86]

■   **140**   ■

As usual, I wrote down the number of our next meeting on a fresh page of the diary, number 140, in red pencil. But the red had to be framed in black. The 140th meeting was the day of his funeral. . . .

That summer he had fallen ill with pneumonia. In June he was taken to Kuntsevo Hospital. There he died on November 8, 1986, at 12:55 p.m.

Izvestia *and* Vechernaya Moskva *ran a brief obituary: "The USSR Council of Ministers sadly announces that on November 8, 1986, at the age of 96, after a lingering and grave illness, there passed away All-Union Personal Pensioner, member of the CPSU since 1906, Molotov, V. M. From 1930 to 1941, the deceased was Chairman of the USSR Council of People's Commissars and from 1947 to 1957 was First Deputy Chairman of the USSR Council of People's Commissars and USSR Council of Ministers.*

—Council of Ministers of the USSR."

At 10 a.m. on Granovsky Street people began to gather. They rode by bus to Kuntsevo. Funeral Hall No. 1. About two hundred people crowded the hall while many stood in the street. At Novodevichy Cemetery I saw many acquaintances. Relatives of Stalin and of Artem-Sergeev, Podvoisky, Tevosian, Bulganin, Kaganovich, and Mikoyan arrived. . . . The guards did not permit members of the public to enter.

Molotov was laid out in a red coffin decked with red carnations, the identification mark of the Bolsheviks. He was dressed in a dark blue suit, grey necktie, and white shirt. His facial features had changed drastically, his face drawn and pinched. Four wreaths had been laid out: from the Council of Ministers; from his daughter and son-in-law; from his grand- and great-grandchildren; and from friends and nearest and dearest. On cushions were the gold star of the Hero of Socialist Labor, Number 79; four Orders of Lenin; the Order of the Banner of Honor; and four medals: "For the Defense of Moscow," "For Victory over Germany," "For Valorous Toil in the Great Patriotic War," and "800 Years of Moscow Commemoration."

The funeral ceremony was brief. Four speakers delivered eulogies: I. Stadniuk; E. Strugov, a veteran of the cruiser Molotov; V. Skriabin, a nephew of Molotov's; and me.

The ceremony was closed by a representative of the administrative director of the Council of Ministers, and we then bore the casket to the hearse. Flashbulbs popped from news cameras. There were many foreigners. The gold star on a cushion was carried by People's Hero G. Baidukov, the celebrated pilot.

At the cemetery the driver of the hearse steered toward the platform where last words are usually pronounced. But someone in an authoritative yet panicky tone of voice hurriedly directed the driver to turn right. The casket was placed on a catafalque, and as it was carried to the grave, Molotov's head shook on a shriveled neck. I could see his cold brow and grey mustache. . . .

Someone in the crowd murmured: this funeral will cost more than the antialcoholism decree!

Molotov was buried and memorialized at the expense of the state.

On the day of his death some KGB men came to Molotov's flat and dacha and carried off two suitcases filled with papers and photographs. . . .

In no time a new master moved into the dacha at Zhukovka. I went there to collect the writing desk at which Molotov had worked. It had been moved to the manager's storeroom. No one needed it. The girl who opened the storeroom said, There was no one like Viacheslav Mikhailovich in our dacha compound. He asked for nothing, much less make demands or indulge in caprices. He did not like or need luxury, he owned neither carpets nor chandeliers. . . .

Molotov lived at the Zhukovka dacha from July 8, 1966, to June 27, 1986. Until the very last day he tried to do everything himself, Tatiana Afanasievna Tarasova, the housekeeper, told us. He was a very strong-willed person. Even when he was almost unable to walk, he tried to walk as far as the sixth post. You would say, stop at the fourth post, Viacheslav Mikhailovich!

No, not until the sixth!

Among the sheets of paper Molotov covered with crabbed writing during his last days, there is one on which he sketched out theses he had intended to work out:

"1. The fundamental principle of socialism (in contrast to communism) is fulfillment of norms of labor established by society.

"2. The Communist party is the party of the working class (not of all the people).

"3. Democracy under socialism."

He returned to these questions time after time during the years of our meetings. Apparently he would have liked to chat with the current leadership about problems of socialism, and he said something of the kind to his housekeeper:

"Phone Smirtiukov, the administrative director of the Council of Ministers. Ask him if Gorbachev could find the time to speak with me."

Nothing came of it.

His mind worked as in former years. It was only at the very end that a decline became noticeable. Shortly before his death, he read the last page of Pravda, *laid down the paper, and said, "Invite Shevardnadze to see me at 5 p.m." Apparently Molotov was agitated over some international problem, and he reverted to his former role as a member of the Politburo, first deputy chairman of the Council of Ministers, and minister of foreign affairs. Members of his household thought he would forget all about it by*

5 p.m., but by that time he had put on his suit and necktie. They told him that Comrade Shevardnadze was busy and could not accept....

He survived eleven heads of the country. He was born under Alexander III and died under Gorbachev.

At his funeral I had said, We bid farewell today to a fighter for communism, to Lenin's last surviving comrade-in-arms.

CHRONOLOGY

Note: Specific days are given according to the Julian calendar, which was in effect in Russia until February 1918, followed by the Gregorian or modern calendar.

1890 February 24/March 9, birth of V. M. Molotov (né Scriabin), village of Kukarka, Viatsk Gubernia (now Sovetsk, Kirov oblast).

1894 Accession of Tsar Nicholas II to the throne.

1905 Revolution of 1905–1907. Russia becomes a quasi-constitutional monarchy. Establishment of Imperial State Duma.

1906 Molotov joins Russian Social Democratic Workers party, Bolshevik wing.

1909 Molotov arrested, sentenced to two years' exile in Vologda.

1911–1916 Molotov enrolled in Saint Petersburg Polytechnic Institute.

1912 Molotov assists in founding of Bolshevik newspaper *Pravda*.

1914 Russian declaration of war on Germany; name of capital changed to Petrograd.

1915 Molotov arrested for organizing revolutionary underground in Moscow, sentenced to three-year term of exile to Manzurka, Irkutsk Gubernia. Escapes 1916.

1916–1917 Member, Russian bureau of the Bolshevik Central Committee in Petrograd.

1917 February Revolution. Molotov joins executive committee of Petrograd Soviet of Workers' and Soldiers' Deputies. Nicholas II abdicates March 2/15. Formation of Provisional Government, composed mainly of Duma deputies.

  October Revolution. Molotov member of Military Revolutionary Committee, headed by Trotsky. October 25/November 7, Bolshevik-led insurrection deposes Kerensky Provisional Government.

IInd All-Russian Congress of Soviets of Workers' and Soldiers' Deputies ratifies Lenin's decrees on peace and land and confirms new government, the Council of People's Commissars (Sovnarkom): Lenin, chairman; Trotsky, commissar for foreign affairs; Stalin, commissar for nationalities.

1918–1921   War communism, civil war, and foreign armed intervention.

1918   Molotov chairman of Northern Region, Council of the National Economy.

1920   Candidate (nonvoting) member of Central Committee of Communist party. Secretary of Central Committee of Communist party, Ukraine.

1921–1928   New Economic Policy.

1921   Member and secretary of Central Committee. Candidate member of Politburo of Central Committee. Lenin's chief of staff of Council of People's Commissars. Marries Polina Semenovna Zhemchuzhina.

1922   Stalin elected general secretary of Central Committee.

1924   Death of Lenin. Struggle for succession. Alexander Rykov is chairman of Council of People's Commissars to 1930.

1925   Molotov heads Stalinist group to remove Zinoviev from leadership of party in Leningrad. Kirov new leader in Leningrad.

1925–1927   Stalin-Trotsky struggle over Stalin's doctrine of "Socialism in One Country."

1926   Molotov elected member of Politburo (position retained until 1952).

1928–1930   Trotsky exiled to Central Asia, then expelled from USSR. Molotov secretary of Moscow Party Committee.

1929   Stalin proclaims Five-Year Plan. Collectivization of agriculture campaign. Bukharin-led right-wing "deviation" defeated.

1930   Molotov succeeds rightist Alexander Rykov as chairman of Council of People's Commissars. Molotov active in collectivization drive, especially in Ukraine, 1932.

1934   Assassination of Sergei Kirov.

1936–1938   "Great Terror." Molotov active with Stalin and secret police heads Ezhov, then Beria, in drawing up arrest lists and signing death sentences.

1939   May: while retaining position as chairman of Sovnarkom, Molotov replaces Maxim Litvinov as commissar for foreign affairs.

August 23: Molotov signs German-Soviet Nonaggression Treaty and secret supplementary protocol dividing Eastern Europe into German-Soviet spheres of interest.

September 1: Germany invades Poland. September 3: Britain and France declare war on Germany. USSR declares neutrality in Second World War.

USSR absorbs Eastern Poland into Ukrainian and Belorussian Soviet Republics.

1940   Estonia, Latvia, Lithuania, Moldavia (Bessarabia under Rumanians), and Karelia (mainly former Finnish territory) proclaimed Soviet republics and incorporated in USSR.

November: Molotov meets with Hitler and Ribbentrop in Berlin to work out frictions over spheres of interest.

1941   May 6: Stalin replaces Molotov as chairman of Sovnarkom.

June 22: German invasion of USSR. Molotov (not Stalin) announces news of invasion by radio to Soviet people. Molotov deputy chairman of State Council of Defense.

1942   May–June: Molotov flies to London and Washington. Signs Anglo-Russian Treaty of Alliance and secures President Roosevelt's agreement "to the urgent tasks of creating a second front in Europe in 1942."

1943   October–November: Molotov at Moscow Conference of Foreign Ministers and seconds Stalin at Teheran conference.

1945   Molotov attends Yalta and Potsdam conferences with Stalin. April: meets President Truman and represents USSR at San Francisco conference founding the United Nations.

1945–1947   Molotov at UN. Also negotiates peace treaties.

1946: Sovnarkom name changed to Council of Ministers— Stalin, chairman; Molotov, deputy chairman and minister for foreign affairs.

1948   Stalin forces Molotov to divorce Polina Semenovna Zhemchuzhina.

1949   February: Zhemchuzhina charged with "treason," arrested, and incarcerated. March: Andrei Vyshinsky replaces Molotov as foreign minister.

1952   Stalin enlarges and renames Politburo "Presidium of the Central Committee." Molotov a member but not included in smaller body, actually a new "Politburo."

1953   March 5: death of Stalin.

Molotov first deputy chairman of Council of Ministers and restored as minister for foreign affairs.

March 6: Membership of Presidium reduced from twenty-five members to eight. Molotov retains membership. Zhemchuzhina released, rejoins Molotov.

1956   June: Molotov removed from position as first deputy chairman of Council of Ministers and replaced by Dmitry Shepilov as foreign minister.

1957   June: attempt to remove Khrushchev from post of first secretary of CC defeated; Molotov and other members of "antiparty group" expelled from CC.

1957–1960   Molotov USSR ambassador to Mongolian People's Republic.

1960–1962   Molotov Soviet representative to International Atomic Energy Commission, Vienna.

1962   Molotov discharged from all positions in the government and expelled from the party. Pensioned off.

1968–1986   Conversations with Felix Chuev.

1970   Death of Zhemchuzhina.

1984   Molotov reinstated in party.

1986   November 8: death of Molotov.

INDEX

Felix Ivanovich Chuev, poet and biographer, was born in 1941 in Svobodny in the Amur Region of the Soviet Union. In the past thirty years he has published some twenty books and collections of poetry on Russian patriotism, nationalism, and communism, including biographies celebrating Stalin's lieutenants and Soviet cosmonauts. His most recent books are *The Russian Flame: A Historical Drama in Verse*, and *Thus Spoke Kaganovich: Confessions of an Apostle of Stalin*.

Albert Resis is professor of history emeritus at Northern Illinois University. Born in Joliet, Illinois, he studied at Northwestern University and Columbia University. He has written widely on Soviet foreign policy and on Lenin. His most recent publication is *Stalin, the Politburo, and the Onset of the Cold War, 1945–1946*.